ARTHUR
AND HIS TIMES

OTHER WORKS BY JACK LINDSAY

Historical

SONG OF A FALLING WORLD
BYZANTIUM INTO EUROPE
CIVIL WAR IN ENGLAND
THE ROMANS WERE HERE
DAILY LIFE IN ROMAN EGYPT
THE WRITING ON THE WALL
SHORT HISTORY OF CULTURE
LEISURE AND PLEASURE IN
    ROMAN EGYPT

Biographical

MARC ANTONY
JOHN BUNYAN
CHARLES DICKENS
GEORGE MEREDITH

Autobiography

LIFE RARELY TELLS
THE ROARING TWENTIES
FANFROLICO AND AFTER

General

ANATOMY OF SPIRIT
HANDBOOK OF FREEDOM

HISTORICAL NOVELS

Ancient World

WANDERINGS OF WENAMEN
COME HOME AT LAST
    (Short stories)
HANNIBAL TAKES A HAND
ROME FOR SALE
CÆSAR IS DEAD
LAST DAYS WITH CLEOPATRA
STORM AT SEA
    (Golden Cockerel Press)
DESPOILING VENUS
BRIEF LIGHT
THE BARRIERS ARE DOWN

English History

THE GREAT OAK
FIRE IN SMITHFIELD
THE STORMY BARRIER
SUE VERNEY
1649
LOST BIRTHRIGHT
THE PASSIONATE PASTORAL
LIGHT IN ITALY
MEN OF FORTY-EIGHT
ADAM OF A NEW WORLD
    (Italy)

CONTEMPORARY NOVELS OF THE BRITISH WAY

END OF CORNWALL
WE SHALL RETURN
BEYOND TERROR
HULLO STRANGER
TIME TO LIVE
ALL ON THE NEVER-NEVER
CHOICE OF TIMES

BETRAYED SPRING
RISING TIDE
THE MOMENT OF CHOICE
LOCAL HABITATION
REVOLT OF THE SONS
THE WAY THE BALL BOUNCES
MASKS AND FACES

Translations of Theocritus, Aristophanes, Catullus, Longus, Apuleius,
Mediæval Latin Poets, etc.

ARTHUR
AND HIS TIMES

Britain in the Dark Ages

JACK LINDSAY

BARNES & NOBLE, Inc.
NEW YORK
PUBLISHERS & BOOKSELLERS SINCE 1873

CONTENTS

ILLUSTRATIONS

To John Pudney

to remind him of what he has left behind
in going to the antipodes

INTRODUCTION

THIS is an account of the Dark Age in Britain, the 5th and 6th centuries A.D., when the Roman imperial organisation broke down and the invading Anglo-Saxons had not yet consolidated their kingdoms. But in order to get at the period, we must work from the known to the unknown; we must have a clear sense of what Roman Britain was like in its last phases, what were the direction and the impetus of the changes already going on, what pattern of the new can be glimpsed under the surface of the imperial system in dissolution.

Indeed, it would be as well to open with a brief sketch of what had happened under the Romans since they had landed in A.D. 43.

By the end of the 1st century they had control of the lowlands as far north as southern Scotland and had subdued the hill tribes in Wales, though there was still trouble among the Brigantians of Yorkshire. Towns were being built across the south, with York, a military headquarters, as the most northerly site. It might well seem that it would not be long before the whole island would be held and Ireland invaded. But about A.D. 100 a serious setback appeared in the north. The advanced garrisons were withdrawn; and when the frontier was re-established, it was by the Hadrianic stone wall running from the Tyne to the Cumbrian coast (c. 122–3 to 128). Under Antoninus Pius the line moved north again and a turf wall was built along what was roughly the earlier Forth–Clyde boundary; but before the end of the 2nd century this wall had to be evacuated. Septimius Severus in his expedition of 208–11 made the last effort to dominate the whole island. He failed, though his settlement in the north secured peace for a couple of generations. (1)

The 3rd century, a time of deep and violent change for the empire in general, did not hit Britain as badly as most provinces; but there was a check to municipal life and its economic bases. And politically there were separatist tendencies. Britain was a member of the independent state-system centred on Gaul in 258–73; and soon afterwards the son of a British schoolmaster, Bonosus, tried to recreate the split with a government at Cologne. The emperor broke him and sent his own governor to Britain, who in turn revolted and was assassinated at the emperor's orders. To help in keeping things under control, Burgundians and Vandals were settled in Britain.

In the later 3rd century the failing imperial power showed in the increasing attacks of pirates, Franks, and Saxons, who filled the Channel. In 285 Diocletian sent his younger colleague, Maximian, to deal with the barbarians on the Rhine, the corsairs and the revolted peasants. Maximian built up the Channel fleet under a Menapian of the Low Countries, Carausius, a bull-necked sea-commander, who followed up his successes by declaring himself emperor and crossing into Gaul. (2) His position was so strong that he had to be tolerated till 293. Then the imperial forces under Constantius Chlorus took Bologne, and soon afterwards Carausius was murdered by his finance minister, Allectus, who was easily defeated by Constantius Chlorus.

Carausius had probably done much to start off the coastal-defence system that now emerged, with great bastioned fortresses set from Wash to Wight along the Saxon Shore. A defence system on lighter lines was also built in the west (for example, at Cardiff and Lancaster); since about 275 the Irish had been raiding South Wales. (3) These developments were typical of steps being taken throughout the empire to construct massive defences in depth all along threatened frontiers. (4)

Diocletian had begun a general reorganisation of the government that was carried further by Constantine the Great, who, after the death of his father, Constantius Chlorus, at York, set out from Britain to gain the empire. The provinces were grouped in larger units, dioceses under vicars, with separation of civilian and military powers; Britain was cut into four provinces under a vicar, who in turn was under the praetorian prefect in Gaul. To offset the emphasis on garrison defences, a mobile field-army was built up: out of which rearrangement came in time a Duke, *Dux*, of the Britains at York, and a Count, *Comes*, of the Saxon Shore. The empire's capital was moved from Rome to Byzantium, and Christianity was adopted as the ideological expression of the new state-form.

The emperors were struggling to organise a society which had undergone drastic changes. The tenant farmer, *colonus*, was tied to the soil; government controls were extended over practically the whole of economic life, which (outside agriculture) was gathered in corporations; the bureaucracy grew in intricacy and power. A new class of landlords, *potentes*, emerged out of the civil wars of the last century, drawing wealth from the colons who gave labour-service and bore the main tax-burden. The cities in the west, which had for the most part an insecure industrial basis, began to decline; they had lived largely on the surrounding countryside, and now met the nemesis of this parasitic existence; they sapped their own sources of life. Municipal life, with the councillors, decurions, who had controlled it, was in a bad way. No longer the organising class of urban forms in co-operation with the government, the decurions bécame a subjected class, forced to carry out imperial policy in taxes and expenditure under conditions steadily more difficult. (5)

About 306 there was trouble in northern Britain from the Picts. (6) At least from the 4th century the Irish, *Scotti*, were attacking from the Bristol Channel to the Clyde. About 342–3 the emperor Constans was in the north fighting; he made a treaty with concessions that doubtless involved permitting Picts and Scots to settle inside the Roman area. He was murdered in 350 by Magnus Magnentius, a Briton or Teuton, who seized power and was hailed in Gaul, Spain, Britain, even Italy. In Britain he was supported by the vicar, Martinus. When he was defeated in 353, the new emperor Constans II sent an emissary, Paulus, who put down the usurper's British partisans with much cruelty.

The year 360 saw more inroads in the north, which were met by a field-army of Batavians and Heruls brought in under a Master-at-Arms. Then in 367 came an alliance between Picts, Scotti, and Attecotti, an obscure folk who provided crack troops for the empire. Together, it appears, with Saxons and Franks, they made a concerted attack. A Count of the coastal defences was killed, the Duke was immobilised, and the Wall fell through the treachery of scouts. (7) Count Theodosius was sent to restore order. The wall-system had been wrecked, and perhaps now a method of using local tribes as Federates was introduced: the Damnonians of Strathclyde and the Votadini of Lothian and Northumberland. (8) Some inland forts, however, were still strongly held—Piercebridge and Malton, for example, with York as their centre; or Carnarvon in north Wales, near important copper deposits. The shore-forts were still garrisoned, and signal stations were set up along the Yorkshire coast, and elsewhere, to tell from their towers of the approach of raiders.

Under Valentinian I, the Alemannic tribe of the Buccinobantes from near Metz were settled in as frontier troops under their king Fraomar, who became tribune or commander. (9) No doubt they were stationed in the north, but we find no trace of them in documents such as the *Notitia*. Then in 378 the empire suffered a great disaster at Adrianople in the East, when it was made finally clear that the old legions were of no avail against heavy mounted troops, here the Goths. In Britain, 383 saw another secession. A Spaniard,

Magnus Maximus, had come over with Theodosius and stayed to carry on some kind of administration in Britain; he now led the main troops of the island over to Gaul, defeated the emperor Gratian, and made himself master of Gaul and Spain, till he was killed in 388. The final imperial reorganisation was made by Honorius, who sent his general, the Vandal Stilicho, to restore order. The poet Claudian claims victories over Pict and Scot, and mentions naval campaigns, 395–9. In 395 the inner strain of the empire had been signalised by a definite division into two halves, with centres at Rome and Byzantium (Constantinople). (10)

Britain continued to be open to sea-raids. (11) In the west the Irish were active; and the increasing danger to Rome had led to the withdrawal of a legion. In the summer of 402, after Stilicho defeated Alaric at Pollentia, Claudian recited his *Gothic War*, apparently in the Library of the Temple of Apollo in Rome:

> First hurry the neighbouring troops, with loyalty proved
> by Raetia saved and Vindelicia's plunder.
> Next the legion left to guard remotest Britain
> that had checked the ferocious Scot and watched in wonder
> strange tattoo-marks on the faces of dying Picts.
> Even the legions that faced the blond Sigambri
> or held the Chatti and wild Cherusci under,
> now turned this way their threatening arms and left
> the Rhine a sole defence: the fear of Rome. (12)

We are now on the verge of the decisive changes that turned Roman Britain into sub-Roman or Celtic Britain; and already some points have come up that are important for our understanding of those changes. First, the tendency to secessions, which, though made in the name of usurpers to the imperial title, must have induced a growing sense of independence; secondly, the advent of the system of Federates which put arms in the hands of Britons and gave their chieftains an increasing sense of power, military and administrative.

With these pointers we can turn to the picture that Britain presents in the later 4th century. We need to know as thoroughly as possible what had been happening to the towns and to the landlords of the countryside, what changes were operating in production and in marketing, and what ideas about the world were developing in the minds of men. We shall find that Magnus Maximus, mentioned above as one of the confused train of usurpers, had a very special importance to the Britons, and we shall need to know why this was so. We shall examine the men whose thoughts are accessible to us:

Pelagius and Patrick among the Britons, and the early Welsh Saints; Victricius, Germanus, Faustus, Virgilius, and others among the Gauls—some of whom may indeed have been Britons and all of whom illuminate the intellectual developments which Britain shared with Gaul.

Used with the requisite caution, such sources can help to cast many beams of light into the Dark Age. "Britain was practically an annexe of Gaul," Rostovtzeff remarked; and of the earlier 5th century Collingwood commented, "Britain, at this late period, is exceedingly poor in literary records of its social condition; but by the evidence of archaeology the likeness between the two countries was so close that Gaulish documents can be used to throw light on British affairs." (13)

Not that we can mechanically transfer Gallic evidences to Britain at any phase; and there were factors at work in the 5th century which rapidly carried Gaul along a different road of development than that followed by Britain. But as long as we take care to bring together those aspects which are demonstrably shared by the two regions, we can find the Gallic materials most valuable. Indeed, between the times of Maximus and those of Saint Germanus (roughly 383 to 445) the cultural connections were in many ways close; and even after that there were lines of important connection between the Celtic areas of Britain and Gaul, especially Brittany, which was being colonised from Britain.

But we are already anticipating the story. Here it is enough to claim that if the Dark Age, with Arthur's victories as the British climax round about 500, is approached with a thorough sifting of the literary and archaeological evidence, it becomes to a considerable extent comprehensible, with clear landmarks and definite lines of development. Far from being an age lost in a dark tumult, it reveals itself as a vital phase in our national history.

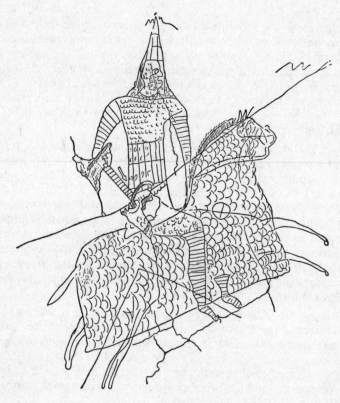

Parthian Knight in full armour on horse in chain-armour; he has a tall helmet with vizor, chainmail coat, and apparently greaves, sword and long spear; no stirrups appear

1

TOWN, COUNTRYSIDE, AND THE STATE

BRITAIN was the least urbanly developed section of the empire, which meant that it was the least Romanised. There was one *municipium* and four *coloniae*, though a fair number of cantonal or tribal capitals for administration and trade existed, and there were two spas, Bath and Buxton. In Britain, as elsewhere, the 3rd century was critical for the towns. Thus Verulamium had prospered in the 2nd century, but weakened by the end of the 3rd; the Constantinian effort of revival had no lasting effect; pavements were patched with clay and the theatre was used for dumping rubbish. Lincoln, a *colonia*, had extended its size to double by the early 3rd century, but by the 4th its fine public buildings were broken down and sites usurped by small structures, shops, and workshops. Wroxeter, capital of the Cornovii, suffered a second large fire in 296 and then made no attempt to rebuild its forum and town hall. At Caister-by-Norwich the guardroom in the main south gate had rubbish tipped across its doorways and was filled in by 300. When bastions were added to London walls, the ruins of near-by houses, including columns and sculptures, were used. (1) The Theodosian Code generalised the state of things throughout the empire: "Towns (*civitates*), deprived of their magistrates, have lost the splendour by which they once shone." (2) The picture of decay indeed needs revision in the light of recent excavations; the pattern grows more complex; but a check, partly overcome, seems sure.

The building of walls showed the failing sense of security. Some larger towns seem walled in the last quarter of the 2nd century—Cirencester, Verulamium, Exeter, Leicester, Colchester, Chichester, Winchester, Towchester, Mancetter, Aldborough, Brough, and Great Casterton; probably London around the same time too. Caerwent, Silchester, Caister-by-Norwich have their walls dated about 200.

In some cases the fortifications fell into neglect; but in the 4th century drastic attempts at reconstruction were made. They had been preceded by the new type of defence systems incorporated in the forts of the Saxon Shore with their high thick walls and their various kinds of bastion. Brough Castle still shows the emplacements for the *ballistae*, swivelling spring-guns, and it was the need for housing such artillery that determined in many ways the type of architecture.

Caerwent had six semi-octagonal bastions projecting ten to twelve feet at uneven intervals. As they were hollow, they must have had a timber platform at the level of the rampart walk; and as they were not bonded in, their artillery must have been fairly light. Their date is 333–50. Aldborough, the Brigantian capital in the plain of York, had four bastions, three of them very large and solid, which are dated about 350. Chichester's bastions were also 4th century. Great Casterton's were built after 337, perhaps even after 350; in a bastion's construction-layer was found, close to the footings, a coin dated 350–60. The previous defences, of the 2nd century, had at least two steep-sided rock-cut ditches; now a rock-cut ditch some sixty feet wide was dug. Thousands of tons were shifted.

Parallels to this great ditch and projecting bastions appear at Ancaster, Horncastle, Caistor-on-the-Wolds, and Water Newton. The latter site lay on the River Nene, some ten miles south of Great Casterton, and enclosed 44 acres; through it ran the causeway of Ermine Street, 40 feet wide, and around it spread the flourishing pottery industry known as Castor.

The bastioned town walls all seem close in date, the product of a single moment of imperial policy; and the time may have been the years immediately following 343, when the emperor Constans considered the British situation sufficiently alarming to come over in person, not even shrinking from what was a perilous crossing, in January. What brought him seems to have been the northern trouble that led to destruction of the forts beyond the Wall. High Rochester was never rebuilt. The Picts, not the British, had been the attackers, and the damage seems to have been restricted to the frontier zone; but Constans may well have seen danger-signs that made him issue a decree promulgating important changes in town defences. The reconstructions would then have gone on about the same time, done by tribal levies under military engineers. (3)

Nearly all the cantonal capitals seem to have shrunk before they gained their 2nd-century walls. But after that they often played an important part in maintaining the economic strength of Britain: thus Silchester's mass of pottery suggests a vigorous 4th-century life, and for a long time Caerwent carried on much trading and manufacturing in its main street. In many places the villa-growth occurs, not around the capital, but near a somewhat smaller town: Ilchester not Dorchester, Rochester not Canterbury, Mildenhall not Silchester. (4)

In the 1928 edition [of the Ordnance Survey Map of Roman Britain] only twenty-one towns were shown apart from Verulamium and the four coloniae. Towns like Chelmsford, Ilchester, Godmanchester, Braughing, and Mildenhall—to name only a few of the more obvious —were classed with Woodyates as "villages," while Towchester, Brough, Ancaster, Horncastle, Great Casterton, Caistor-by-Yarmouth, and Dorchester (Oxon), all now known to be walled towns, do not even attain that status. It may prove that these centres of economic life, well able, behind their massive walls, to protect their citizens against wandering bands of raiders or deserters, formed self-supporting units on which the continued prosperity of the province depended at a time when the larger towns, like Wroxeter and Verulamium, are said to have shrunk and fallen into decay.

The military north had its own kind of village development. A *vicus* grew up round a fort, both market and place of recreation. The houses were mainly long, narrow shops or taverns, with sliding-door fronts and back rooms for stores or service, and with living quarters above. Some soldiers, no doubt, on retiring, settled into businesses; and then, with land settlement for serving soldiers in the 3rd century, these *vici* grew in size and activity. At Housesteads, Chesterholm, Chesters, the village was larger than the fort; and the Housesteads *vicus* had a special gate opening north for trade from beyond the frontier. The depôt town of Corbridge grew as an industrial centre after its military status ended, leaving a late gold hoard and housing craftsmen who made the pots and probably also the Celtic brooches of dragonesque or S-shaped character found on the site. (5)

Settlements grew at Piercebridge (Durham), Old Carlisle, and Old Penrith (Cumberland), with a military road centre giving routes to a market. Binchester (Durham) had many shops and taverns on the same lines. As in Upper Germany, places from which the garrisons withdrew continued to grow: for example, Catterick and Carlisle—though in wilder parts like Wales such a development did not occur.

After the destruction in 367, the *vici* of the Wall were not reconstructed. Now the garrisons with their families lived inside the forts. Roughly rebuilt by local labour, the forts grew like little medieval fortified towns, with the garrisons taking the near land for their services. "Granaries became dwellings and headquarters buildings became half storehouses and half living quarters. A centurion of the old order would have blenched at the sight." (6) At York and Caerleon the farmer-soldiers had their families outside the barracks; at Malton they all lived inside. The troops probably became to some degree British in speech. (7)

The soldiers throughout undertook many industrial jobs, from quarrying to metalwork, and in some respects had set standards of technical achievement. But a slave-economy was unable by its very nature to develop labour-saving mechanisms. The limited extent to which the water-mill was used exemplifies this weakness. Lincoln had a water supply pumped from springs through a water main of concrete-enclosed tile-pipes; also a system of main sewers with manholes and feeders, laid down over an area larger than that of the walled town. Some cantonal capitals had a gravity supply carried underground in timber pipes joined by iron collars: Silchester, Caerwent, Caister-by-Norwich. An open leet, nine miles long, supplied Dorchester in Dorset; a similar one for Leicester seems to have failed, but Greatchesters on the Wall had one. Only Wroxeter seems to have had enough water coming in at a level that made possible the use of leaden and wooden pipes for private distribution—with an overflow for a street-side leet tapped by sluices for flushing latrines.

At three points on the Wall the army used water-power for flour-mills. At Woolaston Pill villa power-driven stones were re-used in a floor near a man-made leet; an iron spindle for

similar stones was found at Great Chesterford. But asses or
decrepit horses, apart from slaves, turned the mills. Ausonius
in Gaul uses words that suggest the terrible picture of racked
slaves and asses in the bakery of The Golden Ass: "From the
millmaze where they turn the stones by the heavy crank, two
three-legged hacks I'll harness, with lashbroken backs" (*ep*. xxv).

A legend tells that Cormac mac Airt in a 3rd-century raid
bore off a Pictish princess. His jealous Queen stipulated that
she should grind daily an impossible amount. So Cormac sent
to Britain for "a craftsman able to make a mill," and the girl
ground her quota. The mill did in fact reach Ireland from
Britain. (8) Lives of 6th-century saints repeat the mill story.

The villas in Britain developed in two main waves. The first,
culminating soon after 200, Romanised the Iron Age farms.
The second wave, starting in the 3rd, culminated in the 4th
century; its houses are usually more complex and comfortable.
Often both phases occur on the same site, but that does not
prove continuity of family occupation. At the conquest the
Belgic south-east was the most advanced area; but Romanisation reached its peak in the south-west, where earlier settlers
(Iron Age B) were located.

It does not seem that in the 3rd century landowners moved
their residences from town to country to avoid heavy liturgy
and tax. Hardly a villa is more than ten miles from some sort
of town: about two-and-a-half hours' walk or a short ride.
Even the towns, Wroxeter and Verulamium, most easily cited to
show the period's decay, do not suggest withdrawing landlords;
they seem surrounded by few and poor villas. Those near
Verulamium appear to have declined in step with the town; they
clearly depended on the town market. (9) We may then surmise
that the first villa phase was linked with insecure urbanisation
and suffered when towns declined in the 3rd century; the later
lift to agriculture came from a new quarter and represented a
sort of new start.

In the 4th century this new start was at work. Britain,
relatively sheltered, could be relied on for crops or textiles
when Gaul was overrun or disordered—as was shown dramat-
ically when Julian commandeered grain for the Rhineland.
Thus, after 369 a new villa was built at East Denton, Lincoln-

shire, a barn-type probably inhabited by a bailiff. At Great
Casterton a villa was reconstructed in the 380s. In East Yorkshire Langton, injured in 367–9, prosperously recovered;
Rudston, founded much earlier, attained mosaics and baths
in the 4th century. A villa at Harpham reached its largest
growth, and that at Old Durham gained bath-house and big
threshing-floor.

Some cantonal capitals benefited: at Isurium of the Brigantes
fine mosaicked houses sheltered the magnates. And agriculture
spread even in some areas of fell and forest. (10) Corn was
needed for the army; and though the garrisons were now rearing
their own crops, some sections no doubt still bought their corn.
And there were the towns. A considerable proportion of harvests must have been taken by the State: requisitioned or paid
for at low rates. Corn-growing was scarcely an easy way to
wealth. The main arable region was East Anglia and East
Midlands; especially the Fenlands and the parts to their south.
Villas, however, were scanty and, apart from half a dozen
exceptions, poor. Great Chesterford gives an example of a town
centre in a corn area, and even here, as well as ploughs, crop-
ping shears for giving a fine nap in a woollen-mill were found.

Orchardry would provide a specialised line. We know from
Pliny that the Romans established the cherry, and stones have
been found at Silchester and Holt. "An apple stall is depicted
in a relief at Arlon, but why should it not also occur at Rochester
or Kenchester? Again, away from farming, what was the organisation of the shell-fish industry (for it can hardly be called
less)?" (11)

There were various industrial possibilities for a villa, not only
round Castor, as is shown at Farnham and Ashtead. At
Borough Farm, Pulborough, the fine house was connected with
the making of Samian ware. An outlier at Magor Farm may
have been concerned with tin; and some good houses (e.g.
Clipsham) with ironstone working—though mining was
mostly carried on in the wilder parts: related to British
villages as on Anglesey, or to officially-controlled settlements
as at Charterhouse on Mendip (with its small amphitheatre for
the convicts or slaves) and at gold-working Dolaucothy with its
baths. Mines were owned by the State, but usually farmed out

to prospectors; the 4th century saw much production of tin, lead, pewter. The villas below Mendip can have had no relation to Charterhouse except as a market. (12)

Woodlands and quarries were also sources of income for landowners; but the main alternative to crops was animal husbandry, especially sheep-rearing. We have many signs of the importance of British wool and woollens in the 4th century. Diocletian's price-list cited the British raincloak, *birrus*, and the *Notitia* mentioned at Venta (certainly Winchester) a Procurator Gynaecii, the official in charge of a State weaving-establishment. Another Diocletianic document, found in Cyrene, dealing with carpets and tapestries, counted as most valuable a carpet of British weaving. (13) We meet very large villas concerned with sheep, as at Bignor, or with processes like fulling, as at Chedworth (which dealt also with wrought-iron agricultural tools). At Darenth in Kent and Titsey in Surrey we again see the change from an ordinary farming villa into something like a big manufacturing site, connected with processing in vats. Silchester in its north-west quarter seems much taken up with dyeing. (14)

We perhaps find animal enclosures at various places, e.g. Soldier's Ring. And in Cranborne Chase we meet in the 4th century a depopulation of the Dorset highlands, a turning from arable to pastoral methods.

But Cranborne Chase is only part of the Celtic field belt which stretches from the Berkshire Downs to the environs of Dorchester, and one would like to know whether the same process took place further south in the interests of such villas as Frampton and Witchampton. An even more profitable field for study might be the area north of Winchester, where also we have villas superimposed on fields of native type. (15)

There is much evidence of the turn from arable in the chalk-lands of Wiltshire; and doubtless the same would have happened also in the Cotswolds if the villages there had not already specialised in sheep. (16)

Who owned the pastoral villas and profited from wool and woollens? The State certainly played its part. At Winchester was the procurator in charge of weaving, an example of the considerable intrusion of the State into textile production in the West at this time. The *Notitia* lists six such procurators in Gaul, at Arles, Lyon, Reims, Tournai, Trèves, Autun (transferred to Metz), another dealing with linen at Vienne, and two dealing with. dyeing at Toulon and Barbonne. In Sicily there was a textile procurator of the last-mentioned kind, while in Spain we seem to find the State after 200 partly controlling the olive-oil trade. (17)

In the Fens the great drainage system can only have been the work of the State. The Romans reclaimed land on a grand scale, building an embankment to protect the flat lands of the Wash from the sea; other dykes enclosed the marshland at the Usk mouth. A canal of eight miles, Car Dyke, joined the Cam below Cambridge with the Ouse halfway between St. Ives and Ely, while a canal, 25 miles long and 60 feet wide, ran from Peterborough on the Nene to the Witham three miles below Lincoln. The Fosse Dyke connected the Witham and the Trent, and a causeway of 60 feet was built along 30 miles of the drainage canal banks. Other such works in the west were the canalisation of a Rhône mouth and dykeworks in Holland, with a canal of 23 miles between the Rhine and the Meuse. (18)

The corn of the Fens was doubtless shipped in part to the Rhine. There is no Roman harbour found in the area, but Caistor-on-Sea (by Yarmouth) was an active port in the 4th century.

An interesting side-light on the level of organisation in industrial matters is given by the use of the coal, which is found (*a*) in the towns and settlements of Wroxeter, Caerwent, Ariconium, Wilderspool, Tiddington, and Heronbridge near Chester—here local coal was used for heating and industrial purposes such as smelting; (*b*) in the outlying villas and villages of Gloucestershire, Somerset, Wiltshire, where it was used for heating hypocausts and suggests wandering pedlars who exploited the Somerset field; (*c*) in the Fens, where the nearest coalfield lies far off in central England; (*d*) on the Wall forts and at the Corbridge depôt—a cartload in the guard-chamber of a Housesteads gate was found in a late context, indicating "an official organisation for the digging and distribution of coal", operated by the quartermasters. (19)

The odd location is the Fens, where at Wyboston coal seems to have been used for corn-drying. The granaries of South Shields, of Severan date, had now been converted to other uses, but there may have been elsewhere a base for Fens supplies. If so, we have an easy route for the influx of coal into the Fens, where charcoal would be scarce.

We gain a hint of the official relation to agriculture, outside the Fens, in the North Midlands. There, away from the region of flourishing villas, each small town or station seems to have one satellite villa: Engleton at Pennocrucium, Shenstone at Letocetum, Sapcote at Venonae, Norton Disney at Crococalana, and so on. The satellite may be connected with the collection of *annona* from the peasantry around.

This would give a context for the third-century development at Norton Disney; and one is reminded of the inscription from the villa at Combe Down, near Bath, which records the restoration of *Principia* in the reign of Caracalla. (20)

A striking indication of State control appears at Bokerly Dyke, north of Woodyates. The first phase of its building runs from 325-30 to after the mid-4th century. The purpose must have been to protect the open pasture-lands lying south between woods; and the earthworks were probably joined at points with forest-sections lined with timber abattis or linked with fences. (21)

We do not know how big an area we should think of. But that the downland estates as a whole should have contained an area of particular importance as an imperial pasture-domain, whether for sheep or for cattle or stud horses, and that the north-western gap in its border of woods should have been held in the earlier 4th century to need earthwork protection, can surely be well credited.

The Dyke seems to have taken in a spring, useful for watering stock; and its construction was devised against raiding—

whether by oppressed peasants—surreptitiously or in such outbreaks as the peasant rebels called Bacaudae so often made in Gaul—or by barbarians if they should ever come; this was a traditional purpose of Roman military barrier-works; and no doubt like the Bitburg walls (in Gaul) it was built by military labour and policed thereafter by a guard. The soldiers would be third-rate troops, peasants themselves, settled on such imperial estates for miscellaneous duties. And a headquarters, responsible for all this part of the district, was close at hand in the Woodyates settlement. (22)

By the early 4th century the growth of Woodyates is shown by an impressive coin concentration; the population seems at its fullest expansion from 275 to 325. A second Dyke, between 364 and 370, was cut across the roadway, then filled in again; its sides were still unweathered when the upcast rampart was shovelled back. It certainly represents an emergency, which soon passed—this must be the attacks of 367–8 by the Picts, Irish, and others, which were over by 370.

(*Left*) Horse with panriers (*Trajan Col.*)
(*Right*) Man in cowl (*from Aesernia*)

2

LANDLORDS AND TENANTS

THE 4th century then saw the growth of large estates and a concentration on sheep and textiles. This development lay behind the rise of Cirencester to the capital of Britannia Prima. The big villas seem certainly to have been owned by landlords: Chedworth, a courtyard-type with a multiple series of rooms connected to front and back corridors; Northleigh with a range of work-rooms added to an earlier house; Woodchester with fine dining-room and gateway, approached through a court of barnlike work-buildings, with corn-drying kiln at the end of one. (1) But the matter of ownership is not so clear, say, at Hambledon, where it is hard to define the building stages in house and corn-drying furnaces. Here again we meet barn-dwellings, and at some time the occupant changed the house-front so as to look away from the area of work. The place seems to have been a slave establishment dealing with corn in a big way, probably run by a bailiff for State or private landlord. (2)

Cranborne Chase, with its change to pasturage, has been conjectured to have been an imperial estate run by a bailiff in Old Sarum and perhaps also in Badbury. (3) This seems most likely, though we cannot disprove the existence of big landlords. Beyond doubt the State did intrude considerably into economic life in Britain, into both corn-growing and pastoral systems. (4) But also beyond doubt the 4th century saw a consolidation of power by the *potentes*, the new big landlords—even though specific factors (the comparative backwardness and the value of Britain in these troubled years to the central government) may have modified the situation. (5) We must not seek precise uniformities between the provinces or within a single province. The large villas of Alsace-Lorraine and the Rhineland were occupied by people who did not farm, though there may well have been owners who were also farmers. In 6th-century Egypt the great man Apion in his villa controlled villages which he did not own. By the 4th century in Sicily the agglomerations called *massae* had arisen in the southern, less mountainous parts. The Massa Pyramitana near Syracuse belonged to the emperor; Constantine the Great gave the pope vast properties round Catana and Panhormus; the churches of Milan and Rome owned estates as large as counties; Lauricius of Ravenna in mid-5th century had a chain of large estates. Senatorials like him or Symmachus leased their land to entrepreneurs, *conductores*, who sub-let to working tenants or colons. At times agents collected rents for *conductores*. Imperial domains in the same way were leased out under *rationales* and procurators. (6) And Roman forms might spread into areas still tribal. Ireland shows villas in its raths. "It looks as if the Celtic system in Ireland was 30 acres of cultivation with waste land around, like the medieval system. It seems to work in groups, like villas." (7)

In Britain, villas cluster in favourable areas: round Ilchester and Bath, or (in a less concentrated way) round Winchester, to some degree at Mildenhall and Sandy Lane. But we need not look for *massae* on the Sicilian scale. Nor do we find such a self-sufficient manor as at Anthée in Gaul, where the villa stands at the head of a 30-acre rectangle with a big gateway separating the inner court from main enclosure; in the latter are some twenty buildings, including smithy, pottery kilns, and so on. (8) What is striking about the clusters in Britain is the businesslike specialisation in sheep and textiles; and though the State, too, was concerned in all that, we can safely see in it the basis of the British class of *potentes*, who were to play an important part once imperial controls went.

The barn-type of building (e.g. at Hambledon) probably signified an estate on which slave-labour was brought together. Such structures were being raised in the 4th century (e.g. Denton) but had also an earlier history. At Llantwit Major in the Glamorgan sea-plain stood a 2nd-century plain courtyard house with farm buildings that included a barnhouse; with the 4th century the main house decayed but the barnhouse flourished for another century at least. (9)

Again, at Brading, I.O.W., with its rich mosaics, there were barnhouses either side. (10) At Clanville, Hampshire, also with excellent mosaics and heated rooms, the enclosed yard and walls suggest a stockyard. The inscription (to the emperor Carinus) may represent a milestone, but may also be the work of an imperial bailiff. "If so, the picture here might be an imperial estate, with native cultivation, later sold or leased off to independent farmers—perhaps to Quintus Natalius Natalinus and his friends, whom we know from the pavement at Thruxton." (11)

The *potentes* appear in texts dealing with the empire in general from 360. With their large estates mainly exploited through the tied-farmers, they grew steadily more baronial and supplied personnel for the highest government posts. The new State had to base itself on them despite the element of rivalry. The emperors complained that they cheated the fisc and drew the peasants into their control away from the tax-collector, yet needed to rely more and more on them for the maintenance of the system.

So integrated in the State were these new lords that they even used its communications for their own economic ends.

It was at this epoch, it seems, that, in default of traders installed in the increasingly weakened towns, the custom arose of confiding to specially commissioned agents the work of buying articles and foodstuffs that could not be found in the local marts. When in the service of the emperors or high magistrates, these agents enjoyed the privilege of the *cursus publicus*: that is, they had official means of transport at their disposal . . . [We thus find] the sovereign providing functionaries for purchases among the producers. (12)

That the landlords had colons working on their lands in Britain we know from the Theodosian Code.

As in Northern Gaul and Germany, the economic development of Britain may have tended towards converting free peasants into *coloni* of great land-owners, if, indeed, they were not already in a somewhat similar position of dependence even before the conquest. (13)

The small farmer becoming a lord's colon had certain gains. He was made secure in his tenure and had someone to stand between him and the crushing state-machine, though in return he had to give rents and services. Still, a vast misery lay behind these developments. As Salvian wrote in mid-5th century in Gaul:

The kind of contract of transference they enter into is something quite new. The buyer gives nothing and gets everything. The seller receives nothing and loses all. This sort of agreement is without precedent; for the buyers' resources grow, but there remains nothing to the seller except poverty. (14)

We can perhaps make out the *fundus*, estate, on lines like those found in Gaul (where it is represented by names ending in -*acus*, which has turned into *ac, at, e,* or *y* in French). It might consist of several small villas. In Oxfordshire some five or six villas at least, with half a dozen other Roman sites, seem to be surrounded by rampart and ditch. Northleigh was the centre. (15)

When villas and villages were mixed in the same area, the villagers were possibly colons on the villa-estate:

African mosaics of the fourth and fifth centuries A.D. display large villas in full working order, with the production of corn left to the *coloni*, who paid rents in kind to the landowners while the more profitable and specialised branches of husbandry were concentrated round the villa itself. (16)

Britain had many social and economic affinities with the Rhineland, especially the right bank of the river. There the farms were mostly large, run for monetary profit, some concerned with corn, some with cattle-breeding; the native population were mainly tenants and shepherds.

In Hampshire, "in the late Roman period a series of satellite holdings sprang up round the larger estate or within its boundaries, and this forcibly suggests colonate tenure." (17) In Gloucestershire, Withington has been thoroughly analysed—and this area specially interests us as that to which we must look for the forces which under Arthur later checked the Saxons. The villa lies a mile south of Upper Withington, roughly on the same contour-line. Beyond lifts the ridge with trackway for Cirencester; it sheltered the villa from the western winds. Between it and the Coln a spring rose, no doubt tapped by a well. (18) Here we seem to meet the centre of an estate with measurable acreage. South, past a wooded ridge, lies Chedworth villa; and the bounds between Chedworth and Withington must have been much the same in Roman days or in the Anglo-Saxon perambulations as at present.

The villa-owner would rely for bread-corn on rents paid in kind by colons, while keeping a staff of shepherds, weavers, and domestic slaves in the villa, and a large sheep-flock on the down. The colons would live in hamlets like Foxcote, paying much or all of their rent in wool: the later yardlanders owed the manor-lord a customary spinning-fee. North Field would be the main arable area, with ploughmen perhaps living in upper Withington. The villa lay a little above the village as prescribed by writers on farming. (19)

In Cranborne Chase we again seem to detect a central villa with dwellings grouped round. The name Anicetis appears in the late Ravenna Cosmography, referring to a site between Shaftesbury and Iwerne. The plural form links with the -acum names so common in Gaul, which, though rare, do exist in Britain. Anicetis was probably the estate based on the villa near Tarrant Hinton with near-by farms (e.g. Chettle) and a road running from Badbury to Bath. The name, it is suggested, comes from Anicetus, Nero's freedman, fleet-prefect at Misenum by Naples; for Nero held estates near Silchester. But a more likely candidate is Q. Pompeius Anicetus, who died at Bath. (Nero's man would be Tib. Claudius.) People dying at spas are often visitors, and there was the direct road from Anicetis to Bath. The name suggests a Greek whose family gained the citizenship in the late Republic. (20) Asianic Greeks we know as contractors working lead-mines in Derbyshire under Hadrian or earlier, e.g. P. Rubrius Abascantus. If Cranborne Chase were an imperial domain, Anicetus would be a *conductor* with a home-farm and with farmsteads of colons as sub-lessees. (21)

We have an excellent picture of a bailiff, *vilicus*, on a private estate in the later 4th century in Gaul. The poet Ausonius of Bordeaux, professor and imperial tutor, gained various high honours and retired in late 379 to his home town, no doubt taking over the estate, Lucaniacus, inherited from his father the year before. His letter shows how local famines could press

heavily on some areas in periods of dislocation. He is writing
to his young friend Paulinus, whose estate Hebromagus
(Eburomagus) is now Bram, near the foothills of the eastern
Pyrenees.

Philon, once my bailiff, after using Hebromagus as a depôt for
goods bought up on various estates, is in peril of untimely ejection
from the entertainment provided by your people. And so, unless
you indulge my plea (that he be let stay on for the purposes of his
visit and that barge or some other sort of craft be allotted to him,
so that a portion of my corn may be carried as far as the town,
rescuing Lucaniacus in time from famine), a literary man's whole
household there will be brought down, not to Cicero's *Corn Supply*,
but to Plautus' *Weevil*.

To gain my way more easily, or to make you afraid of worse
nuisance if you refuse, I send a letter composed in iambics and
sealed, so that you may not accuse the postman (*tabellarius*) of being
suborned if he turns up without a seal's guarantee. Yet I have sealed
it, in Plautus' words, with wax and thread and with expressive signs
—with a poetic stamp: something you may consider more a burnt-in
brand than a surface impression.

> Philon was bailiff of my country-estate,
> an *epitrophos*: that's his word—
> a Greekling likes a pompous term, none better
> than those where classic tones are heard.
> Now his complaint with my appeal he mates
> in this my most reluctant letter.
>
> You'll see the man—here, conjured at my side,
> he typifies his calling fully:
> grey, tousle-haired, unkempt and furious-eyed,
> Terence's Phormio, a bully.
> His hair is ragged with a bristling shag,
> like a sea-urchin, or my verse.
> He, when poor harvests oft belied his brag,
> found the name bailiff prove a curse.
> Through ignorance of the stars he sowed too early
> by far, or else he sowed too late.
> To shift the blame, he swore and shouted, surly,
> against the heavens, harsh with hate.

No earnest farmer, no skilled ploughman, he,
better equipt to spend than earn,
abused the soil for sterile treachery,
preferring a sly business-turn,
in any chaffering forum bought and sold
on Grecian Credit, bartering,
wiser than all the Seven Wise of old,
the eighth Sage, in a market-ring.

And now some grain for mouldy salt he's gained—
see the New Trader proudly stand!
He visits tenants, villages, towns and country,
and travels round by sea or land,
in bark, skiff, schooner, galley borne abroad,
sailing Garonne and Tarn in glee;
turns profit soon to loss and loss to fraud,
grows rich himself and ruins me.
Now in your villa is this chap at large
and there he's dumped the goods he bears,
that grain may be transported down by barge
to meet my needs. So he declares.

But don't be inconvenienced, let the stay
of such a bothering guest be short,
that, entering your boat without delay
and carried to the town's own port,
he may deliver Lucaniacus soon
from famine worsening day by day.
O, you'll be worshipt if you grant this boon
higher than Ceres when I pray.
Triptolemus (Epimenides again
or Buzyges the bailiff's choice)
I'll rank below your godhead. For the grain
will be your gift and we'll rejoice. (22)

Even in Gaul bartering was much carried in the place of
money-sales: Grecian Credit means "no credit at all". Philon,
when making a profit, represents it as loss, while fraudulently
enlarging actual losses. His Buzyges was an Attic hero said to
be the first to yoke oxen to plough and further known as
Epimenides; Triptolemus was also a hero of agriculture.
Ausonius both brings out his own erudition and stresses

Philon's outlandish Greek pride (as in the epistle's opening lines). (23)

We have practically no evidence as to the organisation of life in the villages; but it has been suggested that in an inscription from Beltingham near the Wall we have a clue. This inscription is to an unknown Goddess Saiiada, or Sattada or the like, and is made by the Curia of the Textoverdi. The latter name looks Celtic, but is otherwise unrecorded; and at first glance we should take the dedicators to be the Curia or Council of a British tribe in the north. But in the Celtic provinces the Romans evolved an amalgam of the city-state and tribal organisation. The tribe survived, but was centred on a capital town where its senate or council met. The whole system was called a *civitas*, but the term stressed the capital and in fact underlies our *city*. A tribe, however, might be a large federation of various units which were called *pagi* by the Romans (from which word the French *pays*); but there was still only one capital, and a member of any of the *pagi* was still described as a member of the *civitas* proper, not of his local *pagus*. Normally, a curia or senate existed only at the capital, covering the whole *civitas*. (24)

We have some idea of what the British *civitates* were, and it seems clear that the Textoverdi lay in the territory of the Brigantes with its capital at Aldborough. How then could this group, a unit of the Brigantian *civitas*, have a curia of its own?

There are two possible explanations. One is that the Textoverdians were members of an imperial domain or *saltus*. Decurions of such a *saltus* are known from Germany. True, certain villages in Asia Minor had their senates, but no examples are known from the West. Beltingham is, however, an odd site for a large imperial domain, and we can hardly consider the Textoverdian curia the council of a *saltus*. But Curia is found as a place-name in Celtic Switzerland (Curia Raetorum, the modern Chur), and Ptolemy mentions a Kouria somewhere in the Cheviots, in the territory of the Votadini. He also has a Koria in the territory of the Damnonians, and there is a Corie in the Ravenna list that seems in Brigantian territory. In all these cases we seem certainly to encounter a Celtic root *cori-*, which means Army, the men of the tribe assembled in arms.

The Gallic *pagus* has been seen as a development of the clan, with the tribe as a coalition of *pagi* taking its name from the most powerful member. In this system the *pagi* retained a measure of independence, particularly in military organisation. The number of *pagi* in a tribe varied according to circumstances; but the Roman conquest had the effect of crystallising the relation of *pagi* and tribe (now become *civitas*). We find several tribal names compounded of a number and a *cori-* root, e.g. Petru-corii (Four Cori) from which came Périgord with its four baronies. Such cases make us think that in Gaul the term *pagus* was the Roman version of the Celtic *cori*.

The Curia of the Textoverdians might then be the Cori or assembly-place of the sub-tribal group. Among the Akarnians, the most backward of the Greeks, the capital was still in the 5th century B.C. called *Stratos* or Army, an exact analogy of *Cori*. And as we know that under the empire one of the most vigorous functions of a *pagus* was religious, the Curia on the Beltingham stone fits well into the *cori*-interpretation.

We seem, then, here to touch on local forms of organisation below the level of the *civitas*. The *saltus*, too, would need their council of elders in Britain as elsewhere, so that discussions, when necessary, might go on between the villagers and the official world. In Asia Minor we can see how sturdily the peasants of a *saltus* might stand up for their customary rights, heartened by the fact that the system brought them communally together.

A Phrygian case of the first half of the 3rd century may be cited as showing the sort of thing that must have happened in Britain from time to time. Two villages, Anossa and Antimacheia, were disputing about their respective duties on the highway, which included the provision of animals for transporting men or goods on behalf of the State. The folk of Anossa were plaintiffs and a first inquiry was held at their village in 213 before the procurator Aurelius Threptus. Both sides had spokesmen, Panas for the Anosseni and Alexander for the others. It seems that two or more roads converged on a near *mansio*, road-station, and that Anossa was responsible for the traffic on each road. (25)

Threptus asked for details. How far did the obligation extend? and where were the teams of oxen, used for loads, handed over? Panas replied that his village served a number of short and well-defined stretches of road. Alexander then admitted liability for supplying traffic on the road from Amorium and Ancyra, but protested that his village was poor. (Antimacheia seems responsible for serving long-distance traffic on one route only. Ancyra was nearly 200 miles away.)

Threptus took up the plea of poverty, the relation of obligations to taxes. Figures were bandied about. Threptus then told the villagers that they had accepted the system under many of his predecessors and that the services must be provided in proportion to taxes paid. Panas, dissatisfied, seems to have threatened an appeal to Docimium through an advocate.

Threptus replied, "To what purpose are you going to say more than you have already said?" And repeated his point about the taxes.

The record then picks up a later moment in the argument. Panas seems to have raised the matter of each village's duty to supply the other with the stores necessary for carrying out the services. Threptus goes back on his previous words. "Since it is said that you have also given stores to the Antimacheni, and they turn by turn to you, you will undertake half and they half." He then seems to say that the *optio* (a sub-centurion) will see the award carried out.

Panas makes a last objection. "But if we are to take *angareia* [here, oxen and carts] to Antimacheia, how will this be?"

"You will serve half and half, up to the point where a relief takes over."

Two letters show the *optio* following things up. The first, addressed to elders and people of both villages, indicates that a formal appeal has been made to the procurator. In ornate and servile language the official states that he has been ordered to see the *angareia* or services equally shared and that disobedience will be punished. The second letter bids the Antimacheni "according to what has been laid down in the records of the proceedings to perform the services according to allocation or to take the consequences". On 11 December the procurator Philocurius heard the case anew at Prymnessus. The Antimacheni seemed to be the chief dissidents; and their opponents' spokesman, Valens, asked for a *stationarius* to be put in, apparently for his side's protection.

Nearly a quarter of a century later, in 237, the trouble began afresh. On 10 October, before the procurator Bovellius, at Synnada, the case was tried. Once more the villagers were told that the original decision must hold, and a minor official was charged with its execution. A fine seems to have been imposed.

The independence and outspokenness of the villagers is noteworthy. There is nothing of the serf about them. It is not perhaps surprising that even at this moment many were accepting the individualistic teachings of the Montanist sect. (Frend)

Independent or stubborn would be better terms for heretics like the Montanists, in whom we see the village-community resisting State and Church. Though the Church was not yet part of the state system, it was building the episcopal organisation that made possible the compromise under Constantine. Monks and heretical groups fought the growth of hierarchy which was more and more adapted to the forms of power and property of existing society.

The Phrygian case shows the sort of problem faced by peasants in the 3rd–4th centuries. Under the Constantinian reconstruction the main tax, *annona*, was largely paid in kind and was used to feed troops or officials; there was an increase in traffic burdens. Villages had to provide levies for the *mansiones* strung along the imperial roads and used as *annona* depôts. In Britain, as in Gaul, the chief means of transport would be the four-wheeled waggon; and if plough-oxen were taken instead of the authorised draught-animals, a village could be ruined. The oxen would return unfit for work. A Jewish proverb wailed: "Angareia is like Death." (26)

Britain shared in the general system. We can make out the *mansiones*, doubtless often the administrative centres of *pagi*, though at times mere post-road stations. And we catch glimpses of the *beneficiarii*, soldiers seconded to special duty such as tax-collecting or supervision of road and river traffic. Sulpicius depicts a road-train in Gaul. "A government coach crammed with servicemen ambled along the highway; but when the mules on Martin's side saw him in his shaggy tunic, with his bellying black cloak, they were scared and shied off a bit, then got tangled up in the traces and broke the long lines in which the wretched creatures were massed, as you have often seen them." The soldiers jumped out and lashed at Martin with sticks and whips till he fell down bloody and wounded. The mules refused to budge: "like statues of bronze. The muleteers yelled, but they stood stone-still. Then everyone began beating them and wore out the big Gallic whips. The whole near copse was wrenched down for weapons." At last the soldiers asked the saint's pardon and the mules moved. Whether or not we credit the creatures' piety, we see how the mules or oxen of a levy could come home much the worse for wear.

Only one known rescript is addressed to Britain, dated 329. Though it seems to be partly corrupt, its general point is clear. A decurion is liable to tax on his own property whether held "in hand" or occupied by colons; he is not liable for property and colons of another decurion. (27)

The principle was set out in more recent legislation than that of 319, and these more recent texts are also in the Theodosian Code—for example, two enactments of Africa which reveal an important aim of such rescripts: to guard against tricks by which men evaded the obligation laid on landowners to take over waste plots. (This obligation was one of the means whereby the government tried to raise productivity as the system went down.)

Such laws were never sent out to a single area such as Britain. They were submitted by the chancelleries to the bureaux of praetorian prefects, which sent copies to officials lower in the administrative hierarchy. How, then, did the law get into the Code?

First the Code was a hasty compilation, in which systematic arrangement and elimination of repetitions was not always successful. The law, as it appears in the Code, must have lain in the Roman archives with a subscription as cited by British advocates in a case taken to the supreme appellate court. To get so high it must have been concerned in a more knotty case than one about evading waste cultivation.

The easiest explanation is that there had been some conflict between the rescript and tribal custom in Britain. An archaic system of Welsh land tenure that would suit the occasion was that of *Priodolder*, known in a codification of the 10th century but probably reaching back to the 1st century. By it a remote reversionary interest in land could be asserted. Title was not fixed till the fourth generation; it then held till the ninth generation even if the land were left. The returning Ninth Man had a right superior to any other holders not yet *priodorion*; but if they had also held for four generations, two persons had the same title to the land. The claimant vindicated his claim by a traditional formula, the Cry across the Abyss.

Tribal survivals would certainly be strongest in the wilder parts of the west, where the inhabitants probably had the status of *gentiles*, foreigners. In the rest of Britain, in strict law, Celtic custom was wiped out by the Edict of Caracalla making all freemen of the empire Romans. The *priodolder* custom would give way to the forms of Roman real-property estate. But a case might arise of a Briton founding an estate and going away before the Edict; about 319 his descendant returned with a Cry across the Abyss. No doubt nobody in Britain or at Trèves could answer the conundrum, and so the claim went on to Rome. Counsel argued that no man pays taxes for land not his own; the law declares that a man is only *dominus* of his own estate, and so an estate can have only one *dominus*. Indeed, the final words of our rescript would sound as if bearing directly on the issue: Let nobody suffer injury on another's behalf through this our provision.

Though the Roman municipal system had broken up in many ways, that does not mean that the towns had no part to play in the new development. Recall the small shops huddled at Lincoln. At Verulamium, with all its decay, there were many workshops; the forum failed, but in the theatre and round the rebuilt Celtic temple there was much chaffering in small coins.

Buying and selling went on vigorously, but without its old secure basis in the forum. Many articles were being carried round by hawkers and pedlars with packhorses, who sold coal as well as pottery like that turned out by the New Forest kilns. Charcoal-burners were free workers, semi-nomads of the woods who wandered round with their products. Salt, too, from many a brinepit was needed far and wide. The great Castor potteries must have had an extensive system of chapmen.

At the same time there came a growth of rural markets, connected with local fanes or sacred sites, springs and trees and stones. As in Verulamium economic life was active round the Celtic shrine, so in the country the festivals of the native cults became important fairs. We see this development clearly at Woodeaton near Oxford, where there were no neighbouring towns but the region was full of villages and small villas. The finds establish that the place must have been a market. It was "a convenient spot for traders" from all parts of Britain, situated near the crossing of two main roads. As in medieval fairs, accommodation would be in stalls: which would account for the scantiness of permanent structures. The random distribution of objects over a fairly wide space is consistent with their having been dropped, lost from stalls, in the course of trafficking. The small coins or brooches, falling into the clay on a wet day and trodden underfoot, would be hard to retrieve on Middle Hill. The objects found are almost all of metal; but that does not mean that the trade ignored wooden or woven articles that would have perished in the course of centuries. (28)

From Gaulish art we gain a picture of the wandering pedlars. A stone statuette at Langres shows a hawker on his rounds, bearded, in short belted tunic and loose cloak, with pointed cap; he has a chest on shoulder and a long box under his arm. At Soulosse we meet the woman hawker with a chest on wheels and with wares and longish objects (perhaps tools) hanging from the top, while in the streets of Narbonne we hear the apple merchant, basket slung round neck, cry out: "Apples, ladies my ladies (*mala mulieres mulieres meae*)." On figured vases we see the juggler at cross-roads with monkey, pot, rings, and ladder climbed by a wise dog.

Woodeaton's coins begin with the 1st century or even earlier: all these are much worn. The earliest in good condition are of Domitian; coins of the 2nd century are more plentiful and in better condition still; but it is with the 3rd and 4th centuries that bargaining was at its height. The market probably carried on after the end of the Roman period. There are a few coins of official mintage of the last quarter of the 4th century and a large number of barbarous imitations.

Woodeaton belongs to a group of sites that includes Cold Kitchen Hill in Wiltshire, Beacon Hill, Harting in Sussex, and Lowbury in Berkshire, where a large number of coins and trinkets seem to be linked with festival offerings to a local deity and where we sometimes meet delimiting earthworks without a building. They certainly belong to the Celtic religious system. (29) But similar activities went on at sites with temples, at Verulamium inside a town or at Farley Heath, Surrey, or Lydney, Gloucestershire in the countryside.

In the second half of the 4th century, with such erections as the Celtic temple inside the old earthworks on Maiden Castle and the great temple-complex at the healing centre of Lydney, we can speak of a widespread pagan revival. At Lydney, on a hill by the Severn, soon after 364–7, rich buildings were constructed inside the prehistoric earthwork—large bath-houses, a row of rooms (shops, priest-rooms, or incubation cells), a large hostel for pilgrims to the god Nodens. Some 8,000 coins, mostly of the 4th century or after, have been found here.

Indeed, we are confronting a complex phenomenon: a new rural economy linked with a rise in religious feeling, which in turn helps to consolidate a new awareness of being Celtic as well as Roman, or Celtic rather than Roman, as the imperial structure cracks and times grow more perilous and men are thrown more on their own resources. (30)

The new kind of regional life can perhaps also be seen in the lines of communication implied by the trafficking systems. The administration was based on London, with main lines radiating to nodal points, the *coloniae*, the legionary fortresses, the tribal capitals. But these roads were not those best suited for local trade. They did not, for instance, run along such populated belts as the north or south Downs or the Cotswolds; they cut across, wanting to hurry out of the wooded areas as fast as possible. Local traffic preferred old ridgeways like the Icknield Way on the Berkshire or Chiltern escarpment, or the Harroway of the north Downs, or else roads constructed for local and limited purposes (e.g. the White Way of the Cotswolds). (31)

SOME SOCIAL CHANGES

EVEN the climate seems to have changed in the later 4th century. It was then, not in the 8th century B.C. as has been generally assumed, that the shift from the sub-Boreal to the sub-Atlantic took place. In the Low Countries we find, from the frontier forts of Utrecht, Valkenburg, and Vechten, that in the Roman period no measures were taken against flooding, and no floods are to be found till after the forts were abandoned. Indeed, in the whole alluvial plain along the coast of the North Sea, from France to Denmark, in late Roman or post-Roman times the sea encroached, and on higher ground there was a rise in the water-table. (1)

These climatic changes were no doubt one of the factors in unsettling people in north-west Europe. In Britain, however, it seems that a certain amount of deforestation and drainage of valleys had brought the water-table down. (2) The hill-folk on chalk would be the first to feel the effects; and there was possibly some voluntary removal from the higher grounds into the valleys, as well as a movement from farmlands turned over by the landlords to pasture.

This gradual shift from the chalk- and gravel-lands on to the clays in the lowlands of eastern Britain, and from the open heights to the more sheltered valley benches and lower plateau surfaces in the western uplands, was characteristic of the period; a rise in agricultural techniques lies behind it. (3) The open-field system was already known and practised, at least in the more advanced regions. The arable strip existed as a unit, if not as a system, some centuries before the Anglo-Saxons. (4)

The rural economy had its counterpart in a reassertion of Celtic art forms. The Celtic tradition had never died and had always been ready to show itself in more purely native modes—as in the pottery grotesques of Caister-by-Norwich or the lid which a potter at Linwood in the New Forest scored with his finger-tip in rapid volutes expressing the Mother Goddess whom he wanted to protect his water. We meet the Celtic style grandiosely in the Bath Gorgon, likeably in the Corbridge Lion, powerfully in the intense Severed Heads of stone (e.g. at Carlisle). Certain rich forms of brooches seem to be of the late Roman period—small disks with thin bronze strip embossed in a triskele scroll design, from Silchester, Brough, Corbridge, and perhaps the disks enamelled in two colours, green on blue, deep orange on blue, light blue on red, from Lowbury, Silchester, and Brough, not to mention a five-limbed motive from Lowbury.

We have literary evidence—in the work of the sophist Philostratus—that enamelling was practised round the turn into the 3rd century. His words cannot refer to such things as the horse trappings of the earlier Celtic age; they must concern certain bowls and the like. Triskele decorations, recalling the disk-brooches, appear on a strainer from Carmarthenshire, associated (it seems) with coins of Carausius, on a bronze mount from South Shields and a seal-box lid in red-on-blue enamel from York. It seems clear that the tradition of Celtic design never faded away.

Another Celtic development towards the end of the Roman period is seen in the circular brooches and handpins. They carry on into the 7th–8th centuries, but probably now originated. We find tenuous ribboning scrolls and the like used as a basis for Champlevé enamel; and already in an example from Brough appears a tendency to end scrolls in animals' or birds' heads. The handpin goes back to the Antonines in type, with a circle of bosses forming the head, but it also occurs later. A type with the semicircle of bosses above and a crescentic plate below has been found with coins ranging from the later 3rd century to Magnentius and possibly to the end of the 4th century. (5)

We find the same forces at work if we look at the pottery. Castor ware, produced in bulk on a Romanised business basis, shows in its running animals, leaf-scrolls, and odd humans, a Celticising element of style, flowing and vivid, which transforms the Roman materials. The scrolls in particular tug away from anything like a classical repose. And in the stamped or painted New Forest wares, in a simpler way, the potter reveals a strong

Celtic sense of curvilinear design. He lets himself go in his decoration.

In appearance the British world must have shown a medley of Roman and Celtic elements, the latter growing stronger as one moved into the highlands. The Celtic dress consisted of a short tunic, breeches, and cloak; and still in the 12th century of Giraldus Cambrensis some Irishmen were wearing breeches and shoes. (6) And there would have been many items such as the stool which Sulpicius Severus picks out as specially Gaulish. He records that St. Martin in church never sat in the tribune or bishop's chair—

while lately and not without a blush, God is my witness, I have seen a certain bishop percht aloft on a throne, on a seat so elevated that it was the stand of an emperor. When Martin took a seat, it was on a rustic stool, like those of slaves, one of the seats that we others, Gaulish countryfolk, call tripecciae, and you literary men (or at least those coming from Greece) call tripods. (7)

Even in the 4th century Latin had a limited range. In Britain it was used by the officials and the army, by traders (as distinct from the hawkers and chafferers of the rural markets), and, to a large extent though probably not entirely, by the townsfolk. The governing class was Roman in outlook; the rural upper classes were bilingual. The peasants of the lowland zone, the mass of the population, spoke British and doubtless had a smattering of Latin; in the highland zone, apart from the army and its native camp-followers, the language was British.

The country landlords spoke Latin with a somewhat old-fashioned correctness, "a much more refined and literary, almost archaising pronunciation than the normal speech of the masses which became the ancestor of the Romance languages on the Continent"—though in the cities the middle-class Vulgar Latin lingua-franca would have been heard. The British landlords were not in this matter different from their fellows in Gaul, who spoke in much the same way. The reason why the Continental aristocrats did not determine the basis of French was merely that their speech-forms were swamped by those of the populace.

Some 800 Latin words, Christian and secular, have survived

in the three Brittonic languages (Old Welsh, Cornish, Breton). It was through the landowners that these words reached the British-speakers; only in a few cases did urban or military circles hand a word on. (8)

Christianity had probably made no headway in Britain before the Constantinian epoch, though an occasional trader or sailor may have held the faith in towns like London or Colchester. St. Alban of Verulamium has been claimed as a genuine martyr. (9) If so, he must have been a member of a scanty flock, or, more likely, a chance believer brought in by the army. After the creed was officially championed, it would have spread to some extent; but the strong evidence for a pagan revival in the late 4th century is not balanced by anything as definite for enthusiasm about the new faith.

A fair variety of minor objects with a Christian symbol like the Chi-Rho or a Fish have turned up, but not enough to suggest a pious community. Still, the British Church existed by 314, when it was represented at the Council of Arles by three bishops—from London, York, and a third site which has been interpreted as Lincoln, Caerleon, or Colchester. Again there were British bishops at Sardica in 343, and British bishops seem to have supported Athanasius in his controversies. (10) At Rimini in 359 the British, like the Gauls and Aquitanians, refused to accept government pay for expenses. But three British, having no means, had to make use of the public bounty: "for they thought it more dutiful to burden the Treasury than individuals". This story, told by Sulpicius, has been taken to mean they came from poor congregations; but more likely Sulpicius, an eager supporter of monastic asceticism against episcopalian latitude, was making a point in the debate which was never far from his mind.

Another point can be learned from a scrutiny of Sulpicius' language. He is recounting the troubles in Gaul through the arguments over the Trinity—whether its members were identical or alike in substance.

The struggle went on so long that no part of the world was not involved in impieties of this sort . . . Our Gauls were oppressed by Saturninus, bishop of Arles, an uncontrolled, factious man. The

rumour went that Osius from Spain was also drawn into this vile-
ness, which seems to me remarkable and hard to believe, as he had
been in his time the most courageous man of our parts . . .

Next came the Arian troubles, and the Council was called at
Ariminum. Masters of Offices were sent "through Illyria,
Italy, Africa, the Spains and the Gauls, and soon 400 and more
bishops gathered, enforced or at their own free will". Sulpicius
then goes on to tell about the problem of board and lodgings.
"But our people, *that is*, Aquitanians, Gauls and Britons
thought it incorrect" to take any state aid.

Our church, *our group*, thus includes for Sulpicius Britain as
well as Gaul. And his remarks about the heresies troubling *our
Gaul*, *our parts*, must be taken as meaning that Britain, too, was
shaken. A little later he states that "our part at the Council of
Ariminum" sent delegates to the emperor, having been forced
by him to enter into communion with the Arians. They did not
succeed in winning his grace, so that "almost all ours" (*nostri*)
began to give in; they (*nostri*) began to stop resisting so as to
end the matter at all costs. Then, later, Hilary returned from
his exile and carried the day against the Arians—"he alone".

We can take it, then, that the British Church was entangled
in the Arian dispute about the relations of Son and Father;
and that there lay a true tradition behind the words of Gildas in
mid-6th century:

. . . the Arian perfidy, ferocious as a snake vomiting its transmarine
venom, brought deadly cleavage between brothers dwelling in amity;
and thus, as if a road had been built across the Ocean, all sorts of
wild beasts came inflicting with awful mouth the death-dealing
poison of every form of heresy and launching the lethal wounds of
their teeth on a land always wanting to hear something new and
certainly holding steadfastly to nothing.

Certainly in the latter half of the 4th century there must have
been something fermenting in British Christianity; or such men
as Pelagius and Patrick could not have been produced. But
generally it seems that it was only when the British felt themselves
as Christians, inheriting a great culture and faced with barbarous
pagan enemies, that the creed took deep root. In the 4th century

the national emotions had nourished the cults of Nodens and the other Celtic deities; the same emotions in the period of political independence at least in part flooded into the Christian faith, which provided the idiom of a new social cohesion.

At Silchester what seems to be an early church has been excavated; and a similar building at Caerwent has been also taken as a church. Both structures are small and suggest tiny congregations. The Caerwent place had its foundations in a foot-thick layer of débris above the ruins of Roman baths. (11) Burials discovered in a villa near Llanilltud in south Glamorgan were oriented in an east-west direction—the Christians of this time wanted to be able to sit straight up facing the west on the Day of Judgment—and the graves were cut through the mosaic floor of the villa. Perhaps we here touch the spread of Christianity in the post-Roman period. (12)

In the south-west of Britain there are scattered signs of the faith. The Chi-Rho was inscribed on four stones in Chedworth villa. At Cirencester an inscription records the restoration of the Ancient Faith (paganism), presumably under Julian the Apostate; we may infer that Christianity had previously been dominant. The acrostic *Rotas opera tenet Arepo sator*, found in the same town, has been taken as an anagram of *Pater Noster*. (13)

No monumental tradition among the Christians carries on into the 5th century. One lead coffin is certainly 5th century, probably of the early decades. Such coffins normally die out with the end of Roman rule; and the lettering here is a rough cursive which could derive from the debased Roman-British type seen in an inscription from Ravenhill in Yorkshire—as also could some of the 5th-century stone inscriptions. But the large majority of Roman monuments in Britain are military, and the custom of setting them up had practically disappeared by the 4th century. (14)

THE GENTRY

THE rural lords were not likely to have been so well educated as those of Gaul, so self-consciously inheriting the rhetoric of the Graeco-Roman world. But there were certainly many similarities between the life of the leisured classes in Britain and that revealed in Gaul by Ausonius for the 4th and Sidonius Apollinaris for the 5th century. And the Gaulish country gentlemen often prided themselves on their libraries, on their knowledge of the classics; oratory was highly skilled, especially in the panegyric. The only complete Latin comedy come down to us, apart from Plautus and Terence, is a lively play written to amuse a country house-party about 420–30 in south Gaul: *Querolus* or *Aulularia*, which may be rendered *The Discontented Man* or *The Little Pot*. And Ausonius had a friend, the rhetorician Axius Paulus, who lived near Saintes, south of Bordeaux, and composed a play, now lost, called *Delirus* or *Crazy*.

In the 3rd and 4th centuries there were certainly close connections between both north and south Gaul and Britain. In 237 a leading burgess of two municipalities in Britain set up an altar to the protecting deity of Bordeaux, whose name is cognate with that of the Icenian Queen Boudicca:

M. Aurelius Lunaris, *sevir augustalis* of the *coloniae* of York and Lincoln in the province of Lower Britain, paid his vow to the Goddess Tutela Boudiga, in the shape of an altar which he vowed on his departure from York. (1)

He was clearly a trader who had done well in both *coloniae*: the Fosse Dyke, linking Witham and Trent, made close relations possible. We may suppose that he dealt in wines from south Gaul: low grade for the army and high grade for his clients among the burgesses and landowners. The piece of silver fir found in Silchester may represent the same trade.

Bordeaux with its vineyards is well conjured up by Ausonius:

> Bordeaux's my native soil where heaven's mercy
> is mild, and large the watered earth's good bounty,
> where spring is long and a young sun warms the winters
> and under hills of vines swirl tidal rivers
> foamswept: the way of seas that rise and fall.
> Her foursquare breadth of walls with towers is tall
> and cleaves the clouds light-lost above it all.
> Look admiring on the regular streets, the homes
> well-plotted, spacious squares that suit their name,
> and gates directly opposite their crossroads,
> the springborn stream whose channel cuts the town
> when Ocean brims it with returning tide:
> you watch a whole sea with its fleets come gliding . . .
>
> Hail, fountain of unknown source, deep, holy and gracious,
> bluegreen crystal, unmuddied, murmuring, shady.
> Hail, City Warden with life-giving draughts:
> *Divona* in Celtic, a spring for the god-lists made. (2)

His grandson, writing about 459 but describing events of 379, also stresses the port-aspect:

> Bordeaux I reached, where the superb Garonne
> draws Ocean's tidal waves within the ramparts
> through a shipbearing gate that folds even now
> a spacious port in the spacious city's walls.

Ausonius had a relative by his wife Sabina, the husband of her sister Pudentilla, Flavius Sanctus, who died at eighty years after being a *praeses*, governor, in Britain. He calls on merry-hearted folk who shun lawsuits to honour him, "gently made and bland, dutiful with no tumult but with care". Also, an uncle, Clemens Contemptus, presumably a trader, had grown rich and died in Britain. As the poet was writing in 379–82, this uncle must have been in Britain in the later part of the first half of the century. (3)

A friend of the poet who may serve well for many of the lesser gentry in Britain was Theon, who lived in Médoc, cultivating bees and oysters, hunting and fishing, scribbling verse. (It has been suggested that he supplied oysters to Richborough. (4)) Ausonius calls him rustic, *paganus*, and treats him with bantering good fellowship:

> What course on the earth's last verge do you follow,
> you poet tiller-of-sands whose plough must furrow
> the shore by Ocean's limit and the Sunset,
> whom a poor reed-thatcht hovel clamps,
> a colon-hut that smoke-chokes, smarting eyes?
> What are the Muses up to, and vocal Apollo?
>
> What life is yours there on the Medoc coasts?
> are you zealous in business, grabbing for clipt coins
> goods promptly dumped in sales-rooms at mad profit?
> blobs of blancht tallow, greasy lumps of wax,
> Narycian pitch and scraps of tattered paper,
> with torches stinking rank, your country lamps?
>
> Or have you larger affairs, gone hunting thieves
> who roam your region through, till, cowed and cornered,
> they beg you share their loot? till, tender-scrupled,
> averse from blood, condoning crimes for cash,
> you call them "errors", fine the cattle-reivers,
> and leave the judge's seat to share the guilt?
>
> Are you beside your brother in deep thickets,
> encircling the wild hart with mesh and feathers?
> urging with yells the frothing boar, to ambush
> the beast? I warn you, don't go jabbing spears
> close-quartered with a charging thunderbolt.
> But note your brother's case: he lifts his clothes
> to show the ugly scars in privy places
> and bares a bottom all too nearly pierced,
> then skips away to show his wounds, admired
> by young Gedippa . . .
>
> Or, shunning woodland-chases through these perils,
> have you gone keenly fishing? All the gear
> at Dumnitonus boasts as normal treasures
> the knotted wraps designed for Nereus' creatures,
> cast-nets, drag-nets, lines with bumpkin names,
> wears, and stitch hooks for earthworms. Do you still
> in such equipment trust? The house flows over

with seashore spoils. The waves provide you sturgeon,
the deadly ray and softly-furnisht plaice,
sharp-tasting tunnies and spine-guarded spindles,
and grayling that won't keep six hours when landed.

Or is it your delight to rape with verses
the singing girls of Memory (three or eight)?
    At once produce what I demand:
    only what in your notebook's scanned
    and what the unsoiled sheets display.
    If, poet, this small price you'll pay,
    I'll leave you to your Holiday
    and you'll not fear the people say:
    "That bastard Poet comes along,
    the naughty Pirate of good Song."

We are not without evidence that the literary dabblings of the
Ausonian sort existed in Britain. At Frampton villa, some five
miles from Dorchester, a mosaic pavement of the later 4th
century shows an odd religious compromise. A Head of Neptune is attended by dolphins, with a line of verse either side:

Here Neptune's Top, who won the Moving Kingdom of the Winds,
    is found.
Around his Seablue Shape two encircling Dolphins bound!

The verse reveals classical forms in decay, changing into something new; the hexameter is breaking up and extending into a
jingling seven-beat line. And diction and syntax are peculiar
as well.

Below the Head, a Chi-Rho is depicted in a circle, inside a
large semicircle designed, it seems, to balance the elemental
god with the new cult of redemption. The wish to have the
best of both worlds, mythological and Christian, was characteristic of Ausonius who was deeply disturbed when his young
friend Paulinus decided to give himself up wholly to the new
creed; yet even the sensitive Paulinus could bring in the myth
of Danae to "illustrate the Virgin Birth". In mid-5th century
Sidonius wrote long marriage-poems wholly pagan in idiom,
and Paulinus himself was not baptised till he had reached middle age—perhaps "as the result of political disturbances, such

as that in which his brother was slain, and in which his own life seems to have been endangered". (5) Paulinus, the grandson of Ausonius, was similarly baptised late, and then for the same sort of reason. (The first Paulinus, incidentally, seems one of the small number of people who owned the whole of Bordeaux. (6))

In the cornland of Somerset the early farms of the 1st and 2nd centuries were modest places, with some comforts but no luxuries—e.g. Catsgore, a small half-timbered house on a stone basis. But in the 3rd and especially the first half of the 4th century there was a considerable rise in living standards. At Low Ham, an L-shaped villa with two ranges set at right angles, there were installed by the end of the 3rd century a clumsy mosaic floor and a small bath-block. About 330 the bath was reconstructed with a big cold room and fine heated reception rooms, and with two figured mosaics. The coins carry the occupation to about 370, and the site was probably inhabited for at least another generation. The decoration in the cold room consisted of five panels dealing with the love of Aeneas and Dido, which are the oldest existing series of connected scenes illustrating the *Aeneid*.

There is charm and a distinct delicacy of style in the work. The panel of the embraced lovers in particular has a fine lyric feeling. The proprietor who commissioned the work may not have been an enthusiast for Virgil, but he must have had some sense of the theme and its treatment. At Otford villa a Virgilian quotation has been painted on the wall. (7)

Virgil had throughout the empire's history stood for the high consciousness of a Roman mission; to absorb his work, with the aid of such commentaries as that of Servius, was to become spiritually Roman. The Gallo-Roman Avitus, directing the education of the Visigothic Theodoric II (born *c*. 430), taught him to read Virgil; and Gregory of Tours says of the senator Felix and his slave Andarchius that they studied Virgil, the Theodosian Code, and Arithmetic. Sidonius remarks in astonishment that his friend Syagrius, after having had in youth his Virgil "driven into him with the cane", could bring himself to learn German. (8)

At Aldborough in the dining-room, besides the plain semi-circular margin which held the three couches, nine figures of

the Muses with a Greek inscription fill a centre-piece. Orpheus
was a favourite mosaic subject at Cirencester and in the south-
west, and was certainly savoured for his symbolic qualities
which made him acceptable both to pagans and Christians.
Dionysiac legend appears at East Coker, the Labours of Hercules
at Bramdean, the tale of Cyparissus at Leicester. At Brading a
highly complicated theme drawn from Astrology and the
Eleusinian Mysteries was certainly a special order.

At East Coker, Somerset, the mosaic shows a hunt. Two
men carry a deer slung on a pole on their shoulders. Bare-
headed, they wear short tunics girdled at the waist; one has a
short Gaulish cloak with pointed hood thrown back; both
wear close-fitting breeches and short boots. The man in front
has a spear point-down, and a small dog sits up with tongue out
as if to catch dripping blood. At Pitney, again, is a hunt; and
at Horkstow a chariot-and-horse race.

At Lullingstone in the fine reception room of the 4th century
we meet Bellerophon spearing a rather mild chimera amid
Seasons and Dolphins, and Europa on her Bull going overseas
between Cupids. The latter scene has a couplet in verse, with
something of the scrappy quality of the Frampton lines—the
sort of thing, it has been remarked, that diners might throw
out as an impromptu, deceived by the haze of wine into thinking it witty.

If Juno in her Jealousy had seen the Bull's swimming,
she might have more justly to Aeolus' Halls gone skimming.

Here, too, there seems to have been felt no disharmony between
the pagan jest and the Christian chapel set up later in the
century a few yards away in the same house, with its praying figures, its Chi-Rhos and Alpha-Omega painted on the
plaster.

Perhaps the proprietor rather resembled the Vectius who
lived near Chantelle in the Bourbonnais and whom Sidonius
described about 472. He had two houses, one in town and one
in the country—and it has been suggested that the small
Lullingstone villa, with its scamped sleeping accommodation,
was a country-house for holidays, owned by a man whose main
house would be in a nearby town. (9)

His slaves are serviceable: the country ones obliging, the town ones friendly, obedient, satisfied with their master. His table feeds stranger as much as dependant; there is a large hospitality and yet larger temperance. It is a slighter matter that he of whom we speak is second to none in training horses, judging dogs, hunting with hawks. A supreme stylishness shows in his clothes, taste in his belts, magnificence in his equipment; impressiveness of bearing, gravity of mind: that gains him general respect, this gives him dignity at home. His indulgence does not spoil, his reprimand does not bully, his severity is mitigated, producing tears not fears. Further, a frequent reading of the Scriptures: even at meals he takes much spiritual food. Psalms he studies much, even more chants them; and in a new way of life is a monk complete, not in monachal but in martial cloak. He eats no game but acquiesces in the hunt: with unobtrusive and delicate religious sense he takes this sport without the spoil.

One small girl, left by his wife's decease, is the solace of his widower's life, reared with grandfatherly fondness, maternal assiduity, paternal benevolence. Speaking to servants, he is not furious, to take their counsels thinks it not injurious, in probing faults is not too harshly curious. He rules the level and condition of inferiors not by might but by reason and seems not the owner but the steward of his own house.

To this man Sidonius wrote about one Germanicus, at whose request he had visited the church of Chantelle in the Bourbonnais. "Obviously the big man of the place, with sixty years behind him, in his paraded dress and manner he doesn't only grow younger, he attains a second childhood. With clinging clothes, tight boots, wheel-haircut, each crease of his face searched by tweezers for hairs: by heavenly gift he has joints still firm, eyesight clear, gait smoothly quick, milk-white teeth intact in wholesome gums." Sidonius asks Vectius to give the old chap some advice: he mustn't think himself immune from decay, let him "by good deeds become a new man in old age". A priest's son and a bishop's father, he should look to his own sanctification. (10)

And we can hear the courteous self-assertive tones of the men who dined in the Lullingstone hall, in Ausonius' epistles. Oysters were paid a high regard. To Axius Paulus the poet discourses on their breeds and says that gourmets like both the Amoric Sea's products and those:

that shorefolk pick up on Pictonic coasts
and tides at times unbare for wondering Caledonians.

In the *Moselle* he returns to the latter shore, depicting it green
with seaweed, red with coral, white with pearls. (The Irt and
other northern rivers such as the Tay and the Spey were sources
of pearl in the 13th century when many local shrines were enriched from them. Under Elizabeth, Sir John Hawkins was said
to have gained a patent to pearl-fish in the Irt and in 1865
through a German's enterprise pearls valued at £12,000 were
taken from the rivers, exhausting the beds. Aelian describes the
British pearl as "in a measure rather gold-coloured, with rays
somewhat dull and dusky", but better than those from near the
Bosporus. (11))

To Theon (*ep.* xv) Ausonius acknowledges a receipt of 30
oysters—"large, but O how few!"—and adds a comment on
mussels. With oysters they "make a course for early luncheons,
food that highborns smack their lips at, cheap enough for poor
folk's kitchens" since they are not gathered at any deep-sea
risk but are found in shallows—"in a double shellcave hidden,
till the steam of boiling water spirals out the milky substance".
The Celts were keen eaters. Sulpicius depicts Gauls on their
way to Egypt, who land in Cyrenaica. They meet an old man in
skins at a hand-quern and pray together; then the old man
spreads out sheep-skins and bids them to a meal of bread and
herbs like mint.

I began to smile and turned to our good Gallus. "Well, what do
you say to that? a bundle of herbs and a half-loaf for five men?"
He, in his shy way, flushed a little but did not resent my teasing.
"You're off again, Sulpicius," he replied. "You can't lose a chance
of twitting us about our appetites. But it's rather hard to try and
compel us Gauls to live like angels—though I for one think even
angels get pleasure out of eating. And for this half-loaf of barley,
I'd be afraid of touching it, even if it was all my own. I don't mind
that Cyrenean being satisfied, if it's his vocation to go hungry
through need or nature—or our friend's party either, whom I much
suspect have lost their stomachs through pitching about at sea. But
here we're not at all near the sea, and as I've often mentioned to you,
we're Gauls." (12)

The Celts were hospitable too. Ausonius likes visiting or being visited. He tells Theon that the Médoc south wind will carry him along as he lies under an awning, and will save his big body from being tossed about; then a mule-carriage will convey him to Lucaniacus. Friends exchange gifts, often of food. Paulinus in Spain sends oil and Barcelona fish-sauce (made from brine-soaked tunnies); Ausonius replies that as soon as a cartload of wine comes in to Saintes, Paulinus must get out the ostrich-shell cup "which your steward (*promus*) says was left on the farm in your own Bigorre" (in the Hautes Pyrénées). Again, he sends to his son Hesperius twenty thrushes.

> They tear the glistening clusters from the vine
> and tangle in the net
> that in the evening hour drifts loosely-cloudy
> or tautens with morning dew:
> caught unreluctant in our wintry hedges,
> such birds I send to you.
> For they across the twilight of the dawn
> flew headlong in the snares we set:
> with webfoot waterducks from neighbouring meres
> raided, abounding yet
> in birds whose broad beaks ravage in blue waters,
> whose legs are crimson-wet,
> whose plumes are rainbow-rich with skeins of colour,
> whose throats the throats of doves outdo.

The interest in such verses in precise bright detail was characteristic of the new poetry breaking out in the provinces, in Gaul and north Africa alike; it shows the breaking-up of the classical generalisation now at a dead-end. That the new positions are entangled with a pride in classical allusion and in tags of meaningless scholarship does not weaken their virtue, though in the entanglement we see an opposition which the poets could not overcome—an effort to carry on a classical tradition that had lost its vitality, and at the same time a confused but strong awareness of new forces coming up.

Ausonius' poem on the river Moselle is perhaps the finest example of the new sense of nature. It lacks structure, but has its many fine moments of clear and loving observation. And this new feeling for landscape, with its keen desire to set down warmly and closely the thing seen, has its links with the deep movement of national feeling that we traced in the pagan revival, in the festival-fairs, in the strengthened Celtic motives in art, in Britain. Perhaps, also, the loving sense of the lovely earth is quickened by the sense of danger, of threatening war-clouds over the horizon. Because men's hold on the earth around them becomes precarious, they look on things with a desperate freshness. (Indeed, it has been claimed that the poet paints a dream-picture as propaganda for the recolonisation of a devastated area.)

Ausonius shows a strong sense of family bond and of the people with whom he is in contact. *Parentalia* gives us pleasant vignettes of aunts, uncles, and other relations; the *Commemoration of the Professors of Bordeaux University* has the same friendly emotion, urbanely devoid of intensity. We glimpse a little German slave-girl Bissula, a grandson Pastor (named from a shepherd's flute playing at the time of his birth) who was killed by a falling tile, a wife embroidering verses on a robe. The incomplete *Daily Round* shows the master waking with the swallow while his slave snores on; he calls for shoes and lawn tunic, "all the clothes spread about, neat-set for my going-out". Hands, mouth, eyes he washes in spring-water, then prays in his own chapel. He invites five persons to lunch; with the host they make up six, the right number: more and it's "a mill not a meal". He bids the cook shake the pots, dip his finger in the hot gravy, flick out his tongue in a lick. Then he calls for his expert stenographer. "What theft may your winged hand make in my innermost mind?" With the growth of bureaucracy, shorthand had become important. Special masters taught and practised the art. When Sidonius threw off an epigram on a Towel, a scribe was at hand to take the words down. Bishops, like officials, had notaries, employed to record the proceedings of Councils, the Acts of Martyrs, the historic speeches or sermons. One result is the diffuseness and errors that are found, for instance, in the homilies of Hilary of Poitiers. Prudentius, in verses on the martyr Cassianus, whose tablet stood in a church at Forum Cornelii, shows that shorthand was taught in the schools:

> Youthful studies he guided
> and over large classes as master of letters presided,
> skilled to catch many words in a few brief lines
> and follow speech apace with headlong signs. (13)

After a gap, the *Daily Round* ends with a dissertation on dreams, in which the poet forgets his Christian creed; he sees himself:

> applaud in a crowd of triumph, and again,
> disarmed, through the streets I'm dragged, an Alan prisoner.
> I gaze on the sacred doors and golden palaces,
> the gods' temples, reclined on purple and feasting,
> then I'm eating at some steamy tavern-table.

We feel his uneasiness at the ups-and-downs of his world. For a moment he identifies himself even with a barbarian seen shackled in the street.

We can safely take the picture of Ausonius' world as reflecting generally the life of the gentry in the British lowlands as well as in Gaul. There were many contacts, and conditions had many similarities, though tending in Britain to a lower level of civilised conveniences. In the *Moselle* the poet, promising a poem on the great and learned of Trèves, refers to the local gentry who had been victors under praetorian prefect, "gone governing forth to Italy's folk or Britons born-of-the-north".

One of the main reasons for British relations with Bordeaux, we noted, was the wine trade. By the 2nd century viticulture was carried as far north as the Moselle, and the Bordeaux area was one of the most successful wine producers. On the Moselle, the poet is reminded of home.

> The whole broad scene, with its warm charms, becomes
> an image of my sleek well-tended home:
> the villa-roofs on the hanging banks uplooming,
> the hillslopes green with vines, and the pleasant stream
> sliding below with a dreamy rumour of peace.

Britain could have had nothing quite like this, but there too the vine was introduced. Till the 280s there were restrictions, which Probus rescinded—perhaps to help economic recovery in Britain. He even ordered the army to lend a hand: which so

annoyed the troops that it contributed to his fall. At Boxmoor
villa, Hertfordshire, many vine stalks have been found on a
slope facing south and west; and after 250 the imported amphoras become rare on excavated sites. Vine-growing doubtless
increased in the prosperous 4th-century agriculture, the vines
draped on trellis or tree as Virgil describes. Wine was needed
for the provision of must, which was used as sugar; and with
Christianity came the need of altar wine. Whether viticulture
survived in the Dark Ages may be doubted. But in the Rhineland
and the Moselle valley the vineyards suffered but carried on;
and in Gloucestershire, where villas were so thick, the vine was
much cultivated in medieval days. Alexander Neckham in the
13th century refers to the county as the best wine-producer. (14)

Bronze votive dog from Lydney

COINS AND TRADERS

THE early empire was bimetallic, but its monetary system broke down in the 3rd century. For example, the salary of a trecenar, an officer of the senior ordinary equestrian grade, had collapsed from the equivalent of nearly 70 lb. in gold to a nominal 1½ lb. Indeed, salaries were being paid in food and fodder, *annonae* and *capitus*; gold coins were erratic in weight and a relatively small proportion of the coinage. The volume of the currency had been falling from mid-2nd century, with a climax about 235. The silver *antoninianus* was steadily debased. The bad state of the coinage helped the fissiparous tendencies in the west. Thus, the Gallic Empire of 258–73, which included Britain, raised currency standards. Also, the usurper Carausius began his rule by issuing fine silver *denars*, an effort to return to past standards of value; then, when he was temporarily recognised by the central government, his two mints adopted the imperial *antoninianus*.

The Constantinian reforms made possible certain commutations for cash, and by the end of the 4th century taxes were mostly being exacted in money. Wages, too, were following the same trend. But things were not the same. There was no return to the old bimetallism. Values were counted solely in terms of gold, and the exchange value of the gold *solidus* against the small coins kept on fluctuating. Submultiples were not in lower coin denominations but in *siliquae*, carats, and their divisions. You did not change a *solidus*; you bought or sold it.

We may see in the breakdown of bimetallism the failure of the Augustan attempt to bring the middle classes forward into a place in the state-system without transferring power from the big landowners. While there was vitality and elasticity in the relation of upper and middle classes, the political balance was reflected in the bimetallic balance; when the urban middle class broke down, the silver element in the coinage broke down too.

There was a period of chaos, in politics and in coinage. Then the reassertion of an absolutist state, heavily reposing on the new, big landlords, found its currency-expression in the *solidus*.

A significant aspect of the crisis had been the advent of the bronze *minims*, very small coins, in the last two decades of the 3rd century. These coinages represent the growth of the rural markers, the rise of the fair in place of the forum, the growth of barter and small sales in place of trade within a stable world market.

Constantine brought the bronzes back to metal value in an effort to fight the soaring of prices. For some decades oscillation went on between the attempts to fix prices and over-tariff the coinage, and the letting of coins and prices find their own level. After 348 there was a trend to restrict the volume of currency in circulation for a couple of decades. Then a new ample bronze coinage came from the Gallic mints, Arles and Lyon, with silver, too, from Trèves. Perhaps British silver bullion as well as Gaulish was being used.

Times were prosperous in Britain, and the finds of silver coins and even of gold are unequalled in any other western provinces.

The need for small change was met by continuing to circulate Gaulish radiate issues and by striking small copies of them. In 395 the mints in Gaul ended. Thereafter we cannot expect to find imperial coins in Britain, except random examples of the rare gold and silver issues. Hence one of the major difficulties in dating sites after 400. There has been a tendency to assume that a site promptly ceased to be inhabited a year or so after the last coin of the Theodosian House found there: a quite uncritical assumption. (1)

The virtual monopoly by Britain of silver hoards may derive from the considerable independence of British garrisons from 383 for more than two decades. It seems as if the areas where the hoards are found were cut off from the process of withdrawal that was going on elsewhere. (2)

The Roman aristocrat Symmachus noted in one of his letters the scarcity of gold; and the last emperors of the 4th century forbade traders to buy goods from barbarians with gold. (3) Stilicho in his campaigning took measures to get as much bullion as possible from the provinces to Rome. After 366–7 gold went direct to the Sacrae Largitiones, where a department dealt with its recoining. In 365 and 369 the Senate gave anyone the right to prospect for gold at a yearly fee of eight (later seven) scruples of the metal. But the work soon proved disastrous; all prospectors and their sons were tied for ever to their profession; if they fled, they were brought back like deserters. Soon after 376, in Thrace, they ran off to the Goths, to whom they were useful as guides. In Gaul and Italy, in 378, others tried to escape to Sardinia and heavy penalties were decreed for them and their abettors. (4) Yet there was still much gold available, as the number of workshops for coining it shows. (5) The zeal of tax-collectors in nosing it out was one reason for the dread of their visitations.

The quest for the much needed gold was carried out with ruthless thoroughness—Leontius of Neapolis was later to compare Roman fiscal severity to the inexorable terrors of the Last Judgment. It is not without significance that the text of the medieval *Dies Irae* abounds in metaphors derived from the technical vocabulary of tax exaction. (6)

Since the taxes had so much to do with popular discontent and revolts, we must grasp their crushing nature. The more the State found the old market system failing, the more it extended its bureaucracy to extract from producers and traders the means for keeping itself intact. At the same time the big landowners wielded so much power that they were able to throw the tax-burden from their own shoulders on to the peasantry's. No wonder the tax-collector was a sort of devil haunting men's minds and making them ready to do anything to escape or limit his menace: flee to the barbarians, rise in revolt, enter a monastery. By getting outside the empire the Britons were saved from the five-yearly levy of gold and silver on traders, the land tax, the supertax (laid on all classes at first, then in 450 lifted from the senatorial landlords), voluntary taxes (i.e. forced levies) on accessions, anniversaries, and victories, the rents of state-lands, various revived indirect taxes (e.g. sales tax, 444–5), customs dues, licences like those of the prospectors, the compulsory buying of gold by towns (in return for small change at government rates). (7)

The 3rd-century crisis had drastic effects on trade. In 326 Constantine gave privileges to the corporation of *navicularii* who kept the shores of Narbonne and the Arles quays busy. These shipowners escaped the fiscal charges that bowed the citizens; but they were tied to their trade, with a service-turn for the State every two years and savage penalties for embezzlement or delay. Every wreck was investigated and the crew questioned under torture. The river-men, *nautae*, disappeared and their place was taken by a militarised state-system of transport—fleets like that of the Anderetiani at Paris. (8)

Trade went on, but under many difficulties. Syrians, Egyptians, Jews were more than ever to the fore; but not only foreigners held the field. From Sidonius we learn of Amantius of Clermont, who acted as a small trader at Marseilles and carried letters among other things. Winning Sidonius' trust, he was recommended as a Reader to Graecus, bishop of Marseilles: a keen merchant who didn't mind the profit going to others, so honest that people lent him money without security. Sidonius adds that he had only recently come to know the man but found his good name so general that he did not hesitate to back him. In the next letter, however, he apologises for misleading Graecus. Amantius had been kept down by his respectable father, a small business-man of Clermont; he ran off to Marseilles where he soon wormed into the good books of even the local authorities and won the hand of an heiress:

He started attracting the girl by genial greetings and by giving her (as at her age he correctly might) the trifles and trinkets charming a maiden's fancy; by such slight links he strongly bound her heart to his. Time passed. She reached a marriageable age. You guess already the event. This young fellow, without visible relations or substance, a foreigner, a minor who had bolted from home without his father's leave or knowledge, asks the hand of a girl his equal in birth, his superior in fortune. He asks, and more, he gets. He is accepted as suitor. The Bishop strongly abets his Reader, the Count supports his client, the mother-in-law-to-be does not bother to look into the applicant's means, the bride likes his person.

The marriage contract was drawn up, and some little suburban plot at Clermont was put into settlement and produced with much theatric declamation. This legal chicanery and solemn sham completed, the penniless lover bore off the golden bride. He lost no time in going into all his father-in-law's affairs and extracted some excellent pickings, helped all along by the credulity of his compliant and free-handed mother-in-law. Then, and only then, the peerless swindler beat a retreat and disappeared into Auvergne. Too late, the mother thought of suing him for the ridiculous exaggerations in the contract. But what was the use of bewailing the smallness of his settlement when she was already rejoicing at the prospect of a plethora of little grandchildren? (9)

But the cheerful scoundrel seems to have weathered his troubles and to have ingratiated himself afresh. The next letter of Sidonius to the bishop begins: "Here is Amantius again, carrier of my trifles, off as usual to his Marseilles to bring home his pickings from the city."

Towns like London or Colchester must have known countless sailors and traders from the East. In the area of the Wall, Barates of Palmyra married a British woman, and there were other Easterners such as Salmanes, with various Greeks. There were also visitors from Gaul at the Bath spa, and travellers or traders such as Verecundius Diogenes from the Bourges area at York or Nonnius Romanus from the Moselle valley at Caerwent. (10)

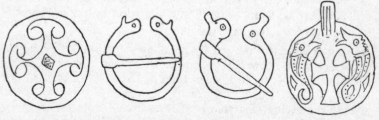

(*Left*) Disc from hanging-bowl, Sutton Hoo
(*Centre*) Pennanular brooches from Lydney and Llanferres (*Denb.*)
(*Right*) Hanging-bowl escutcheon, Faversham

MAGNUS MAXIMUS

BEYOND the Forth were the Picts. (1) Between the Forth
and the Wall were Britons, of the same general stock as
those of the south. We may call them Cumbrians: their own
name for themselves was *Cumbri* or *Cumbrenses*, latinising the
native *Cymry*, Fellow-countrymen. These lowland folk had
been much influenced by Roman contacts and trade; and in the
Ravennas list we meet *loca* that seem to be authorised meeting-
places cited in treaty or frontier regulations—perhaps in the 3rd
century when the region was patrolled as far as the Tay, rather
than garrisoned. (2–3)

If we may judge by the relative thickness or sparseness of
garrisons, the Votadini of Northumberland and Midlothian
were better treated than their neighbours the Selgovae. A dis-
crimination, not so clear, seems also to occur between the
Damnonii and Novantae. The Votadini were allowed to stay
on in their hilltop town of Traprain Law, but there was little
Romanisation. No such licence seems given to the Selgovae,
whose main hill forts, Ruberslaw and the North Eildon, stood
vacant and were taken up by Roman signal-stations. (4–5)

About the years 222–35 a Caledonian seems to have been serving
in the Roman army, Lossius Veda, Clansman of Vepogenus. His
name seems to mean the Knowing Crooked One, and he "pro-
claims his genealogy with all the pride of a barbarian chief". (6)
In the later 4th century there were the regiments of Scotti and
Atecotti, but we do not know if they were levies exacted after
offensive action or if they had been drawn over by Roman
gold. (7)

The events of 367 underline the fact that close relations had
grown up between the soldiers on the Wall and the folk beyond. The frontier-guards for bribes betrayed information
about the Roman defences. Their job had been "to traverse the
country far and wide, and report movements of the near peo-

ples". *Areani* is their name in Ammianus, amended to *Arcani*, though the word occurs nowhere else—it suggests a connection with the secret police, *agentes in rebus*; and they have been thought to be the same as the *Angarii* in charge of the courier service. But there is no need to make the emendation. *Areani* has been interpreted as military slang derived from the term *area* for a milecastle with its enclosed plots like garden-patches or sheep-stalls. *Areani* would then mean Milecastle Garrisons (who now were local levies, we must remember, designed perhaps by Hadrian the Philhellene on the model of the Athenian ephebate). (8)

There were cases of desertion also in 367. But at this period it was not unusual for officials to conspire with the barbarians beyond the frontier. We find them letting looters in and taking a share of their booty as they slipped out again. (9)

Around 450 we meet kings in the north, in Strathclyde and Manau, with the title of *guletic*, maybe the equivalent of Roman Count or Duke. One of these kings, Cunedda, had a grandfather Patern Pesrut, Paternus of the Red Tunic (which may or may not mean the Purple Robe); the other, Ceredig, had a grandfather and great-grandfather named Cinhil and Cluim, which have dubiously been taken as Quintilius and Clemens. These ancestors of the kings would have been flourishing around the turn of the 4th century. (10)

Certainly some tombstones in Latin over the border have names borne by Romans on the Wall, e.g. Carantius and Cupitanus. Also it has been noted that St. Patrick's father was Calpurnius, and his mother Concessa (according to Muirchu), while a dedication at Hexham by a prefect of horse, made not later than mid-3rd century after a victory over raiders, reveals the name Q. Calpurnius Concessinus. (11)

We saw above that at some time in the later 4th century the situation in the north was stabilised by taking the North Britons into the imperial service as Federate Troops. The date can hardly be earlier than the Theodosian construction of Strathclyde and Manau (south of the Firth of Forth); otherwise the Picts in 369 would have destroyed the new States in bursting over the Wall. It has been suggested that Theodosius, carrying war into enemy territory, secured the frontier by setting up buffer-states of treaty-bound allies at each of the Wall's ends. Not that such a thesis implies an abandonment of the Wall. We may plausibly conjecture a partial occupation for at least a quarter of a century after the 380s, previously put forward as the date of withdrawal. (12)

There is much to be said for this Theodosian settlement. But Magnus Maximus, a Spaniard like his master, seems to have played an important part in the matter. Indeed, the federate system may not have been finalised till he made his bid for the empire and needed to secure his rear. Certainly the Britons held him in some special reverence. It may even be that it was he and not Theodosius who carried out the northern campaign of 369, and that his rôle was omitted by the historian Ammianus who composed his work when Theodosius was emperor. There are definite statements in a Gallic Chronicle that Maximus fought a war against Picts and Scots, in Gregory of Tours that he saved the Britons from being oppressed by tyrants (usurpers), and in Gildas that the Picts invaded Britain after he crossed to Gaul. (13) Gildas' chronology seems wrong, and it is hard to make out when the other writers placed Maximus' wars in Britain. Certainly it is easiest to make sense of the statements by deciding they embody a tradition that Maximus had played an important part in breaking the Picts and in restoring order in Britain, and by putting the date of these actions in 369. It is perhaps significant that, when he made his bid for empire, he is described as being animated by envy and jealousy in fighting the emperor Theodosius, the son of his old commander. If he had done all the hard work of 369 and gained little credit for it, he might well have felt resentful.

What is certain is that Maximus stayed on after 369. The Greek historians deny that he held an honourable office in Britain; he cannot, then, it seems, have been Count or Duke. His close link with the British tradition suggests that he was the Roman in charge of the local militia in Wales. Such militia had become more important after the occupation of Caernarvon stopped about 340. Maximus, governing Wales, may have resided in that fort after some reconstruction there. *Wledig* (*guletic*) was possibly the title given him among the Britons: a title which may have been the same as the unusual title *Protictor*

which turns up later among the Britons. But all this is a philo-
logical guess.

After his downfall his enemies painted him a mere scullion
in the Theodosian employ. The orator Pacatus, who felicitated
the emperor Theodosius for having ended his usurpation, remarks scornfully: "That man was once the most obscure
slave-nursling of your house" (*vernula*), who waited as sutler
(*lixa*) on the servants' tables. He adds that he gained at first
some credence by bragging of his relationship and favour with
the emperor (*affinitas* and *favor*). When he claimed the empire,
"who did not at first laugh at the news of the new crime? the
matter seemed below the dignity of anger." And he uses the term
"exiles" to express contempt for the soldiers kept in Britain.

Ausonius, in verses written after Maximus' fall, praised the
city of Aquileia where he had perished:

> Famed for your harbour and walls, but more your praise
> for Maximus' death when in these latter days,
> Sutler who posed as Warrior, here he fell,
> paying for five long years that wrought us harm.
> O joyous witness, him you punished well,
> the Rutupian Brigand whelmed by western arms. (14)

But all we can surmise from such abuse is that he had originally
held some lesser office under Count Theodosius.

It seems certain that he married into one of the princely
British families. If so, he was only doing what the great landlord
Aetius did later in Gaul; for Aetius' second wife was a woman
of a royal Gothic family. Merobaudes hymns her: "Spouse not
to be sung by light Muses, Descendant of Heroes, Offshoot of
Kings." Maximus is incorporated into the genealogy of Dyved
and appears as the founder of an unidentified northern dynasty.
Elsewhere his name has been substituted for that of Ceredig
Gwledig as ancestor of Rhydderch Hael and founder of the
Strathclyde dynasty. In the traditions of the kings of Powys we
find a descent from Vortigern and his wife Sevira, who is
described as Maximus' daughter: and this relationship is inscribed on the pillar-cross near the gates of Valle Crucis Abbey,
by Llangollen. Here Concenn, who died at Rome about 854,
celebrates his line in round half-uncials:

Concenn son of Cattell, Cattell son of Brohcmail, Brohcmail son of
Eliseg, Eliseg son of Guoillauc: Concenn therefore being great-
grandson of Eliseg erected this stone to his great-grandfather
Eliseg: It is Eliseg who annexed the inheritance of Powys . . .
throughout nine (years?) from the power of the English, which he
made into a swordland by fire: whosoever shall read this hand-
inscribed stone, let him give a blessing on the soul of Eliseg: It is
Concenn who . . . with his hand . . . to his own kingdom of Powys
. . . and which . . . the mountain . . . the monarchy Maximus . . .
of Britain . . . Concenn, Pascent . . . Maun, Annan: Britu moreover
(was) the son of Vortigern, whom Germanus blessed and whom
Sevira bore to him, the daughter of Maximus the King who slew
the King of the Romans: Conmarch painted this at the command
of his King Concenn: The blessing of the Lord upon Concenn and
all members of his family and upon all the Land of Powys until the
day of Judgment Amen

The cross records the exploits of Eliseg and Concenn (in fragmentary form) in driving back the English, and finds space to
point proudly to the origin of the Powys line in Maximus and
his daughter. (15)

In the medieval tale, *The Dream of Maxen Wledig*, Maximus
dreams a dream that leads him from Rome over many lands
and seas to claim his bride at Caernarvon and make her empress. In a late medieval Cornish play he appears as Massen
Mytern, Maximus the King. (16)

In the *Dream* his wife Elen is the daughter of a chieftain at
Caernarvon. He sees her in the fairest fortress he had ever beheld, at a river-mouth: in a hall roofed with gold and vaulted
with glittering gems. There two youths play chess, an old man
carves chessmen, and Elen sits beautiful on a golden throne.
When he embraces her, he wakes. Messengers search a year in
vain; then they follow the route of the dream and find the
Caer. Maxen sails with a great fleet and finds Eudef the chieftain,
his two sons, and the girl.

She is Helen Luyddog, Helen of the Hosts (who appears in
the Dyved dynasty where Maxim Guletic is interpolated seven
generations before her). She was connected with the construction of Roman roads in Wales. From Caernarvon Roman roads
went over the mountains to Chester in the east, and to Carmarthen and Caerleon in the south; parts of these are still

known as Sarn Elen, Elen's Causeway. The meaning of her epithet is lost in legendary distances and is not likely to derive from her confusion with the Helena, mother of Constantine the Great, who was said to have been sent "with a great army" to seek for the wood of the Cross. In her mythic aspect she seems affiliated with the Breton deity Ahés, who also in medieval sources is associated with the building of Roman roads. (17)

We may take her, however, as an historical person. That she would become blurred in legend with the Helena who bore Constantine the Great was natural; and indeed another Constantine, the usurper of 407, came in to entangle things further. Geoffrey of Monmouth tells of two Constantines, the great emperor and Constantine of Brittany; the latter had three sons, Constans, Aurelius Ambrosius, and Uther; Uther was the father of Arthur. (18)

Geoffrey also states that Maximus was persuaded to take over the rule of Britain by wedding a British heiress, the unnamed daughter of an upstart ruler, Octavius Dux Gewissei. *Gewissei* is Asser's name for the West Saxons: compare the Welsh *Iwys*. But Geoffrey is dealing with pre-Saxon times. The *Bruts* gives *Ery(n)g ac Yeu(i)as*. What confusion has gone on here, it is hard to say; but the story of the inheritance by marriage is not without interest. However we interpret the evidence, in Geoffrey or elsewhere, the importance of Maximus is evident. No other character in Roman Britain has left anything remotely like his mark on Welsh tradition; and there must have been a good reason for this.

Caernarvon clearly played a large part in his legend. It lay at the base of Snowdon where the Seint flows into Menai Strait, and the ruined fortress of Segontium in this remote region (deserted by the time of Nennius) had a strong evocative effect on the Britons. (19) Its last buildings had been erected later than 364, probably after 367–8, with a section called the Commandant's House that was quite palatial for such a site. (20) "Certain structural details suggest the possible presence or even prevalence of local elements in the latest garrison." (21) The intensive occupation ceased in 380–5, but even after that a smaller force probably held the fort. Here seems the Welsh residence of Maximus.

Four sons are credited to him. Victor perished in Gaul, cited only in a few late pedigrees as Gwythyr. A fragment of *The White Book* tells of "Saint Peblic in Caernarvon, son of Maxen Wledic emperor of Rome, and Helen daughter of Eudaf was his mother"—the Peblig (Publicius) of Llanbeblig church by Caernarvon.(22) *The Red Book* and a pedigree give us Owein. Then there is a Custennin or Constantine buried at Caernarvon. Nennius (with MSS. making him son or father of Constantine the Great, or Constantius son of Constantine) declares "his tomb is shown near the city which is named Caer Segeint, as the letters which are on his tombstone show." (The tomb may have been a milestone, misinterpreted by the Welsh of the Dark Ages.) *The History of Gruffyd ap Kynan*, known only in a Welsh version of the 13th century, but perhaps composed in Latin a century earlier, speaks of Arvon, "the old City of Constantine the Emperor, son of Constans the Great". Finally, according to the *Chronicle* that goes under the name of Matthew of Westminster, in 1233 Edward I went through Wales collecting treasure: Arthur's crown, a piece of the True Cross, "and many famous relics". At Caernarvon "the body of Prince Maximus, father of the noble emperor Constantine, was found and by the king's command was deposited with honour within the church". (23)

Nennius adds, "He sowed three seeds, that is gold, silver and brass, on the pavement of the said city, so that no poor man should ever dwell there." This tale doubtless reflects the fact that many coins were found in the area; well over a hundred coins of the two Constantines have turned up round Segontium in modern times.

MAXIMUS AND ST. MARTIN

GRATIAN, the young emperor against whom Maximus rose, was accounted amiable; Ambrose praised him for lying only with his own wife. He carried the victory of Christianity to a new level by discarding the title of Pontifex Maximus, and, against the wishes of the aristocracy of Rome, overthrowing the Altar of Victory there. An ardent hunter, he took part in the wild-beast fights of the amphitheatre. But he had sown discontent in the army by favouring Germans and dressing in furs, reclining with Alans in the parks and spending lavishly on them. (1)

With winter scarcely gone, Maximus landed at the mouth of the Rhine, where the troops hailed him. (2) He then marched to Paris, where after five days' skirmishing he won over the imperial Moorish horse. Gratian saw his army fading away and fled for the Alps with 300 cavalry. At his approach the cities closed their gates. At last he was let into Lyon, with Andragathius, Maximus' Master of Horse, in pursuit. Lulled by a solemn oath of protection, he was stabbed at a banquet on 25 August, 383—perhaps by Andragathius himself. (3)

We have some lines by Ausonius, a fragment "copied from a rough draft", recording his shattered state when the news reached Trèves. He sent his son home, but himself stayed on. The boat carrying his son faded into the dim distance:

> Then among crowding friends
> I stood alone . . .
> Now I lash down the upthrusting willow shoots,
> now trample beds of turf and through green sedge
> I poise my slippery foot on scattered pebbles . . .
> I'd buy with death the sight of you, my son,
> if you still lived to watch my obsequies.

Life has suddenly become a strange thing; he distrusts the new shoots and finds his balance precarious. (4)

The historians define Maximus as a vigorous, shrewd man. Orosius calls him a strong, righteous man raised to power against his will; Socrates sees him as ruthless against Gratian, but subtle in gaining his end; Ambrose of Milan, who went on two embassies to him, detested him and was ready to put the worst interpretation on any of his acts. (5) But he does not come too badly out of the detailed picture given by Sulpicius Severus, though he seems a trifle shifty, unstable despite all his keen energy.

He appears to have carried out systematic confiscations. Pacatus in his panegyric of the winning Theodosius states:

Shall I recall the cities emptied of their citizens and the solitudes crowded with the fugitive nobility? Shall I tell of the public auctions of the goods of persons who had filled the highest offices, their dignity fallen, their lives assessed in so much gold? We have seen the honourable ranks reduced in number, the consulars deprived of their insignia, the old men surviving their good fortune . . . (6)

We must take such comments with a grain of salt; but they do indicate a definite policy of expropriation and economy. We have no evidence, however, that the commoners had their burdens lightened as a result.

Pacatus draws a picture of the Brigand in Purple standing by the coffers, presiding over all the details of confiscation. The Imperial Residence seemed rather a Brigand's Storeroom. "All our goods went to the treasury along a single unending road," from which there was no return. (7) On the other hand, Maximus seems to have had no use for the more Oriental forms of etiquette that had grown up round the Sacred Palace, with its rigid ceremonies, protocols, genuflections, prosternations. He refused to be served by eunuchs. (8) And it is of interest that the latest extant milestone in Spain records a comprehensive repair made by the local governor, on the road from Pompaelo to Bordeaux in his name. (9)

Sulpicius tells us how his hero, Martin, confronted Count Avitianus whom Maximus had charged with a commission for ferreting out partisans of Gratian. "One day he entered Tours followed by a lamentable procession, files of people in chains. He ordered various tortures to be prepared for them." The town was stupefied. Martin, as soon as he heard, hurried to the Count's house; but as it was past midnight all doors were closed. So "he lay down before the threshold of the Palace of Blood". The Count was roused by an angel's buffet and told, "The Servant of God lies at your threshold and you sleep." He sent slaves to look. "But they, resembling in this all slaves, went scarcely beyond the inner doors, laughing at their master as the dupe of some delusive dream." Also they could not believe that in the dreadful dark a bishop could be lying at the door of a strange house. Again the Count slept; again he was awoken by the angry angel. He went to the door himself and found the saint. In terror he swore to do what Martin wanted if only he would go away. Martin departed and the Count freed all prisoners. Friendly now, he did no more harm to Tours.

Later Martin visited him at his home and saw a demon behind him. Blowing hard, he dislodged the demon, though the Count was puzzled by the saint's peculiar way of breathing on him. (10)

We are not told if the episode at Tours occurred before or after Martin went to Trèves to appeal to Maximus for clement behaviour. Maximus, "a man of fierce nature, pufft up by his victory", had gathered the bishops from all over his empire, and they vied in flattering him:

Martin alone sustained apostolic authority. In spite of needing to intercede with the emperor for others, he commanded rather than requested. Often invited to table, he refused, declaring that he could not dine with a man who had taken one emperor's dominion, another's life.

Maximus replied that he had not voluntarily assumed the empire, but that after being forced to it by his soldiers with God's will he had only defended his position by arms, and that God did not seem opposed to a man who gained victory in conditions so incredible. None of his adversaries had fallen save in battle. Won over at last by pleas and prayers, Martin attended his table and the emperor was delighted at gaining his end.

The diners, invited as to a festival, were great persons, illustrious men: Evodius both prefect and consul, one of the most righteous of men, and two all-powerful Counts, brother and uncle of Maximus.

The old way of reclining three to a couch had given way to the stibadium or crescent-table. The two horns were the places of honour; there lay Maximus and Evodius as consul; the inner places were taken by the Counts, with the priest between them. Martin, as an ascetic, refused to lie down and sat on a stool by the emperor. About midmeal a customary goblet was brought, which Maximus directed to Martin, hoping to receive it back from his hands. But Martin, to the court's amazement, gave the goblet next to his priest. "The tale was enthusiastically repeated: Martin had done at the emperor's table what no bishop had done at the least magistrate's dinner." (11)

He was a Pannonian. His father had risen from the ranks in the army to the position of tribune; when Martin tried to evade being called up as a veteran's son, his father handed him over to the authorities. While serving "he contented himself with one servant", and himself usually took off the man's boots and cleaned them. "They had their meals together and it was mostly the master who did the waiting." One wintry day he gave half his cloak to a shivering beggar by the gate of Amiens. Then, baptised, he stayed two more years in the army till on a day when donatives were being distributed he told the emperor, "I am Christ's soldier, I may not fight." He was put under arrest, but the next day the invading barbarians sued for peace and he was let go. He went to Hilary of Poitiers (appointed bishop 350–3), then was sent by a dream to his homeland. On his return to Gaul he spent some time on an island with a priest, then was pressed against his will into the see of Tours. He established the monastic system in Gaul, building on the bases laid by Athanasius and Hilary. That he did so as a bishop shows the fluid conditions of the later 4th century. His settlements at Ligugé and Marmoutier became the models for the new wave of Christian fervour rising up from below. He had begun at Tours by living in a small hut by the cathedral, but to escape visitors he fled to a remote spot where he was joined by some two dozen disciples. He dwelt in a timber cabin; his followers built similar cabins or dug hollows in rocks. There was no system of rules; but everyone gave up private property and buying-and-selling. The younger monks did copying; for the rest the monks came out of their cells for services or communal meals. Wine was allowed only to the sick; the sole clothing was of coarse goathair. (12)

Maximus seems to have convinced Martin of his own piety. They had long talks on the glory of the faithful and the eternity of the saints. (13) These themes were for Martin millennarian themes. We find him announcing the imminent advent of Antichrist. In an admirable speech to the Devil he promises him salvation if he repents, and adds that this event can happen "even at this late moment with the Day of Judgment at hand". Elsewhere Sulpicius himself takes up the theme. In his *Chronicle*, dealing with *Daniel*, he details his interpretation:

It is thus that the Roman land has been occupied by strange peoples, whether they took it by force or had it given up under the appearance of peaceful concession. And we see the barbarians, in particular the Jews, mingled in our armies, cities, and provinces and passing their lives with us, yet not adopting our ways. These are indeed the Last Days announced by the prophets.

As for the stone snatched without hands and braying in the dust, gold, silver, brass, iron, clay, it is a figure of Christ. For he is not produced from the human condition; he is born not from the desire of man, but from God. This world, in which are the kingdoms of the earth, he will break to nothing and he will found that other kingdom, incorruptible, unending: I mean the future age prepared for the Saints. (14)

Maximus must have convinced Martin that he had similar views; for the saint unbent with him to an unparalleled degree. We cannot tell if it was shrewdness or sympathy, or a mixture of both. Maximus must have wanted to win Martin over or at least to neutralise him; for he was staking much on his position as a defender of the faith. Martin was a tricky customer; strongly opposed to bloodshed and to state-interference in religion, he clashed with Maximus on important points of policy, and yet Maximus did not want him as an open enemy. At the same time, Maximus, claiming a special divine favour, perhaps had points of contact with Martin's ardours.

The extent to which Martin was charmed is shown by his behaviour to Maximus' wife, whom unfortunately Sulpicius does not name. She had an extreme veneration for Martin. "She hung on his very mouth." He could not escape her, though "till this time no woman had ever touched him". Careless of her imperial dignity, "prostrate on the ground, she could not snatch herself from his feet". She persuaded her husband to join her in begging Martin to come to dinner; and "despite his firmness, the blessed man had to yield". She sent all the servants out, made all the preparations, covered a small seat with a cloth, and served the dishes that she herself had cooked. She stood at a distance, "showing in all things the reserve of a woman serving at table and a slave's humility". She mixed the drinks and held out the cup; then she collected the crumbs, "in her ardent faith preferring these remnants to imperial banquets".

The comments in Sulpicius' *Dialogues* are no less interesting than the story itself in revealing the attitudes of the period.

There a speaker objects in dismay that this story is liable to set a bad example and be used by men who like women's company; and Gallus has to make a long defence, pleading that the woman was an empress acting with her husband's consent, not a widow or a wild girl, that she acted like a slave, and that Martin succumbed only once in his life—and that in his sixties. (15)

Maximus had arrived amid the Priscillianist controversy. Gratian had been inclining to the dissidents. As the trouble began in Spain, Maximus, a Spaniard, may have known about it all the while; or he may have seen the chance, after he settled in at Trèves, to justify his usurpation with the aureole of religious orthodoxy. He wrote to pope Siricius that he would allow no innovation in faith or church-order; and claimed that in view of the bishops' unreliability (*inconstantia*) he had changed a charge concerning faith and morals into a criminal charge. He was crushing the Manicheans "who endangered the Catholic Faith with destruction". The charges were proved and confessed, but he blushed to detail them. Later he again made it clear that he meant to make political use of the situation in Italy, where Arians or semi-Arians were strong at Milan. In terms unctuously menacing he wrote to Valentinian II that if the government could not protect the true faith, he, Maximus, would regretfully have to do so. (16)

His foes accused him of double-dealing. The orthodox said that he sought support from the pagan aristocracy at Rome;

the pagans blamed him for not turning to the gods; Ambrose declared that he had become King of the Jews, because he had won the Jews' co-operation. But for a while his tactics succeeded. He sent his chamberlain to Theodosius of the East to ask for recognition and alliance. (17) The imperial court noticed with a shock that this man was not a eunuch, and learned that Maximus refused to have eunuchs about him. Theodosius, cautious as usual when not infuriated, felt the need to hedge. There were threats on the eastern frontier from nomad Saracens; the Persian situation was unclear; the Balkans needed watching. He acknowledged Maximus as his co-Augustus; and we hear of a statue of the emperor from Britain set up with acclamations in Alexandria. (18)

In Italy also there were confusions that aided Maximus. Valentinian II had acceded on his brother Gratian's death and a struggle to dominate him had opened between his mother Justina and Ambrose. The latter, son of a praetorian prefect of Gaul, had been present as a government official at the election of a new bishop for Milan in 374, and had found himself forced into the seat; he was still a statesman as well as a bishop. Now at Justina's request he went on an embassy of peace to Maximus.

Maximus suggested that Valentinian should come himself into Gaul. Ambrose objected that it was winter. Maximus then sent his son Victor (soon to be made Caesar) to Milan; but Valentinian was not persuaded. On Victor's return, Ambrose left for Italy. In the meantime Count Bauto, a capable soldier, had occupied the Alpine passes and spoiled any plans that Maximus had for invasion.

At Rome the pagan party of the nobles was again hopeful; two of them (including Symmachus) had been raised to high office. They appealed in vain to Valentinian for the restoration of the Altar of Victory; and they thought they might win Maximus over. Ambrose again went on an embassy, to ask for Gratian's corpse to be buried in Italy. Maximus refused; he was heard to regret not having invaded Italy at once after Gratian's fall. (19)

It is time now to look more closely at the Priscillianists. The Cordovan bishop, we saw, had started things off and, despite his repentance, could not hold them up. Hydacius of Merida was ruthless. A council was held in 380 at Saragossa, where among others was present Delphinus, bishop of Bordeaux and friend of Paulinus of Nola. The Priscillianists did not dare appear; but two bishops, Instantius and Salvian, and two laymen, Priscillian and Helpidius, were excommunicated. Ithacius, bishop of Ossonoba in Lusitania, was empowered to make the sentence public. (However, a treatise which seems drawn up by the Priscillianists for the pope denies any such sentence.) The two attacked bishops promptly consecrated Priscillian bishop of Avila. Their opponents appealed to the emperor Gratian, who forbade the Priscillianists to enter the churches or the towns. Instantius, Salvian, and Priscillian set out for Rome. Refused permission to pass through Bordeaux, they halted at Elusa, won many partisans, and were entertained by Euchrotia, wife of the orator Delphidius. Euchrotia was so moved that she and her daughter Procula went on with the travellers to Italy. At Rome Salvian died. Refused access to the pope, the others went on to Milan, where Ambrose also refused to see them. The Master of Offices, however, restored them to their sees.

Ithacius, against whom a charge of disturbing the peace of the churches had been made, fled meanwhile to Trèves, where he was well received by the bishop and the prefect. Gratian, however, persuaded by the Master of Offices, ordered his arrest; but was then himself overthrown by Maximus, who took up the cause of Ithacius. At a Bordeaux council, in 384, Instantius was deposed from his see. Priscillian appealed direct to Maximus. Ithacius and Hydacius, perhaps to help in justifying themselves for bringing two fellow-bishops before a secular court, put in a double charge of magic and immorality. In the winter of 384–5 occurred the trial at Trèves, where the Priscillianists were condemned. (20)

The Priscillianists may have been linked with the sect of *Abstinentes*; they were passionately ascetic, opposed to marriage. According to Orosius, they laid stress on unity and saw in the Trinity only a Single Christ. They had Gnostic types of creation-myth, considering the soul a part of divine substance captured by the powers of evil and jailed in the body; but they held that even the Prince of Darkness could be redeemed. As with many extreme sects who rebelled against any acceptance of the existing world, they tended to dualism and were specially interested in the teachings of St. Paul.

Sulpicius, with every chance of observing them during a week's stay near his home, called them Gnostics and described Priscillian:

noble in rank, extremely well-off, keen, restless, eloquent, learned from a full reading, very prompt to argument and discussion; happy if he had not corrupted a first-rate character with perverted occupations. You could indeed see much good in both his body and mind. He could endure long vigils, bear hunger and thirst, had not the least desire for property, was most sparing of display; but he was deluded, excessively inflated with secular knowledge. It was even believed that he had practised magic arts from his young days.

A mixture of humanism and asceticism, humility and wild aspirations, such as we find among many leading heretics of the era. A blank rejection of the State and all that holds together the existing system; a deep sympathy for all that struggles towards the time when even the Devil is redeemed and the ruling divisions are wiped out. A harshness and a sweetness. (21)

Sulpicius goes on: "Women in hordes were drawn towards him, avid for novelties, with insecure faith and curious in spirit about everything."

Apart from Gnostic oddities, the Priscillianists aroused the antagonism of most bishops by their *ascesis*. The fierce total rejection of the existing world in monachism and allied trends was a grave danger to a hierarchical Church which had come to an accord with the State. For many long years after the Constantinian settlement the bishops had a difficult problem in taming the monastic or ascetic movements till they fitted into the pattern of the establishment, serving the Church instead of challenging it.

Martin must have made now a second visit to Trèves. We cannot conceive the long intercourse with Maximus and his wife, which Sulpicius describes, as taking place amid the agitations of the trials. But either Sulpicius has confused the times when Martin came to see Maximus or the troubles of Gratian's supporters had dragged on a long time; for we find in his pages the latter intruding among Martin's cares together with the Priscillianist persecutions.

Martin opposed himself flatly to the bishops. "If you want my opinion, the accused and the accusers displease me equally. Ithacius above all. I say that he has no scruple, no respect for anything. He's full of effrontery, a babbler, impudent, wasteful, reducing everything to a matter of belly and gullet. He's grown so stupid he accused all honest folk, even holy men, with a liking for reading or a steady design to vie in fasts. He denounces them as accomplices or disciples of Priscillian." (Jerome said likewise of the worldly clerics of Rome: "They call a Manichean anyone they see pallid and grave." (22))

Ithacius made a public accusation of heresy against Martin. Martin went on asking Maximus to shed no blood and to content himself with expelling the heretics from their churches. Maximus hedged and adjourned the proceedings, "and even at the moment of his departure Martin extracted a promise that no blood would be shed." But the two bishops managed to get the proceedings transferred to the prefect Evodius, "a harsh and pitiless man". Priscillian denied that he held meetings of lost women or prayed naked. (23) (From his *Apologeticus* we know how he answered those accusing him of sorcery: "Nobody will succeed in overthrowing the tabernacle of Christ, the temple of God that is in me.") Evodius condemned him; and Sulpicius says that to keep the bishops well away from the final sentence, a further trial without them was held, this time one Patricius, *patronus fisci*, being accuser. Maximus imposed the capital sentence. (24)

In his *Dialogues* Sulpicius elaborates. Martin arrived as the bishops had things well under way and Maximus was about to send tribunes armed with full powers into Spain to round up the heretics. The bishops had a simple test of heresy: pallor of face (that is, any suggestion of fasting). They feared Martin would refuse communion with them and be followed by large numbers of people, so they asked Maximus to send to the Master of Offices and have Martin forbidden entry to Trèves unless he declared himself at peace with the gathered bishops. Martin merely answered that he came in peace with Christ; and this reply appears to have satisfied the simple policemen. He entered in the dark and went to pray in the church, then next day visited the palace with many requests for mercy—especially for Count Narses and governor Leucadius of Gratian's party. But most of all he wanted to stop the tribunes going to Spain with swords. (25)

For two days Maximus warded him off: to make his favour seem more precious, or out of obduracy induced by the bishops, or out of greed for the estates of the condemned. ("This man," comments Sulpicius, "who was endowed with many good qualities, was, it is said, defenceless against greed. It was perhaps necessity of government." The treasury was exhausted and the likelihood of further warfare was always present.)

Martin refused communion with the bishops, who ran to Maximus. The latter called Martin in and tried to soothe him. Everything had gone by due process of law; why blame the bishops? The synod held a few days before had exonerated Ithacius. Martin was not won over, but Maximus went ahead with his plans for extirpating the heretics. Martin, hearing of it all, burst into the palace, though it was at night. Spare the men and call back the tribunes, he said, and he would communicate with the bishops. Maximus agreed, and next day Martin went into communion with the bishops, though he refused to sign a document stating that he had done so. The following day he left Trèves, sad at having communioned with guilty men. By a small township, Andethanna, in a corner of a lonely forest, he sat grieving and saw an angel who told him to cast regret aside, but, "taking courage, return to your usual firmness or otherwise you will imperil not your fame but your salvation". So, henceforth, he took care not to compromise himself in communion with the party of the bishops. But he felt a diminution of his power and kept away from all synods and gatherings of bishops. (He may in fact have been excluded from such gatherings.)

The political success had been with the bishops; but Martin remained the hero of the people, and in many ways his example had a powerful effect in Britain and Ireland. (26) The Celtic Church, with its monastic basis, was at root a development of Martin's way of life as opposed to that of the compromising bishops. The confrontation of Martin and Maximus, both figures who were to have such potent influence in Britain, has therefore much interest.

Ambrose had returned to Milan convinced that Maximus meditated attack. "You will be safer opposed to this man, who hides war in a wrapping of peace." (He had been on his way home when he met Hyginus, the bishop of Cordova who had begun the denunciations of the Priscillianists, then changed his mind. Maltreated and dying, the old man begged for a cloak and a mattress; but the guards, driving him on, pushed Ambrose aside.) The situation was being complicated by barbarian inroads in Raetia; and at Bauto's suggestion Alans and Huns nearing Gaul were diverted into the territory of Maximus, who complained. Valentinian had to buy the retreat of his own allies. In the East, Theodosius, seeking to extort extra taxes for his war preparations, provoked a revolt of the populace of Antioch.

At Milan the conflict between Ambrose and Justina, who favoured the Arians, continued. Ambrose was besieged in his cathedral, where he taught his flock antiphonal singing in the Eastern way and wrote hymns for them. He was now discarded as ambassador and Domninus of Syria was sent by Valentinian to Trèves, where Maximus offered or agreed to supply troops for aid in threatened Pannonia.

A part of Maximus' army was thus sent on into Italy, while he himself followed with a larger body. He was able to force the passes in the Cottian Alps. Justina and her son fled from Milan to Aquileia, then crossed the seas for Thessalonica. There it seems that Theodosius received an embassy from Maximus, who no doubt argued that he had only acted in defence of the Nicean Creed and so deserved the support of the East. Theodosius, while trying to convert Valentinian to orthodoxy, built up his army through the winter.

Rome had now fallen to Maximus, whose fleet was cruising in the Adriatic. Agents of his worked on the Germans in Theodosius' army, and a plot to murder the latter was discovered in time. The invasion of Italy proceeded by a crossing of the Save, where it seems that Andragathius was killed. Then at Poetovio the brother of Maximus, Marcellinus, was defeated and many of his men went over to the other side. Aemona (Laibach), which had been fiercely holding out, welcomed

Theodosius in; and Maximus retreated to a camp around
Aquileia. Theodosius came hot upon him. Maximus fought
hard but was driven back into the city and surrendered. Three
miles out, he was carried before Theodosius, then hustled off
to his death—probably on 28 July, 388. Only a few of his
followers, including the Moorish Guards, were also executed. (27)

Orosius says rather untruly that the "ruthless Maximus" with
his terrible Germanic troops was cooped up and beaten "without any strategy, any dispute", so that "a most formidable war"
ended without a drawn sword. Ambrose comments, "The power
that he had wickedly seized, he let slip in fear, in a sort of
feminine way." He adds that Theodosius supported the old
mother of Maximus and brought up his orphan daughters. (28)

Maximus' fleet was defeated off Sicily, and his son Victor,
who had been left in Gaul as Augustus, was killed by Argobast.
The troops brought from Britain did not return. We may suppose that it was men from Segontium who figure as Segon-
tienses in the Balkans. Theodosius must have sent them there,
to use their arms in imperial defence far from the temptation to
revolt. (29)

Claudian contrasts Maximus with Eugenius, the next
usurper in the West, a puppet set up by the Frank Argobast in
392–4 and also defeated by Theodosius:

> Out of these sunset-lands, by various crimes
> two tyrants emerged. One was wild Britain's spawn,
> the other a Frankish outlaw's dangling puppet.
> Each dared to sin, with his Lord's innocent blood
> each stained his hands.
>   This, risen abruptly, felt
> a boldness; that learned caution from his fall.
> This rushed to arms; that prudently attempted
> slow steps. This outwards spread, that gathered strengths.
> This burst across the land, that skulked in ramparts.
> Unlike, but brothers in death. They might not flee
> dishonoured ends by dying amid battle-noise.
> With glory and armour all gone, they met again
> their powerless state. Arms knotted, out they stretched
> their shivering necks beneath the uplifted sword
> and begged for pardon and life.

While Theodosius, he says,

> faster than rumour of his coming, trampled
> the closed mountains like plains, and suddenly struck.
> Rear up your toppling crags, drive towers to heaven,
> stand girt with rivers, spread deep forest-barriers . . .
> You'll find no locks for guilt. The avenger comes.

Before we pass on, Sulpicius deserves a word for himself. A friend of Paulinus of Nola, he had his home in that part of Aquitaine which lent support to the Priscillianists. About 392, on Martin's advice, despite his father's opposition, he renounced the world, sold most of his property, and became a presbyter. He had finished his *Life* when Martin died in November 397; he revised and published the work in 400 with three Letters, which gave an account of the death and obsequies of the saint. His *Chronicle* we may date 403, and his *Dialogues* the following year. A pleasant writer with a clear, amiable style, he passionately expounds the monastic ethic, with its belief in world-end and the rule of the saints, as against the compromise with the State that the bishops now embodied.

Thus he ends the second book of his *Chronicle*. The persecution of the Priscillianists, he says, strengthened the sect.

The bodies of the executed were taken back to Spain and given great funerals there: even to swear by Priscillian became the height of religion. And among us this stirred up a ceaseless battle of discords, agitated by foul disputes that have lasted already fifteen years without any lull.

And now everything we see has been confused and entangled by the discords of the bishops; everything has been perverted through them with hate or back-scratching, fear, fickleness, envy, faction, lust, greed, arrogance, torpor, idleness.

Finally, against the small group of persons of true insight the majority strive with lunatic aims and pertinacious efforts. And in the midst of it all the People of God and every single man of genuine goodness are held in scorn and mockery.

That passage shows the man. His impetuous intensity, his independence, his sharp opposition of the creed of Martin to the corrupted world (in which he includes the hierarchical Church), are all there. And it is of interest to find that he considered the controversy still raging in Gaul (and *inter nos* would in his idiom include Britain). He can hardly mean the direct Priscillianist issue; he therefore sees that issue as only one aspect of a general struggle between what we may call monastic and episcopal Christianity.

It is worth noting that Sulpicius with his resolute opposition to all the powers of the world, episcopal or monarchical, has an element of regard for Maximus—while he carefully omits saying anything of Theodosius where he might well do so (*Vita* xx). His interest in Maximus is thus a considerable tribute; for so strong was his anti-monarchical position that he was cited and used by later rebels, especially in the 15th and 16th centuries:

[A critic] points out with surprise the use made in England and Denmark, in the revolutionary eras, of certain passages from the *Chronicle*. What would he have said if he had known the prodigious crop of pamphlets which came out indefatigably over three-quarters of a century on the soil of the Republic of the Seven United Provinces. To struggle against the ambitions of Leicester, to fight the covetousness of the son of the Silent, five to six texts drawn from opuscules served as ever-ready weapon, first for nationalist Republicans, then for Calvinists opposed to the Stadholder. There it was that Milton learned to represent the judgments of our author on royalty as an echo of the general sentiment of the Fathers on the subject. (After analysing chapter I of *Kings* 8 and giving it, as Sulpicius does, a democratic colour by enrolling Samuel in the Republican ranks, Milton adds: "Thus also the ancient Fathers interpreted this place," and he cites the wise and judicious Sulpicius Severus, "one example among many".) (30)

More stories might be cited from Sulpicius to show the consistency of his views and his unrelenting antagonism to all elements in the Church which compromised with the world. He tells how once in winter a half-naked beggar approached Martin, who bade the archdeacon provide clothes; but the latter scornfully did nothing. The man came into the sacristy weeping with cold. Martin at once took off the tunic from under his surplice and gave it to him. The archdeacon entered to say that the congregation was waiting; Martin replied that the poor must first be clad; the other replied that the beggar was gone.

"Well," said Martin, "as the clothing is ready, bring it in. I'll find the poor man who needs it." The archdeacon ran to a near shop and bought some Bigorre cloth, short rough stuff, for five silver pieces, and cast it at Martin's feet. "Here's the cloth, but no poor man." Martin said nothing, but went aside and clothed himself in the coarse cloth.

The tale, however, which gives the core of the position of Martin and Sulpicius is that of the saint's temptation by Satan in the guise of Christ. This Satan-Christ "wore a royal robe and was crowned with a diadem of gems and gold, and gold gleamed on his shoes; his face was serene, his expression joyous . . ." Martin recognised that the insignia were of the Devil—of the imperial power—and rejected the vision. The glittering figure went out in a stink.

In Britain the tale went that after Maximus' death in 388 his widow returned to Wales and was there regarded as a saint. (31) As St Elen she had several churches dedicated to her: Llanelen near Llanrhidian in west Gower, Llanelen in Monmouthshire, Bletherstone in Pembrokeshire. There was once a Capel Elen in an Anglesey parish (Penrhosllugwy). And she was the reputed mother of saints, the Constantine and the Peblig we have already noticed. (32)

Dedications to the family of Maximus are mostly in areas where Gallo-Roman memorials are found. There is a western concentration; but in south-east Wales there are also groupings, linked with others in Monmouthshire and west Herefordshire. It seems that here we touch the earliest level of dedications in Wales and that there is a close relation between this development and Martin's monasticism.

In every way, then, it is sure that Maximus and his family are of the utmost importance for our inquiry into the dark age of Britain. By forming or building up the Federates, Maximus laid the political basis from which the kingship of the dark age grew; he enabled the Celtic kings to feel themselves the inheritors of Roman tradition, so that as much continuity in culture as the circumstances permitted was brought about. Through his connection with Martin, he and his wife instituted, or at least greatly strengthened, the links with Gallic monasticism that were of the utmost importance for Celtic Christianity. He became a focal figure for the new legends born from the Celtic struggle for independence and survival. In a sense he is the prototype of the Arthur of legend; for the real Arthur fought against the Saxons, but the Arthur of medieval fantasy, like Maximus, fought and "killed the King of the Romans".

THE SCILLIES, NINIAN, AND
PEASANT REBELS

THERE were direct links of the Priscillianists with Britain, since some of the condemned were exiled to the Scillies. At the 384–5 trial at Trèves, seven persons were found guilty as Manicheans (dualists) and Melefici (magicians)—that is, on both religious and civil charges. They were Priscillian, Instantius, Euchrotia, a poet Latronian, and two clerks, Armenius and Felicissimus. Instantius was exiled to the Scillies and the others beheaded. Martin not only failed to save the lives of those executed, he failed also to prevent the harrying sword. Other Priscillianists were arrested, done to death, or condemned to confiscation and deportation. Among the exiles was the writer Tiberian, who went like Instantius to the Scillies. The orator Latinus Pacatus Drepanius, in his panegyric on Theodosius in 389, gives a detailed account of the indignities and decapitations inflicted under Maximus on the sect. This orator, to whom Ausonius dedicated three poems, suggests that the fault of the sufferers was that they held to "an excessive religion and too diligently exercised worship". (1)

They certainly included many highly cultured people. Priscillian was a remarkable man. Latronian is described by Jerome as of great learning, comparable in his metrical skill with the ancient poets. Tiberian seems to have been a skilful writer, though Jerome refers to his swelling style. Euchrotia is called by Pacatus the wife of a famous poet. Another victim, Urbica, said to have been stoned outside Bordeaux, was the daughter or close relation of the poet and orator Urbicus, a freedman, who was one of Ausonius' colleagues: a voluble declaimer in Greek, weak in Latin. In the Scillies the exiles lived out their days; and we catch one glimpse of them when we hear from Jerome that, after the death of his friends, Tiberian was "overcome by the boredom of exile". (2)

Even so the Priscillianists may have affected the intellectual life of Britain:

We have to bear in mind that casual contacts between Britain and Gaul will generally have passed unrecorded. Occasionally we get significant glimpses. . . . What was the nature of the connection of Scilly with Gaul? It must have been close, yet we hear of it merely incidentally. We may suspect that the connection was a Breton one, and that the close connection of Britanny with western Britain had already begun in Roman times. (3)

The Scillies had been used in the 4th century as a place of political exile, e.g. for the Pannonian Valentinus.

It is unlikely that there was much Romanisation of the islands. At Halangy Down, St. Mary's, we find structures close to those of Chysauster and Porthmeor in west Cornwall; the pottery, too, is similar: a courtyard-house culture. Oval rooms, a smaller opening from a larger, a massive entry, a dished post-base retainer, paving at entry and beyond the wall, tanks and drainage system, and hillside location. Terraces point to cereals—as also does the lower stone of a rotary quern; whorls and a button point to textiles; slag, slate for a few articles, gritted wares apparently from the Cornish mainland thirty-five miles away, with some yet more heavily-gritted and poorly-fired vessels probably made on the spot, help to build up the picture. (4)

From the extreme south we must now move to the north again. In the 390s an obscure figure seems to have been at work evangelising among the Picts of Galloway, Ninian by name. The sole sources for his work consist of a brief note in Bede's *History* and a *Life* of the 12th century by a Cistercian monk Ailred, who had been brought up at the court of David I in Scotland. Bede merely tells us that he was the apostle of the southern Picts, that he had been instructed at Rome, that he built Whithorn, gave it St. Martin's name, and was himself buried there. Ailred, writing at the request of the Whithorn officials, composes a panegyric with elaborate miracles; but he claims to use an earlier work, and there may be old traditions in his *Life*. He makes Ninian a Briton, son of a Christian king (presumably by the Solway), who was consecrated in Rome, called on Martin at Tours, took away monastic ideas and masons, and built the Whithorn church. While building, he heard of Martin's death and dedicated the church to him. He also founded a monastery at Whithorn, modelled on Marmoutier. (5)

Not many of these statements bear scrutiny. The attribution of high birth is a common hagiographic fiction; the visit to Rome suggests a late interpolation meant to respectabilise a Celtic saint; it is unlikely that a church would be dedicated to a just-dead bishop; and the movement of masons from Tours is ridiculous. The one detail in Ailred that may be old is the conversion of a prince Tuduvallus. The name is Celtic and other sources locate the man in Strathclyde. (6)

Today Ninian's name is scattered over Scotland, even beyond the Grampians in the land of the North Picts. But many, perhaps all, of these place-names date from the 12th century when David I popularised Ninian in his important work of reformation—Ailred's *Life* being a main instrument in spreading the saint's fame. But Ninian may have evangelised in Galloway and the Wall district; certainly about this time a widespread effort of conversion was made in those parts. (7)

We can hardly accept the dedication to Martin. All dedications to him, including that at Canterbury, seem to come after Bertha's marriage to Ethelbert of Kent in the later 6th century when there was an expansion of Frankish influence. Bertha had her chaplain Luidhart and used the Canterbury chapel before the papal mission under Augustine arrived. Still, there was perhaps a link between Ninian and Martin, as in the case of the saints of Maximus' family. Indeed, the evangelisation among the South Picts was going on at the same time as that in south Wales, and there may well have been connections. (Note, too, that at this period even the living could be prominently linked with a church. Paulinus of Nola mentions a picture of Martin on the wall: "even amid the splendours of the holy things he shines forth with conspicuous clarity", while a painting of himself stood on an adjoining wall.) (8)

Gildas in mid-6th century recalls the pagan days. Still, he says, one sees the ugly lineaments of idols, "inside or out of their abandoned walls, still with fierce features as was their customs". He mentions also the honours paid to mountains, valleys, and rivers "once deadly, now useful to men". In the

390s, and for long after, large pagan areas persisted. We can gain some idea of what Ninian and his fellows faced from Sulpicius' contemporary account of Martin in the more Roman-ised Gaul. In one town the saint started destroying a pine by a sanctuary and was attacked by priest and crowd; he argued and they agreed to cut the tree down if he stood ready to receive it; but the tree fell away from the steadfast saint. Elsewhere, as he burned a shrine, the flames threatened the next house; he climbed on the roof and forced them back. At Leprosum the people drove him off; for three days he prayed in ash and haircloth; then, guarded by two angels, he was unmolested. Aeduan peasants assaulted him as he pulled a temple down; he offered his throat; a man with a sword swung it so furiously that he fell over backward; another man drew a knife but it vanished. At Amboise a tall cone-topped tower of smooth stone "drew local superstitions by the beauty of its work"; the priest, told to erase it, pleaded that he would need the army and a host of workers; Martin prayed all night and a storm toppled the tower. Once he overthrew a Jupiter Column. The Devil took the form of Roman gods to deceive him, pretending to be Mercury, Jupiter, even Venus and Minerva—but mostly Mercury. We learn that Mercury often worried him, but that Jupiter was a heavy, stupid fellow. (9)

Having demolished the gods, the saint was expected to take over their curative and fertilising powers. Sulpicius says that Martin saved the Senones (round Sens) from hail-devastations after a prefect led a deputation to him; his informant was the prefect's son. After Martin's death "he trembled for his future harvests as you yourself saw".

But the peasants of Britain and Gaul were not merely becom-ing serf-tenants and changing their religion; they were also from time to time breaking into revolt. And it is essential to grasp how bitter and deep was the tradition of struggle. The uprisings go back to the 3rd century, merged with rebellions of the soldiery (themselves mainly of peasant stock) that shook the empire. Indeed, they go back to the 180s, the War of the Deserters, the revolt of runaway slaves and farmers, labourers and army deserters in Gaul and Spain. Nearly twenty years later four legions were needed in Gaul against the unbeaten peasants. (10) About 283–4 large-scale rebellion broke out afresh, and we hear for the first time of Bacaudae. This was the trouble in which Carausius and his fleet played a key part. The 260s saw the peasants raiding estates and towns, then retiring to forests and wastes. (11) Historians disliked mentioning such things; Ammianus shamefacedly states that Valentinian I in the early years of his reign fought more than barbarians. "There were other battles less worthy of being recounted, waged through various districts of Gaul. But it is superfluous to describe them, as their outcome produced nothing worth remark, and it is unseemly to prolong a History with ignoble details." (12) The anon of *De Rebus Bellicis* says that poverty "often inflicted grave losses on the State by laying the fields waste, broke the peace by starting off brigandages, stirred hate by inflaming people, and by the rising scale of lawlessness encouraged usurpers". (13)

A small band could be called brigands; when large it became a horde of Bacaudae. Anyhow, the authorities preferred the term "brigandage" for peasant revolt; it sounded less disturbing. The peasants set ambushes along the highroads of Spain and Gaul, they caught and killed the emperor Valentinian's brother-in-law. After striking, they retired (as Merobaudes says) with their spoils to the woodlands. When the 367 attacks were made by barbarians on Britain, peasant revolt was in full swing in Gaul. Sections of the Wall garrison worked with the attackers, and beyond doubt the peasants joined in sacking the big villas. "A rising of Bacaudae is a regular consequence of barbarian inroads into Gaul," and only lack of records fails to show the same sort of things in Britain. When Count Theodosius arrived with a field-army at Richborough and marched down Watling Street to London, he found the countryside swarming with bands who were loaded with captives and booty, and London in a state of siege. Among these bands must have been slaves, colons, and servants, as well as Scots, Picts, or Saxons. We hear that the Pannonian exile Valentinus tried to put himself at the head of an uprising amid all this confusion. Who were the disaffected groups? Valentinus must surely have been hoping to use the inflamed peasantry while stirring sedition in the army. (14) The evidence provided by Bokerley Dyke for the fear of peasant attacks, especially in 367–9, we noted above.

In Ausonius' poem on Theon's busy life in Médoc, we met the local "brigands", with whom it is jestingly suggested that Theon the small squire is in collusion. Hill country was naturally favourable. When Martin, ordained exorcist by Hilary, was paying his visit home, he lost his way in crossing the Alps and encountered brigands. One man brandished an axe, but another prevented the blow. Martin, with his arms bound behind his back, was left under a single guard in a lonely spot; and soon in argumentative fearlessness he had converted him. (15)

Sulpicius further tells how Martin once suspected a false cult at an ancient tomb, interviewed the priests and clerks there, inquired into the martyr's name and date, and then stood on the tomb, demanding the true name and merits of the dead man. An ugly spectre rose and confessed that he had been a brigand, executed for his deeds. (16)

Sarmatian horseman in mail (*Trajan Col.*)

VICTRICIUS OF ROUEN

THE close links between Gaul and Britain in the ecclesiastical and cultural spheres, which we traced in the careers of Maximus and Martin, are shown clearly in the life of Victricius. Born about 330–40, he may indeed have been a Briton. His friend Paulinus of Nola describes him as from the World's End, *de extimo orbis*: which could mean anywhere in the arc from Brittany, through Britain, to Belgica and Germania II. Most likely Paulinus refers to Normandy, where Victricius evangelised the Morini, and alludes to Virgil's phrase: "Morini the furthest of men." In any case, the area of the Morini, through its port of Gesoriacum (Boulogne), had age-old connections with Britain. The Augustan poet Grattius in his *Chase*, describing British dogs as bold and tough, though lacking looks and graces, writes:

> What, if the Morini's tideswept wayward straits
> you visit and even penetrate among Britons . . . (1)

Victricius was one of the saints from the army, like Martin and his disciple Victor, like Januarius of Naples, or Pachomius who played a key part in founding Egyptian monachism. The tale of Martin's defiance of the emperor must have long been repeated in the ranks in Gaul, losing nothing in the telling. (2) Victricius chose a day of Army Council when the soldiers were under arms. Breaking ranks, he went to the commanding officer and offered up his arms. "I leave these arms of blood to assume the arms of peace. Free me from the oaths (*sacramenta*) that bind me to the service of Caesar." He was seized and beaten, then flung into prison—into one of the army cells paved with broken pots with the jagged ends uppermost. Next he was sent before the Count and condemned to death; but as he was led off, the executioner made an insulting gesture and was struck blind. The chains fell off Victricius; and the Count, informed, let him go.

Such is the account by Paulinus in a letter addressed to the saint himself. (3) As with Sulpicius' tales about Martin, we can only say that men in this difficult period of violent change were so moved by the symbolic meaning they saw in events that they insensibly remoulded those events closer to that meaning—not with any intention of deceit, but in a desperate need to dramatise the moment of choice, the birthpang of the new out of the old.

In 380–5 Victricius became bishop of Rouen. About 356 Paulinus met him in Martin's company at Vienne. The occasion was a governmental division of the province of Lyonnaise II, which distributed the towns taken from it among the metropoles of Rouen and Tours. Vienne was the seat of the vicariate of the Seven Provinces; and the two bishops had come to discuss the administrative issues. We seem to have a memento of the visit in the epitaph of a woman named Foedula who, buried at Vienne, had been baptised by Martin.

Also, in a tale by Sulpicius, we meet Victricius and Martin together again, with the local bishop, when, about 395, Martin cured a dumb girl. (4) Profoundly enthusiastic for Martin's monastic ways, Victricius introduced them at Rouen, propagated the ascetic cult, and instituted a choir of virgins. Ambrose of Milan, his other model, depicts the rite of Veiling, which was solemnly carried out amid a host of white-clad neophytes with lighted candles. The girl received her veil at the altar as a Bride of Christ; if she fell away, she was rated an adultress. A female Soldier of Chastity, she had to endure mortifications in food, bathing, sleep; she was forbidden all festivities or family parties, and spent her days in exercises like reading, labour, prayer. (5) Victricius speaks with pride of the veiled maidens and widows, the chosen ones of his congregation; and his success was such that the church became too small, so that he decided to build a new one. This he dedicated to the saints Gervasius and Protasius, whose remains, of giant size "like those of the primeval times", were found in June 386 as Ambrose and his flock were besieged in the Portian Basilica at Milan by the Arian troops of the empress Justina. The discovery of these saints with their lack of any history, their suspiciously rhyming names and huge bones, was very heartening for the faithful; and their fame spread through Gaul and Italy, helped by the hymn that Ambrose composed in their honour. Victricius' choice of them brings out his admiration for Ambrose and the cult of virginity. (6)

Bishops all over Gaul and Italy were anxious to gain some scraps of the new saints. Lacking the martyrs who were so plentiful in the East, the West wanted to make the most of the Milanese chance; and Ambrose shared out fragments to many towns. In Gaul, at least Vienne, Tours, and Rouen received a piece. In the epitaph of Foedula of Vienne we read:

> Foedula's left the world in the mercy of God
> she lies in this tomb that fostering faith has given.
> Bathed by the hand of noble Martin she shed
> her sins in the font, in God reborn to heaven.
> And now the martyrs yield her a fitting seat,
> noble Gervasius and Protasius she adores
> By her right of faith her merited rest she meets
> here in the saints' society evermore.

In the midst of his building Victricius was called to Britain. The year was 396. Furious dissensions had broken out in the British Church and the bishop of Rouen was considered the best man to settle them. Two passages in his one extant work, *The Praise of the Saints*, tells us all we know of his journey.

I filled the wise with the love of peace, I gave it to the submissive, I inculcated it in the ignorant, I made it penetrate with force among the recalcitrant, persisting in season and out of season, according to the advice of the Apostle. In short, I entered into their souls by doctrine and suggestion.

When human weakness betrayed me, I called the spirit to my aid. I did what those do who sail the sea in the extreme fury of a storm; they do not trust to the skill of the pilot, but call on the mercy of the sovereign majesty. The Jesus who is in us can calm the billows and hush the winds, but human art cannot. After that, I had no more need to occupy myself with those fallen away by breaking the bonds of discipline. (7)

Forty miles from Rouen on his way home, he heard that one Aelianus had arrived with the relics from Ambrose. Hurrying on, he burst into tears before the relics.

Here a large part of the celestial militia deigns to visit our city so that henceforth we shall needs dwell among crowds of saints. By the joy that I now feel, I measure what I have lacked till this moment.

But, saints and venerable martyrs, my delay, if I do not deceive myself, is pardonable and you will forgive me for it; if I have gone to Britain, if I have stayed there, it is to carry out your own orders. The bishops, my brothers in the priesthood, called on me to make peace there. Could I, your soldier, have refused them? It does not show lack of respect to obey orders. In Britain I was always at your service, and, though separated by the surrounding ocean, I was held by the duty I owe you. For you I went away, for you I am here, returned. (8)

Two other events in the bishop's life are of much interest. The Church in Gaul was still only beginning to expand outside the large towns, the seats of bishops. By 314, at the Council of Arles, we find rural parishes growing in the south; but the north was much slower. At Tours, such parishes arose only near the end of the century, built by Martin; in Limousin they developed only in the 7th–8th centuries after work by hermits and monks. For evangelising the countryside, Roman roads were of high importance; the five or six *vici* that Martin turned into parishes were at crossroads or along highways. (9) Victricius had a very large area formally under his control, and he set to work on Martin's lines, operating in both the land of the Morini (the Boulonnais, Morinie, Artois Flamingant, west Flanders) and the land of the Nervii (Bavai, Hainaut, Brabant). Paulinus declares that he made monasteries rise, not only in the towns, but also on islands and in forests. Thus, "instead of barbarians from without and brigands from within, now venerable and angelic choirs of saints fill the whole region". An exaggerated picture no doubt, but reflecting a zealous work of conversion. Note that the evangelisation hopes to end "brigandage".

The Church in Gaul still lacked central organisation as much as rural parishes. The bishops were more or less independent; no metropolitan system imposed uniformity in action and procedure. Obviously Britain must have shown the same position, in sharper form.

The end of Victricius underlined the condition of things in Gaul and the impending changes. About 403 he went to Rome, not on a pilgrimage, but summoned. He was in some sort of trouble, as we know from the letters of Paulinus. He may have fallen under suspicion of heresy; perhaps affected by Apollinarism (which, denying Christ's humanity, had made some headway in the West). But what happened at Rome shows that doctrinal issues were not directly at stake.

The papacy was determined to clean things up in Gaul. The Council of Turin, about 400, had discussed metropolitan controls, but not clearly. In such a situation the independent methods worked out by Martin were a nuisance. The more orthodox bishops considered that that saint brought the Church into disrepute by his odd behaviour, his monastic emphasis, his disdain of all shows. Sulpicius stresses his disordered and dirty appearance: "despicable of visage, foul of clothes, tangled of hair." He went "in shaggy dress, draped with dark and hanging cloak". A small man, almost shrunken, a *homunculus* with sin withered out of him. Here Sulpicius follows an apostolic tradition which insisted that Christ was ill-favoured in order not to be loved for extraneous reasons. (Origen, arguing with Celsus, concedes that Christ was ugly, *dyseides*, a man of mean build and ignoble looks.) Victricius, carrying Martin's methods into his diocese, was liable to episcopal disapproval as unbalanced in his concern about fasts, veils, vows, and worldrejection, to the detriment of building up the Church as a governing body inside society. (10) Further, his close relations with Ambrose may have been felt to accentuate his errors.

For a period which, it is true, was short, yet which was important, it seems as if the western episcopate recognises a double hegemony: that of the pope and that of the bishop of Milan. This situation arises at the time of St. Ambrose. . . . His influence makes itself felt in the affairs of the Eastern Church, at Antioch, Caesarea, Constantinople, Thessalonica. He it is who is charged with giving a bishop to Sirmium at a critical moment. At Aquileia he directs a council where are settled the final problems left by the Arian crisis in the land of the lower Danube. But it is above all in Gaul and in Spain that the ecclesiastical authority of Milan seems taken as a higher and normal tribunal. (11)

We may safely add Britain in that last sentence.

A.H.T.—4

The high esteem of the see of Milan derived at root from the fact that the city at this time was the official imperial residence in the West. For a while the see was as serious a rival to Rome as later was that of Byzantium; and the popes lost no chance to sap the position of their rival. They helped, in creating the metropolitan diocese of Ravenna, to weaken Milan. And Innocent in his Letter to Victricius showed his preoccupation with stopping the bishops of Gaul from turning to the tribunal of Milan in major cases.

But the issue of Milan, important as it was, was only one of those that had to be raised if the Church in Gaul were to develop a hierarchical system directly obedient to Rome in small as in large things. The methods of Martin, which brought monastic ideas and forms into the heart of the diocese and the parish, had to be ended. Generally, the line of the bishops had to triumph over the line of Martin.

The hostility of the Gaulish bishops towards the new ascetic and monastic movement was widely known in Italy and the East. In A.D. 392 St. Ambrose makes the episcopal quarrels his excuse for not going to Gaul. Again in 406, Jerome, in his treatise against Vigilantius, refers, with bitter abuse, to the opposition to asceticism in Gaul. . . . [Again there is] Sulpicius's undoubted unpopularity, which is clear throughout his own writings, and also from a letter of invitation from Paulinus, in which he urges Sulpicius that a visit to Nola would allow time for the hostility of the Gaulish bishops to abate. What the exact charge against Sulpicius was we do not know; but his own attitude was anything but conciliatory. Indeed, he never loses an opportunity of pressing home a thrust against the bishops and the clergy. (12)

The pope had summoned Victricius because he was now the leading exponent in Gaul of Martin's positions, with much influence also in Britain. The Letter of Counsels which he received had nothing particularly new in it. Its aim was simply to introduce into the Gallic Church an order acceptable to the papacy and the imperial State. (13) It thus stressed that no man might be granted ordination if his duties as a civil magistrate held him—that is, men must not be let run from the crushing burdens of the town council into the Church. No man who had served in the army after his baptism must be accepted, or any man whose wife had been previously married, or any twice-married man, and so on. (14)

Victricius had the task of circulating and propagating the contents of the Letter in Gaul; and he carried out his orders. In the Merovingian epoch at a Council of Tours the Letter's regulations were cited as binding. And the *Anglo-Saxon Chronicle*, under the year 403, has the entry: "Pope Innocent sent a decretal letter to Victricius, archbishop of Rouen." This unusual intrusion in the *Chronicle* shows that the tradition of the Letter's importance had been carried into Britain by the Roman missionaries.

We can now make a reasonably safe guess as to the nature of the debates in Britain which Victricius had been called in to settle. The British Church must have been reproducing the struggle between the monastically-minded and those who saw the bishop as an ecclesiastical official of the empire, concerned with organising a Church adapted to existing society, not with drawing people out of society in groups of *abstinentes*.

While at Rome, Victricius was in touch with his old friend Paulinus, who expected him to visit Nola (near Naples). But he rushed away to Gaul after receiving the decretal Letter. It looks as though he did not want to discuss his experiences at Rome with a fellow-disciple of Martin. (15) The impression one gains is that he lacked the rugged, uncouth simplicity of Martin. Though deeply devoted, he was of slighter stuff, more intellectual and exalted, not made to withstand the sort of pressures brought to bear on him at Rome.

There remains his composition on the *Praise of the Saints*. A highly skilful piece of writing, it reveals a man thoroughly trained in the schools; its diction is concise and carefully chosen, its rhythms elaborately cadenced. (16) In argument it shows a deep grasp of the neoplatonic way of thinking that was richly veined in Eastern theology, but not at all characteristic of the West. Once again one sees how Gaul's connections were with the East rather than with Italy; not only with the thought and practice of Egyptian monasticism, but also with the more abstruse and often deeply poetic tradition where Greek philosophy merged with Christian theology.

We find the commonplaces of monastic thought, the stress

on life as a ceaseless struggle; but Victricius works out the
transposition of military life into the spiritual sphere with his
own vigour and colour. "The quest for truth is a joy to the
seeker." (17)

Further, he is aware of the philosophical problems be-
queathed by Neoplatonists like Porphyry to Christian thought:
the relation of particular and universal, individual and species,
which provided the main basis for the debates of medieval
schoolmen. He firmly takes the position later to be called
Realist. Every individual existence, he says, holds in itself "the
force and the definition of its whole kind". On this basis he
develops his argument for the worship of relics.

If you ask to what species belong human beings, you will find that
from individual Adam is become species. For how can he not be
species, who has provided the substance from which has been produced and diffused among all men the principle (*foetura*) of the
human body? . . . For we must know that men do not differ one
from another by nature, but only by time, place, deeds, and thoughts.
The eyes of reason see clearly that all men are only a single body. (18)

From this passionately held belief—that all men are one body,
differentiated by the particular experience of each individual in
his time and place—he builds his case for the virtue of the saint
still vital in the mortal fragment. The unity of Adam in the
body reflects the unity of Christ in the spirit; the martyr's
blood still burns with the gift of the new life.

Though he tries to guard himself against the charge of a
pantheist glorification of all living, in his ardent vision of unity
he comes near to forgetting the Nicean Creed with its precise
Trinitarianism. (19) His words burn and pulse with his exalted
joy as he moves to the climax of his argument, turning to the
sun and seeing all things dissolved in the unity of light.

We say that the flesh is held in the essence of the blood, and we
declare that the spirit, dropping entire from the dew of blood, has
received from the Word its enflamed ardour. . . .
In saying that the whole is included in the part, we do not open
the gates of the bodily lights, we open the eyes of the heart. . . .
We speak of the brightness of fire; we speak of the colour of fire.
And yet in nature it is one and the same thing, there is no distinc-

tion except that of name. Light begets splendour, and yet there is no real distinction between light and splendour. Man himself, as man, holds a common origin with all beings. Brass, gold, all the kinds of metals, though variously torn from earth by the sharp talons of greed, have still the quality of identical substance. . . .

We see only little relics, only a drop of blood. But the truth beholds these trivial things more shattering than the sun. . . . (20)

Such passages suggest the sense of organic unity that bursts through works like *The Heavenly Hierarchies* of the pseudo-Dionysios, which seems to have been composed in the 5th century to combat the still-potent ideas of solar monotheism. But what Victricius most suggests are the alchemists with their insistence on a single substance differentiated by the circumstances of particular mixture and their hope of rediscovering the pure source of unity. "For it [the body] had put on the light of divinity and darkness had departed from it, and the body and the soul and the spirit were all united in love and had become one, in which unity the mystery had been concealed" (Archelaos). (21)

The links of Gaul with Eastern Christianity went far back. The confessors of the persecution at Lyon in 177 were mainly of Anatolian origin. In the old diocese of Paris the region of Deuil was evangelised by Syrians who were later confused with the bishop of Toledo, Eugenius (whose body was brought there in the 8th century from near an old Gallo-Roman pagan cult-place). (22) Athanasius had been exiled to Trèves in 336, where he introduced *The Life of St. Antony* and gave the first stimulus to Gallic monasticism, beginning the work that Martin carried on. Augustine describes how at a crucial moment in his own life a friend, Pontitianus, was discoursing:

He told us how one afternoon at Trèves, when the Emperor was taken up with the Circensian games, he and three others, his companions, went out to walk in gardens near the city walls, and there as they happened to walk in pairs, one went apart with him, and the other two wandered by themselves; and these in their wanderings lighted upon a certain cottage, inhabited by certain of thy servants, poor in spirit, of whom is the kingdom of heaven, and there they found a little book, containing the life of Antony. This one of them began to read, admire, and kindle at it; and as he read, to meditate. . . . (23)

Hilary of Poitiers, exiled to the East, brought back the lore he had there acquired. The intercourse of Gaul with the Egyptian monks never slackened; and Sulpicius, as compensation for his difficulties at home, had the news that his *Life of Martin* was a best-seller in the desert and that the monks were asking for a sequel. (24) Britain was certainly sharing in all this development.

In ports such as Narbonne sailors and travellers from Spain or Britain met others from Syria or Egypt. Ausonius writes in hyperbole, but his point holds:

> What of your folk so varied in clothes and speech? . . .
> Enriched from the Eastern Sea, the Spanish Main;
> Sicilian deeps and Libyan send you fleets,
> all freights by varying routes of river and sea,
> all argosies of the world come steering hither.

Throughout the 5th and 6th centuries the Eastern element remained strong in Gaul. St. Caesar, bishop of Arles (who died in 542), wrote hymns in Latin and Greek for his flock; and Gregory of Tours tells of the Greek merchants of Orléans advancing with song to meet the Frankish king. There was a stylite (a saint living on top of a pillar) at Yvoy; and the Gaulish churches enjoyed as extensive a right of asylum as the Eastern churches. We hear in Gregory of a Syrian *negotiator* who bought a bishop's see for himself, and constituted a *scola* of his own, made up solely of Syrians. Thus, the elements flowing in from the East did not lessen in the 6th century, though the control by Rome had then tightened. (25)

The arrival of the cat in Gaul shows direct relations with Egypt. Four funerary monuments depict a child with a cat; and there are two statuettes, one of a collared cat, another of a young man (perhaps Priapus) holding a cat with a belled collar. The locations are Lyon, Montceau, Dijon, and Bordeaux; Auxerre and Alise. The concentration in the east of Gaul, in Burgundy and the Lyonnais, suggests that the domestic cat was introduced by the valley of the Rhône and the Saône. Monuments, texts, and excavated bones alike reveal the cat only very rarely in Italy. Latin, indeed, had only the name *feles*, wild-cat; *cattus* appears at the end of the 4th century and seems to be Celtic.

The cult of Isis, organised in several towns, from Marseilles to Lyon, and the Egyptian or Egyptianising figurines found notably in the Bouches-des-Rhône, the Gard, the Vaucluse, the Drome, and, more north, at Lyon, Trévoux, Anse, Belleville, La Chapelle-de-Guinchay, La Truchère, Ouroux, Saint-Germain-du-Plain, Chalon-sur-Saône, Autun, Bourg, Vésines, and Conliège, provide evidence that can scarcely be contested, at least during the Roman period, of connections between the banks of the Nile and Rhône basin.

Come from Asia Minor. Christianity will take the same route, the sea and the navigable rivers being then the great ways of communication, those followed by trade and ideas.

It is sufficiently striking also to note that, towards the mouth of the Garonne, we find together, although to a lesser extent, at Royan and at Bazas, Egyptian or Egyptianising objects—with the cat on the funerary slab at Bordeaux. (26)

The domestic cat has been supposed to have entered France towards the 9th century. Clearly, however, many cats had come to south Gaul from the 2nd to 4th century, together with papyrus, ushabtis, and Isiac figures, not to mention Christian ideas. They must have been smuggled or come as stowaways, for the Egyptians held their cats in such high regard that they prohibited their export.

The advent of the new creature met a new need. Half-wild weasels had been used to keep down vermin—mice, field-mice, and the like. The black Asiatic rat seems to have come swarming with the barbarian invaders of the 3rd and 4th centuries; and cats were needed to deal with it.

THE END OF ROMAN RULE

WE now reach the point where we can discuss the breakdown of the imperial system in Britain. The deepening crisis is uttered in the verse of Claudian, the poet from Egypt, in whom the panegyric stirred with something like epical verve and sweep. He has more references to Britain than any other Roman poet. (1) He looks back to the days of 367–8 when Count Theodosius "pitched camp in Caledonian snows", "Terror of Moors and Conqueror of British coasts, Devastator of south and north alike".

> What barrier stands in eternal snows, skies frozen,
> uncharted seas? The Orkneys with stricken Saxons
> reddened, Thule with Pictish blood was warmed,
> ice-clamped Hibernia wept for her heaped-up Scots. (398)

And he depicts the Emperor Theodosius in similar terms:

> The nimble Moor and the pictured Picts he beat,
> he chased the fugitive Scot with his wandering sword,
> clove the Hyperborean sea with adventurous oars,
> and gleaming with spoils of northern skies and southern,
> he trod the flowing sands of either Ocean. (396)

And again the general Stilicho:

> Next Britain, clad in Caledonian beastskins
> with tattoed cheeks and azure cloak billowing
> down to her feet with the swell of ocean, cried:
> "When I lay helpless to the neighbouring tribes,
> Stilicho saved me too. When Scots had roused
> Ireland, and Tethys foamed with enemy oars.
> Now, through his care, I dread no Scottic weapon,
> I tremble at no Picts, nor watch along
> my shores for Saxons careless of the winds." (399)

Despite the conventional terms, we get some feeling of what the British frontier meant to the beleaguered empire; and it is

fitting to watch the last days of Roman rule in Britain through
the eyes of the last vigorous poet of imperial Rome. In a poem
written about 393 for his colleague Palladius who was marrying
Celerina, he says of the bride's father that as *primicerius
notariorum* he dealt with the location of garrisons:

> He ordered the defences of Sarmatia:
> which legions face wild Getae or hold the Scots
> and Saxons in check, how many cohorts border
> the Ocean, how large a force keeps Rhineland peace.

And in a panegyric on the consulship of Fl. Manlius Theodorus,
who held office in Africa and Macedonia, rose high in the
treasury, and then became praetorian prefect, he writes:

> . . . set you to rule the rulers of the earth.
> The Seas of Spain and Germany now obeyed you
> and Britain cut so deeply from our world.
> Rivers of all lands duly kept your statutes,
> slow Saône, headlong Rhône, and golden Ebro.
> How often did Rhine, where the barbarian went,
> moan that that one bank yet lacked your fostering rule.
> One man controls the reddening Sunset-lands,
> all that is snared in the last lengthening rays.

In *The Gothic War*, as well as the passage cited in the Introduction, there is a significant passage which tells of the barbarians watching the inner strife of the empire and biding their
time.

> Reflect that all of Britain's ferocious tribes,
> the tribes that Rhine and Danube rear, lean watching,
> prepared. A victory now wins many wars.
> Restore Rome's glory, on your shoulders upheave
> the toppling empire. All goes well if this
> goes well. One triumph earns a world of peace. (c. 402)

And rumours indeed of the fall go west and north:

> Did not rumour with her darkening wings of panic
> sweep all before her from Cadiz to Britain,
> scaring the Ocean, and beyond our world
> shake distant Thule with strange battle-echoes?

While in *Stilicho's Consulship* he has one of his fine passages
which seize on the positive side of the Roman achievement:

No halt at Ocean. Passing the deep with oars
she sought in another world for Britons to master.
She alone welcomed the conquered to her bosom,
fostered mankind with a common name, a Mother,
no Empress, calling the tamed to citizenship
and uniting sundered folk in a loving faith.
We all of us owe to her rule of peace that still
the world, wherever we roam, our home we meet;
where we desire, we settle; we find it sport
to visit Thule and dare her lairs once dreadful.

The year 407 was a crucial year. The attack of Irish freebooters
was nearing its climax. The raid in which the high-king Niall of
the Nine Hostages met his death has been dated 405, though it
probably occurred in 427; but in any event Niall did much
raiding before his death. His mother Cairenn seems to have been
a British captive, so that he was in fact half a Briton; and it was
perhaps on one of his raids that the boy Patrick was carried
off to Ireland. (2)

In 406–7 barbarians poured over the Rhine—Vandals,
Suevians, Alans. The date is controversial: the moment of
break-through was the last day of either 405 or 406. In any
event there were sharp reactions in Britain to the increasingly
dangerous situation. Sometime in 406 a usurper Marcus appeared; he fell and a civilian (*municeps*), Gratian, was elevated,
apparently early in 407; then he was brought down and a
soldier, Constantine (III), was chosen. (3) However we analyse
the dates, it is clear that this rapid succession of claimants to
the purple was brought about by the situation in Gaul and the
need of Britain to look to herself. We know that the raiders
over the middle Rhine turned north-west and that bands reached
Amiens, Arras, Therouanne, Tournai. It must have seemed that
they were swerving up towards the ports that faced to Britain. (4)

Constantine crossed to Gaul with most of the troops left in
Britain. But we get no hint of trouble on the borderlands. For
a while Constantine did well. He defeated the invaders and
guarded the Rhine more securely, says Zosimus, than anyone
had done since Julian. In central and west Gaul, however,
Vandals, Suevians, and Alans were unchecked. When Constantine took Arles, the imperial government sent a Goth,

Sarus, against him; but though Sarus won a battle, he failed to take Valentia and returned to Italy. Constantine went on to occupy Spain through his son Constans and his lieutenant Gerontius.

Honorius, the emperor at Ravenna, harassed by Alaric, agreed to recognise Constantine in return for aid in defence of Rome. But after the latter had crossed the Alps, Honorius put to death the Master of his Horse, Allobich, on a charge of conspiring with him. Constantine withdrew into Gaul. In Spain trouble had been caused by allotting barbarian mercenaries to guard the Pyrenees instead of the Spanish legions, who revolted. Gerontius, left in command, was superseded in favour of one Justus; he retorted by setting up his own emperor, Maximus (perhaps his son).

For a while there were six emperors ruling some section of the empire: Theodosius in the East, Honorius at Ravenna, Maximus at Tarragona, Constantine and Constans at Arles, and Attalus (set up by Alaric) at Rome.

Gerontius tried to out-manœuvre Constantine by drawing into Spain the Vandals, Suevians, and Alans who had been ravaging Gaul—an act that led to the loss of Spain and of Africa. Constans retreated before such a force, was captured at Vienne and put to death; Gerontius then besieged Arles. Meanwhile Honorius had sent an army under Flavius Constantius and Upfilas. At its approach Gerontius hastened back to Spain. There his own troops attacked him in a house which was set on fire. With his Alan squire he fought long and hard, then he stabbed his squire and his wife Nunechia at their own request, and killed himself.

Constantine held out more than three months in Arles, with his second son Julian. Then his Frankish general, Edobich, who came up with barbarian reinforcements enlisted beyond the Rhine, was defeated. Constantine fled to a sanctuary and was ordained priest. Under promise of safe conduct he was sent on to Honorius, who, recalling his cousins whom Constantine had slain, had him and his son killed in September 411. (5)

Meanwhile in 408 the Saxons had raided Britain in its weakened state and must have reduced the garrisons yet further. And now the disaster of 409 meant that there was no strong force on the Continent as a bulwark. The result was that the people broke out in rebellion, not this time setting up yet another usurper, but rejecting the Roman system altogether.

Our source for this event is Zosimus. He is an unreliable historian; but for his western events he largely follows Olympiodorus, an Egyptian Greek, who, born about 365, dealt in his history of twenty-two books with the years 407–25. And Olympiodorus seems a particularly valuable and trustworthy writer. We may assume that Zosimus, in his clear statement of what happened in Britain in 409, is transcribing him:

The barbarians from beyond the Rhine (? Saxons), ravaging everything at will, drove both the inhabitants of the British Isle and some of the peoples of Gaul to secede from the Empire of the Romans and to live in independence, no longer obeying the Roman Laws.

The people of Britain, therefore, took up arms and braved every peril, freeing their cities from the attacking barbarians. And the whole of Armorica, and other provinces of Gaul, imitating the Britons, liberated themselves in like manner, expelling the Roman officials and setting up a civil policy according to their own inclination.

This secession of Britain and of Gallic peoples took place during the time of Constantine's usurpation, the barbarians rising up in consequence of his neglect of the government. (6)

We can verify this statement as far as Gaul is concerned, which increases the trust that we may put in the part dealing with Britain. The peasants of Gaul, and above all of Armorica, broke out this year into a furious revolt, which continued till 417. The poorer classes rose against the officials and the landed gentry, drove out the first and enslaved the second. (7)

The precision of the terms used by Zosimus are remarkable. He speaks of many other revolts and usurpations, but never in such words. Further, the Gallic *Chronicles* define the aims of the peasants in the same definite way. We are told that during the Bacaudan movement in 435 Armorica "seceded from Roman society". And the poets Rutilius and Merobaudes speak of the suppression of the revolt as the Restoration of Roman Rule. (8)

Zosimus sees the revolt as arising from the failure of the imperial government to protect the people, who decided to take their destiny in their own hands. It might be argued that he is here merging the events of 407-8 and those of 409 together. But we can surely conceive that the fears of attack in 407, followed by the collapse of Constantine after harrying attacks by Saxon raiders, brought about the frame of mind that hardened into a resolution to achieve complete independence. It is unlikely that the raids of 408 took place in a neat co-ordinated campaign; they may well have straggled on into 409, at least in some regions. We get rather this impression from a chronicle entry in Gaul:

The multitude of the enemy so prevailed that the strength of the Romans was enormously diminished. The provinces of Britain were laid waste by an incursion of the Saxons. (9)

The picture that emerges, then, is of a disorganised province without effective means of defence, recently harassed and still fighting or expecting to fight in various quarters; of converging angers and determinations; of intense conflict between the conservatively-minded who wanted to cling to the name of Rome and the rebellious who wanted to throw off the Roman tax-collectors and take their own measures of self-protection. In such a situation we can imagine the landlords fleeing to their cities with their retainers, the peasants fiercely up in arms, the townsfolk divided in their counsels.

It is against this background that we must consider the statement which Zosimus goes on to make: that the emperor Honorius wrote to the cities (*civitates*)—that is, to Canterbury, Silchester, Caister-by-Norwich, Leicester, and so on—to look to their own safety. The imperial message has been taken to mean only that the emperor wanted the *civitates* to organise their own militia against raiders until such time as the central government had restored order in Gaul and could send forces over the Channel. No doubt Honorius was saying all that, but in view of the peasant revolts there can be little doubt that he was also bidding the cities to put the peasants down as best they might. When we realise that his government was puzzling out how to deal with a Gaul in which barbarian tribes and insurgent peasants were alike seething, we can put no other interpretation on his words. (10)

The Britons seem to have clung to the tradition that they had thrown out the Romans. In the 8th century Nennius declared:

The Britons overthrew the dominion of the Romans, neither did they render tribute to them, nor receive their kings to rule over them, nor did the Romans dare to come to Britain to rule any longer because the Britons had slain their leaders. (xxviii)

The central government could not hope to get a footing again in Britain with the peasant revolt unbeaten in Gaul. There the fight went on till 417. The Tractus Armoricanus, the core of the rebellion, had a large extent. Much wider than Brittany, it took in Tours, Orléans, and even Auxerre.

In 411 Fl. Constantius was fighting in Gaul, invested with the functions of Count and Magister Utriusque Militiae, a generalissimo. In 415 he fixed his headquarters at Arles, but had to move about fighting in Africa and Spain as well as Gaul. By the end of 415 he rose to the patriciate and on the first day of 417 he married the emperor's sister, Gallia Placidia. This year order was finally restored in Gaul and a reorganisation carried on. From 13 August to 13 September, 418, the Council of the Provinces sat. (11)

In 417 a rich landlord, who was a poet, Rutilius Namatianus, left Rome to return home to the Toulouse region. All was now safe there and he wanted to play his part in the reconstruction. He wrote a travel poem recording the day-by-day events and unpacked something of his hatred he felt for the insurgent peasants. It is perhaps significant that the only body of men he hates as much as the peasants are the monks. (12)

About 417–18, then, we would expect the central government to begin thinking seriously about Britain again. What had happened there? We are without any decisive literary or archaeological clues; but we may surmise that a complicated situation of struggle had continued—the peasants asserting themselves, and the big landlords or leading citizens of the *civitates* taking what steps they could to put the peasants down and revive their rent claims. But we can leave further surmise along those lines for the moment, and consider only how far the central government was able to re-enter Britain and re-impose its system.

We know that the signal stations in Yorkshire were held till 395 or later—probably several years later. And tiles stamped with the name of Honorius have come from the Saxon Shore fort at Pevensey.

The *Notitia Dignitatum*, a register of imperial officers, throws some light on the situation, though not much. The work has been thought to be a revision of 428 on the basis of earlier documents, with additions made even after 430. (13) It gives a survey of the forces under the Duke of the Britains: fourteen units stationed in what seems Yorkshire, County Durham, and Westmorland, then forts on Hadrian's wall with some others. Certainly this section is out of date, but we can only guess how much. However, if we ignore the forts, we get a disposition of troops that is not unlikely for the end of the 4th century, based on the defence of the Vale of York—with the north-western coast left out of the picture. The west in general, indeed, is omitted; but we might interpret this state of things as meaning that both west and north the system of Federates was in operation. (14)

But there is a reference to a Count of the Britains, *vir spectabilis*, who seems to belong to a small group of officers created 410–20; and this Count may have been the commander of a field force sent into Britain some time after 410—perhaps in 417–18. (15) That some sort of action was taken about this time is suggested by an entry in the *Anglo-Saxon Chronicle* under 418:

In this year the Romans collected all the treasures which were in Britain and hid some in the earth so that no one afterwards could find them and some they took with them into Gaul.

There is a mournful note about this entry, which suggests that it does record some sort of evacuation. (16) No doubt an effort was made to remove bullion or objects of precious metal—we saw earlier how such an action would accord with the imperial policy of building up gold supplies for coinage. Further, there is some suggestive evidence from coin-finds for a partial re-occupation. Richborough shows signs of a revival of Roman trade; and we have a glimpse of renewed commercial life within an area enclosed by a line drawn roughly from Weymouth to the Wash. The coin-series are composed of Roman money in use during the period 417–25. The boundary of the area where

Roman coins are once more active runs south-west along the Icknield Way and the Berkshire Ridgeway, then goes on via Warminster to the mid-Dorset coast. (17)

Perhaps something like this area in the south-east was for a while governed by a vicar with his seat in London. The Saxon Shore forts do not produce the same run of coins as Richborough; but then we should not expect them to leave the same sort of remains as a busy trade-port of entry.

The coin evidence, however, is purely economic in its bearing; the political additions are mere guesswork. There could have been a renewed commercial connection with Gaul after 417 without any reoccupation. On the other hand, the existence of the Count and the passage in the *Anglo-Saxon Chronicle* do suggest that the central government restored some sort of limited control in Britain.

For the economic activity we have the further evidence of the silver hoards of worn and clipped *siliquae* which served as money in the absence of new supplies. These fan out from the Home Counties to Somerset, Lancashire, and north Yorkshire, and indicate provincial communities still active till round 420–30—whatever their political organisation may have been. (18)

Before we leave the coins we must, however, stress that there is little weight in the negative conclusions which have been drawn from the omissions. In 395 the western mints ceased producing copper coins, and issues of all sorts grew much rarer. Thus in Noricum Ripense the coin-series comes to an end about 400, yet the literary evidence shows that till about 480 the area was occupied by regular Roman troops and must have been administered under the central government. As late as 460 the towns of the area were provisioned in a famine by cornships coming from Rhaetia by way of Inn and Danube. (19)

We may, then, on the balance of probabilities hold that Britain was partially and loosely reoccupied by the central government for a period that perhaps ran from 417 to 427. This period could not, however, have seen anything like a firm reorganisation on imperial lines. The movement to independence and all it implied could not be checked; in the wilder parts the struggle of peasants and landlords must have been going on;

raids by the Irish and probably by others continued. But for the moment we had better leave the developments of the 420s till we have, first, considered further the ideas and methods of the peasant rebels as we know them from Gaul, and, secondly, glanced at the remarkable figure, Pelagius, who emerged from the intellectual and religious life of Britain to shake the Roman world in the second decade of the century.

THE BACAUDAE

FIRST, then, the Bacaudae. What the name means is not clear. Constantius, about 480, calls them "an unstable and undisciplined throng (*populus*)"; and the writers in general who are brought to mention them define them as brigands. But a different picture is drawn by their actions and by the one writer, Salvian, who belongs to the monastic dissident tradition and who has much sympathy for them. He and others speak of men escaping to freedom among the Barbarians or the Bacaudae. (1)

Salvian was perhaps born at Cologne. Educated at Trèves, he saw in his youth the great invasions that devastated the Rhineland cities. He sought refuge in the south, where he found men to his heart in the scholarly monastic society of the Isle of Lérins. (2) He composed in the 440s the treatise going under the name of *God's Government* (rather, *God's Pilotage*). Augustine and Orosius had tried earlier to answer the jeers of the pagans that the adoption of Christianity had brought the State to disaster; Salvian wanted to help the Christians who felt crushed under accumulating troubles. But, more deeply, he was moved by the great historical changes of his age and felt the need to grasp and understand them, to denounce the social sins that he considered responsible for the breakdown. So far from minimising the dark situation by pointing to past miseries, as Augustine did, he was keen to stress the pangs in order to make men face themselves and the nature of the society they had built up. (3)

He was revolted by the ruling class's cruelty and indifference: prefects and governors venal and ruthless, lesser officials parodying their example, the town decurions so many tyrants, pressing the taxes on the back of those least able to bear them. Any state relief went to the richest landlords. (4) Even men who had turned to a strict religious life carried out the grossest oppressions when they had the chance. "They refrain from lying

with women, but not from property-lust" (*rapina*). (5) Dressed
in ostentatious asceticism they argued that Christ needed no
gifts; but Christ was the neediest person in the universe since he
felt the needs of all who suffered privations.

He could never forget how in his youth he had seen the main
citizens of Trèves sunk in drunken debauchery with the barbarians at their gates. (6) With an unslackening indignation he
felt the miseries of the poor. The landlords, pampered by the
law, passed all their burdens on to the labouring farmers;
they took everything from the poor man; and so the farmers
turned to the barbarians. "The enemy is kinder than the tax-
collector." (7)

The fear and hate of the tax-collector had much to do with
causing the peasant revolts. In the later 3rd century Lactantius
was writing:

The tax-registration, carried out simultaneously in the provinces and
the *civitates*, was a thing of public calamity and the common misery
of all. The officials spread out on all sides and disturbed everything.
What happened was a hostile tumult, a sort of horrible captivity. . . .
No excuse of age or health was accepted. The sick and the weak
were not spared, the age of each person was calculated, years were
piled on the young and old men were entered as much younger. The
world was full of moaning and misery. (8)

Then more officials were sent out in the tracks of the others,
who, to prove that they had been needed, added many more
extortions.

Salvian drives the moral home. "Are you surprised at not being able to defeat the Goths when the Roman people of Gaul
prefer to live with them than with you, Romans? . . . Are you
surprised at seeing our towns taken and destroyed when for a
long time we have prepared this disaster by the oppression of
the masses of the people? In reducing our fellow-citizens to
captivity, we have prepared our own loss of liberty." (9)

These comments go to the heart of the matter and touch on
the main reason why the empire had lost its powers of resistance.
And they are important further for us, since we have in this book
to answer the question: Why, when Gaul and other provinces
of the West put up no lasting fight against the barbarians,
did Britain alone wage an unrelenting war against the invaders?

Salvian insists that the Goths were far superior in humanity and justice to the Romans, and that many of the poorer classes were glad to turn to them. An interesting sidelight on this insistence of his is given by Paulinus of Pella, which shows that even members of the upper class, caught in the general tumult of misery, might feel as did the embittered monk. Paulinus speaks of his ancestral estate "lost through barbarians, who by laws of war pillaged, or Romans who with wanton greed robbed me at different times against all rights. This guilt clings even to my near relations." He feels much more angered against his fellow-Romans than against the barbarians. Later, when he had given up hope of getting anything from the wreck of his grandfather Ausonius' estate,

> and all the land I, poverty-stricken now,
> held at Marseilles was under written contract,
> the freehold being lost, you raised me up
> a buyer from the Gothic folk who wished
> to purchase the small farm now wholly mine
> and of his own free will sent me a sum
> not indeed all its worth and yet to me
> a godsend, I admit, which gave me means
> to prop the ruin of my tottered fortunes.

And here are some more passages from Salvian which will serve to show how strongly he feels the plight of the peasants:

What else can the wretched people do, driven to periodic or rather unceasing ruin by the exactions of the public taxes, perpetually menaced by a heavy and unslackening proscription? They desert their homes so as not to undergo tortures in those very homes; they choose exile to escape cruel treatment. The enemy are kinder than the collectors. The facts prove it. They take refuge with the enemy to evade the violence of the taxes.

Most of them abandon their plots of ground and huts to avoid the law's violence. Would they not prefer to take with them, if it were possible, that which they are forced to abandon? But, unable to do what they would, they do the one thing they can. They deliver themselves up to someone stronger in return for being warded and protected. They become the subjects of rich men and pass as it were under their power and authority.

They submit to a humiliating yoke, they are reduced to the extremity of seeing themselves not only deprived of their goods but of their very condition in life, they lose not only their land but themselves. And losing themselves, they lose all that was theirs: the ownership of their property and their right of freedom.

They are received as strangers, they become natives by reason of their establishment: as once the powers of that Witch, it is said, transformed men into beasts, so all the poor folk taken into the estates of the rich are changed as if they had drunk Circe's cup. . . . They were free men, they turn into slaves. . . .

Now let us speak of the Bacaudae. Despoiled, beaten, slaughtered by wicked judges, by bloody judges, they lose first the right of Roman liberty, then even the honour of the Roman name. . . .

What, in fact, has created the Bacaudae? Is it not our iniquities, the criminality of our judges, their proscriptions, their rapines? Is it not the work of our judges who use the tax-system for their own enrichment and the tax-lists for their own exacted booty? Like wild beasts they have devoured the men whom they should have governed. Not even satisfied with plundering men, as robbers generally are, they tear their victims to pieces and, so to speak, feed upon their blood. Thus it is that men, strangled and crushed by judicial brigandage, begin to be barbarians since they are not permitted to be Romans. . . . They are compelled at least to preserve their life since they see that they have wholly lost liberty.

The poor people are broken down, the widows weep, the orphans are trampled underfoot; and so a large number of these victims, and of persons not at all of obscure birth, persons who have received a liberal education, flee to the enemy to escape dying from the blows of the state's persecution. Yes, they seek among the barbarians a Roman humanity since among the Romans they have found barbarous inhumanity intolerable.

Though they differ from those with whom they take refuge, in religious rite, though they differ in language, though, as I may assert, they are unlike bodily and suffer from the smell given out by the barbarians, yet they prefer among the barbarians to endure a strange way of life rather than among the Romans to submit to a ravening injustice.

That is why, all round us, they go over to the Goths, to the Bacaudae, to the bands of barbarians who control various regions; and are glad that they have gone. They think it better to live free under an appearance of captivity than to live prisoners under an appearance of freedom. So we behold this name of the Roman Citizen, once so esteemed and even so dearly bought, repudiated and evaded like a thing not only valueless but almost abominable. (10)

Paulinus of Pella gives us an example of the sort of broils that
kept breaking out. The Visigoths had sacked Bordeaux in 414;
his house was burned down, and he fled to Bazas, only to find
himself besieged there:

> For when we were driven
> from our ancestral home and our rooftops burned,
> Siege by the enemy caught us in the town,
> Bazas, close by (our family's original home),
> and, far more dangerous than the encircling foe,
> a slave-conspiracy aided by senseless fury
> of youths who, freely born, had sunk to crime,
> armed specially to slaughter the nobility.
> You, righteous God, shielded the innocent blood
> and quelled the peril with deaths of a guilty few,
> ordaining the murderer aimed at my heart should die
> by another's avenging hand, unknown to me. (11)

St. Orientius in his poem, *Commonitorum*, writes also: "to
many persons Civic Treachery was the cause of death." And
Sidonius in 474 describes Clermont after the Visigothic siege
when Constantius, biographer of Germanus, visited the city.
"You found it no less desolated by inner dissension than by
barbarian assault; but you conciliated all, renewed their
harmony, restored to the country her sons. The walls are re-
manned, the people returned to unity, all thanks to you." Here
Constantius acts a part in the key of his hero Germanus.

Sidonius, too, illustrates Salvian's generalities with the por-
trait of a magnate in high office driving men to the woods.
Seronatus, it seems, was governor of Aquitanica Prima:

Openly malign, he basely deceives; swaggers like a slave, indicts like
a judge, orders like a despot, lies like a barbarian; goes armed all
day in fear, starves from miserliness, glowers terrible in greed, is
ruthless from vanity, and keeps committing or punishing thefts. In
public, amid grins of listeners, he belches of battles to civilians, of
belles-lettres to barbarians. Not even properly schooled in the
alphabet, he dictates instructions before all out of brag, corrects
them out of effrontery. When he covets a thing, he makes pretence of
buying, too stuck-up to pay, too cautious to make a contract. In the
council-room he shouts orders but has no counsel to urge; in church
he jests, in the dining-room sermonises; snores in court and in
bedroom condemns.

Daily he fills the woods with fugitives, the farms with barbarians, the altars with criminals, the prisons with priests. Exulting to the Goths, insulting to the Romans, he makes fools of prefects, tools of public accountants. He tramples the Theodosian Code and substitutes the Theodoric; he noses out old offences and thinks up new taxes. (12)

Salvian in four books, *Ad Ecclesiam*, denounced greed and declared, "The poor man buys blessedness by beggary; the rich, torment by property." (13) He cried: "You see Christ in need and leave your wealth to people who are not poor." Again, "Christ is hungry and you prepare delicacies for those already well supplied. Christ complains that he lacks even water and you heap with wine the cellar of those drunken." St. Valerian of Céméle, also probably trained at Lérins, in his sermons reiterates less furiously the same message. He bids his congregation that to give to Christ is to give to the poor, and appeals to them not to delay in the good work. He calls on his beloved ones to keep practising the Christian life as a raw recruit before going into battle "practises his strength against the stump of a tree". (14)

Salvian shows us how the farmer and craftsman felt; Rutilius, how the landlord. His nicely-detailed *Itinerary* has several illuminating items. In Tuscany he met a Victorinus who (before 407) had held a high office, presumably the vicariate, in Britain, then retiring as a Count of the Third Class to Toulouse. When Ataulf in 413 took that city, Victorinus fled with his household to Tuscany:

> His wisdom was bright when life was prospering duly
> and still it shone unquencht in hardships now.
> His virtue's known to Ocean and to Thule,
> and all the fields ferocious Britons plough.
> He earned the esteem that grows each steady hour:
> the Prefect's deputy, with self-checked power.
> On the far edge of habitable parts
> he ruled as if at the active centre of things.
> The more the merit to have wooed the hearts
> of men whose hatred would incur no shame.
> Now Count of the Sacred Palace he's become
> but mocks in his dear country-lair at fame.

The bitter tone and the adjective *ferox* must reflect the narrative of Victorinus; Rutilius seems to keep a verse diary, jotting down couplets fresh from each recounted episode.

Rutilius also tells how, waiting a fortnight at Tiber's mouth for his ship to sail, he had with him young Palladius, "the hope and glory of my house", who returned to Rome for his studies:

> This gifted lad was sent from Gallic fields
> to study law at its true source of late.
> Deep love to him my heart in gladness yields,
> such a close relative as my son I rate.
> Exuperantius his father gave
> the charms of peace back to Armoric folk.
> Law he restored and Liberty he saved;
> and slaves who had made the free men slaves, he broke.

Exuperantius, Duke of the Armoric Tract, had been prominent in quenching the Bacaudan revolt in blood; he was to be murdered in 424 in Arles while Prefect of the Gauls.

Rutilius went by sea. The land route was deep in floods and Goths had overrun the Aurelian Way with "fire and sword". But his home area, though ravaged, was pacified:

> It's time to tend the burnt-out farms again,
> at least to raise the shattered shepherd's shack.
> The springs, if they had voices, would complain;
> the trees, if they could speak, would call me back.

Besides his hatred of monks and hermits, this poet with his fervour for the Rome of Law seems to have been an obdurate pagan. (15)

We gain some idea of the aims of the Bacaudae from his comments. They "enslaved" the free men (the landlords) and made an end of all he considered law and liberty. They abolished Roman Law and put in its place a law of their own. Some slight idea of what that meant is given in the comedy, *Querolus*. The critics are divided on the question as to whether this work was written in trochaic verse or rhythmical prose; it seems best to take it as verse, based on the Plautian system, with deliberate irregularities. The style is clear, concentrated, witty; and though the theme no doubt derives from a lost Greek original, the author has thoroughly adapted it to his own place and time.

Querolus is discontented with his lot, which seems that of a minor landowner. His domestic Lar, acting as a sort of guardian angel, decides to take a hand and help him to what he wants out of life. Querolus' father, an old miser, has died on a journey, after confiding to a parasite that there is a treasure at home, buried before the Lar's altar; he gives a sort of contract or will to the fellow, stating that he is to have half if he gives up the rest to Querolus. The parasite, disguised as a magician, enters the house, and with the aid of two accomplices obtains the chest under the altar. Opening it, he finds a funerary urn, which he flings back into the house. The urn breaks and scatters gold at the feet of Querolus.

The characters are well worked out and maintained, and the fun is kept going. Pantomalus, the impudent slave, puts the slave point-of-view vigorously and yet amusingly. Altogether, the comedy is an impressive work of its kind, and shows the liveliness to which Gallic culture of the late 4th and early 5th century could rise.

It opens with a long discussion between the Lar and Querolus, in which the Lar tries to probe the reason for the man's discontent. Querolus admits that he is envious; he is worse off than worse people. Pressed to say what he would like, he replies that he could do with the wealth and esteem of an army officer. But he admits that he doesn't want to do any fighting, so asks for an advantageous civilian place. Then he admits that he can't see himself a tax-collector, and suggests that he be made a simple citizen, but one with power (*potens*): "throw down those not my own, despoil and knock over the neighbours." The Lar says that that is brigandage (*latrocinium*), and then has a proposal:

> *Lar.:* I've got it, just your thing. To the banks of the Loire.
> *Quer.:* And then?
> *Lar.:* Folk live there by the Law of Nature.
> No guile. Capital sentences are pronounced
> under the Oak and written down on bones.
> Peasants are lawyers, ordinary citizens judge.
> All as you wish. If you were rich, you'll there
> be called *patus*. That's how our Greece talks.
> Woods, Solitudes, who said that you weren't free?
> Larger matters I've omitted. That will do.
> *Quer.:* But I'm not rich. I want no Woodland Laws. (16)

The Bacaudae are thus represented as having their own system of laws, by which they try the landlords. There is a remarkable suggestion of what happened in East Anglia when the uprooted peasants and craftsmen rose under Ket in 1549, broke down the fences and hedges, and tried the landlords under the Great Oak. *Patus* is presumably some Gaulish word to which we have no clue; "our Greek" simply means Celtic—the Greek of the original play transposed into the local dialect. (17)

Querolus goes on to ask for a good court job and is told of the troubles he'll meet: short tunics in winter and double clothes in summer, wool highboots and stick-in-the-mud shoes. He'll go bare-legged in cold and cover his knees in heat; his time, his soul won't be his own. "Aye, sell your voice and sell your mouth, your anger lease out, even your hatred!" Then retire with "a little cash and much malevolence". No, "better bury than harry" the persons he'd meet in such a job. So he asks for a place with the red-tape men of the treasury, and is again warned of the results. "Skilful calculator, raw farmer, a stranger to your neighbours, hated through life to find a costly funeral." He counters by asking for the fat purse of the trader from over-seas; but admits a dislike of wave and wind. "Then give me Titus' cash-box." "And his gout?" He asks for the girls kept by the foreign usurer, and the Lar bids him take them if he owns "Nestor's sinewy length". Besides, "With cash you have charm; your charm goes with your cash." The discussion ends fruitlessly and the Lar moralises, telling Querolus that he can recognise wealth but not health. "How weaker yet is the mind. Hope, fear, desire, greed and despair, leave no man happiness."

The comedy is dedicated to a Rutilius, probably the poet of the *Itinerary*, who had been prefect of Rome in 416, controlling the shows and theatres. The Rutilius of *Querolus* is an impor-tant man with pretensions to literature and philosophy, in re-turn for whose generosity the play had been composed; it seems produced to amuse the guests after dinner. (18)

The playwright's urbane satire accords, we may note, with what Salvian bitterly says of the careers open in his world: "The traders' life was nothing but a tissue of fraud and lies; that of the curials nothing but injustice, that of the officials devoted to collusion, the career of soldiers is one of rapine."

Now to return to the Bacaudae. Their plebeian democracy is suggested by their refusal to set up usurpers in the normal way of rebels. We hear later of a leader Tibatto, but no title is suggested as claimed by him; his commanders are merely called *principes*. (19)

One of the acts of the central government after regaining control of Gaul in 417–18 is important to us. The Visigoths were recalled from Spain and the Patrician Constantius settled them in the rich province of Aquitanica Secunda, on the western seaboard between the mouths of the Garonne and the Loire, and in some near *civitates*. One of these latter was Toulouse, in Narbonensis Prima, which became the capital of the Visigothic kings. The Visigoths seem to have held no land north of the Loire. (20)

The Visigoths had been moving about for some forty years. In 365–7 they were in Wallachia and Transylvania, fighting the Romans; beaten because the Romans broke off all trade-relations. They found themselves in an "utter lack of the necessities of life". By 376 they were on the move around the empire, still much dependent on trade: e.g. in 414 the Romans blockaded the coast of Gallia Narbonensis where the Visigoths then were; the latter's settlement collapsed and the men rushed off to Barcelona. Once more blockaded in Spain, they tried to get away into Africa, and in 416 capitulated. Thus rendered amenable, they were brought back to south-west Gaul and settled down. (21)

The act of putting the Visigoths into Aquitaine was, then, official and Roman. The government wanted the tribesmen in the area. But why? There was no obvious frontier relation, nobody whom the settlers were to block—except the Bacaudae across the Loire. If the new farmers defended the rights given under the rule of *hospitalitas*, they would in effect be defending the Roman landlords too.

The same situation, we shall find, recurs in 443 elsewhere in Gaul, with the settling of Burgundians and Alans.

If this explanation is correct, we may well admire the brilliance of the diplomacy of Constantius [in 417] and Aetius [in 443]. At one stroke they converted wandering and hostile masses of barbarians into settled and on the whole contented communities of agriculturalists; they broke the alliance of the invading barbarians with the restless elements of the Roman countryside; and they provided themselves with an effective military force which would defend southern Gaul from the uprisings of the indomitable slaves and their allies who had caused so much damage earlier in the fifth century.

It could be further shown, I think . . . that by these settlements also succeeded in splitting the ranks of their barbarian enemies, for they set the interests of the tribal nobility once and for all in conflict with the interests of the rank and file of the warriors. The nobility were no longer simply the "leading men" of the people. They were now a landed gentry whose manner of life would become increasingly different from that of their followers; it had become something like the relationship of landlord and tenant. (22)

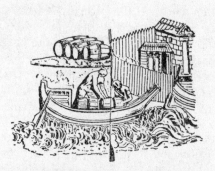

River traffic (*Trajan Col.*)

12

PELAGIUS

IN the later 4th century Gauls were ardently making pilgrimages to the holy places of the East; and we should guess that Britons certainly were among them even if we had not the explicit statement by St. Paula (writing from Bethlehem to Marcella in Rome): "Even the Briton remote from our world forsakes the setting sun and seeks the spot he knows by fame and from the Scriptures." She herself and Jerome had gone sightseeing through Syria and Egypt. The Lady Melania was putting up pilgrims in Jerusalem; and the main roads were still in good order, especially the trunk road from Bordeaux to Milan, on via Aquileia and Nish to Byzantium. Letter-writing from one end of the empire to the other was practised as part of the new cultural life promoted by the spreading faith. Hedibia, a member of the Bordeaux University circle of Ausonius, wrote to Jerome about the husband, Rusticus, of a relation Artemia who had fled from troubled Gaul to a Jerusalem convent; and Jerome in turn wrote to him—though we do not know if he was persuaded to follow his wife.

A woman pilgrim "from the ends of the earth" (possibly Britain, but more likely west Gaul) left a record of her visits to sites in Egypt and elsewhere in the East. She went to pray, she says, but also because she was sufficiently curious. She climbed Sinai and was pleased with a gift of apples and the broad view. (1)

But the strong-minded girls and ladies who intrude with questions on the zealous solitude of Jerome, his Amazons, were all of the upper classes—as were men like Sulpicius, Paulinus of Nola, Priscillian. Only gradually was the example of men like Martin, Ninian, Victricius, spreading among the commoners. The discontented peasant or artisan, the embittered slave, was still in the West more likely to flee to the barbarians or the wildwood outlaws than to become an enthusiastic (that is, monastic) Christian.

Sulpicius tells us that the discords and agitations in the Western Church (which included the British) went on unabated after the Priscillianist trial. We saw them rise into view in Britain in the life of Victricius. And we gain another clue from the fact that a governor about this time was Chrysanthus, who in 407 became bishop of the Novatians at Byzantium. (2) Socrates says that under him the Novatian Church flourished, that he was the first to give gold to the poor out of his own estate, and that on Sundays he ate only two loaves of blessed bread. Such a man, who had a high respect for learning, must have left his mark in Britain.

The Novatians held views allied to those of the Donatists of north Africa. They denied the efficacy of Penitence: that is, they closed their ranks against apostates and compromisers. Such creeds were developed during the persecutions against the time-servers who conformed to the State's demands as soon as things grew difficult; and so, though Penitence was the theme of argument, what was at stake was the question of true devotion, true struggle to follow the Christian ethic, as against the diluters and opportunists. The latter had vastly increased with the mass baptisms of people with little knowledge of the faith and no inner impulse of conversion. Donatus had asserted: "What has the Emperor to do with the Church?" On this basis, political as well as theological resistances were mustered; and the Donatist Church fiercely persisted till outlawed and broken by the State.

Now from the spiritual wrestlings of the British Church there emerged a man who was to shake the whole Christian world. Though his teachings were condemned, they forced Augustine to define his position ever more firmly and clearly; they thus played a crucial part in the definitions which were to determine the whole development of Latin Christianity. Pelagius fought for Free Will, for a belief in the possibility of harmoniously integrated personality; Augustine defeated him with his theses of Predestination, Grace, and Original Sin.

He was certainly British, though we have no idea from which part he came. Attempts to describe him as an Irishman born in

Britain are sheer guesswork. The only probability we can urge
is that he came from one of the large towns, London, York, or
Cirencester. The many allusions in his works to medical matters have suggested that his father was a doctor: a guess that
would fit in with his Greek name. (3) Efforts to translate
Pelagius into Morgan or Muirchu and make him a Celt must
be resisted. He seems rather to come from a Greek or Eastern
family living in Britain, a family already Christian. The one
sure point is that the conflicts in the British Church must have
played a part in the early formative years of his mind.

"Pelagius called the Briton," says Augustine. "The monk
Pelagius, British by race," adds Mercator; and Prosper,
Orosius, Gennadius all agree in naming him Briton. "A per-
fect dullard weighted down by Scottic porridge," shouts
Jerome, and makes some obscure comments on "a brood of
Scottic folk from near the Britons". But he merely feels it more
insulting to use the Irish label, since he looked on the Irish as
idolatrous cannibals. (4)

Pelagius arrived in Rome at dates estimated between 375 and
400, probably for secular studies. (5) His writings show that he
had deeply pondered upon Roman Law. His rigorous method of
exegesis, his pervasive concept of Justice (*aequitas*) which
largely determines the application of his thought, his views on
the absolute binding character of contractual obligations freely
entered into and of the responsibilities of the free person—all
these point overwhelmingly to legal studies. As the *prudentes*
defined the validity of constitutions or fixed the circumstances
under which an edict ceased to apply, so he noted in history
what he called Conditions of Times: the period at which a
law came into being, the period when it ceased to bind. (6)

He also certainly studied Lucretius' poem *On the Nature of
Things*, with its atomic materialism, its sense of evolutionary
process, its passionate effort to penetrate the fears which the
poet held to lie deepest in religion and to obstruct human
happiness and progress. And in the rhetoricians' schools he
lost any provincialism of accent and acquired the art of
argument.

He also deepened his sense of the injustices perpetrated by
the law, and by the State of which the law was the mouthpiece:

His personal writings give a strong impression of a man who has known at close quarters the façade and the facts of the legal apparatus. He has witnessed exactions and cruelties that have moved and repelled him. He knows the diversity of the means of torture that Roman procedure put at the judges' disposition. Those arbitrary imprisonments, those confiscations, those summary executions of which the sole motive was greed, have wounded him in the deepest levels of his emotions of humanity; and before even knowing the verse of the Bible: "You shall not afflict any widow or fatherless child; if thou afflict them in any wise and they cry at all unto me, I will surely hear their cry; and my wrath shall wax hot, and I will kill you with the sword; and your wives shall be widows and your children fatherless," he has had to promise never to lift to the Lord "hands tainted with rapine and blood."

His criticism makes him ask on what basis can a man claim the right to judge his fellow or to pronounce on goods that are not truly ours; his psychology shows him all the influences which intervene in a judge's mind and determine his verdict. But most of all the cruelty of the punishments have made the exercise of judicial functions odious to him. . . . (7)

Pelagius thus sees his world rent by intense contradictions: a concept of universal and equal justice (which implies the brotherhood of man and the rejection of all consideration of person) and the actual procedures of the State, which he feels to embody injustice and to rend the seamless garment of human unity. The conflict he defines in legal terms (for in the Law itself was a contradiction between Stoic ideas of the Law of Nature and the regulations preserving inequality of status and property); but it is in Christian terms that he feels the whole thing.

How deep went his horror of the State and its methods of force can only be realised by reading through his powerful work *De Divitiis*:

How can we look for the rule of Christ in such a rich man, or his pattern in such a possessor of wealth? . . .

Let us see if there can be any likeness between the character of the rich man and that of Christ.

From the attack on riches he moves to the attack on the State which sustains the rich man:

Under your very eyes the bodies of men, sharers of your own nature, are lashed with leaden scourges, broken with cudgels, crushed under the Claw, or burnt in the fires. And your holy eyes bear to watch this; you a Christian allow yourself to stare at this.

And not to stare only, but in the rôle of oppressor to inflict the tortures of the executioner.

To stare at it is horrible enough, but what can I say of him who orders it?

Answer me, O earthly judge, has some strange hardening of the soul made you exempt, immune from fellow feeling with one of the same nature as your own? or how is it that the sufferings of a human body do not rouse the feeling of a human heart?

Any Christian after it all feels such pity that he cannot even sleep till he has done the offices of compassion on those whom you have bidden be tortured so often and punished in so many brutal ways. And he is stricken with fear of divine judgment at the thought of not showing he man some mercy. Do you fear nothing, at whose command he has suffered all this?

You at times thrust even the innocent into jail, driven by motives of gratitude for others or a sense of personal wrong; and you appear very important to yourself when your injury is revenged. Yet Christians feel not only an enormous concern, but also a haunting fear of divine anger if they do not strive for the man's freedom. Do you enjoy entire peace of mind, at whose command he is imprisoned?

It takes too long to list all the horrors, the scourging, the dungeons, the darkness, the hard bonds of fetters—under such a judge there can be no punishment without torture and death. Then there is stirred in Christians a complex anguish urging to acts of succour when they see themselves in the persons of their own kin torn and devoured by birds and beasts—even burial being often refused.

But you, the upholder of wealth, trafficker in offices, after these cruelties you recline at ease, lolling on piled-up embroideries; you entertain your guests with the story, telling how you tortured and mangled the man, before the people, and with what manner of death you broke him and laid him low, as if you were a general celebrating his triumph; and in case anyone at your table should be horrified at the tale, you assert that you had to carry out the law, you who shortly before were boasting that you lived according to Christ's law and were a follower of the gospel though rumour calls you a swallower of it.

How is it, I ask, that there is so great a discrepancy among those who share the name of Christian and are bound by the same religious obligations, that some are so steeped in merciless brutality they do not fear to oppress, rob, torture and even kill, while others are so dominated by pity that even the wretches whom the others do not shrink from slaughtering appear pitiless in comparison with themselves?

Such words convey to us the quivering repulsion that gripped the man as he wrote. And we may well feel some pride in the fact that the first Briton who emerges out of history as a fully-drawn character was a man so passionately humane, whose words come straight from his own heart to ours.

No doubt it was with his baptism that he broke from the legal world, carrying into the Christian sphere the conflicts and aspirations discovered in his secular studies. (8) He now felt that *aequitas* could not be realised in existing civil society. The justice he wanted could only be expressed in the Church in its opposition to that society. But by giving his ideas this focus, he had to accept the creed of Chastity and Poverty; no other way in his era could the total rejection of property-greed and the State be expressed. Thus a new conflict was set up, between the way of sharp renunciation and the vision of an earth of fulfilled humanity. With his clear mind Pelagius was calmly aware of this. "Is there anything so hard, so iron-hard, as to deny nature?" When the earth heaps up before us its riches and splendours, can we cruelly refuse our spirits the right of access? The very nature of man, Pelagius says, is to rule the elements. Then, when we see man at his work of dominating matter by transforming it, changing the whole face of the earth through his labours, is it not a sad thing to cut our senses away from the joys of life, to resist the impulses that turn us into the masters of nature, and to set all our hopes on the other side of death? It is hard and grievous, he replies, but it must be done. There can be no complicity with iniquity, and we become accomplices as soon as we have any part in the existing system. (9)

He gathered disciples: Leporius, a Gaul of Trèves; Julian of Apulia, bishop's son and future bishop of Eclanum, a talented but vain, spoiled youth; probably Sixtus of the priestly aristocracy, who was to be bishop of Rome; and no doubt Britons such as Agricola who later championed his doctrines. His main follower was Celestius, often called an Irishman, but apparently

Campanian or African, who was "born a eunuch from his mother's womb", and who, before meeting Pelagius, wrote three letters of incitements to virtue, dedicated to his parents, from a monastery. (10) There was also some protector of high rank, probably a member of the Anician *gens*, the first noble family to come over to Christianity, which had grown in political importance through the 4th century.

The Pelagian party preached the rejection of property and sex, the two main forces tying men to the world. Like other ascetics they believed in continual prayer and meditation on the Scriptures, abstention from all oaths and tribunals of the law, refusal to call any man Father; they denied the worth of infant baptism. (11) Though influencing some of the clergy, they were a movement of lay men and women. They did not broadcast their views, but used oral propaganda, and if they wrote tracts, put no names to them and confided them only to tried-out persons.

Pelagius' first important work was a *Commentary* on the Epistles of Paul; an earlier treatise on the Trinity we know only from fragments. (12) The commentary is sober, concentrated, realistic in method; it rejects allegory, prolix citation of texts, or elaborate glosses. Digressions are exceptional. Pelagius seeks to get at the heart of Paul's meaning and to find the relation of the words to life. (13) He minimises the elements that could be used for a dualistic view of the universe. Thus, when Paul opposes works and faith, he defines works there, not as moral activity, but as acts in the narrow legalistic sense, in the letter of the Mosaic Law. He accepts the contrast of Adam and Christ, but not in the sense of Original Sin opposed to Grace; he finds a purely ethical distinction. He strives to banish all Manichean tendencies that regard nature and the body as innately evil; and is so successful in this aim that he is accused of throwing out the Mystery of the Cross. (14)

The first scandal came with his attack on the Magnates. Ever since Clement of Alexandria had made it possible for bankers to join the Church by allegorising away the texts against the rich, most leading ecclesiastics had compromised on the issue of the great landlords. In place of the doctrine of Restitution they set that of Stewardship. Ambrose pronounced along these lines; so did Augustine. A doctor had recently written a thesis on the legitimacy of wealth, saying that if the apostles gave up their property it was because of persecution. Abraham was rich and the Old Testament saw wealth as the blessing of God. Maybe the rich would not be let into the Kingdom, but there was no reason for forbidding them entry into the Life.

Pelagius burst out against this apology. Basing himself on Christ's command to sell all and give to the poor, he repeated without qualification: Woe to the rich! He however permitted men to keep a sufficiency. Equality of goods would be desirable and logical, but if a mistress of a house had only two or three slaves she did not come under the apostolic condemnation. What he denounced absolutely was greed (*avaritia*), the will to possess. In his eyes it was insatiable and inhuman, essentially bad; it showed itself in the huge inheritances, the anxious grabbing of lands and goods, the cynical usurpation of the substance of the poor by powerful judges. (15) He exclaimed in horror at the violences loud all around him, and stated the utter incompatibility of being both Christian and rich.

Proba, a wealthy woman of the Anician *gens*, was alarmed in her conscience, and Augustine had to reassure her. (16) But others were enraged; most of all, says Pelagius, his fellow-doctors resented any attack on their gains. They encompassed him "with a deadly hatred".

The assault on riches, however, was simply an aspect of his fundamental position: that faith without works is no true faith. He demanded an entire concurrence of theory and practice, and with his cool, clear mind pounced on the least infraction. Now he began to hear the word *heretic* thrown at him. Disquieted, he tried to find ways of stating his views that would cause the least misunderstanding and produce the most persuasion. In a long letter to Paulinus of Nola in 405-6 he still evaded coming quite to the point in defining Grace and Free Will, but was contemptuous of a blind, broken appeal to the Will of God. Some time before 410 strong discussion began at Rome about his ideas. Pope Innocent asked for clarifications, which, when received, were not as definite as desired.

Offence was being given by Pelagius' concept of *impeccantia*, the power of men to rise above sin, to achieve human perfection. (17) He accused his opponents of wanting an excuse for remaining sinful and imperfect. Not only was it possible to break the bond of sin; it was obligatory on a Christian to do so, as precisely stated in the precept of the evangel and the message of Paul: Be you perfect. Not that a Christian could simply, by one moment of decision, throw sin out for ever; the achievement of perfection was a process of continuous development in which effort was always needed. What Pelagius claimed was that the effort could be made, that men could go on becoming ever more securely human, oriented to goodness and *aequitas*. He denied that mankind was divided into good and bad, that virtue was a gift to some chosen persons, that there was an elect. Grace was open to all men equally; the obligation to grow perfect was laid impartially on all. To prove his point he published *Witnesses*, passages from the Scriptures collected under headings. (18) And in *The Good and Nature* he set out his ideas, with man's freedom defined as the governing principle. Even before Christian law there were thoroughly good men and women, upheld by the light of their conscience. Using the categories of Aristotelian logic, he argued that sin could not constitute a real thing (*substantia*) or a sanction (*vindicta*) or a source of further sins; it was only an act of disobedience, a free manifestation of our pride, for which we were personally responsible. Body dominated spirit? How could there be a pernicious fight between two elements that were alike the work of God?

But now Alaric's invasion of Italy disturbed the great families at Rome, who fled with as many dependants as they could muster, several going to Jerusalem. The last of the Anicians, a young girl Demetrias, was taken by her mother and grandmother to Africa; on the point of marriage, she chose perpetual virginity. Jerome, with his usual vehemence, says that all the African churches leaped with joy, even the nomads were overcome in their huts, and the whole of Italy forgot its woes. (19) Pelagius and Jerome were both asked by the family to draw up rules for confirming the young aristocrat in her vocation.

Pelagius restated his main ideas, using a more varied and enriched style. (20) He stressed that the conscience was a thing naturally man's. Man alone in the universe had succeeded in freeing himself from necessity and becoming the voluntary executor of justice. Evil came from willing bad things; we grew habituated to it from the world around us till it became a second nature; then virtue seemed something cut away from us and we imagined holiness as brought to us from without. (21) He did not hesitate, indeed, to proclaim man's Natural Holiness. (22) Why stress to Christians the difficulty of avoiding sin when even pagans have achieved a steadfast goodness? "How many has one seen of philosophers chaste, patient, modest, generous, disinterested, charitable, scorning the honours and pleasures of the world and enamoured only of justice and truth?" (23)

He had shrewdly linked his thought with those parts of other Christian writers that looked in the same direction: passages from Ambrose, Lactantius, Pope Xystus, St. Paul, even Jerome and Augustine. But his conciliations were nullified by the blunt and crude form given to his doctrine by Celestius, who for twenty years (411 to 431) was "master and leader of the whole army", as Jerome put it. (24) He and Pelagius had left Rome in the exodus and went via Sicily to Hippo, where Augustine was bishop—though at the moment in Carthage at a conference on the Donatists. Pelagius went to Carthage and spent some time with Augustine in friendly intercourse, then departed for Jerusalem, leaving Celestius behind.

The Donatists, demanding rebaptism for apostates, had sharply raised the question whether baptism conferred remission of sins. Celestius, flatly denying the efficacy of infant baptism, increased the difficulties of the orthodox; the deacon Paulinus, a sort of representative in Africa of Ambrose, took the matter up. Called before a Council, Celestius declared Adam's sin his own sole affair; but he refused to name any others supporting his position except a priest Rufinus. He was excommunicated and went off, saying that he would appeal to Rome. He seems to have paused in Sicily, where soon Pelagianism was thriving, then he arrived in Ephesus where he was admitted to the priesthood (413–14). He seems to have had some success in Rhodes; but reaching Byzantium, he was expelled by the patriarch.

Augustine was growing more concerned about the situation; but as it was hard to pin Pelagius down to bald definitions like

those of Celestius, he set about a refutation with some caution
In 412 he still spoke in laudatory terms of Pelagius, but was
steadily advancing his argument for Original Sin. His agitation
was worsened by a questionnaire of five points submitted by a
visiting Syracusan, which summed up the main Pelagian ideas
(including the prohibition of riches). In his reply he made a
strong defence of the wealthy and said that they must be accepted whether their wealth was justly or unjustly gained. Then,
in 415, two disciples of Pelagius, afraid of the tendencies in their
master's teaching, brought him their qualms. Augustine, while
strongly urging his own viewpoint, still left a reconciliation
open.

But the difference between the two thinkers was impassable.
Augustine himself tells an anecdote that brings out well their
deep opposition. An African bishop at Rome had been reading
some passages from the *Confessions*. When he came to the
words, "Give what you command and command what you
will," Pelagius burst out, "I cannot bear it!"

Meanwhile Pelagius was in Jerusalem, on the best of terms
with John, the bishop of that busy pilgrim centre. A young
Spanish priest, Orosius, feverishly disputatious and ambitious,
arrived with all the details of Celestius' career in Africa.
Jerome in his intellectual cell at Bethlehem was suspicious of
Pelagius, whose creed he crudely saw as a form of Stoicism. (25)
He launched one of his ferocious attacks, directed at Pelagius
and intended to catch him "like a rat". A synod was convened
at Jerusalem, at which Orosius did his best to blacken Pelagius,
but to no effect.

From Orosius' writings we gain a picture of Pelagius, a
shambling, bulky man. Enemies said that he ate too much, and
Jerome depicts him as plodding along at tortoise pace.

But now a new accusation came in, drawn up by two aged
bishops of Gaul—Heros of Arles and Lazarus of Aix. It was
sent to the metropolitan of Caesareum, who called together the
bishops of Palestine at Diospolis in late December 415. Pelagius
extricated himself, but it seems at the cost of denying what he
had himself written in *On the Christian Life*. The issue at stake
was the possibility of perfection, of moving beyond sin. He
could have argued that his words were simply meant to define

the condition towards which the righteous man must tend; but perhaps he was wearied-out and afraid of having his words twisted. The Council vindicated his name.

The Africans were dismayed, affronted. Two Councils, of Carthage and of Milevum (for Numidia), denounced Pelagius and Celestius; and a letter was addressed to the pope. The Africans knew that Pelagius still had strong support at Rome and that to defeat him they must defeat him there. So, while he was working at a book on Free Will (in which he insisted on the blamelessness of birth), in January 417, pope Innocent excommunicated him and Celestius, insisting on the need for "daily Grace".

The volatile crowd of Jerusalem—that "populous city with its senate, his squadron of soldiers, its whores, mimes, drolls and everything else", in Jerome's words—assaulted the Latin monastery and sacked it. Jerome and Eustochium and the other devotees took refuge in a fortified section of their domain, a tower. Eustochium was a high aristocrat; Jerome was looked on in the west as one of the Latin patriarchs; and so the affair had its repercusions. Pelagius could not be explicitly blamed, but Augustine demanded immediate sanctions in a note added to his recension of the Acts of the Council of Diospolis.

In March 417 Innocent died and the new pope Zosimus was no member of the coteries of Rome. An impulsive man, he responded to the appeals of the Pelagians. Celestius presented a statement of his creed; and Zosimus held a public inquiry, which in effect cleared the applicant. Then in September a statement from Pelagius was read, which brought tears of indignant sympathy to the eyes of those present, who included the pope.

The Africans, however, refused to budge on their decisions. They had been taking various steps ever since the summer of 416, working on the priestly aristocracy and gaining support at court. The Pelagians themselves were propaganding at Rome; Julian of Eclanum was stirring up the students. On the grounds that disorders were provoked, the emperor was drawn in and the pope began to weaken. On 30 April, the emperor ordered the immediate expulsion of the heresy's ringleaders, laid on everyone the duty of denouncing them, and directed that all partisans have their goods confiscated and be themselves deported. Thus "the necessary unity" would be established.

On 1 May, at Carthage, a Council again condemned Pelagius and Celestius. And finally the East conformed. At a synod of Antioch, Pelagius and his teachings were repudiated. Mercator, one of his foes, says that he was excluded from the holy places. Perhaps he tried to enter Egypt; for a letter of the coarse-tongued Isidore of Pelusium seems addressed to him:

The host of years has gathered round you, but you still have an unbending spirit, passing from one lodging to another in search of all dishes. If then you interest yourself in the smell of kitchens and in sauces, make rather your court to those who rule, and seek the towns with their chimneys, for hermits are not in a position to give you hospitality. (26)

Perhaps he spent his last years on his *Commentary on The Song of Songs*, in which he celebrates the nobility, the endless strength of true love, and once more attacks the Manichean opposition of body and soul. (27)

Anyway, he faded out, unbroken but defeated. Some of his disciples gave up; others carried on the struggle. Anianus, for example, translated the homilies of St. John Chrysostom in which many of the Pelagian pleas for active virtue, for a rejection of pessimism, could be found. In Campania and in north Italy organised resistance was made to the imperial rescript and the decisions of Carthage and Rome. Eighteen bishops refused to accept the *Tractoria* setting out the papal position. (28) Protests were circulated; Julian wrote to the pope and to count Valerius who had busied himself against Pelagius at court. In 419 a document was sent around, meant to affect the new pope Boniface; it demanded the right to speak out against the "Manicheans". (29) The Pelagians wanted a General Council to be called at which their position could be effectively discussed.

The defenders of Original Sin were taking no chances. A close friend of Augustine went to Ravenna and pulled all possible strings; he distributed among the high officials more than eighty magnificent horses. The Pelagians vainly pleaded that they were being silenced by the shouts of the mob and the force of arms, the call of the trumpet; they vainly set out precedents for their request for the calling of a General Council where they could freely propound their views before thinkers concerned with such matters, not before an ignorant crowd and a browbeaten episcopate. The dialectics of the Pelagians repelled the unlettered faithful who wanted the magical efficacy of baptism upheld and who were infuriated at the thesis that death was a natural fact and not necessarily an evil or a punishment. (30)

The eighteen refractory bishops were exiled—though some in the end recanted. Florus, Orontius, Julian remained firm. Imperial letters of June 419, January 421, July 425 show us the progress of the repression. In 423, taking advantage of the quarrel between the emperor Honorius and his sister Placidia, and the confused state at Rome through Johannes' usurpation, Celestius dared to reappear despite threats of a death penalty and to demand without effect the reopening of his case.

The constitution of July 425 bade the Pelagian bishops of Gaul renounce their errors before the bishop of Arles within twenty days or fall under the displeasure of the prefect. This imperial measure, taken with the surprising step of Heros and Lazarus in writing to accuse Pelagius in the East, shows that Pelagian ideas had a wide currency in Gaul. But it was not so easy to deal with the same ideas in Britain, where imperial controls had wholly or largely fallen away. There were, however, ways and means of trying to assure uniformity there as well. Agricola, son of bishop Severianus, had gone across from Gaul to propagate Pelagianism; he seems to have been a Briton. And Prosper of Aquitaine, the chief watchdog on behalf of Original Sin in Gaul, recorded, "Enemies of Grace had taken possession of the land of their birth and the Pope succeeded in getting them removed even from that remote part of the Ocean." He refers to the mission of St. Germanus with which we shall deal in a later chapter. (31)

The Pelagians went on trying to gain support in the East, where orthodoxy was less sharply and narrowly defined than in the West. John Chrysostom in his social attitudes had links with Pelagius, and Theodore of Mopsuestis had a strong humanist and rationalist element; he had, for instance, written a book in favour of the innocence of babies. Nestorius at Byzantium had indeed come out in support of the universal inheritance of Adam's sin; but Eastern thought was so much more nuanced and sensitive to philosophic argument than Latin thought that the Pelagians still had hope of prevailing there. In 429, the year of Germanus' visit to Britain, a group of important Pelagians, led by Florus and Julian, arrived in Byzantium. Celestius was with them, but holding (or held) back. Nestorius was undecided; but he himself was in dogmatic conflict with Rome and at the Council of Ephesus in 431 the trinitarian issues he had raised were in the forefront. He was defeated; and at the same time the denunciation of Pelagianism was renewed. (32)

Julian continued writing in support of his beliefs; but he was a shallow thinker by the side of his master. He and Augustine went on arguing about Marriage and Lust. Julian lost himself in scholastic issues, trying to determine exactly at what moment the Devil was able to insert in a babe the seed of sin; and in defence of nakedness he claimed that Adam and Eve on leaving paradise put on clothes, not because they were ashamed, but because they felt cold. Florus attempted a sort of coup to regain his bishop's seat at Misenum, which occasioned scenes of convulsions round the shrine of Sisennius. Julian the abstruse intellectual also made efforts to gain popular support, but was driven again out of the Church.

The Pelagians had been defeated in the head-on conflict. They managed to preserve and hand on many of their master's works by attributing them to others; perhaps by a complicated sense of humour they even put the names of Jerome and Augustine on some of the compositions. To carry on direct propaganda was now impossible. (33) But Pelagius' influence was not simply dissipated. In modified forms it entered into the work of many Gallic thinkers, who struggled against the unadulterated Augustinian doctrines of Predestination and Original Sin. We shall glance later at this development. For the moment it is enough to note that Severus Sulpicius in his later years fell under strong suspicion of Pelagianism. Gennadius tells us:

In his old age he was led astray by the Pelagians, and recognising the guilt of much speaking, kept silence till his death, in order that by penitent silence he might atone for the sin which he had contracted by speech. (34)

There is no need here to consider theologically the positions of Augustine and Pelagius, but we must have some notion of the cultural bearings of their thought. For in the conflict between them we touch the deepest elements of their world, its sense of hopeless collapse and corruption, its resolute quest for the good life and the reaffirmation of human values. If Augustine can be criticised for the Manichean trend in his ideas, Pelagius can be criticised for failing to enter fully into the tragic situation of the people of his world. Men needed a creed that embodied the anguish which they felt, the intolerable sense of loss, the conviction of a headlong fall; by a subtle paradox the pessimistic creed of Augustine gave men a power of endurance through centuries of bitterness and darkness. (35) But it would have been a sad thing if no voice had been raised in defence of humanism and earthly hope. As we have seen, Pelagius made no simple rehash of Stoicism, as Jerome thought he had; he was a Stoic in one sense, but he was also a Christian. And there was in his thinking a series of vital contradictions as considerable as any traceable in the thinking of Augustine, where the pessimism is linked with a vision of the organic fellowship of the faithful. For the medieval world that was opening up the inner conflicts of Augustine were more fruitful than those of Pelagius—though the Briton had a contribution to make which mankind could ignore at its peril and which came again to life in certain aspects both of the Protestants and the Humanists of the 16th century.

Relief of young girl with cat from Bordeaux

13

TOWNS AND VILLAS IN THE
EARLY 5TH CENTURY

WE now come back to the scene in Britain, first to what was
happening in town and countryside, and then to the
political forms growing up out of the broken imperial system.
Despite raids and harryings, the towns and villas did not suffer
much. Neither now nor in the later Saxon invasion was a town
sacked. At Silchester and elsewhere a gateway was half blocked
with masonry as it now seemed too wide for easy defence.
There are signs of damage at some places, but not such as to
suggest any large-scale assaults and demolitions. At Caister-
by-Norwich human remains have been found in a burned-
down house; at least thirty-six persons, perhaps refugees, met
their end there. (1) The house seems to have been inhabited till
400, perhaps much later. Colchester in its specially exposed
position may have come under attack. (2)

But generally the towns were too strong to be stormed. The
only reference to a Roman walled structure being assaulted and
taken occurs in the *Anglo-Saxon Chronicle* under the year 491:
"Aelle and Cissa besieged Andredesceaster [the fort of Anderida,
Pevensey] and slew all the inhabitants." The walled cities of the
south and the south-east may be considered to have stood in uninterrupted though weakened life throughout the 5th century. (3)

The road system remained in use for such trade as was carried
on, for evangelists or pilgrims, for military bands. Even in
Wales it seems to have been used till into the 7th century. (4)

In the first years of entire or partial independence the failure
of the old forms of centralisation must have forced each *civitas*
back upon itself in many ways, with resulting conflicts and
rivalries as well as isolation:

What the cities lacked was a co-ordinating power; they must therefore have run on more or less parallel but unconnected lines, always
in danger of getting to cross purposes, and also in danger of becom-

ing the tools of ambitious men bitten by a desire for local greatness. They continued also to raise and employ local militia; but these forces, adequate for a defence of town walls against casual barbarian raids, would be useless for a campaign and therefore unable to drive an enemy out of a countryside. (5)

But there were counter-forces making for an over-all control, which we shall discuss in the next chapter.

Some villas may have been roughly fortified; but such earthworks as are at times found around them may have been meant only to prevent cattle from straying, not to meet any determined attack in force. (6) A few villas were certainly burnt in the later 4th or early 5th century: for example, a cellar granary near Verulamium (about 367); another (earlier) in Kent; a Sussex villa (about 367); a villa at Great Weldon (two fires in late 4th century). There was a fire at Lullingstone villa before the 4th-century dining-hall was built; and fires at Verulamium. (7) But fires can be accidental. In the *Life* of St. Martin we read how the saint was once in winter visiting one of his parishes—"as it was his yearly custom, and that of bishops to visit their churches". He lodged in the sacristy. A fire had been lighted in the hypocaust. The surface of the flooring was thin and cracked, and the flames came up through the *tesserae* and set fire to the straw, which he, preferring the bare ground for bed, had shoved aside. (8)

Besides the raids by Saxons there were still raids by the Irish in the west (and perhaps along the south coast) and by Picts or Britons in the north. On Traprain Law, south of the Forth, a hoard left by raiders has been found—fine silver flagons and dishes, many of which had been hacked in two. Two bands had probably co-operated and then divided the loot; one band, surprised in its hill-lair, buried the silver in haste, then were killed or driven far away. (9) Similar halved objects have been found in Gaul.

Then there are the two Irish hoards of Coleraine and Balline that belong to this period. (10) And it is more likely that the high-king Niall was doing his raiding now than in the earlier years of the century:

According to a poem attributed to Cinaed ua hArtacáin (*c.* 975), Niall led seven expeditions across the sea. On the last of these

Eochu of the Lagin slew him out of love for the Saxons (whom the poet evidently believed to have been in possession of England in Niall's time). His men brought his body home, fighting seven battles on the way.

There are later prose accounts which tell the story more fully, but no longer place the scene of his death at or near Muir nicht (the sea of Ictis, the Isle of Wight). Niall, we are told, set out with the intention of conquering Gaul and Italy. On his way to the Alps his march was held up by a great river (the Loire), and while he was there an envoy arrived from the Romans to offer him hostages (in token of submission).

His enemy Eochu had taken refuge with the king of Alba (here understood to mean the Scottish Dál Riata); and tradition hesitates as to whether Eochu followed Niall to Gaul and slew him there, or whether Niall returned from Gaul and was slain by Eochu near the house of the king of Alba. As in the verse account, his men brought his body home to Ireland, and fought seven battles on the way. (11)

It seems that by the time the legends were written down, Gaul was the land of the Franks and the Romans were thought of as in Rome or Italy. Hence the tradition that Niall fought the "Romans" is interpreted as an advance somewhere towards Italy. But however that may be, Niall has become a sort of Maximus or Arthur. In one text there is a mention of the mountain-range which in the 6th century separated the Irish colonists in Scotland from the Picts; and this suggests, as is otherwise likely, that Niall had raided in north-west Britain as well as in the south. (12)

All over south Britain, and especially in East Anglia, treasures were hidden and never recovered in these years, reminding us of the lament in the *Anglo-Saxon Chronicle* of 418. The Mildenhall treasure found at West Row is a splendid example:

In the immediate neighbourhood of Mildenhall alone, I have records of the discovery of eight hoards. If the area is extended a few miles into the Fenland and along the Icknield Way belt, the number rises to twenty. Many of these hoards consist of pewter table-vessels, others of pots full of late Roman silver, including coins of Honorius. One of several finds near Icklingham, in Suffolk, consisted of silver coins, brooches, rings and a spoon, together with gold beads and ingots. (13)

In the bed of the old Croft River at Welney in the Fens two complete vessels were found in the earlier 1940s, and when the site was later examined a small dish was brought up from the river-bed, cut in two with shears, and doubled up.

Raiders had been sacking the Romano-British buildings which stood on the river-bank. They had found the pewter, which they thought to be silver, and were cutting it up to be shared out, when someone came along who recognised the character of the metal. "You are not going to carry that heavy old stuff home with you?" he asked. Whereupon they threw it all in the river in disgust. (14)

At Silchester a family treasure-chest was buried in a flint-lined cavity under a tesselated floor, standing on pieces of flanged tile to protect it from the damp earth. Three strong iron bands and hinges reinforced the lid. These, with the lock-plate, key, and iron handle survived, but the wood had decayed away. The contents had been removed or rifled. Remains of another iron-bound box were found at Brislington villa in Somerset. (15)

A trace of the Picts was left in East Anglia, an ogam-inscribed knife from the heathland at Weeting in southwest Norfolk, a region with débris of a Romano-British peasant holding. The parish bounds follow the Devil's Dyke or Foss-ditch, an earthwork some $5\frac{1}{2}$ miles long, which runs from the Wissey in the north to the Little Ouse in the south. The earthwork's date seems late Roman or sub-Roman; and the knife with a reindeer antler-tine for handle and the remains of an iron tang was found some 300 yards east of it. Ogams on portable objects are recorded only in Ireland, the Hebrides, and Orkneys. The latter areas have each turned up knife-handles with ogams. The Weeting ogam is certainly Pictish, though 500 miles more south than its fellows. Such a knife is unlikely to have been sold or given away. Its owner must have been a Pict, perhaps a mercenary—though it may be significant that his knife was found on the enemy side of the earthworks. (16)

But where we gain the most vivid signs of the raids is in the Yorkshire signal stations. At Huntcliff the station went up in flames and the building toppled southwards, littering the yard with charred wood. The defenders were killed and tossed with their women and children into a well. At Goldsborough also the end was sudden—perhaps the raiders coming up with a yell out of the dead of night or one of the thick sea-mists called frets, or else unheard amid the crashing of a storm. The well-preserved skeletons in the south-east corner of the tower had been covered by a total collapse of the structure. In the north-west corner, there were signs of a staircase, and close by the socket-stone was found a human skull; in the north-east the lower half of a quern was bedded in the floor with the upper half lying nearby. In the south-east:

a short thickset man had fallen across the smouldering fire of an open hearth, probably after having been stabbed in the back. His skeleton lay face downwards, the left hand, on which was a bronze ring, behind the back, the right touching the south wall.

Another skeleton, that of a taller man, lay also face downwards, near the feet of the first, his head pointing south-west. Beneath him was the skeleton of a large and powerful dog, its head against the man's throat, its paws across his shoulders—surely a grim record of a thrilling drama, perhaps the dog of one of the defenders, the man an intruder. Near the feet of the second skeleton were two silver coins of Eugenius and Honorius.

The coin-series reaches up to late 394. To surmise, therefore, that the stations fell in 395 or thereabouts is to go far beyond the evidence. They may have lasted a decade longer, or even two or three decades. (17)

The specialised systems in the big villas could hardly carry on when the army market broke down and the links with the general market of the empire ended or were seriously impaired. The clearest sign of the changed times appears in the fading-out of the imperial coin-series and the expansion of the minute coinage that is connected with the rural markets and fairs. The very nature of the way of life in the 5th and 6th centuries means that definite archaeological evidence is hard to assemble; the lack of dateable materials associated with the coins makes it hard to date the coins themselves. But on general grounds it seems obvious that the sub-Roman period would need something just like these coins, the small barbarous copies of Roman mintings in base metal, the minims or *minissimi* (of which fifty could be spread on a halfpenny).

They fall into two groups, those with radiate portraits imitating 3rd-century models and those with diademed portraits mainly copying the Return-of-the-Happy-Time (*Fel. Tem. Reparatio*) or Fallen-Horseman models of about 348. (18)

We would be much helped if we knew how long the types of late Roman pottery went on being made or what new sorts we should look for as the products of the early 5th century—such as the pottery from a post-Roman stratum at York, "quite good in quality, which looks like an unfamiliar kind of Romano-British ware". From the late 3rd century, wares called Romano-Saxon were being made, mixing Roman technique with Saxon decoration. They were particularly used in the region of the Saxon Shore, which suggests that Saxons had already begun settling there, that the garrisons were supplemented by Saxon Federates planted along the coast, or that trade was very brisk with the tribes beyond the North-Sea frontier. The issues raised by the wares are complex, but point to cultural fusions of Romano-British and Saxon elements long preceding the invasions. "When finally Roman commercial manufacture ceased, many of the same elements in purely Anglo-Saxon form were reintroduced by the new settlers, but among the cremation pottery of their cemeteries it is still possible to recognise, here and there, pieces directly reminiscent of the Romano-British or even the pre-Roman past." (19)

An interesting example of a Britain abroad is given by a stone found at Salonae in Dalmatia, dated 424, which records a Dumnonian woman—a member of the tribe of Devon–Cornwall: *clarissima femina, civis Dumnonia*. She died at the age of thirty.

A key question is what was happening on the villas and the farms. On the one hand the farmers were now relieved from the heavy burden of requisitions for the army. No doubt the landlords pressed for as large a share of the tenants' crops or flocks as they could; but how much they got in such a period would depend on the force at their disposal, and we have no reason to think that the "ferocious Briton" was less likely to fight for freedom from levies or rents than he had been to fight for the end of the tax-collecting nightmare. In unravaged areas it is unlikely that production went badly downhill, even if the problem of markets increased.

Gildas has a clear tradition of a great period of prosperity in Britain; we can most safely locate this period as following 409–10 when the controls of the central government broke and there must have been for some decades no strong imposition of fresh controls—though local landlords, based on the nearby town, or rising tribal chiefs, based on the wilder uplands, would be doing their best to extract tribute one way or another from farmers or shepherds. Probably the era of prosperity ran from 410 to the Saxon inroads and the plague of 443. (20)

In the west at Compton Abdale, Combend, and Foxcote (Gloucestershire) coins of Gratian have been found; at Whittington and Wycomb, coins of Honorius. At Lydney and Bourton, we saw, the minims have been plentifully excavated. (21) Lysons noted that one compartment of the 4th-century Orpheus mosaic at Withington had been cut out and a new border inserted at what seemed a much later date. Near the close of the 4th century on the east side of Withington villa a hall was built and linked with the house by a corridor, some seven by thirty feet. Villas at Hucclecote and Bourton are known to have been repaired at the very end of the century. (22)

Therefore, while the evidence is consistent with the supposition that monetary traffic dwindled, and finally, in the sub-Roman period, gave way to a system of barter, it lends no support to the idea that the Cotswold villas were generally deserted by 400, or even by 450.

Nor is there any reason to suppose that the villa-estates were broken up when the houses themselves were abandoned. . . . We may picture the Withington villa-owner, in the disturbed state of the sub-Roman period, withdrawing to the shelter of Corinium, and thenceforth paying only occasional visits to his old home, but continuing to draw an income from the estate.

For want of maintenance, the house would fall gradually into disrepair. It might after a while be invaded by tramps or squatters, who would light fires on the mosaic floors, as they did at Withington, using the rafters for firewood; and the end of it all would be a conflagration leaving clear traces of itself in the mass of burnt timber, melted lead, and broken walls that Lysons found when he dug up the site. (23)

True, the tendency of the large landlord had long been to use a bailiff to run the estate; but we can hardly picture the gentry now as simply withdrawing to the towns. They had a tradition of country ways which went far back on both the Roman and Celtic sides. Thus Ausonius writes to his friend Axius Paulus that he has at last got away from Bordeaux's soft blandishments and is on his farm near Saintes. Come quick, he calls, as he must get back to Bordeaux to celebrate Easter.

> Harness the cloppity mules on a four-wheeled car,
> or a jump in a three-horse gig if that's your choice,
> bob on a cob or a hack with broken back,
> come anyway if it's quick, and I'll rejoice.

Again he writes to the same rhetorician, slanging town life:

> The heaving crowds, the sordid crossroad brawl,
> I'm sick and weary of them all.
> Echo confuses all the rumbling air:
> Hey, give it, strike, get on, take care!
> A mad dog or a sow comes wild with muck,
> the waggon with its oxen's stuck.
> Your house won't save you, not its innermost room,
> still through its lairs the noises boom.
> These, and what else offends with tedious riot,
> drive me beyond the Walls for quiet.
> I seek the country's peace where, free from stress,
> I turn to serious idleness. (24)

Recall, too, Rutilius' friend the Count who left the court for his "Beloved Countryside". Later, Sidonius writes to Syagrius, occupied on his estate near Autun.

Tell me, Flower of Gallic Youth, how long, busying with rural labours, will you turn up your nose at urban matters? how long will those hands, once worn only by dice-tossing, against all right keep grasping field-tools? how long will your Taionnacus fatigue you, a farmer of patrician breed? how long, no cavalier, a plough man instead, will you bury in the winter fallows the spoil of the tress-waving meadow? how long, with the hoe weighing in your hands, will you scrape at the earth along your vine-rows? . . . (25)

This was the Syagrius who was as much a master of Burgundian as of Latin; he became indeed secretary to the Burgundian king. We see in him and others a return to the countryside, to the Celtic background, and a capacity of adaptation to changing circumstances. We find this change especially among men "whose homes or ancestral lands were in the old territory of the Aedui, and the upper waters of the rivers draining from this area, a kind of Highland zone. Yet these men were among the most cultured of their age". (26)

Again Sidonius complains that a noble friend Eutropius is immersed in farm matters, buried among cow-keeping rustics and grunting swineherds: "as if you were blessed in all your hopes if you feel plough-handle quiver over cleft furrow, or, bent on sickle, spoil the flower-wealth of meadows, or hoe the sprouting vines. . . ." Eutropius did in fact leave his estate to become Prefect. Some landlords, such as Maurusius, are depicted as being happy on their farms and vineyards. "When your granaries and garners are packt, you may resolve to pass in rural ease the months of snow. . . ." Others such as Eucherius seem ready to take office, but cannot obtain it—"what wonder when a breed of uncivilised allies directs the Roman Power, likely to bring it grounded with a crash?"

There is no reason for doubting that these men loved the countryside as well as wanting to make it profitable. There is a genuine note in many lines from Ausonius:

> Now, cut from Bordeaux and the common throng
> by hills and threefold streams, I am here at leisure
> with vine-thick slopes, the peasants blithe along
> the generous glebe, the meadows of green, the copse
> of dancing shadows, the crowded village church,
> all my farms close by Norvarus clustered,
> where every season of the year brings pleasure,
> warm amid wintry frost, in summer-sweats
> cooled by the northern breezes gently blustering. (27)

We may note there also the picture of his various farm-estates, *praedia*, grouped round the village of Norvarus, inside its territory.

The account of Germanus in 429 conveys the impression that the magnates had a town base but lived outside. Germanus pays his homage to the shrine of St. Alban, and then attends a synod at which a host of people appear, with some arrayed in splendid clothes. It is generally assumed that the synod took place at Verulamium, and indeed it may have done, since the proximity to the shrine would make that town a suitable place for settling a vexed point of religion. But there is nothing in the text to say so, and the synod may in fact have taken place in London for all we can tell. (28)

Still, it is worth while looking again at Verulamium with its derelict theatre used as a rubbish-dump and with a Celtic temple remodelled about 380 and showing many signs of a thriving market. The coin-series comes down to the last copper issues of the West (about 395) and includes the minute types. (29)

This kind of life was going on in 429, though repairs were made in a summary way and broken floors roughly clay-patched. In one house was found an urn of coarse gritty ware formed vaguely in the Roman mode but not wheel-made; under it lay a lid of normal Roman fabric, scarred by fire and evidently reused. (30)

The later Saxon town grew up across the valley. Probably by the 6th century Verulamium was abandoned, but the shrine of St. Alban seems to have been frequented all the while. In the 11th century the Roman town was used as a quarry by Saxon abbots. (31)

Further indications as to the way that things carried on both in town and villa appear in Patrick's *Confessio*. Though his dates are not certain, we may take it that after he escaped from being a slave-swineherd in Ireland on a boat carrying Irish wolfhounds abroad for sale, he arrived back home about 414–15. He had been about sixteen when rounded up with large numbers, "thousands" he says, of Britons. His father Calpurnius was a deacon, one of the sons of Potitus, a priest. (32) (Elsewhere he writes, "I am born of a father who was a decurion, but I sold my noble rank . . . for the profit of others.") The town system with its councillors responsible for the taxes must have been functioning to some extent, however incapably, in his home area. Even when writing in the mid-5th century, Patrick felt that his words needed no gloss.

Also, on his return he found things in order; he makes no lament over changes or devastations:

And again after a few years I was in Britain with my kindred, who received me as a son, and in good faith besought me that at all events now, after the great tribulations I had endured, I would not depart from them any whither.

His relations thought that the conditions in Britain, or at least in their region, offered compensation after the years of slavery. Later (perhaps about 231-2), when he heard the voices of the Irish crying across the sea, he felt it necessary to vindicate his going to live "as an exile among barbarians". He looked on Britain as still a place of civilisation—indeed too cultured if anything, since it abounds in "lordly rhetoricians" whom he fears would laugh at him.

It is, then, of some importance to establish where his home area was. Because, about 461, in writing from Ireland (if not still in Armagh, in semi-retirement at Saul) in a letter addressed to the king of Strathclyde, north and east across the waters, he refers to the king's people as Fellow Citizens, he has been taken to claim the North as his homeland. But he is speaking quite generally to his fellow Christians of Roman Britain.

In the *Confessio* he names his home as Banavem Taberniae, where his father "had a small estate, *villula*, close by, and there I was taken captive". The site is also spelt Bannavem in one MS., and is so given by Muirchu who wrote the first *Life* in Ireland; the second part of the name is varied as Taburniae and Thaburinde. Muirchu adds, "We have ascertained repeatedly that this town is unquestionably Ventre"—Nemthur in Fiácc's hymn. (33)

Where, then, was Banavem Taburniae Ventre? Efforts to link it with Bonnaventa of the Antonine Itinerary, which was near Daventry, are useless. We seem brought nearer to its area by the fact that three sites in Glamorganshire have the Welsh name Banwen. (34) But we can come closer yet. Ventre suggests Venta (Silurum), Caerwent, in the form Ventae. (35) We may then amend the name of Patrick's home town to Venta Sabrinae, Caerwent on the Severn. Even if we may not see in *Venta* the meaning of barter or sale, the Welsh cognate *Gwent* was used for a district and has been explained as having a root-meaning of *field*, with secondary meaning of *market-place*. (36)

Venta Silurum was a market-town with decurions, connected with the Channel ports by two roads—one via Gloucester; one by the ferry, *trajectus*, and on through Bath. (So Patrick could easily have got there from the Continent.) And in the 5th century the western routes were also open—a road ran to Caerleon and on through the Vale of Glamorgan to Carmarthen; another from Caerleon went north-west through Abergavenny and the hill-country of Brecknock to the Towy valley, to unite with the first road at Carmarthen. The united road then ran west by a small station at Castle Fleming to the shore at Whitesands Bay, where a small creek ran into the sea and there was a good haven for small boats, Porth Mawr. St. David's Cathedral was built a mile or so away in the sheltered valley, straddling the main British-Irish route of the period. Also, in its valley-lair it was out of sight of sea-raiders. Porth Mawr was still a sailing station for south Ireland under Henry II.

In the later 11th century, before Norman influences invaded St. David's, a clerk Rhigyvarch wrote a life of his saint, in which he says that thirty years before David's birth, Patrick sailed from Porth Mawr at the end of the Roman road. There was perhaps at that date an early sanctuary still there. In any event the medieval clergy held to the tradition, as they built a chapel on the spot—the remains still lie under the sand by the beach of the Porth. (37)

The Irish texts (Muirchu and the Tripartite Lives) show Patrick sailing up the Irish coast south to north, with his first land-fall at the mouth of the Wicklow River. Muirchu adds that he came "with all speed and a fair breeze". These details fit in with Porth Mawr as the sailing-point.

We noted above that the dedications to the family of Magnus Maximus were largely grouped about the western land-routes here discussed, both in the area of the Severn valley and in Pembrokeshire. The importance of the routes for the diffusion of Christianity is also shown by the cult of St. Brychan, who with his sons receives the other main body of early dedications. His mother Marchell travelled from Brecknockshire to Porth Mawr on her way to be married in Ireland; her father Tewdrig, founder of the early post-Roman kingdom of Brycheiniog, must have come along much the same route in the opposite direction. He was a chieftain of one of the many bands of Irish adventurers entering south-west Wales in these decades, and had pushed on to settle in the upper Usk basin. Along the same lines came the Ogams, and soon along them were also to come men from Gaul with their own brand of Christianity. (38)

Marchell's son, Brychan, appears in medieval hagiography as the begetter of a very large family of saints: sons and daughters.

The relationship of these dedications to the Roman road system and the routes leading therefrom to the western seas . . . is remarkably clear. We have, thus, every reason to associate the establishment of these and other churches dedicated to the children of Brychan with an early rediffusion of Celtic Christianity from Breicheiniog in the fifth and sixth centuries. (39)

In the Usk and Severn valleys, then, we find a comparatively sheltered region (though exposed to a certain amount of Irish depredations) which suits excellently with the background to be inferred from Patrick's writings. Both Roman culture and Roman agriculture were alive, even if undergoing strains. Patrick's father had a small villa-estate near Venta, at the village Banna-Venta-Sabrinae, Hill-market by the Severn, and there it was that Patrick was seized by freebooters. There it was he returned to the bosom of his family; there it was that he meditated over his experiences and felt how much better the world would be if the Irish were converted to the same creed as himself and his neighbours.

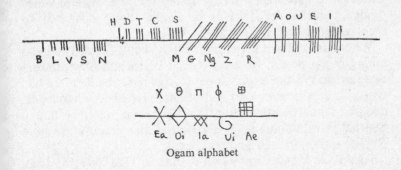

Ogam alphabet

GERMANUS AND VORTIGERN

WHILE Patrick on the one hand speaks of a small villa and a town council, on the other hand he addressed a king in Strathclyde; and in his world there seems nothing strange in the mixture of Roman survivals and tribal kingships. Within a few decades of 410 it is clear that the kingship had reached a flourishing state, and we may surmise that it was the development of Federate Troops under local chieftains which provided the half-way house between Roman government and the maturely independent kingdoms. In the sub-Roman period there must have been a welter of competing powers, one group based on the *civitates* that had kept a strong position, the other based on the highland chiefs who had been Federate officers. The *civitas*, a small limited republic ruled by the neighbouring big landlords, gave way to monarchies of varying size and importance. (1) A new term for king comes into use: *ti(g)ern* which originally meant landlord as in Gaelic. Later displaced by *brenhin*, it survived in derivatives. (2)

We can make out a kingdom of Powys being formed and first taking in the Severn basin in central Wales and Shropshire— close in form to the *civitas* of the Cornovian tribe that had had its capital at Wroxeter. Vortigern seems to have been its founder; and the name Gwrtheyrnion (Vortigerniana) suggests that it was his private domain. (3) His father and grandfather have Roman names (Vitalis and Vitalinus).

Again the kingdom of Gwent seems to take its name from Venta the capital of the Silures, Caerwent. It was founded in the early 5th century by a Caratacus known in Welsh tradition as Caradawc of the Strong Arm, *Vreichvras*. We can perhaps read the new nationalism in the revival of the name of the king who had fought valiantly against the Romans in this area some 400 years before. Caradawc's son Ynyr (Honorius), however, has the name of the emperor then ruling in Rome—imitation

or emulation? Soon after, the name Cynfelin (Cunobelinus)
turns up, suggesting again a return to the names of early
Celtic kings.

In Dumnonia (Dyfnaint and Cernyw), too, we meet princes
who belong to the last decades of Roman Britain. (4) At
Byzantium, the seat of the central government in the East, the
tradition arose that Britain to all intents and purposes fell out
of the empire after 407. Any unofficial contacts or temporary
occupations seemed unimportant beside the main fact of loss.
About 550 Procopius referred to the revolt of 407 and added,
"The Romans were never able to recover Britain, but from this
time it continued to be under tyrants" (rulers not of the central
government). By his day, the island was closed in dim mists, a
land of the Dead out in the West; but his statement about the
tyrants fits in with the picture we get of rising local dynasties.

Now let us turn to Saint Germanus, whom we have met at the
429 synod. His connections with Britain and King Vortigern
are of much importance; and his career illustrates what a deep
change had gone on in the Gaulish Church since the days of
Martin and Victricius. (5)

Here is the educated and conforming Roman who moves
without much dislocation from a secular to an ecclesiastical
career. His biographer Constantius, writing about 480, thus
begins:

Germanus was born at Auxerre of highly illustrious parents. From
early youth he was absorbed in the study of the liberal arts, and,
as learning cultivated the richness of his spirit, art and nature contributed together to make of him a well-instructed youth. After
attending the Schools of Gaul, in his desire for the fullness of knowledge he went to Rome, where he crowned his attainments by
mastering law. As a lawyer he adorned the tribunals of the Prefec-
ture. He shone in this sphere and was exercising his skill to the
plaudits of all when he married a lady distinguished by her family,
her wealth, and her pure morals. He was toga'd in all the lustre of
his renown when the State raised him to honours, conferring on him
the dignity of Duke and confiding to him an administration that
embraced several provinces.

His duchy included Auxerre and was very likely that of the
Armorican March. (6) Ardent in the hunt, he used to hang the

heads of his spoil on the branches of a big pear tree in the midst of the city. Such a procedure had its roots in very ancient Celtic custom; the early Gauls were head-hunters who hung the heads of slain foes on their doorposts and whose art is to a considerable extent dominated by the cult of the Severed Head. The bishop of Auxerre, Amator, objected to Germanus' practices and one day had the tree felled while the duke was away. The latter was so enraged that he decided to kill the bishop and moved on Auxerre with his retainers. Amator went to Autun, where he was told that the prefect had received a revelation naming Germanus as his (Amator's) successor. (7) The prefect agreed to release Germanus from his dukeship and Amator returned to Auxerre, collected the people in his house, and announced his nearing end; then he led them all to the church, Germanus and his henchmen included. After ensuring that all weapons were left outside, he seized Germanus, tonsured him, dressed him in religious garb, and inducted him into orders. (8)

Germanus, now (418) perforce a bishop, lived chastely with his wife. "He left the army of this world for the heavenly army." He gave up changing his clothes, wore only tunic and cowl (*cuculla*) in all seasons till they were in rags, kept a hairshirt next to his skin, and slept in his clothes on a bed of ashes framed with four boards. Thus he gained "a refined sanctity". His house was open to all, and he washed the hands and feet of all guests. Across the Yonne he established a monastery. (9)

After some not very remarkable miracles—driving spirits from a deserted roof-fallen house and restoring the power to crow to the roosters of a district—he went to Britain. (10) Constantius says that envoys had come complaining that "the Pelagian heresy was very widely spread in their land and that the Catholic faith needed prompt succour". A Council was called and the bishops voted unanimously that Germanus and Lupus be sent to Britain. (11)

We have independent testimony in Prosper's *Chronicle*. Prosper of Aquitaine had dedicated himself to attacking Pelagianism; he was therefore much interested in all steps taken to defend the dogma of Original Sin. Under 429 he wrote:

The Pelagian Agricola, son of the Pelagian bishop Severianus, corrupts the churches of Britain by insinuating his doctrine. But at the suggestion of the deacon Palladius, pope Celestine sends Germanus bishop of Auxerre as his representative, and after the confusion of the heretics guides the Britons to the Catholic faith.

Constantius sets the journey in winter, with a bad storm in mid-Channel. Germanus took charge, but grew so tired that he slept; things worsened; then, woken by Lupus, he succeeded in mastering the elements. In Britain the two bishops spoke "not only in the churches, but also at the crossroads, in the fields and the by-ways". We should like to know the language used—Latin, presumably. The Pelagians at first kept away, then decided to challenge the bishops. "They came out, flaunting their wealth, in resplendent clothes, surrounded by a mob of flatterers." A huge concourse of men, women, and children gathered out of curiosity. The Pelagians spoke first, then the bishops, and the heretics were confounded amid loud applause.

Suddenly a man of tribunician power advanced with his wife in the midst of the assembly. He presented to the two bishops his daughter, aged ten years, who was blind.

The Pelagians failed to cure her, the bishops succeeded. Then they went to St. Alban's shrine. Afterwards Germanus slipped and hurt his foot. As he rested, a nearby house was set on fire and the wind drove the flames his way. Then they parted and went harmlessly round his house to the farther side.

"During this time the Saxons and Picts united their forces to make war on the Britons," who, incapable of meeting the attack, appealed to the bishops. The time was Lent and the bishops preached. A large number of soldiers asked to be baptised and an oratory was built of tree branches; then, still wet with the baptismal waters, the army marched. The Saxons and Picts, hearing what had happened, rushed to battle. The British scouts reported their movements and Germanus assumed charge.

Taking with him some light-armed troops, he reconnoitred the country and noted a valley cleft between high mountains, which opened from the side where the enemy were expected. Here he drew up under his command an army on a new model.

The savage host drew near. Germanus quickly sent round the order that everyone should repeat in unison the call he made as battle-cry. Then, while the enemy came on confident of a surprise

attack, the bishops thrice shouted Alleluia! As one man the army
repeated it and the shout they gave went ringing through the air,
echoed on several times in the closed space between the mountains.
At this uproar there was such a panic among the enemy that they
imagined rolling on their heads not only the overhanging rocks but
even the sky itself.

They fled, throwing away their weapons, and a bloodless victory
was won—though some of the enemy drowned themselves in
the hasty retreat over a river. The Britons collected the spoils
abandoned by the fugitives; and the two bishops, their duty
done, sailed back through calm weather to Gaul.

Despite the fantastic details, the account seems based on
genuine traditions. We can assume that the mission against
Pelagianism was carried out and that during it a defeat of the
Picts occurred, in which Germanus played a leading part. The
appearance of a man of tribunician power is also of interest.
"*Tribunus* is a recognised title of certain administrative officers
in the later empire, and Germanus' host was no doubt simply
the chief magistrate of the municipality."

Germanus, before becoming a bishop, had been a fiery-tem-
pered hunter and commander, reaching a high rank, *ducatus
culmen*. Constantius keeps thinking of him as a military man.
His defeat of the storm-demons brings him the phrase "duke or
priest" (*dux ipse vel pontifex*), and he is said to visit his church
and monastery like a Duke of the Heavenly Hosts. (12) No
miracle is called on to explain the defeat of the Picts and Saxons.
The Germans were well known for their terrifying battle-yell;
and the saint merely uses their own trick against them in a
magnified form made possible by an intelligent grasp of terrain.
Whether or not we credit the tale, it is not miraculous.

For the next sixteen-odd years of the saint's life Constantius
has little to tell; the important items pack into the last year or so.
After such a space of time, he says, "It is hard to recover the
facts darkened by silence." But after all he wrote only some
thirty-five years after Germanus' death; and Lupus was still
living, a member of Constantius' own literary circle. He himself
would have been near thirty at the time of the second voyage.
We may take it that the *Vita* does record the main exploits
and interests of Germanus.

Auxerre was delighted, Constantius says, at his return. In his absence the townsfolk had been submitted to heavy exactions and he agreed to go to Arles on their behalf. Sailing down the Saône, he won over the prefect Auxiliaris by curing his wife of a fever, and Auxerre had its taxes lightened. This episode seems dated 440-1, so there were some dozen years or more left vacant in Constantius' narrative. (13)

The second visit to Britain seems to break in at once. Pelagianism had again become active. Constantius gives no idea who called or sent Germanus; and since, to preserve the plausibility of his tale, he has to state that the heresy, crushed in 429, had in fact been revived by a mere handful, it is hard to see why the British bishops should not have been able to deal with it themselves. Yet Constantius says appeals poured in from all sides. This time Germanus took bishop Severus (hard to identify) with him. An easy crossing was made. Germanus rigorously sought out the few heretics and had them deported (? to the Scillies). Elafius, the first man (*primus*) of the region, brought him a son with contracted knee, who was cured. (14)

Prosper does not mention this second voyage. His *Chronicle* indeed makes little reference to Gallic affairs after 440, when he probably left Marseilles for Rome—though he would still hear important church news from Gaul. But it must be realised that he calmed down considerably after he entered the pontifical chancellery. The policy of Sixtus III (432-40) and his deacon Leo who succeeded him was to maintain the positions against Pelagianism, but with a minimum of bitterness. A letter by Leo or someone close to him, written to Demetrias, shows the changed tone; the Pelagians are described as men with many virtues but over-trustful of human nature. Prosper responded to this atmosphere. His *Replies to Objections of the Gauls* is more conciliatory, less rigidly Augustinian, than his earlier works.

It has been suggested that Germanus' second visit did not actually take place at all. But we must reject this view, No doubt the second visit had less dramatic incidents, and Constantius tried to eke out the bare available details by giving it something of the same structure as the first. But he could hardly have invented it.

Germanus had scarcely returned to Gaul when he was met by

envoys from Armorica. Aetius, the great magnate who dominated Gaul, was launching the Alan nomads on the peasantry
there, "angered at the insolence of the arrogant folk". Germanus, knowing the ironclad Alans were already on the march,
lost no time; he intercepted them and bearded their king Goar
amid his bodyguard. Through an interpreter, he at first spoke
mildly; then as the king paid no heed, he upbraided him and
grasped his horse's bridle, halting the whole army. Goar, as-
tonished, paid heed and after discussion agreed to camp without
attacking the Armoricans on condition that the terms of peace
were ratified by the emperor or Aetius.

Soon after, Germanus set off for Italy to gain the emperor's
support. Crossing the Alps, he arrived at Ravenna on the feast
of Gervasius and Protasius, 19 June. Valentinian and his regent
mother Placidia were there, and Germanus won pardon for his
Armoricans. But almost at once came news of a fresh revolt,
which enraged the emperor. The Armoricans, says Constantius,
would have to pay for their rash perfidy. Germanus, however,
weakened and died. (Constantius does not make the dates of
these events clear; but, as we shall see later, we had best date the
saint's death in 445.) (15)

The striking parts of Germanus' biography are all connected
with Armorica and Britain. He was obviously a vigorous and
capable man, who remained much of a soldier under the cowl
and whose political interests did not end when he became
bishop. If, as seems probable, he had been Duke of the shore-
defences in Brittany and Normandy, he would have had connections with the British side of the Channel. The way that the
Armoricans appeal to him, fresh from his journey to Britain, is
surely significant. (16)

The year of his first visit, 429, is of interest. The partial re-
occupation of Britain was then nearing its end, or had just
ended. A worsening situation is suggested by the inroad of
Saxons and Picts. In such a situation heresies would thrive; and
a political bishop like Germanus, ready to tackle any emergency,
was the man to bring in. He could take charge where imperial
officials would be impotent or liable to meet trouble. Some sort
of government functions in Britain—there is the man of tribunician power and the primus (of a region, not a town)—but

it is indistinct. We hear of no tribal kings, unless Elafius was indeed one of them; but we may guess that the saint's dealings were with *civitates*, not tribal kingdoms.

But though the ecclesiastical sources are mute about the kings, the British tradition tells at length of the fight between Germanus and King Vortigern. Here we lack contemporary sources, but the tradition yields some interesting sidelights on the situation. Vortigern (Guorthigirn) we have met as a king in east-central Wales; but he seems to have wielded some sort of supreme power. His name means Overlord, Highlord, and may originally have been a title though now a personal name. (17) His wife seems to have been the daughter of Magnus Maximus, and we may date his reign from about 425.

The *Historia Britonnum* of Nennius, compiled round 800 from all sorts of traditional materials, depicts saint and king as violently hostile. The king has committed some heavy but undisclosed sin in relation to the saint and is accused of incest with his daughter. The saint pursues till the king is consumed by fire from heaven; then he goes home. He also struggles with a wicked tyrant Benli whose fort seems in Powys on the east borders of Wales. Benli the inhospitable is destroyed and a slave takes his throne. (18)

No historical details can be extracted from these tales, but we can still look for the originating cause. Vortigern must have been an important figure in these years and the clash with the saint must arise from some real opposed interests, however fantastically understood. Germanus obviously stands for the Roman interest, for the Catholic faith, and the imperial government; he strikes down heresy because it breaks both the faith's unity and the ideological cement of the imperial State. The *Vita* brings out his duality by making him both propounder of the one true faith and the bold general who demoralises the barbarians. The rallying faithful are those still looking to Rome, to emperor and pope—or who at least want to conserve as much as possible of the old governmental methods for their own benefit. These are the men of the *civitates*, landlords who, while seeking to draw rents and exactions from the peasants, are organised in the *civitas* in forms borrowed from the imperial days.

On the other hand there are the tribal kingdoms. They, too, in their own way draw on the Roman past, but have a new national sense (even if we must in the context of our period always modify *national* with the term *tribal*). They belong mainly to the highlands, but in the disintegrated situation may have been extending their power into the lowlands. How far Vortigern had asserted himself as a sort of supreme king in 429, it is hard to say; but by 441–2 he seems certainly to have a high prestige and wide powers.

Constantius in his 429 narrative defines the Pelagians as richly dressed, surrounded with followers. They are no mere scholars or poor monks. For the heresy to have become such a danger as it was declared in 429, it must have had strong protection; and it is tempting to suggest that Vortigern, no doubt with others, was backing the native heresy against the Roman-minded orthodoxy of the towns. (19)

Another reason for thinking that strong forces were at work to baffle Germanus is the fact that he does not seem to have had any lasting effect on British Christianity. (20) True, Pelagianism in its direct form also soon ceases to dominate the scene; but that was because of a complex of social and political forces, not because of theological argument. Efforts have been made to argue that Germanus went west as well as east in Britain, and even that he took the western route. But all that is sheer guesswork. The dedications in Powys to Garmon are not his. (21)

We see how thoroughly Germanus represented the Roman school of thought when we consider his biography. Constantius had a definite aim in writing it.

The evidence of the *Life* seems to me to suggest that the reputation of St. Germanus was deliberately exploited in Gaul for the following reasons. First of all the Pelagian question was all important. We have a large body of information relating to the controversy in the south, but little for northern Gaul. The *Life* by Constantius is perhaps the most important contribution to the literature relating to the subject for the north.

In the second place it must have been felt desirable to create a new popular saint to rival the cult of St. Martin in order to exalt the metropolitan see of Lyon and check the growing prestige of Tours. Finally, by creating a saint who belonged to the local aristocracy,

Constantius was ranging himself on the side of pope Celestine and those Gaulish bishops who sought to check the increasing tendency to elect monastic bishops—peregrini of no particular rank or local connection—to fill the sees of Gaul as they became vacant. (22)

In short, the stress on Germanus was to be at the expense of the tendencies embodied in Martin. We are at a further stage of the cleaning-up process met in the career of Victricius. Pope Celestine had stated in a famous letter to the bishops of Narbonne and Vienne, dated 26 July, 428, his view of the need for the churches of Gaul to fall into line with the Roman usages:

It is not a matter of surprise that those who have not grown up in the church act contrary to the usages of the church and that, coming from other customs, they have carried their own traditional ways into our church. Clad in a pallium and girdled round the loins, they consider they will be fulfilling the letter rather than the spirit of the Scriptures. . . .

Such a course may be taken perhaps as a result of custom rather than reason by men inhabiting remote areas and passing their lives far from their fellow-men. But why should they dress like this in the churches of Gaul, changing the usage of so many years, of such great prelates, for another habit? (23)

Note the dates. This call for uniformity was made in July 428. Next year Germanus went over to Britain at the pope's command. The Letter and the journey were part of the same programme.

It is instructive, too, to find that Nennius, in whose pages we meet the tales of the conflicts between Germanus and Vortigern, was, like Constantius, a propagandist of the Roman discipline. He wrote about 800 at the request of Elvodug, bishop of Bangor, who finally effected the belated union of the Churches of North Wales with the Anglo-Roman Church, at least as to Easter observances. Elvodug was the first Welsh bishop to be styled Archbishop of North Wales in the Welsh annals (year 809). It was natural, then, that Nennius should embody traditions that showed Germanus as the enemy of Vortigern—if we are correct in seeing in those two men the protagonists of Roman and heretical views. (24)

Vortigern, the man blamed for introducing the Saxons into

Britain, was considered to be the particular foe of the Roman dispensation, political or religious.

An event which seems to fit into the pattern we are discussing was the movement of the Votadini from north Britain to north Wales.

This movement was made under the king Cunedda. (25) At least one motive of the emigration from Manau was to drive out Irish who had settled in north-west Wales. The king's eldest son Typiaun with a part of the people was left behind, but the majority seem to have gone south.

We know little of the Irish invasion in north Wales, but no doubt it was one of the troubles that Gildas bewails in generalised language. What Nennius tells us is that the Sons of Lethan, an Irish family, established themselves in Dyfed and other regions, Gower and Kidwelly, till expelled by Cunedda and his sons from British soil. And that Cunedda (Cunedag), ancestor of king Maelgwn, who died about 548, had come with his eight sons from the north 146 years before Maelgwn's reign. "They expelled the Irish from these regions with a very huge slaughter; and they never returned to dwell there." In 380 the area was certainly under Roman control; the Irish invasion and settlement must have taken some decades at least—we cannot therefore accept an early date given for the Votadinian migration which would allow the Irish only four or five years to move in. A date at the turn of the century—during the time of Stilicho— would be barely possible; but the most likely moment is the 440s. The Irish invasion had been thorough and prolonged.

Welsh tradition which preserved a clear memory of the Irishman's huts, and which, moreover, ascribed the final expulsion of the Scots not to Cunedda himself, not even to his sons, but to his grandson, Cadwallon the Longhanded, is evidence that the Scottish [Irish] occupation was not something which lasted only half a dozen years. (26)

There is a big difference between the Christian traditions of north and south Wales. In the north were a relatively small number of Irish proto-Christians who moved along the seaways, the old trackways, and the Roman roads, leaving fewer ogams. There was nothing like the wealth of dedications centred on the family of Brychan Brycheiniog and their associates Brynach and Peulin in the south. (27) The north coastal plain faced towards Yorkshire and north England; the intruders who in north-west Wales built unenclosed hut-groups in the period between the 1st–2nd centuries B.C. and the Dark Ages arrived by sea from the north. Concentric hut-circles that may be the settlements of Cunedda's people are found in much the same positions; we may assume that the new migration came by sea. (28)

Were the migrators already Christian? It is most likely that they were. There is archaeological evidence for the conversion of the Scottish Lowlands south of the Forth–Clyde line after Ninian. And a great saint-family was soon to appear in the invaded part of Wales, claiming descent from the Votadinian princes. These persons built up the Church in the north and their influence later went southward. There was a wide cleavage between the Brychan and the Cunedda families, bringing out the division between the cultural traditions of north and south. (29)

The migration of the Votadini was no random movement. It suggests some co-ordinating control of British policy; and it has been conjectured that Germanus on his second visit pressed for the migration as part of his political policy. (30) But it is hard to see how the Roman party to which he was attached could have been in a position to persuade or force a tribal king of the north to make such an important decision. It may well be, however, that the question of defending Britain against the Irish was one of the matters with which he was concerned.

We may take it that the Irish in north Wales were not yet converted. This would explain why strong measures were taken to protect north Wales, while we know of nothing commensurate done in the interests of the south, where Irish raiding and penetration had gone on for so long. In the south the settled Irish had been converted and were no longer felt to be a danger, while the pagan Irish of the north were perhaps encouraging unrest and revolt among the hill-tribes. They may also have been threatening to move eastwards, towards Chester and the Midlands. Certainly the question of large-scale defence of the island was now coming up. Gildas tells us of a Council of the rulers being summoned; and the Saxons were called in as Federates to defend the north.

But now the problems raised by the career of Germanus are widening out. In 441–2 there had been big Saxon attacks of some kind on Britain. Germanus was certainly concerned with the issues that they raised. What was to be done if Britain were to remain an orthodox Christian country? The question of Pelagianism was entangled with the question of national defence.

There was, further, the question of internal strife, the persistent revolt of the peasants, which was going on in Gaul and can hardly have slackened in Britain.

Before, then, we come to the question of the Saxon attacks in 441–2, we must further examine what was happening among the Gaulish peasantry, and what steps other than the Votadinian migration were being taken in Britain against the Irish menace.

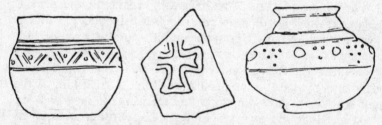

Tintagel stamped ware (*fragment*) between two pieces of Romano-Saxon ware, Abingdon and Colchester

MORE BACAUDAE

ONCE we let the rebellious peasantry out of mind, we cannot keep a truthful picture of this world. In 435–7 the Armoricans were again up in arms, under a leader named Tibatto. "Western Gaul followed Tibatto the head (*princeps*) of the revolt and withdrew from Roman society," and as a result "almost all the slaves of Gaul conspired in a Bacauda". The word used is *servitia*. From the 3rd century on it grows harder to tell the slaves from the serfs in the countryside; both tend to come together under terms like *servi* or *servitia*, which are contrasted with *ingenuus*, freeborn. *Rusticus*, countryman, and similar words cover poor *servi* and *ingenui* alike in contrast with the rich nobles or with the townsfolk, or with both. (1)

Under 437 we read: "Tibatto was captured and the other leaders (*principes*) of the sedition were partly defeated, partly slaughtered, and so the Bacaudan tumult quieted down." (2)

Aetius, held in Belgica by fighting against the Burgundians, had charged Litorius, then perhaps Master of the Soldiers, to reduce Armorica, and had lent him a section of the Huns in his service.

> Litorius after his victory in Armorica
> led his fast Hunnish horsemen against the Goths
> under the Walls of Clermont,

so declaimed Sidonius. After defeating Tibatto, the general had gone by forced marches towards Narbonne, which was near surrender to the Goths after a month's siege. As the Visigoths held the direct route through Aquitaine, he moved via Clermont. Reaching Narbonne, he loaded each horseman with two bushels of corn. They charged and scattered the Goths, then revictualled the town. (3)

In the early 'forties Aetius again feared trouble in Armorica and established north of Orléans the Alan nomads under king

Goar, who were to settle and keep a watch over the native peasantry. In 444–5, despite the Alans, the peasants rose. (4) King Goar was leading his men against them when the deputation from Armorica reached Germanus and drew him in to plead their case. Exactly whom did this deputation represent? Hardly the more resolute rebels, since we find them soon again in the field. We may conjecture that it was the landowners and perhaps some less bold farmers who wanted Germanus' intervention. They may well have feared that the fierce nomad horsemen, now settling down, would take the better parts of their lands. It seems clear that Germanus had had connections of some sort with Armorica, presumably when he was Duke; and the deputation, relying on his interest, convinced him there were better ways of dealing with the Armorican question than by massacre and devastation. It seems unlikely that a tried and capable politician like Germanus, who was near his end, would have gone all the way across the Alps to ask the government at Ravenna simply to pardon the Armoricans; he must have had some further scheme of settlement. With his experience of handling similar difficult situations in Britain, he must have decided to take his suggestions direct to the imperial court. Whatever he had in mind, it was thwarted by the peasants in Armorica refusing to abide by the truce he had extorted from Goar. (5)

By the first day of 446 the Alans had broken the peasants and restored peace and order. Merobaudes in a panegyric announces that the farmer again works on the Armorican *saltus*, taught to become somewhat milder; instead of hiding criminal loot in the woods, he sets himself to make the uncultivated fields bear crops. (6) These words suggest that there had been a lengthy period when the estates were producing nothing for the landlords, and may explain what plea the deputation made to Germanus.

In 448 there was further widespread uprising, but we do not know if the Armoricans were involved. A doctor Eudoxius, a man of acknowledged skill in his profession, was accused of complicity in Bacaudan revolts and fled to the Huns. (7) The peasants were up in force and even laid siege to Tours—in the midst of winter, for Sidonius says that the Loire was frozen. (8)

These 440s were the years when Salvian was stirred to speak out against the landlords whom he considered to be driving the people desperate. The revolts were so strong in Tarraconensis that in 441 the Master of Both Services, Flavius Asturias, had to travel to Spain to take the field there.

He slew "a multitude of the Bacaudae of Tarraconensis", we are told, but evidently he did not slay enough (from his own point of view), for his successor and son-in-law had to continue the work of "maintaining order". This was the poet Merobaudes "who in the short time of his command broke the insolence of the Bacaudae of Aracelli" in 443. But even then they were as active as ever about half-a-dozen years later, if not before. For in 449 one Basilius collected the Bacaudae of the neighbourhood, entered Turiasso, and killed the bishop Leo in his church; and in 454 the Romans set some Visigoths upon the Bacaudae of Tarraconensis.

The two places with which they are specifically associated, Turi-asso and Aracelli, lie in the uplands at the head of the Ebro valley; but *circa* 456 they are also found far away in the distant north-west of the peninsula in the neighbourhood of Bracara, where they were sufficiently active to find a mention in our meagre chronicles. Bearing in mind how scanty are our authorities for fifth-century history and how reluctant they are to record the struggles of the oppressed classes, we need have little doubt that Spain and Gaul swarmed with peasants in open revolt as Western Imperial history drew towards its close. (9)

In the tactics of planting the Alans round Orléans, the policy which we inferred for the settlement of the Visigoths south of the Loire was openly avowed. Another group of Alans were settled in *agri deserti* round Valence in 440. (10)

Similarly, in 443 Aetius called Burgundians from Upper Germany and settled them in Savoy. Three years later, with the agreement of the Visigoths, they expanded and divided the land with the Gaulish senators in the area. A tradition ran that the Romans of the provinces of Lugdunensis invited them in. (Further expansions were made under king Gundobad, *c.* 480–516; then in 534 the kingdom was destroyed.) (11)

In these settlements the treasury lost. The Visigoths seem not to have been subject to imperial taxes, though how things were arranged with the Burgundians is not clear. The barbarians were settled under the system of *hospitalitas*, whereby the *hospes* got two-thirds of the arable ground on a Roman estate, one-half of pasture, woodland, and so on. (12) The Alans, till attacked by the Huns about 370, were pastoral nomads beyond the Don, unaccustomed to agriculture; we saw how about 444 they were riding off in war-array. The more civilised German settlers, however, would have quickly found their place on the land.

Savoy was a strategic area, holding the key to some of the main Alpine passes. Why hand over such an area to a barbarian people? Aetius was an extremely astute politician as well as an excellent general. If he had wanted to block out the Alemanni, who seem by 406 to have reached north Switzerland, he could have settled the Burgundians on the Swiss sector of the road linking Lyon with the Danube. We can take it that social and economic considerations, rather than plain strategic ones, governed his action.

Savoy had presumably been drawn into the general Bacaudic movement of 435. In 408 there were large forces of Bacaudae in the Alps, who forced a powerful body of troops under a renegade Visigoth to give up the booty taken in Gaul. (The troops had been besieging Valence where in 440 Aetius settled Alans: they were moving back into Italy along the very line that these later Alans were set to guard.) We hear nothing of the Bacaudan mountaineers ever being put down; and as conditions had kept on deteriorating, we may assume they were still fiercely at large.

There also seem to have been independence movements, which may well have had a Bacaudic character, in Vindelicia and in Noricum, Aetius was obliged to undertake campaigns in both these areas in or about the year 430. Is it credible that with Bacaudic movements west of Savoy and with what may have been Bacaudic movements east of it, Savoy, which had had its own Bacaudae in 408, remained unaffected?

If, then, we try to give the reasons for the settlement of Sambida's Alans at Valence in 440 and of the Burgundians in Savoy three years later, our safest course would seem to be to suppose that the description of Gaul in general as given by Salvian in 440–1 was true also of Savoy: and that Aetius' purpose was to protect the Rhône valley and Savoy itself and the Alpine passes against attacks of rebellious peasants and shepherds in the Alpine region. (13)

The land taken was that of the great Gallo-Roman senators, not that of the humbler curials. The smaller landowners indeed seem free from the requisitions. A man with twenty-five Roman acres could qualify as curial, and many curials had estates of this size; if they gave up two-thirds arable, etcetera, they would have been beggared. And what would a Burgundian want with such a morsel of land? (The Burgundians divided a property among the sons.) There must indeed have been very strong reasons to make senators gladly acquiesce in the substantial loss of land. The magnates must have been afraid of the peasants taking everything—a fear no doubt accentuated in Savoy by the possibility also of Alemannic attack. The ever-present danger of the peasants was something far worse than the danger of passing barbarian attacks.

The large landlord's personal attitude to the Burgundians is given in some lines written by Sidonius to a senator Catullinus:

> How, even if I owned the craft,
> could I compose a Venus Song,
> stuck here amid the long-haired throng
> with German talk that sends me daft,
> praising wry-faced the things they sing,
> these gluttonous barbarians
> with rancid butter in their hair?
> What is then that verses bans?
> Her sixfoot lines the Muse puts by,
> defeated by their barbarous thrumming
> and blencht at patrons sevenfoot high.
> Happy your nose I must declare,
> your eyes and ears, so far withdrawn
> from garlic breath and onion reek
> belched from ten breakfasts in the morning.
> You're not hemmed in before the dawn
> (like an old grandpa or foster-father)
> with hordes of giants rowdily come . . . (14)

Certainly not the guests that would be chosen except out of sheer necessity.

These years of drastic reorganisation and settlement in Gaul, we must remember, were those of Germanus' second visit to Britain, when the Votadini seem to have moved and the fatal step was soon to be taken of inviting in Saxons as Federates. The picture of Britain makes sense when we see it, with all its variations, as part of the wider range of dislocations and adaptations. (15)

The Armoric question, we may note, was like the British, complicated by sea-attacks. (16) In 455 Aetius was assassinated by his master Valentinian, who was himself in turn assassinated. With the masterful Aetius gone, the situation in Gaul grew acute. All the barbarians were agitated. The Franks occupied Germania I and Belgica II, the Alemanni extended their domain over the left bank of the Rhine, the Visigoths were threatening, and the Saxons increased their attacks from the sea on the Armorican March. Indeed, from early in the century the Saxons had been established in the Boulonnais and the mouth of the Loire. In 463 they assaulted Angers.

A letter of Sidonius, dated about 472, shows brigands at work in the Auvergne. The name now given them is Germanic, *Vargi*; in Old Icelandic *vargr* means wolf and is a technical term for outlaw. They had stolen a woman travelling on the roads and sold her in open market. Sidonius' letter is addressed to the Lupus who went with Germanus to Britain in 429. (17)

Mailed soldier and imperial protectores (MSS. and Kresch disc)

ST. PATRICK

WE now approach another matter closely bound up with the complex of events we have been unravelling. Prosper, in a treatise, after mentioning the banishment by pope Celestine of Coelestius, Pelagius' follower, goes on:

Nor was he less persistent in freeing the Britains from the same disease as certain men, Enemies of Grace, had taken possession of the land of their birth; and he drove them from their lair of Ocean and ordained a bishop for the Irish, so that while he took zealous steps to keep the Roman island Catholic he also made the barbarian island Christian. (1)

Enemies of Grace was the orthodox term for the Pelagians. And we may note that Prosper still looks on Britain as a Roman island without feeling any need for qualification. In his *Chronicle*, where he tells us that Celestine sent Germanus to Britain in 429, under 431 he adds: "Palladius, ordained by pope Celestine, is sent as the first bishop to the Irish who believe in Christ." The Palladius can hardly be other than the man of the same name whom he mentions in 429 as advising the pope to send Germanus. (2) Palladius was someone specially interested in British affairs.

Prosper clearly considered Palladius as successful in converting the Irish. His *Chronicle* also suggests strongly that there were already many Christians in Ireland. Patrick in his *Confessio* conveys the same impression. He says that he journeyed to outlying regions "where no one had ever come to baptise or ordain clergy or confirm the people"; and thus infers that in less remote areas the creed had made some progress. In fact he seems to have worked only in the north and west of Ireland, as the records show, together with his choice of Armagh as the seat of his ecclesiastical jurisdiction. (3)

It would indeed have been surprising if the close relations between south Ireland and south Wales had not led to a certain amount of conversions among the Irish in both areas. And there were direct contacts between Ireland and Gaul. As early as about 350 there seems to have been an Irish bishop of Toul, Mansuetus. (4) Michomerus, an Irishman, is cited in the appendix to the metrical of life of Germanus by Heiric as a disciple of the saint; he lived at Auxerre about 430 and the Irish form of his name was probably Míchomairle. Corcodemus, who is brought into the *Life of Germanus* by Constantius, was probably an Irishman. (5)

In later times efforts were made to take Patrick to Rome or at least to the Auxerre of Germanus, in order to tie him up with the Roman system. There is no reference of any kind to such journey in the *Confessio*; but in one of *The Sayings of Patrick* (in *The Book of Armagh*) the saint is made to state: "I had the fear of God as the guide of my journey through Gaul and Italy, and moreover in the islands which are in the Tyrrhene Sea." (6) Tirechan declares that he was seven years wandering and spent thirty years in one of the Islands called Aralanensis—which is taken to be the famous monastery of Lérins off Marseilles. Muirchu, however, knows nothing of Aralanensis or the Tyrrhene Sea. He says that Patrick went off with the intention of visiting Rome but stopped with Germanus at Auxerre—ignorant that Germanus was an unconverted young noble at the time. Patrick remained in Auxerre thirty or forty years till a man Victoricus, who in Ireland had foretold all things and had often since visited him in dreams, announced that the time was come to return to Ireland. So Germanus, who knew of Palladius' mission, sent Patrick away. But as the latter was travelling, he heard of Palladius' death, turned aside, and was made bishop by the chief bishop of the neighbourhood, Amathorex; then he went on to Ireland. (7)

Amathorex is Amator, the bishop of Auxerre who conse-crated Germanus, and his introduction is the last touch needed to complete the confusion of Muirchu's narrative, which seeks at all costs to harmonise the facts of Palladius' mission with the legends about Patrick in Gaul. It is much more in the key of the *Confessio* to believe that Patrick was consecrated in Britain by some obscure local bishop or bishops and "more in accordance with contemporary practice". (8)

But what happened to Palladius? Prosper, we noted, suggests that his mission succeeded; but in the later form of the Patrick legend he scarcely begins his work before he dies. Muirchu says that Germanus knew of his mission and therefore sent a priest with Patrick because Patrick was not ordained "to pontifical rank". Why Germanus did not ordain Patrick is left unexplained. But

when tidings came of the death of St. Palladius in Britain (because the disciples of Palladius, i.e. Augustinus and Benedictus and the rest, returned and told in Ebmoria of his death) Patrick and they who were with him turned aside to a certain famous man, a chief bishop, Amathorex. . . .

Palladius himself had quite failed:

God prohibited him; because no one can receive anything from earth unless it were given to him from heaven. For neither did those wild and rough people readily receive his teaching, nor did he himself desire to spend a long time in a land not his own; but he returned to him that sent him. Returning from hence, he crossed the first sea; and continuing his journey by land, he died in the country of the Britons.

Nennius, perhaps getting his idea from Muirchu's description of "this island lying under the rigour of winter", interpolates that "God hindered him by means of various storms", and makes him die in the land of the Picts. (9)

Both Muirchu and Tirechan belonged to the party wanting to Romanise the Celtic Church; hence their efforts to link Patrick with Gaul and Germanus. (10) But it seems that in the contrasted mission of God-hindered Palladius from Rome and prospering Patrick from Britain there lies an earlier tradition of clashing purposes and ideas, which the Romanisers confuse but do not eradicate. (11) This interpretation is aided by the fact that Patrick in the *Confessio* shows himself persecuted by some opposing group of Christians in Britain, who look down upon him.

And when I was assailed by several of my elders, who came to urge my sins against my toilsome episcopate—certainly on that day I was sore thrust-at that I might fall both here and in eternity. . . .

For after thirty years had passed they found as an occasion against me a matter which I had confessed before I became a deacon. . . .

On that day when I was rejected by the aforesaid persons, during the night I saw in the night visions. There was a writing without honour against my face. And meanwhile I heard the Divine Answer speaking to me, "We have seen with wrath the face of so-and-so." I suppress the name. He did not say, "You have seen with wrath," but "We have seen with wrath," as if in that matter he linked himself with me. (12)

What lies behind the attack on him it is hard to make out; but it may well have been entangled with the controversies which, often doubtless in confused and erratic ways, were penetrating his world.

He protests that he long hesitated to make a written statement. "I feared to come under the censure of men's tongues, because I am not learned as others are who have imbibed in the most approved ways both Law and Holy Scripture." He says that his speech "is translated into a strange tongue", and he is illiterate, unlearned.

Therefore, be you filled with wonder, you that fear God, both small and great, and you lordly rhetoricians, listen and search it out. Who was it that called me up, fool as I am, from the midst of those who seem to be wise and skilled in the law and powerful in word and in everything? (13)

We feel a sharp sincerity in these words, and yet they show that Patrick too was caught inescapably in the net of the rhetoric he disdained. In a reaction against the rhetorical methods on which secular education was based, the Fathers developed the mannerism of proclaiming their rusticity. Gallus in the *Dialogues* of Sulpicius insists, "If you call me a disciple of Martin, you must also allow me the right to follow him in scorning the faldelals of speech and the ornaments of words." (14) A sermon attributed to Caesarius repudiates the élite audience and the secret satisfaction that comes from a superior training:

And therefore I humbly ask that the ears of the learned bear patiently the rustic words if only the whole flock of God may partake of spiritual food by means of speech unadorned and (if I may say so) pedestrian. (15)

Ruricius, bishop of Limoges and contemporary of Sidonius, speaks of his "inept rusticity", his "rustic style". "My rusticity I prefer to betray than to lose charity." (16) Here the claim begins to be an affectation. It merges with the idea that letter-writing between gentlemen should be negligent, thrown off; and the more painfully elaborated the letters become, the more abased the protestations. (17) "My countrified style," says Sidonius, torturing words with all available rhetorical devices. "In this style of mine there is no urban suavity, but only bump-kin rusticity." (18)

Patrick has absorbed much of the Christian learning of his day, but on lines that we would expect from a Briton struggling in his own land without any special advantages. He shows no signs of the ideas being worked out at Lérins or Auxerre; (19) and no bishop brought up in Gaul, where Celestine was attempting to bring about uniformity of Church practices, could have acquiesced in the kind of Church that looked back to his teachings in Ireland. He was akin to Martin in his simple evangelism, and it may well be that the Martin tradition, brought into south-west Wales, had much to do with the outlook he had developed. (20)

Tirechan keeps telling us that at various centres in Ireland he taught the elements, taught the alphabet. This insistence shows at least the tradition that he had started the learning of Ireland.

For one important event of his later life we luckily have the documentation of his own Letter. About 459 the soldiers of a king of Strathclyde, Coroticus (Ceredig), had made a raid in Ireland and carried off many newly-baptised converts. Patrick wrote a letter of protest the day after the raid; then he composed the extant letter, to be read in the presence of the king and his men. The most striking thing is that he considers them all as Romans:

With my own hand have I written and composed these words to be given and delivered and sent to the soldiers of Coroticus: I do not say to my Fellow-citizens or the Fellow-citizens of the holy Romans, but to those who are fellow-citizens of Demons because of their evil deeds.

A priest who had taken the first letter with a request to be handed some of the booty and the baptised captives, had been jeered at. Patrick remonstrates:

This is the custom of the Roman Gauls, they send holy and suitable men to the Franks and other heathen with many thousands of solidi to redeem baptised captives. You rather slay and sell to a foreign nation that knows not God. . . .

Freemen are put up for sale, Christians reduced to slavery, and worst of all to the most degraded, most vile and apostate Picts. (21)

(The Picts are apostates as having apparently fallen away from the conversions brought by Ninian.) Patrick denounces Coroticus and his men as rebels against Christ, "handing out baptised maidens as gifts". There is throughout an especial emphasis on the stolen women; but though there is a fine indignation against selling Christians into slavery, the saint does not rise to a condemnation of slavery itself.

The Roman *imperium* has become for Patrick the world that carries on ancient culture as embodied in the Christian Church; he sees no distinction between political and religious meanings. But his appeal to Gaulish practice shows that he is no lost backwoodsman. Within his limits he is aware of his inheritance and its implications.

But this proud claim to the Roman name is made about 459 when for some years Britain had been subjected to Saxon invasions. In the *Gallic Chronicle* for 441–2 we read that "the provinces of Britain which up to this time had been on all sides harassed by various slaughters and disasters, are brought under the dominion of the Saxons". And a later chronicler (about 511) says of the same year, "The provinces of Britain are lost to the Romans and yield to the rule of the Saxons." (22) Against these flat statements we have the fact that nowhere in the *Confessio* does Patrick show the least awareness that the life of Romanised Britain is seriously threatened. Germanus on his visit of 444–5 carries on with his business, meeting an important Briton of some kind (*primus*). Further, his biographer, about 480, describes Britain as a most prosperous island (*opulentissima*) without the qualification we would expect if he looked on the place as devastated and lost.

Clearly, however, something important happened in 441–2, which to observers in Gaul might seem at the moment to have ended Britain's independence—though to Patrick in Ireland, with connections in south Wales and Strathclyde, it might not seem so tremendous.

But before we turn to consider 441–2 in detail, it would be worth while to look at the writings of Gildas in which, dated mid-6th century, we can see how the events after Maximus were handed down in tradition. Gildas was a learned man, passionately serious, and though his aim was not directly historical, he was concerned to get the facts down as fully as possible to illustrate his moral thesis. (23)

Thickets of tyrants, he says, had kept on growing up and bursting into a vast forest. "The land kept the Roman name, but not the morals and law." Maximus crossed to Gaul, a man of cunning rather than valour. As a result, Britain lacked soldiers, vigorous youth, and even rulers ("cruel though they were"). So for the first time the island was trampled by two foreign peoples of extreme cruelty, Irish from the north-west and Picts from the north, "and for many she lay stunned and groaning". She sent an embassy with letters to Rome, vowing submission in return for aid. A legion was sent, which drove the enemy over the borders. The inhabitants were then bidden to build a wall from sea to sea, using turf not stone, and so the wall proved of no use to a populace "lacking reason and a leader". The legion went home and the wolves of the enemy rushed over the frontiers, "carried across by wings of oars, rowers' arms, sails bellying in a fair wind. They slay everything and cut down all met like a ripe crop, trample, pass through." Again suppliant messengers were sent to Rome and again help came. The Romans now urged the Britons not to lie at the mercy of marauders; they must learn how to fight and preserve "their land, property, wives, children, and what is still greater, their liberty and life". Another wall was built, now of stone, "by public and private contributions", in the "accustomed method of structure, in a straight line, from sea to sea, between cities which had maybe been situated out of fear of the foe; they give bold advice to the terrified people and leave patterns for the manufacture of arms". They also placed towers at intervals along the south coast where ships came in. "Then they bid the Britons farewell, like men meaning no return."

Gildas has telescoped events widely separated in time; he

huddles them all in the last few years of the occupation. And he continues with a picture of desolation brought about by Picts and Irish, in which elements from the immediate post-Roman period are mixed with memories of other sufferings and the result enlarged to cover the whole of the country:

As they were on their way home, the dreadful hordes of Irish and Pict eagerly emerged from the currachs (*curuci*) in which they had been carried over the sea valley, as when Titan is on high and heat waxes, dark swarms of worms come wriggling from the narrow crevices of their holes. Differing to some extent in manners, but alike in their thirst for blood, also in covering up their villainous faces with hair rather than their indecent parts with decent clothes: these, having learned of our aiders' departure and their refusal to come back, grew more assured than ever and seized the whole north region of the land as far as the Wall to the loss of the inhabitants.

Against them was stationed on the height of the stronghold a force slothful for battle, unhandy for flight, incapable with trembling bosoms, which languished day and night in its stupid watch. Meanwhile the barbed arms of the naked men are still at work, by which the miserable citizens are dragged from the walls and dashed to the ground. This penalty of untimely death was a benefit to those cut off with such a demise, a quick end saving them from the unhappy tortures menacing brother and close relations.

What more? They abandon their cities and tall walls and again there are flights of citizens, again yet more desperate dispersions, again pursuings by enemies, again yet crueller slaughters. And as the lambs by butchers, the pitiable citizens are torn asunder by the enemy so that their lives might be compared with that of wild beasts.

For they even began restraining one another by brigandage of the small means of subsistence for meagre living which the wretched citizens owned. Disasters from without were worsened by inner tumults (*motus*) as the whole region was being emptied of every sort of food-supply, omitting the relief that came from the craft of hunting. (24)

The last sentences can only refer to Bacaudan risings.

THE SAXON ADVENT

SO far our picture has been one of the breakdown of Roman administration, with rulers from the *civitates* or the tribal areas filling the place of that administration, a movement towards a supreme kingship, a tumult of religious ideas with an expansion of evangelist activities. A man like Patrick was clearly dominated by a single-minded religious zeal; but to the more politically-minded prelates of Gaul, such as Germanus or Sidonius, the problem of converting the barbarians and of maintaining a uniform Roman cult was seen also as a problem of preserving as much as possible of classical culture and imperial organisation. Sidonius, writing to bishop Basilius of Aix about 472–3, depicts the collapse of the Church in the Gothic area and makes an appeal:

Do what you can, as far as there is amity and royal assent, to gain for our bishops the right of ordination, so that we may hold the people of Gaul, who are enclosed in the Gothic boundaries, by bond of faith if not by bond of law. (1)

The first visit of Germanus was connected with the dislocations, political and spiritual, following the final Roman withdrawal. The collapse of imperial forms led to the drive by the new centralised ecclesiastical system to control the situation. Then about 444 came the second visit, straight after violent and sustained attacks by the Saxons, which must again have produced considerable derangement of all kinds; on the Gaulish analogy it would certainly have created new unrests among the peasantry of the sort with which Germanus became entangled immediately on his return to Gaul and which sent him on his last journey, to Rome.

First let us look at the account by Gildas of what happened after the irruptions by the Picts and the misery and civil conflicts that they brought about. He again seems to have packed far too much into a few years, lacking any secure basis of chronology; but that one way or another what he describes did happen we need not doubt. He declares that as a result of the sad state of the country the British appealed to Agitius in his third consulship: he must here mean the great magnate Aetius of Gaul:

The miserable remnant sent a Letter to Agitius, a man of high Roman power, speaking as follows: To Agitius in his third Consulship the Groans of the Britons. And after some remarks they complain: The barbarians drive us into the sea, the sea drives us into the barbarians; between these two kinds of death we are cut down or drowned. (2)

In desperation the people, carrying on guerilla warfare from the hills and forests, inflicted a heavy slaughter on the enemy (still the Irish and Picts) who had been pillaging for years. "Their trust was not in Man but in God." So the enemy withdrew, "but our citizens did not withdraw from their sins. For it was the unchanging way of our people, as it still is to this day, to be weak in returning the missiles of the foe, but strong in sustaining civil strife (*civica bella*) and the burdens of sins". The Irish, he says, now went home, but the Picts began settling for the first time "in the furthermost part of the island". (3)

Now, too, began an age of prosperity such that "no age afterwards remembered the possession of such abundance". Luxury grew, and with it "hatred of truth together with those who defend it, love of falsehood together with its fabricators, undertaking evil for good, respect for wickedness rather than for kindness, desire for darkness instead of the sun, the welcoming of Satan as an Angel of Light".

In such a writer these comments can only refer to an expansion of heresy; the reference must be to the Pelagianism that Germanus came twice to extirpate. The placing of the epoch of prosperity at this point, after the Appeal to Aetius, gives it an impossibly short span. We may infer that, in the tales which Gildas had heard, a great period of abundance followed a successful defeat of the Picts and Irish, and that he has got his pattern confused. But we must take his account as a highly valuable and authentic picture of the way in which the Britons of his period looked back on the preceding two hundred years; the essential experiences are there, and a general structure with its resemblances to the historical facts, but with the proportions emotionally elaborated and following no clear chronological system. (4)

Gildas goes on to say that cruel kings emerged, who were soon put to death by the men who had anointed them, "without any inquiry as to truth, because others more cruel had been chosen". Leaders who were of a milder disposition and "more attached to the truth" were attacked by all. Not only the laity, not only the men of the world, but also the pastors and their flocks were confused "by the swelling of animosities, the clashings of contention, the rapacious talons of envy, the blurred judgments of good and evil". Then rumours came that the old enemies were meditating an attack which would ravage the land from end to end, and that after it they would themselves inhabit Britain. But no notice was taken of the danger till a plague arrived.

Here at last is an event to which we can attach a definite date. Hydatius states that the plague came immediately after the appearance of a comet, which is dated both by astronomical and contemporary evidence at the end of 442. We cannot estimate how fast the plague spread, but we may roughly put it in Britain at 442–3. (5)

The *Anglo-Saxon Chronicle* under 443 has an interesting entry:

In this year the Britons sent oversea to Rome and asked them for troops against the Picts, but they had none there because they were at war with Attila, king of the Huns, and then they sent to the Angles and made the same request to the princes of the Angles. (6)

We have no other account of such a call by the Britons to Rome; but it ties in both with Gildas' tradition of an Appeal and with the visit of Germanus about 444. And however we juggle with the dates it is certain that about this time, 441–3, someone in Britain called in a body of Germanic troops as Federates. In doing so, he was doing exactly what was being done in Gaul at the moment and as had been done by the Roman central government for many a long year. In 443 the Burgundians were being settled by Aetius in the Savoy and in 444–5 Germanus met the Federate Alans, on the move from their area of recent settlement against the Armoricans.

Thus Gildas describes the way in which the foreign troops were introduced. A Council was held to deliberate on the best steps for averting the ceaseless threat of invasion. All the members, including the Proud Tyrant (who presumably dominated the proceedings), were so blinded as to decide that "those wild Saxons of accursed name, hated by God and men, should be called into the island, like wolves into sheepfolds, to drive back the northern nations".

There is a difficulty here, however, that the Angles who were called in came as friends, under the control of the Britons. The *Chronicle* gives no suggestion that the invitation resulted in anything but the amicable agreement of the Angles to co-operate with the Britons. Yet in Gaul, according to the chronicle writer we have cited, Britain appeared as though attacked on all sides and falling to the Saxons in 441–2. Even if we take this as an exaggeration, we can hardly see the Britons as calling in Saxons or Angles after having just been badly mauled by them.

It seems best, then, to follow Gildas in the broad lines of his account—that the attackers over these years had been the Irish and the Picts, that there was a flare-up of warfare in the early 440s (with which we can link the movement of the Votadini from the north into north Wales against the Irish), and that the British leaders had plans of using the Angles for their own purposes.

Where, then, does the Appeal to Aetius fit in? This, with the plague, is the only dateable event in Gildas. It was made during Aetius' Third Consulship, i.e. between 446–7 and 450–1. The inference in Gildas is that it was an appeal against the Irish and Picts, of the sort that is mentioned in the *Chronicle* under 443. (7) But if it were made after 446, it was made well after the Federate Angles had been brought in.

We must then ask: Who sent the Appeal? Just as we asked above: Who were the Armoricans who appealed to Germanus? Aetius was the leader of the senatorial magnates in Gaul, and any group who appealed to him must have had an outlook and a social basis similar to his own. What would have been the political consequences of an intrusion of Aetius into Britain's situation, and who would have profited by such an intrusion?

The magnates, the large landlords, are the group likely to look to him; not a would-be independent king such as Vortigern. There can be no doubt that the Proud Tyrant of Gildas was Vortigern; Nennius and Bede both name him as the person mainly responsible for bringing the Saxons in. Gildas apparently loathes his memory so deeply that he cannot bear to write his name. We have conjectured that two forms of rival leadership emerged in the sub-Roman period, one based in the tribal kingship and derived from the Federate troops with whom Magnus Maximus was connected, and the other based in the *civitates*, in the magnates of the areas prospering during the late Roman period. The first group, that of the tribal kings, seems to have rapidly become the dominant power, with Vortigern its most outstanding figure. Gildas tells us that these kings or princes had a Council at which they could discuss large-scale problems; and from the later 420s this Council may well have become the ruling power, controlled by Vortigern. Such a Council was perhaps responsible for moving the Votadini under Cunedda from the north to drive the Irish out of north Wales and remove a base from which fresh invaders kept coming in.

How would the local magnates operate when the Roman army and the forces of compulsion based in it were no longer present? How would they extract taxes or rents from a restless and rebellious peasantry? They must have followed the trend of the times by collecting bodyguards of retainers to frighten the farmers and make them yield up rents in kind. In such retainers we see the beginnings of the system that Arthur was able to turn into a mobile mounted army. In the unstable situation, with raiders threatening and peasants grumbling, only the bigger landowners would be likely to survive; and we can imagine the smaller men, including such of the town curials as survived, enrolling under the banner of magnates who had built up bands capable of keeping the local peasantry in subjection. In some areas, no doubt, at times the peasants slipped away from all controls, but in the richer districts a steady effort would be made by the magnates to maintain their position in the changed circumstances. Thus their system of forced rent-payments would begin to correspond to the system of levies or dues exacted in tribal areas, but would not be quite the same. The magnates with their retainers would try to keep up the Roman tradition and would look across the Channel to their friends and fellows in Gaul, with whom communication would not be difficult.

We may then conjecture that the men who appealed to Aetius were the magnates, who opposed the supremacy of Vortigern though unable to do much to disturb it, and who looked on themselves as Romans. We find, indeed, something very like this situation suggested by the words of Nennius.

. . . after the death of Maximus the Tyrant, the rule of the Romans in Britain being finished, they lived in fear for forty years [i.e. till about 428]. Guorthigern [Vortigern] reigned in Britain, and while he was reigning he was beset with fear of the Picts and Scots, and by Roman aggression, and also by dread of Ambrosius. (8)

Note how the date of 428 fits well in with the thesis of a political and religious crisis around that time, bringing about the visit of Germanus in 429. Ambrosius seems the leader of the Roman party. Gildas calls him the Last of the Romans, and it is from his quarter that Arthur emerges as the victor over the Saxons. Note also that Nennius mentions the fear of Roman aggression. This would have a clear meaning if the Roman party were working to secure yet another return of imperial power, closely watching, as they must have done, the way that things were going in Gaul, and beginning to see in Aetius the successful politician and general who would yet break both barbarians and peasant rebels with his astute and vigorous manœuvring.

In this context, too, the picture already drawn of conflicts between Germanus and Vortigern will be found to make much more sense than it may at first have seemed to make. The visit of Germanus must have been engineered to some extent by the Roman party, and the paucity of events that Constantius has to record may well come from the fact that Germanus was able to make little headway against the now-established power of Vortigern. No doubt the situation in Britain, as much as that in Armorica, entered into the report and the plan that he set before

the government in Ravenna. It was to the secular power, not to
the papacy in Rome, that he went.

In Gaul the events of 441–3 might lead a pessimistic observer,
basing his views on stories of the discomfiture of the Roman
party and the movement of Angles into eastern England, to
decide that Britain, beset by barbarians, had come under Saxon
domination.

We may then accept the date 442–3 as that of the Saxon
Advent, if by that we mean the achievement of a decisive foot-
hold by the Saxons. What they had not been able to achieve by
raids, they gained as a gift. (9)

Our next problem is to decide where the Saxons first came and
what was the enemy they opposed. Because we know most of
the events in Kent, there has been a tendency to think of the
Federates there as the main body. Bede assigns the Advent of
the Angles to the year 449 and says that they arrived "in the
eastern part of the island". There they fought the foe coming
from the north and defeated them. Gildas gives us few geo-
graphical clues. (10)

Then there breaks out a brood of whelps from the den of the barbarous Lioness, in three keels (*cyulae*) as it is said in their language,
but in ours in warships under full sail, with omens and divinations
in which it is prophesied (by a presage held certain among them)
that they will occupy the land to which their ships' bows are turned
for 300 years; for 150 (half the time) they will often lay it waste.

And so they sailed out, and at the bidding of the Ill-omened
Tyrant they first fixed their terrible talons on the western part of the
island, like men meaning to defend the land, but more truly to
assault it.

To these the aforesaid mother, finding that things had prospered
with the first troops, sends out a more bursting gallows-crew of
accomplices and curs, which, borne on ships, join with their bastard
comrades.

Nennius, however, says plainly that they were installed under
their leaders Hengist and Horsa in the Isle of Thanet. There
they were multiplied, presumably by new arrivals, and demanded food and clothing as had been promised. The Britons
demurred at the increased numbers "and they took counsel

with their elders to break the peace". But Hengist saw that he had stupid and unarmed people to deal with, so he suggested bringing in yet more men to fight their battles. Envoys returned with sixteen keels full of picked soldiers and a lovely girl, Hengist's daughter. Then Hengist gave a banquet for Vortigern, his soldiers, and his interpreter, and Vortigern fell in love with the girl. Hengist and his elders demanded Kent as a marriage-price; and Vortigern agreed without consulting the king of Kent, Guoyrancgonus. Hengist promised Vortigern to sustain him and said that he would call on his son and his son's cousin to fight against the Scots. "So give them the regions which are in the north by the Wall." This pair were Octha and Ebissa, who sailed round the Picts, wasted the Orkneys, and held many regions . . . even to the borders of the Picts. And all the while Hengist went on bringing in more men from overseas. (11)

It is clear that this account, concentrating on Kent, gives a lopsided picture. If the Federates were wanted against Picts and Irish, they would have to go far afield from Kent.

In the north there has been found a group of English cremation urns which have been called Anglo-Frisian (that is, they are related both to the Anglo-Jutish peninsula and to the Frisian Low Countries). This group is shared by east Kent as well as east Yorkshire—not to mention East Anglia and Lincolnshire. (12) And pottery of the same kind was used domestically in Canterbury, where it is found in early post-Roman levels, within the walls. (13) In the north the remains of the Saxon pagan period cluster to a considerable extent round York.

From the Wolds it will suffice now to refer to cremation urns from Sancton and Broughton by Malton and to the dwelling site at Elmswell, near Driffield, where the Roman and Anglo-Saxon period of occupation have been found to merge into one another without any perceptible break. (14)

Cremation burials from two, perhaps three sites, have been found within a mile of York Minster. They were thus close to the old legionary fortress, set on its low ground and more or less surrounded by marsh and woodland, and are among the earliest Saxon remains in the whole of Britain. We have seen above how late the Roman defence system was functioning in

Yorkshire, and there is every reason to believe that York and Malton were held throughout the sub-Roman period. (15) The cremation-burials must represent the Saxon troops brought in to defend the north, with York as their base and the rich cornlands of the Wolds for their supplies. (16)

Early pottery similar to that of Kent and Yorkshire has been found at Ancaster, Lincoln, Caister-by-Norwich, and other places north of the Chilterns in east England, as well as in north-east Kent and at Lackford in Suffolk. The distribution is "consistent with the settlement of a screen of Teutonic mercenaries to oppose the Picts". (17)

It seems, then, that Gildas correctly described the Federates as called in to deal with the Picts in the north. However, there can be no doubt that Angles were brought into Kent as well, and that if they were not the first comers they were among the first. Our Hengist seems to be the Hengist of *The Lay of Finn* introduced into the epic of *Beowulf*, where this Jutish warrior joins in killing the king of the Frisians after making terms about the killing of his own lord. Such deeds would lead to banishment, and Nennius in fact calls both Hengist and his brother exiles. (18)

Hengist, then, we may take to be one of the peninsular Jutes, who seem culturally much like their neighbouring Angles. In Jutland of the time indeed creation had become rare: the reason seems to have been the arrival of Danes, practising inhumation, from south Sweden, and the moving-out of the Jutes who refused to become half-Danes and join the intruders. For such Jutes, Frisia was the halfway halt on the journey to Britain. Thus it appears that the leadership in the Federates in Kent was Jutish, though elsewhere Anglian; and that Frisians, too, had been drawn into the adventure. (19)

But why were Federates needed in Kent at all? Here was the last place where Picts were likely to appear in numbers—though we must recall the Pictish ogam-knife from Norfolk and the fact that a ruler with a Pictish name Natanleod is found south of the middle Thames about 500. (20) There may well have been a union of Picts and British Bacaudae in the wilder parts, which meant that pockets of marauders or brigands were liable to irrupt at any favourable moment in small raids on the farms.

The Isle of Thanet still remains an odd place for the concentration of Federates if we are thinking only of Irish and Picts as the foe. If, however, we follow Nennius and see Vortigern as worried about Roman aggression and the Roman party, we can make sense of it. The Federates were close to the ports where any landing from Gaul would be attempted, particularly close to Richborough. And in 448 Aetius was in the north of Gaul, not far from the crossing-points. This year may well have seen Vortigern's acquiescence in reinforcements for the troops of Hengist. Also, it would be useful to have the Federates in a position to overawe the peasantry of the rich southeast area. That a coup was effected against the Roman party is suggested by the tale of the "gift" of Kent being made secretly, over the head of the Kentish ruler. In such a Romanised area he would probably be a member of the Roman party; and Vortigern's marriage, if not a monkish accretion to show his sinfulness, may have indeed represented an effort by Vortigern to weld the Federates under Hengist, grown uncomfortably strong, into his system in the way that Aetius was welding Alans and Burgundians into his.

Along these lines we find in fact that the whole tangled skein of events and evidences unravels into a comprehensible system.

But Vortigern had made a bad mistake. The fierce pagan Angles and Jutes were not so easily drawn in as the far more civilised Visigoths and Burgundians in Gaul. The lure of loot and land was too strong. In 455, according to the *Chronicle* (the year of the murder of Aetius and of much movement and tension in Gaul) the Federates revolted. This date fits in so excellently with the whole situation in the West, that we may accept it. (21)

Sidonius thus depicts the confused and dangerous state, with Aetius' murder promptly followed by the murder of the emperor who had killed him, and with the *imperium* insecurely held by a noble, Petronius Maximus, who joined forces with the followers of Aetius:

> The mad eunuch murdered Aetius.
> Scarce was the diadem set on Petronius' head
> than gushed the barbarous flood, the Goth had visions
> of Rome fallen, the earth to his fury yielding . . .
> The Armorican March awaited the Saxon pirate

who thinks it a sport to plough the British sea
with hides and cleave blue waters in stitched boats.
The Frank was laying low Germania One
and Belgica Two. Bold Alemann, you drank
the Rhine from the Roman bank, on both sides swaggered,
turned citizen, and conqueror. (22)

Gildas says that the Federates complained of lack of supplies:

The barbarians, admitted into the island, demanded provisions
(*annonae*) as soldiers and as men about to undergo (as they lied)
great hardships for their good hosts. Which provisions, gathered for
a long time, closed (as the saying goes) the mouth of the dog.

They complain again of their monthly supplies not being copious,
colouring their chances deliberately, and they declare that if bounty
is not more profusely heaped on them, they will break the treaty and
waste the whole of the island. And with no delay they follow threats
with deeds.

He then bursts into one of his passionate passages describing
the devastations that the Britons by lack of foresight and by
disunion have brought on themselves:

For the fire of just vengeance, provoked by earlier crimes, was fostered from sea to sea, piled high by the sacrilegous hands of eastern
men; and so, devastating all the near cities (*civitates*) and lands (*agri*),
did not pause, once kindled, till it burned almost the whole surface
of the island and licked the western Ocean with red and ruthless
tongue. . . .

Thus were all the *coloniae* levelled with incessant battering-rams,
and the *coloni*, with the bishops of the churches, with the priests and
the people, were cut down amid gleaming swords and crackling
flames, and, grievous to see, there appeared in the midst of the
streets the bottom stones of towers with tall beam wrencht out, and
of lofty walls, sacred altars, pieces of bodies strewn with clots as of
curdled red blood, in confusion as in some sort of horrible wine-
press, and there was burial of no kind except in the ruins of houses,
or in the entrails of wild beasts and birds in the open. . . .

Some of the unhappy remnant were thus caught on the mountains
and slaughtered in heaps. Others, defeated by hunger, surrendered
and gave themselves up to be the slaves of their enemies for ever, if
they were not promptly murdered (which stood for the best service
that could be done them). Others sought regions beyond the seas,

with loud lamentation, singing instead of sea-chanties such words as these below the bellying sails: Thou hast given us like sheep appointed for eating, and among the gentiles hast thou scattered us. Others, confiding their lives, always with apprehensive mind, to rugged hills, beetling, precipitous and defended, and to thick forests and rocks of the sea, remained fearfully in their own land. (23)

Bede follows Gildas, thinning down his vehemence; but Nennius has much more to say. Vortigern's son Guorthemir, he asserts, thrice drove the rebels back into Thanet and held them there. But they called in reinforcements. Still, he fought four battles with them. (24) The first may have been on the Darenth; the second was at Aylesford, where Horsa fell; the third was by the shore of the Gallic Sea (the Channel) where the rebels were driven into the sea. The fourth Nennius omits to name, perhaps because it was a defeat. The *Chronicle* has under 457, "Hengist and Aesc fought against the Britons at a place which is called Crecganford [Crayford] and there slew four thousand men; and the Britons then forsook Kent and fled to London in great terror."

It seems, then, that from Thanet the invaders spread along the Medway valley, lopping off a neat territory with the desolate weald to the south; they thus effectively cut Britain from any easy contact with Gaul. But what happened after the conquest of east Kent is more difficult to make out. Canterbury became the capital of the conquerors.

Something of the battle mood of the invaders is shown by the cemeteries at Mitcham near Croydon and at Girton near Cambridge, where some of the warriors were interred with a head that must have been the head of a Briton they had slain in the fight. (25)

Nennius goes on to say that Guorthemir died after the victory on the coast. (26) The victory availed nothing, for uxorious Vortigern let the invaders land again. Then Hengist decided to entrap him by craft. He invited him to peace-parleys, bidding his own men to hide knives in their boots. Then, in the midst of the feast, he gave the signal-shout: "and all the three hundred elders of King Vortigern were massacred. And he alone was taken and chained. And for the redemption of his life he gave them very many regions, to wit Essex and Sussex."

In the *Chronicle* under 465 we find: "Hengist and Aesc fought against the Welsh near Wippedesfleot and there slew twelve Welsh nobles; and one of their thanes, whose name was Wipped, was slain there." And in 473 the same two leaders "captured innumerable spoils, and the Welsh fled from the English like fire". (27)

There is one more movement of the period that we must look at before the full pattern emerges. Gildas mentioned the flight of people oversea. He was thinking of the migrations to Brittany which intensified about this time, though there is reason to think that there had been for some time a drift across the Channel. Both British and Breton traditions carry the beginnings back at least to the time of Maximus. "It was certainly not due to Saxon pressure in Britain, nor to Scottic; all one can say is that it reaffirmed in a new way a certain solidarity of culture and population which always unites the sea-divided fragments of the British highland zone and tends, whenever opportunity offers, to embrace Brittany as an outlying part of the same zone." (28) But what were the special circumstances now linking the two areas?

Early in the century the peasant revolt in Britain had ignited a revolt in Armorica; there was clearly close contact as well as fellow-feeling. And we have surmised more than a chronological connection between Germanus' second visit to Britain and the deputation from Armorica which met him on his return. There seem to have been many points of contact between both the commonfolk and the landlords of Brittany and south Britain, especially the south-west.

If the migration from south-west Britain was not mainly a matter of flight from the Saxons, what was its motive? The Britons wanted "to better themselves in the devastated and vacant tracts" of Armorica? (29) That seems hardly a good enough reason until we realise that the vacancy in question was largely one of landlords. The repeated uprisings had clearly shaken the whole system of landlord-control in Armorica; and the British magnates, feeling unsure in their own land, thought it a good idea to come closer to Aetius and the remnants of central government in Gaul.

It may be suggested as at least a possibility that the exodus of British gentry to Armorica followed quickly on the failure of their appeal to Aetius in 446. Under heavy pressure from the barbarians and perhaps also, as we have ventured to suggest, from sections of their own peasantry, numbers of the British landowners along with their dependents fled to Armorica in and after 446, subjugating the dangerous peasantry of that region, and so caused the name of Bacaudae to disappear from Gallic history. (30)

We then understand why, after 450, the Armoricans play a new rôle in Gaul. From the most rebellious folk they become allies of Aetius and the imperial government. We find them fighting under Aetius against Atilla; and in 467 a British king Riothamus was active in Gaul on the government's side. He was commander of an Armorican force helping against the advance of the Visigoths and had been given the defence of Berry. Meeting Euric before Roman supports could come up, he was defeated on the Indre and took refuge among the Burgundians.

We have a letter to him from Sidonius written about 472:

The bearer of this letter, humble, obscure, so insignificant as to invite the exploitation of his harmless helplessness, moans that his slaves have been carried off, enticed by the Britons. I have no idea if his plaint is well founded; but if you decide the case with equity before the confronted antagonists, I think this wretched man can prove his charge: if indeed among keenwitted armed rowdy folk contumacious in spirit and in their force of numbers, there can be justice and a fair hearing for a lonely feeble abject rustic and penniless stranger. Farewell. (31)

Previously in Armorica slaves slipped away to join the lads of the greenwood and had to be hunted down; now the sharp-practising landlords are building up their estates by luring slaves or serf-farmers away from other areas.

And the name Armorican is giving way to *Britanni*. (32) I have translated the word as Britons, for it is the same as that which Sidonius would use for the folk of Britain; but he is certainly referring to the British migrants in Armorica. (33) The Breton kingdoms arose in the 5th century, as all traditions agree, Frankish, Breton, and British; and all evidences support the tradition. By the 6th century Gregory of Tours refers simply to Armorica as Britannia; and in the lives of the Breton Saints the area is known as Britannia Minor. (34) Of the three chief Breton kingdoms, Dumnonée in the north recalls the Dumnonii of the Severn Sea in Ptolemy, whose name survives in Britain in Devon; Cournouaille in the south-west recalls Cornwall, both names being found first in the 9th century; and Bro Weroch or Vannes in the south and south-east, traditionally derived from Weroch, the founder of the ruling dynasty, less certainly suggests Viroconium, Wroxeter. "It seems to be from the ruling family of this latter district, later known as the kingdom of Powys and Gwrtheyrnion, and of the little neighbouring kingdom of Brycheiniog (modern Brecknock) that Breton tradition derives the earliest saints of Bro Weroch."

The movement into Brittany, then, was not a haphazard flight across the sea; the rapid co-ordination of the new Breton forces with the strategy of Aetius and the central government precludes such an idea. We see in it a concerted move of the Roman party in Britain, which began, at least in its organised form, with the agreement and collaboration of Aetius. The Britons came in from the north and west to complete with the Alans from the east the encirclement and crushing of the rebellious peasantry.

Further, having dealt with the peasants, the new lords would be able to organise defence against Saxon attacks, which had been going on for some time. About 463 the Saxons besieged Angers, reappeared next year and exacted hostages; Chilperic had to take the town from them in order to recapture the "islands" they occupied. The *Vita* of St. Vivian of Saintes, who was known to Gregory of Tours, tells a tale of the Heavenly Militia manning the wall at Marsas in the Gironde against the Saxons and winning a "bloodless victory".

The considerable migration of the magnates with their bodyguards from south-west Britain must have weakened the forces of resistance to the Saxons. However, sufficient strength remained under Ambrosius and Arthur to show how easily the invaders could have been repelled if a united movement had been built up and sustained. The complaisance which Nennius stresses, of Vortigern towards the barbarians, can be best explained as deriving from the need he felt to use them against the Roman party and the restless peasantry; but in the disunited situation the Federates soon began acting independently. The magnates of Gaul, with their much more highly developed system and with more civilised tribal groups to handle, were able to dominate things long enough to bring about an integration of the settled tribes with the Gallo-Roman system of agriculture; but in Britain nothing similar occurred. The magnates could not command sufficiently Romanised forces. Some fled to Armorica; others stayed on and put up a good fight, which, led by Arthur, had powerful effects on history. But in the long run the struggle was between the redeveloped tribal kingdoms of the Celts and the rapidly developing Germanic tribal kingdoms.

Sidonius gives us a remarkable picture of the emotions of the Gaulish nobles in the year 455. The murder of Aetius and the general disorder following had broken the last spell of the central government upon their minds. Petronius Maximus had ruled for little more than two months when he was defeated by the Vandals and stoned to death by the mob at Rome; Rome fell to the Vandals. The Gallo-Roman magnates met hurriedly at Beaucaire near Arles and elected Avitus as their leader. Sidonius describes their motives:

> Lately a rich chance glittered out
> while Maximus grasped the panicked City: Gaul
> might then have shown her thews, have owned the world
> if, you as Master, she'd regained her rights,
> her lands. Aye, it's no secret who aroused
> the Armoric shore, the Belgic fields, the wraths
> of Goths. To you we yield in these fierce struggles
> the pride of place. Now supreme office calls . . .
> Why check your country's will?
> Now she commands you to command. We each
> cry out: *Be Lord, then I'll be free.* (35)

The British nobles or kings could not make such a bid now to control the empire; but they could share this strong sense of independence in a world where the central government no longer held anyone's respect or awe.

THE SAXONS

BEDE says that the Federates in Kent were Saxons, Angles, and Jutes—respectively from the north German coast between the Elbe and the Rhine, from east Schleswig (a part of which is still called Angeln), and from Jutland. Archaeological evidence makes the picture more entangled. Already, it seems, the Angles had partly merged with a wider grouping for which, after the Conquest, Anglo-Saxon becomes the obvious term. Also the Saxons had reached down as far as the Rhine and had even sent settlements on as far as the Seine and Loire. Mingled with them were various peoples: the Chauci and Frisians of the coast along which they were moving, and, besides the Angles, sections of several northern tribes—including possibly the Saxones Eucii, who may have been Bede's Jutes. (1)

The Saxons were still not profoundly affected by contacts with the Roman world. Their tribal system was in some ways breaking up, but had not reached anything like the level of movement towards a central military monarchy found among the Franks. (2) Sidonius depicts them as drowning every tenth captive as an offering to the sea. He stresses a combined canniness and tenacity. "He spoils the unguarded, from the ready recoils; watch-keepers he slights; the sleepers he fights. What he chases, he catches; what fleeing he races, he outmatches." (3)

In Kent we meet a mixture of groups, with Jutes no doubt as the leaders. The pottery and brooches might, however, be those of Angles as much as Jutes, and in west Kent or Surrey the saucer-brooches suggest Saxons. Frisians we would expect to be present, and Franks, who held the area next to the Frisians on the mainland, and who were only beginning the movement that was to change Gallia into Francia—though in the south-east the Ripuarian section were pushing into what had been Roman Rhineland. (4) These latter Franks are the ones who seem to have contributed to the ranks of the Germanic invaders in

Britain, though they are not archaeologically important in the first phases of the occupation. (5)

Kent presents several problems, which hinge on the part played by the Franks in the conquest and settlement there. The institutions which survived were largely unlike those in the rest of Saxon England. The unit of settlement was the hamlet of free peasants, the unit of cultivation the ploughland tenement. The kindred had a common right of inheritance in the system of customary tenure called Gavelkind. The kingdom itself was divided into provinces or lathes; there were ten in Kent. Each lathe had as its centre a *villa regalis*, and owned its portion of woodland or weald. (6)

Traces of the system occur in Sussex, east Surrey, and south Hampshire, suggesting a single primary settlement. (7) It is quite unlike the open-field system and the nucleated village with its self-sufficient basis. On the Continent, however, we encounter similar forms, not in Jutland or Frisia, but among the Ripuarian Franks of the Rhineland. Another detail to be found in Kent and the Frankish Rhineland is the *leude* or bloodfine for the death of a noble rated at three times that of a ceorl. Among the Saxons it is rated at six times: the free warrior has a higher status. (8)

It has been argued that in Gavelkind we meet a Celtic survival. If there were indeed British customs allied to Gavelkind in Kent, they merged with the older Rhineland survival which had played its part in building the Frankish nation. They would then have helped towards an assimilation of Britons with the invaders in Kent. (9)

It seems certain, then, that a large section of those invaders were Franks of the lower Rhine, who at this time were especially hostile to Aetius. The systematic land-seizure that went on after the first successes was carried out in Kent by Frankish custom, while in the Saxon and Anglian areas of east England the custom was that of the north or north-west Germans. But further inroads were made in west Kent and Surrey under Saxon leadership; in Sussex after 477; and later in what was to be south Wessex, where we trace both Jutes and Saxons as leaders. The degree of approximation to the Frankish custom was then determined by the numbers of Franks in the groups.

For a while in Kent the northern rite of cremation was carried on by the Jutish leaders and their Frisian associates, using Anglo-Frisian urns and putting early cruciform brooches among the grave goods.

But these burners of the dead were never more than a minority, and soon the main rite in Kent was that of burial.

In the Jutish homeland, during the second generation of the invasion, Danes from south Scandinavia were entering in larger numbers and already getting into contact with the English in East Anglia. The ruling class in Kent kept in touch with their home area and soon a Danish element was thus brought into the Kentish kingdom. The type of animal ornament which the south Scandinavians were developing about 490 was taken over and worked out in a lively way; for the square-headed brooches were also taken over from the Danes. By 520–5, however, the Frankish majority of the settlers, who had now found their roots in the soil, began strongly asserting their culture. (10)

Along the south coast, in the Isle of Wight and Hampshire, the invasion under Jutish leadership continued. South Saxons landed near Selsey Bill, according to the *Chronicle*, in 477, and are described as having by 491 mastered the coastland as far east as Pevensey where, under Aelle and his son Cissa, they stormed the fort. The Roman name of Regnum disappeared, making way for Chichester, the *ceaster* of Cissa. (11) The West Saxons traced their kings' descent from chiefs who landed near the head of Southampton Water and made their way in towards Salisbury Plain late in the 5th and early in the 6th century. (12)

Also, beyond the settlements in west Kent, a large group of invaders occupied the dry soil in the Croydon area, cut off from London by marsh and forest. They seem to have been kinsmen of the Saxons ploughing the coastlands and river valleys of Sussex, though separated by the Weald; no Saxon settlement of the pagan period has been found along the wealden section of Stane Street, and communication between Sussex and the Thames valley may have been by sea. (13)

There is a tradition of a high-king at this time, the first of seven whom Bede names. Aelle of Sussex (*c.* 477 to *c.* 514) is the man; but there can hardly have been a consolidated territory accepting his rule. He probably had an acknowledged but undefined position as the outstanding war-leader. (14)

The kingdom of Essex, of the East Saxons, grew to take in not only the county to which it gave its name, but Middlesex and most of Hertfordshire. By the 7th century it controlled London and place-names suggest a widespread pagan occupation of the coastline, which reached into the woodlands. (15) The fate of London in the period 450–600 is not at all clear; but though the city must have declined heavily, there is no reason to think of it as at any time a broken place with a few miserable squatters. When it comes up again into view, the Frisians are connected with it; and these busy traders may have been using it for many years before we sight them. Probably what happened after the first decades of shock and isolation was a slow re-development as a trading-place, with Frisians infiltrating and a British-Germanic population growing up with no allegiance to Christianity.

But besides the south-east there were two major areas of invasion—that radiating from the Fens and the river-valleys running into the Wash, and that of the river system of the Humber estuary. (16) In the Fens the newcomers passed through to the gravelled terraces and more drainable soils beyond. They moved into west Suffolk by the Lark; settled along the upper Cam; wandered up the Ouse into Bedfordshire; more north, they worked up the Nene and took in much of Northamptonshire; went by the Welland into Rutland and Leicestershire—perhaps even crossing the watershed and making for the Trent—or ventured up the Witham and the Slea towards Ancaster or the south Lincolnshire wolds. (17)

Generally, the Saxon settlements fall into the same pattern as those of the Roman period—except that the irrigation controls of the Fenlands are gone, an industrial area like that of Castor ends, and the penetration into the woodland which the Romans had begun is temporarily held up. (18) The Roman road system, however, could not but affect the movements and the choice of sites.

In the Humber area the more northerly settlements developed into the kingdom of Lindsey. (19) In Bede's day, and perhaps as early as the mid-7th century, the Humber estuary was taken as a dividing line between the southern and northern English. (20) But the developments in the north are obscure for many years and hardly concern us in this book; we can therefore turn from them to East Anglia.

Invaders had come down the Lark and elsewhere from the waters of the Wash; they also used the estuaries of the Ware, the Wensum, and the Tas, which gave safe entry through the windy shingle and swampy lagoons of the east coast. They also sailed to the low stretch between the Alde and the Orwell. (21) At least three lines of movement, from west, north, and east, can be detected in Norfolk, and two in Suffolk. East Anglia was largely cut off by fenland or wooded clay-land from the rest of England. There was only one long narrow passage of open country marked by the ancient Icknield Way. Here was the line where later Mercians and East Angles were to fight for command of Middle Anglia; here, too, was the one important route from the Fens to the Thames valley—and beyond that valley the chalk uplands that were to be Wessex.

The well-drained soil of the upper Thames was soon a point at which bands of invaders aimed. Here, near Dorchester, we noted some of the earliest Saxon remains. The focus of the area

lay, not as in later times at Oxford, but some ten miles farther south in the triangle of country which contains, in close proximity, the prehistoric hillfort of Wittenham Clumps; the Roman market-town of Dorchester, which became also the seat of the first West Saxon bishopric; the great manor of Bensington, a villa regalis of the early Saxon kings; and the later stronghold of Wallingford, the site of a tenth-century burh at a vital crossing of the Thames and the head-quarters of an important medieval honour.

This district, which has been described as the strategic centre of southern England, dominates the intersection of two of its natural lines of traffic, for it is here, between Wallingford and Goring, that the Icknield Way crosses the river route of the Thames where the latter passes between the Chiltern Hills and the Berkshire Downs. (22)

Here was the area to be most fiercely contested by Saxons and Britons, the area that Arthur won back.

There were three possible lines of approach for the Saxons: the Fenlands to the north-east, the lower Thames valley to the east, the uplands to the south. Many striking cultural similarities have been noted between the settlements on the headwaters of the Ouse and those in Oxfordshire; the distribution of saucer-brooches is particularly suggestive. However, the connection is by no means sure.

On all the cremation-sites of the upper Thames there are at least a few objects which link with the graves in Bedfordshire and Cambridgeshire; yet no settlements have been found in the intervening space of the Icknield Way. The invaders may have hurried down the Way, burying a few men by the roadside and perhaps afraid of lighting a pyre that would attract the notice of the Britons of Buckinghamshire and east Oxfordshire. For in those latter areas there seem large persisting pockets of Britons, who may have been ready to let Saxon bands through unattacked if they did not loiter. On the other hand, there are cremation-sites along the Thames that suggest the riverway as the main line of advance.

But, after all, the explanation of the evidence may lie in the fact that cremation was a fairly elaborate and skilled job, perhaps available only at definite centres. For quick disposal of a body, inhumation was the obvious way. (23)

It is thus easiest to cover all the archaeological suggestions by agreeing that migration into the upper Thames valley came by both the Way and the riverside.

We must then imagine the Anglo-Saxons in the decades after 455 swarming in all along the east coast, moving up the accessible rivers and settling on attractive soils. In the process many Britons must have been killed or enslaved. In the first movements the tendency no doubt would be to knock natives on the head; only as things grew more secure would there be much likelihood of using them as slaves or selling them abroad. However, we must not visualise anything like large-scale campaigns or organised occupations over wide areas with a definite policy.

Let us, then, look closer at these intruders. Their clothes were still much what we see the south Germans wearing on the column of Marcus Aurelius—a tunic or shirt to the knee, coats buckled on right shoulder, long trousers to ankle. (24) The sleeved tunic was girded at the waist; hide-bindings or metal clasps might be attached to the wrists; the breeches or leggings were close-fitting. A sort of phrygian cap was pulled over the long hair. The upper classes had decorations on cloak or tunic; red, blue, and green seem common colours.

Women wore a long gown with wide, open sleeves, or a gown covered by a short upper tunic or mantle—all of which might be in bright dyes. A hood, short or long, might be gold-embroidered. The sleeves were caught at the wrist with small clasps and girdle-hangers jangled from the belt. Fashions varied. At Sleaford in Lincolnshire the early-comers wore beads slung in festoons from shoulder to shoulder, the ends pin-fastened to the tunic. The women's workboxes of bronze were sometimes gilt; into them went bronze needles, small tweezers, or knives, threads of silk, or wool.

In the Nydam bog one of the boats has been preserved. Low amidships, it is 77 feet long by 11 feet, and clinker-built. Five planks a side: held by large iron rivets which are fixed within by washers or nuts, and tied by bast ropes to the ribs. The rowlocks for the fourteen oars a side were also tied to the gunwale, and each oar went through another rope (tied to the rowlock, which had a sloping shape). As a result, the rowers could row only in one direction; the ship was steered by a large back-paddle. And there was only scanty manœuvring power; the buoyant frame could take neither mast nor sail, and needed much ballast. Some forty persons could probably have crushed in for the chancy sea voyage.

The weapons from the same peat consist of swords that are mostly imports, barbarian-Roman from the Rhineland, and spears with shafts mainly of ash, eight to ten feet in length— the chief fighting-arm. There were also spears for throwing, and hunting spears; and long bows and arrows—the bows about five feet, with arrowheads of iron or bone; the shafts generally marked or notched as signs of ownership, so that they could be collected and claimed after a fight. For defence there were round wooden shields, which would have been covered with hide and armed with a boss; they were held in the left hand. Mailcoats and helmets were worn when obtainable from the Rhineland; but as the supply had failed in the 5th century, we must picture only a few of the warriors invading with such armour. (25)

Kingship had long been known to the Germans; but Bede says that "the Old Saxons have no king, they have many chiefs each set over his own tribe". (26) For the movement across the seas the essential thing was a war-chief with his *comitatus* or bodyguard of picked warriors. These men might have originally been the chief's hearth companions, given board and lodging with occasional largesse such as bracelets of gold and silver; after the fighting they would expect land—and so in time the close-knit tribal links of comradeship would give way to feudal networks of obligation and service.

The bond of chief and *comitatus* supplied the highest moral ideas of the tribal group in this phase of transition. Loyalty at all costs was expected; the virtues of courage, honour, fidelity-to-death were exalted in a deeply-felt and thoroughly worked-out code of the heroic life. The image that keeps coming up out of the songs is tragic, the figure of the lonely fighter in a hopeless place who goes down without a flaw of regret. A haunting loneliness is the profoundest note, as if at the heart of the fierce exultations there was a deep sense of loss, of nothing sure in a shifting world.

As in all breaking-up tribal groups, there were kindred systems of varying scope, held together by the need of every man within the kindred to feel a complete solidarity with the others against attack—to exact vengeance by blood or fine wherever the attack was made. Precise wergild calculations defined the degree of responsibility or of recompense for injuries. Such systems are always liable to breed criss-crossing feuds that can end by undermining the whole of social life; and the rise of the king and the king's law is the necessary answer. The kindred system thus, in such a phase of tribal disintegration and reorganisation, plays both a cohesive and a divisive part; and the tension between its dynamic energies and the efforts of the war-chief to develop into a stable king, with his pervading peace, becomes one of the driving forces of society. (27)

Another source of valuable tension lay in the institutions of kingship and popular assembly:

Many factors had combined to create such assemblies. Even in the smallest kingdoms the administration of the customary law cannot have waited for the occasions when, in King Aethelberht's words, "the king calls his people to him". The history of the Kentish lathes illustrates the way in which the popular assemblies of a folk had maintained its primitive interests in march and forest. From the earliest phase of permanent settlement the need must have arisen for local assemblies where, as in the later hundred courts, men might "defend" their holdings against the king's ministers seeking the king's dues. (28)

And so, despite the various forms of inequality emerging at each phase of the historical growth of the nation, the tension between the free community of equals and the system of unequal rights or powers continued to operate:

The institution of slavery was part of the earliest English law, and in view of later evidence there can be no doubt that the primitive English ceorl was usually a slave-owner. Like their descendants in every age, the English peasants of the earliest time were very sensitive to diversities of rank, and in particular to the distinction between themselves and those whose birth entitled them to a place among the retainers of the king. Through grants of rents and services once due to the king, men of this higher class had become lords of innumerable villages long before the end of the seventh century. The beginnings of a manorial economy are clearly visible in Ine's laws. Nevertheless, it is not the manor, but the community of free peasants, which forms the starting-point of English social history. (29)

In religion there was no central organisation or site, but only local enclosures where sacrifices were made. We hear later of a chief priest (in Northumbria), but he seems no head of a system. No doubt a landowner set up his own shrine, though we find pagan priests in London in the early 7th century.

Woden and Thunor were the main gods, and there were lesser figures like Frig and Tiw. Woden appears primarily as a war-god and is associated with earthworks, e.g. Wansdyke or Woden's Dyke. Thunor we know in Britain only as Thunderer. Tiw was a war-god who seems to have dimmed before Woden; Frig was a fertility goddess. But we also hear of corpse-choosing witches, Waelcyrian, and giants, Eotenas. A goddess Rheda was connected with March; Eostra of April (reappearing in the Christian calendar as Easter) seems akin to the Greek Eos of Dawn. In midwinter was the Mothernight, which reveals the cult of the Mothers. The folk told tales of Weland the Smith, of Sceaf the sheafchild come miraculously in a ship, of Wyrd the Fate, of elves, nightmares, dragons, and sea monsters (Nicors). (30)

The Saxon farmer had no use for towns; he wanted land. Ammianus remarks on the reluctance of German tribes to settle inside the walls of the captured Rhineland towns. (31)

The lord needed a hall where he could hold feasts and accommodate his retainers. Round such a hall would be a timber enclosure. The first Saxon village in Britain to be found was that of Sutton Courtenay in 1921. Close to the Thames, the huts were set in straight rows with some attempt at a rough plan. Ground-plots were irregular, though mainly rectangular; the largest was some 16 by 11½ feet. The rule was one small chamber for living, eating, and sleeping in; but one hut had three rooms—fragments of the same cooking-pot found in all three demonstrating that they were being used at the same time. (32) From post-holes we may reconstruct a pair of gable-posts supporting a horizontal roof-ridge about 11 feet high. The walls were of rammed earth, or mud and straw; there were no signs of wattle and daub.

The folk lived amid accumulating débris, but the huts were snug in their way, with well-sunken foundations and with the eaves of the penthouse-roof almost reaching the ground. Folding doors of wood with stone stops and locks were known, and windows or shutters. Braziers were possibly used with charcoal to supplement the hearth-fire.

The food included venison, pork, mutton, and beef. The marrow was extracted from the long bones of the ox, and hand-made pots were used for cooking and serving food. In one hut was a large collection of rings of baked clay (that had various uses as fishnet-sinkers, pot-rests in or by the fire, loom-weights to hold the warp-threads taut); here they were associated with the post-holes of an upright loom and the stone seat of the weaver who had worn holes in the gravel as she bent to her work. (33)

These, then, were the hard-living folk who had challenged the Britons for the right to occupy Britain.

We have seen through Sidonius' eyes how disagreeable the

Romanised gentry in Gaul found the barbarians, even when allies. We can read in the rage of Gildas how much more monstrous seemed the pagan bands that ravaged Britain.

> Amid Gothic hails, *scap jah matjan jah drighan*,
> what worthy verse can sound when such cries thicken. (34)

So sang a poet on the Continent; the Gothic he cites seems to mean: "Hail, provide us with meat and drink!" But even Sidonius had his moments of sympathy. He says of the Franks that death may overcome them, but not fear; "their courage almost outlives their lives". (35) And he gives us a little vignette of a marriage party broken up at the battle of Vicus Helena:

> There, by the river, on the slopes, it chanced
> wild songs were echoing from Frankish dance-rings,
> a blond bridegroom was wedding a blonde bride.

Marjorian, posted at the bridge, charged in:

> The dancers he scattered. On his helmet clanged
> blow after blow; his scaled coat turned aside
> the thrusting spears, until the foe at last
> turned backs and fled. There in the waggons were cast
> redly the sprawled adornments of the wedding:
> captured salvers and viands spreading, dropped,
> and wreathed servants with winebowls on oiled topknots.

After Auvergne was ceded to the Goths, the poet was imprisoned for some time near Carcassone; and the worst memory of his cell was the noise outside his window at night of two old Gothic women: "more brawling, boozy and nauseous creatures we shall never see again." (36)

But the Saxons, like the Franks, had their songs. In *Widsith*, perhaps the earliest of their minstrel chants—dated about the 7th century, but with much earlier memories in it—we hear the tumults of the epoch of wanderings and endless battles. Amid its catalogue it gives us a glimpse of a king Offa who ruled in Angel before the invasions began—who won his kingdom while a boy and drew the boundaries between his people and the Myrgingas at the river Eilder. "No man of the same age achieved greater deeds of valour. . . ."

Thus I travelled through many foreign lands, through this wide world; good and evil I suffered there, cut off from kinsmen, far from those of my blood; I served far and wide.

Wherefore I may sing and utter a measure; recite before company in the mead hall how the noble ones were liberal to me in their generosity. I was with the Huns and with the glorious Goths, with Swedes and with Geats and with South-Danes. . . .

So it goes on, the endless wanderings of folk. "Full often from that band the yelling spear flew screaming against the hostile people. . . . Wudga and Hama, wanderers, had sway there over men and women by twisted gold." And the minstrel roams among them, looking for the man who "performs valorous deeds until light and life fall in ruin together". (37)

(*Left*) Scot from *Book of Kells*
(*Right*) Warrior from stone in Eglwysilam churchyard,
7th–9th centuries (Nash-Williams No. 195)

HILLFORTS AND AMBROSIUS

THE walled towns were too strong to be normally taken by the Saxon if at all resolutely held; but a strategy based on a passive town-defence would obviously lead only to the collapse of the towns through starvation. In Gaul the manning of the walls might have its points in a more complicated situation, though even there it could be depressing and futile.

Inform us hastily if all these things are fact, that they may be a moment's rest in the unending watch for those whom neither a day of snow nor a night without stars drive from the walls. For though the barbarians withdraw to winter quarters, the most our men can do is to defer the heart-rooted fears that cannot be removed.

For me, shut in the half-burnt narrow space of feeble walls and terrified with the war around me, I cannot satisfy the desire I have to see you. (1)

But in Britain it was necessary to have recourse to rougher methods. In many cases the old hillforts were reconstructed. Thus, Cissbury on the South Downs, after being turned over to the plough, which produced lynchets inside and up against the backs of the ramparts, was put into condition again. Yarnbury too was reoccupied. (2) At Lydney-sanctuary the worshippers thought it best to strengthen a prehistoric earthwork. Cadbury hillfort has late pottery inside it. (3) In the north a rude fort like the castles near Hamsterley in Co. Durham seems to tell the same tale. Hidden among deep woodland and valley, it was built on a Roman plan but with stones not squared or cemented. (4)

Even more striking are the large-scale earthworks that seem to belong to the period. Bokerley Dyke has shown us that great dykes could be constructed by the Romans; but a considerable number of these obstructions are clearly Dark Age. Wansdyke is a massive rampart reaching from Inkpen near Newbury almost to the Severn. The ditch on the north side demonstrates that the structure was meant to bar out attacks from that quarter; and the excavations prove that its makers used Roman pottery and wore boots with Roman hobnails. A third dyke was now built at Bokerley.

"Scattered lengths of earthwork along the eastern slope of the Pennines play a part for the northern sector of the Highland Zone parallel to that of Wansdyke in the southern." (5) Linear earthworks covering the north and west approaches to Silchester have been proved to be post-Roman. (6) Round London also the same sort of precautions seem to have been taken by the citizens. Grim's Dyke running from Ruislip across north London to Potter's Bar may well be a Dark Age construction. (7)

Let us look back at Bokerley, where the dyke is the best attested of all these earthworks. The third structure was certainly built after 393-5; in or under the rampart have been found coins of Gratian (ten, with one in the ditch), Valentinian II (one), Maximus (one), and Honorius (two). The date is probably before 405-7. All the first dyke and most of the second were still standing after 367 (the only levelling of which we are sure is the short section where the road was restored). The new dyke, over a mile long, is on a more advanced line north-west from the junction and gives an improved tactical command of the area. It is built in the old style, revealing official engineering methods, and is perhaps part of Stilicho's reorganisation.

And for official Roman power here it was final crisis; for the road remained cut, leaving traffic, presumably, to go round past narrower check-points on the Ox Drove ridgeway. But for a while there would be little traffic. The pony-trains of the New Forest potters ceased to ply, and the highways would be ways where fools might err, but the unclean barbarian pass all too ravenously—to say nothing of the revolted peasant. The immediate crisis for the Dyke-builders, indeed, might be their combination. (8)

From Bokerley in Wiltshire we may turn west to Wansdyke, with its great length reaching from near Clevedon on to Marlborough Down and near Newbury. It, too, was built against a threat from the north or north-east, and can best be dated as around mid-5th century. It seems certainly orientated towards the Thames valley, and we may assume that it was a defensive rampart thrown up at the time when the Saxons were pouring into and along that valley and settling strongly in its upper regions.

The ramparts rise to a considerable height by the important trackway which breaches them near Wodnes beorg above the Vale of Pewsey. Traces on the edge of Savernake Forest point to the use of woodland, while isolated sections of the dyke at Ham and Buttermere closed a gap where the high chalk outcrop gives easy southward access between Savernake and the greater forested area yet more west. The superimposition on a Roman road for some twelve miles from Morgans Hill to the environs of Bath proves the post-Roman origin. (9)

Such an earthwork was not something lightly undertaken. It shows that there were still large reserves of manpower and the capacity to direct them. Whose was the strategic mind that devised and carried out the construction? who had sufficient political power to muster the men and equipment?

The two names that stand out in our confused literary evidences as wielding power in the mid-5th century are Vortigern and Ambrosius Aurelianus—the tribal king based on east-central Wales and the Last of the Romans. Probability points to Ambrosius rather than Vortigern as the builder of a great defence line protecting the Salisbury area and the further south-west region from the Saxons. Gildas names him as the leader of the successful resistance to Saxon aggressions, while neither he nor Nennius gives any hint of Vortigern having played such a rôle.

There seems no doubt that Vortigern and Ambrosius stood for different traditions, that they had different ideas of the best way of meeting the crisis come upon Britain, and that they were based on somewhat different social and economic systems.

Nennius thus recounts the end of Vortigern:

Saint Germanus used to preach to Vortigern that he should turn to his Lord and separate himself from his unlawful marriage. And he fled miserably to the region which takes its name of Guorthigirniaun, Gwrtheyrnion, from his own name, that he might there hide himself with his wives. And saint Germanus pursued after him with all the clergy of the Britons, and there he sojourned forty days and forty nights and used to pray on a rock and used to stand day and night. And again Vortigern withdrew ignominiously to the citadel of

Guorthigirn, which is in the region of the Demeti, Dyfed, by the river Teibi, Teify. And in his wonted manner saint Germanus pursued him, and fasting there with all the clergy he sojourned for his cause three days and as many nights. And on the fourth night about the hour of midnight the whole citadel fell by fire sent suddenly from heaven, the heavenly fire burning it. And Vortigern, together with all who were with him and together with his wives, perished. This is the end of Vortigern, as I have found it in the Book of the blessed Germanus. (10)

Another tradition, he adds, made the king wander from place to place, after a general revolt (of powerful and weak, slave and free, monks and laity) against his "crime", until his heart broke. Yet another tradition said that the earth swallowed him up on the night of fire. (11)

He had three sons: Guorthemir, already mentioned; Categirn; "Pascent, who reigned in the two reigns of Buelt [west of the Wye] and Guorthegirniaun after the death of his father, Ambrosius bestowing them on him, who was king among all the kings of the British nation." (12)

After discounting the myths and the animosities, we may deduce that Vortigern did fall into discredit and disaster, and that Ambrosius, the Citizen, the Last of the Romans, who had assumed the leadership of the resistance to the Saxons, became a sort of supreme king. The latter was able to map out provinces and to undertake such large works as Wansdyke. Gildas thus describes him:

After some time had gone, the relentless robbers returned home. Then, with the strengthening of God, a Remnant—to whom miserable citizens gather from various lairs on all sides as keenly as a hive of bees under threat of storm, praying him at the same time with all their heart and, as it is said, burdening the air with innumerable prayers [*Aeneid*, ix, 24] that they might not be wholly wiped out— take up arms and challenge their victors to battle under Ambrosius Aurelianus.

He was an unassuming man who alone of the Roman Race chanced to survive in the clash of such a tempest (his parents, indubitably clad in purple, having perished in it), whose offspring in our own times has greatly fallen away from the ancestral virtue.

To these men with the Lord's assent victory came.

After that the citizens were at times victors, at times the enemy, so that the Lord in his wonted way might try in this nation the Israel of today, whether it loves him or not. And so it went on to the year of the Siege of the Badonic Mount and of almost the last and not least destruction inflicted on the villains. . . . (13)

It may be significant that Gildas calls Ambrosius *dux*, not king.·

Nennius incorporates a Latin version of a tale, *cyfarwydd*, told in Wales in the 8th century, and perhaps then quite old. It narrates how Vortigern, consulting his magicians, fled to the mountains of Snowdon and sought to build a tower there, but every night the materials were taken away. The magicians told him to sprinkle the blood of a fatherless child on the site. He sent messengers all over Britain to find a boy with no father. In a part of south Wales (roughly Glamorganshire) they found boys playing ball and one boy calling the other, "Fellow without a father!" They inquired and learned that the unfathered boy's mother claimed never to have lain with man. They brought the boy to the king, where he showed himself superior to the magicians, telling them that amid the pavement was a pool, and in the pool two vases, and in the vases a tent, and in the tent two badgers. They found the badgers, who were fighting. The boy interpreted: "The tent is a figure of your kingdom. The two badgers are two dragons. The red badger is your dragon and the pool is a figure of this world. And the white dragon is of that nation which has seized nations and regions very many in Britain and almost from sea to sea will they hold it. And afterwards our nation will rise and will violently beat away the nation of the Angles across the sea." (14)

He then told Vortigern that he was Ambrosius, son of a Roman consul; and Vortigern ceded to him the site and "all the kingdoms of the western side of Britain", and himself went with his magicians to the north (perhaps of Wales).

This tale is important, not merely because it presents in a new form the clash between Vortigern and Ambrosius, but because it shows the popular hopes gathering round the latter as a prelude to their settling on Arthur. The prophetic rôle here played by Ambrosius was later taken over by Myrddin, Merlin; and after Geoffrey, about 1150, wrote his poem *Vita Merlini*, the figure of this prophet was to have a vigorous life in Welsh and English popular literature. (15)

Nennius preserves yet one tradition about Ambrosius. "From the reign of Vortigern to the discord between Guitolin and Ambrosius are twelve years, which is Guoloppum, that is, Cat Guoloph" (the battle of Guoloph). This enigmatic statement seems to mean that in the twelfth year of Ambrosius' reign, about 467, he had to fight with one Vitalin. It looks as if the Vortigern family tried to reassert itself; for Vortigern's father was Guitaul, Vitalis, and his grandfather Guitolin, Vitalinus. Anyhow, Ambrosius' supremacy was being challenged, and the conflict seems fought out at Guoloph. We should expect such a battle to be in some part of the south-east unmastered by the Saxons, or in the Severn valley where the Vortigern family still held power. Candidates are the river Wallop in Hampshire and the river Wallop in Shropshire. If the name can be interpreted as the Empty or Dry River, the Hampshire site is the more likely, as streams would dry easily in chalk country. (16)

Slight, then, though the reliable details are, we cannot doubt that there was a man named Ambrosius Aurelianus who played a highly important part in rallying the Britons after the shock of the Federates' rebellion. He was a member of one of the *civitates* of the west, Winchester or Cirencester or the like, and he brought to bear on the situation all that survived in Britain of Roman strategy and technique. The tribal kings, proved to be inadequate, acquiesced in his overlordship—though after twelve years, presumably during a lull in the war with the Saxons, his title was challenged by what must have been a large confederacy: otherwise it is hard to see why the event has come down so definitely in the almost empty chronology of the 5th century in Nennius.

ARTHUR

GILDAS does not mention Arthur; but a scrutiny of his language shows that he does not necessarily claim the victory of Badon for Ambrosius. Nennius, however, brings Arthur full into the picture:

When Hengist was dead, Octha his son passed over from the northern part of Britain to the kingdom of the Kentishmen and from him are sprung the kings of the Kentishmen.

Then it was that Arthur was wont to fight against them in those days along with the kings of the Britons, but he himself was leader of the battles (*dux bellorum*).

The first battle was at the mouth of the river which is called Glein. The second, third, fourth, and fifth on another river, which is called Dubglas and is in the region of Linnuis. The sixth on the river which is called Bassas. The seventh was a battle in the wood of Celidon, that is Cat Coin Celidon. The eighth was the battle at Castellum Guinnion, in which Arthur carried the image of saint Mary ever virgin on his shoulders, and the pagans were put to flight on that day and there was a great slaughter of them through the power of our Lord Jesus Christ, and through the power of saint Mary the virgin his mother. The ninth battle was fought at the City of the Legion. The tenth battle he fought on the shore of the river which is called Tribuit. The eleventh battle occurred on the mountain which is called Agned.

The twelfth was the battle on mount Badon, in which there fell together in one day nine hundred and sixty men in one onset of Arthur, and no one laid them low save himself alone.

And in all the battles he remained victor. (1)

Before we turn to the battles, let us see what we can make of Arthur. First, it is clear that he belongs to the same line of development as Ambrosius; the way in which Gildas tells the story is proof of that: Badon was the great triumph of the Roman party.

Arthur was *dux*; but Ambrosius had a similar title according

to Gildas and was certainly a king of kings. Arthur may have
been the same or he may have been a special sort of war-chief
who was supreme during operations in whatever part of Britain
he was carried by the war-needs. Bede calls Germanus *dux belli*,
implying a special military command. On the whole, it is best
to consider Arthur a brilliant general who won his reputation
under Ambrosius and who was entrusted with an overriding
commission during a period of pressing danger from the Saxon
invaders. He does not appear in any early genealogies.

We may take him, then, as the commander of a mobile force,
no doubt wholly or mainly of horsemen, which moved around
to meet any new threat, owning the right of entry into any
British kingdom and co-operating with local levies. He was the
direct descendant of the Roman Count of the Britains. He and
his force must indeed have been what the *civitates* asked for in
their appeal to Aetius; not gaining a mobile army from the
imperial government, they devised one themselves. Arthur, like
Ambrosius, we may consider a member of one of the western
civitates, son of some magnate family, though with less of a
purple glow.

The Roman party in Britain were certainly in contact with
Gaul and would know a good deal about the army methods and
systems of the imperial government. Though there had been
heavy setbacks, the amount of craft-skills still available in the
area that included the Cotswolds and Salisbury, Caerwent and
Bath or Cirencester, must have been large. There would be no
difficulty in turning out effective chain armour and the other
paraphernalia of the cavalry troops of the imperial army. (2)

Ambrosius or Arthur realised that if they were to check and
drive back the Saxons they needed shock troops of the most
efficient and well-armed kind. The Saxons, like most barbarian
tribes, were not capable of waging war except by means of arms
bought or looted from the Romans. We see the same weakness
exemplified in the Huns, the Avars, and later the Turks. A
decisive blow was struck against the Huns in 455–6 when
Marcian in the east of the empire addressed an enactment to the
Prefect forbidding all export of weapons to barbarians. (3)

The Roman party saw how to turn their superior culture
against the invaders. They built up a force of heavy cavalry in

chain-mail, knowing that the Saxons, with their comparatively weak armament and lack of horse, would be unable to withstand the attack of such a force. (Already, in the 4th century, the Count of the Britains had commanded six regiments of cavalry to three of infantry.)

The local militias were composed of footmen, and the highland tribes would have owned no horses capable of bearing a well-armed man into battle—while the Saxon spearmen, with little or no body armour, only later acquired from the Britons the habit of mail-shirts, and they never became horse-troops. The Franks, too, on the mainland were slow at mounting.

A great change had come about in the equipment and tactics of armies. The Franks of the 5th and 6th centuries were, among the barbarians, with the Anglo-Saxons, the last good infantry. Everywhere else the decisive arm was the heavy cavalry. . . . The power of the heavy cavalry charge proved itself so irresistible that little by little the Franks themselves had to adopt the tactics of the new army. The change was completed by the middle of the 8th century. (4)

If the more developed Franks in Gaul, right up against the imperial troops, were so slow in changing, we can be sure of a yet greater conservatism among the Anglo-Saxons, whose personal courage and hardiness were considerable but whose sense of tactics was elementary.

Arthur, then, was the leader of the Roman party, proud of Roman traditions and learning everything possible from developments inside the empire; a man with a strong tactical sense, and, to judge by his success, of equal strategic insight. He must have had a good intelligence system which enabled him to know where the invading forces were gathering dangerously, where to break their communications, drive them into a corner, and crush them.

We may now turn to the battles. Where did Nennius get his list with the suspicious legendary number of twelve? Perhaps from some *Annals*; more likely from some catalogue poem like those attributed to Taliesin on the victories of Urien and Owein, or the poem addressed to Cynan Garwyn. Or he may have had the figure twelve from some tradition, which he filled in as best he might, bringing in battles actually fought by other leaders.

The *Annals* generally gave not more than one battle a year, and if he drew on such a source he might have gathered a list stretching over much more than a dozen years. (5)

The names are oddly hard to locate; and this is a tribute to their genuineness, or at least to their antiquity. A compiler making the whole thing up would select well-known sites, as Geoffrey of Monmouth did later in his *History*.

Glein may be the Northumbrian river Glen, though the Glen happens to have no mouth: *ostium* is the Latin word, which may possibly be used for junction. The region of Linnuis may be Lindsey in Lincolnshire, though no river Douglas is known there. *Douglas*, however, Celtic for Black Water, is a common name for streams, used particularly for brown waters coming down from peat-moors; rivers once so called are found all over Britain with variously metamorphosed names—Dulas, Dowles-brook, Dalch, Dawlish, Devils brook, Divelish. Bassas may contain the word *bas*, shallow: there is an Eglwseu Bassa in a poem, identified as the Baschurch in Shropshire.

Celidon seems to refer to the north. Welsh tradition set the Wood of Celidon in or near Strathclyde, though if the name is connected with the Dicalidonae whom Ammianus mentions, the site may be yet more northerly. However, the Welsh *celli* means a wood; and a site-name embodying some cognate form of it may have been dislodged by a name famous in Welsh legend.

The eighth name seems to refer to some Roman fort, and efforts have been made to tie it up with *Vinovia*, Binchester, in Co. Durham; but they are not convincing. The City of the Legion is the one obvious site; it must be Chester. Later in 616 there was a decisive battle there, which went against the Britons; but it is strange to find the Saxons penetrating so far around 500. Still it is perhaps not impossible that a raiding band reached Chester and was there caught. There may even have been, though it seems unlikely, an attempt already to drive a wedge in, cutting the Celtic zone into two.

The tenth battle is quite obscure; and after that the manuscripts become confused, reading Agned, Bregouin, and Agned Cat Bregomion. In any event, we have no idea where the site or sites lie. It has been suggested that Badon did not occur in the original dozen and that two battles have been telescoped in order to take it in; but this seems unlikely. (6)

We come now to Badon. Many efforts have been made to identify this battle-site. Almost any place-name in the south that starts with something like *bad* and can boast a hill—for instance, Badbury Hill near Faringdon or the hill above another Badbury near Swindon—has found zealous champions. But there is no need to seek out some particularly impressive hillfort; and the place was after all most likely located near the Severn estuary or round about Bath. (7) From the description of the conflict as a siege we may surmise that the Saxons, making a desperate attempt of retaliation, managed to catch Arthur and his men in a hillfort encampment—whether it was their chief headquarters or merely the one they were using at the moment for some special purpose. However, the Britons broke out and completely destroyed the attacking force. The statement that Arthur all on his own killed 960 men, we may take to mean that this time there were no local levies involved; the fight was wholly between Arthur's horsemen and the Saxons.

There is one interesting displacement. Nennius says that at the battle of Guinnion Arthur bore an image of Mary on his shoulders. We have here a clear instance of incorrect translation from the Welsh. Nennius or some previous redactor has confused *ysgwyd* shield and *ysgwydd* shoulder, which could both have been written *iscuit* or *iscuid* in Old Welsh. It was on his shield that Arthur bore the image, not perched on his shoulder. The *Annals* transfer the episode to Badon and try to make the shoulder-burden more comprehensible: "The battle of Badon in which Arthur carried the cross of our Lord Jesus Christ for three days and three nights on his shoulders, and the Britons were victorious." (8)

The *Annals* date Badon as 516. Gildas gives a cryptic date: "And this begins the 44th year as I know with one month elapsed and it is also that of my birth." If he means that Badon occurred forty-four years before the moment when he is writing, the battle must have been fought before 503, since his work was composed before the death of one of the princes it attacks, during the plague of 547. The *Annals* date Gildas' own death as 570, so that we have little idea how many years before 503 he was born; it may have been as early as 490 or roundabouts. (9)

Bede, using a manuscript that was at least some 300 years earlier than any of ours, reads a text that interprets Badon as coming forty-four years after the Saxon Advent. And Gildas' difficult Latin has been unravelled to mean that he was 43 at the time of the battle; if the battle was 516, he would have been nearly 98 in 570. Also, various efforts have been made to amend his text, which still further perplex the matter.

It is best, then, merely to consider that Badon took place somewhere round the turn of the century. The battle itself was a definite setback to the Saxons in the upper Thames valley; it gave the Britons in the west two or three generations in which to develop their way of life. And though they failed to throw back the Saxons when a second main wave came westward, the cultural consequences of the respite were of the utmost importance. In the later 5th, and throughout the 6th century, the Celtic way, canalised most richly and powerfully in its Church, was steadily developing, enriching its resources and preparing for the time when it would conquer with the arts of peace the military conquerors of so much of the island.

We cannot hope to make out anything of the personal features of Arthur, despite the tremendous part his legend was to play in Celtic and medieval literature. His name seems to originate in the Latin gens-name Artorius, which would normally undergo aspiration in passing into Welsh. There was a Lucius Artorius Castus at one time in the Roman forces in Britain, who led an expeditionary force into Armorica in the 280s against the Bacaudae. He died in Dalmatia, and it seems unlikely that he left any descendants in Britain. (10)

There may be a connection with the Celtic *artos*, bear. A 13th-century manuscript of Nennius glosses a passage by remarking that "Arthur translated into Latin means *ursus horribilis*". This Arthur is described as "cruel from his boyhood, a horrible son, a horrible bear, an iron hammer". But all these terms no doubt derive merely from the bear-association. (11)

Apart from Nennius we have, however, the references in Welsh poems, the legends that are entangled with the poems and passages in several saints' *Lives*. Though these are of the utmost interest as revealing some of the ways in which a great heroic myth was evolved, they throw little light, if any, on the historical Arthur.

There is, however, yet one more detail in Nennius, which seems historical. Under the year 537 in the *Annals*, we find: "The action of Camlann in which Arthur and Medraut fell. And there was a pestilence in Britain and in Ireland." (12) It, would appear, then, that for more than twenty years after Badon Arthur remained alive and dominant. The Camlann battle then represents the inevitable revolt of discontented princes, with resulting anarchy. The name seems to include two common Celtic words, *camb(o)* curved and *landa* (later *lanha*) enclosure, e.g. Vindolanda, Chesterholm, which means the White Enclosure. We know of no Cambolanda, but there was a Camboglanna on the Wall, at the start of the Roman road going north to Bewcastle. The name means Curved Glen. In the Ravenna List there is a Cambroianna, which may be amended to Cambolanna, exactly corresponding to Camlann; but we do not know where it was. In its context it suggests Selkirkshire, and more doubtfully the fort of Camelon near Falkirk. (13)

Though generally the locale of Arthur's war-deeds must be sought in the regions encircling the upper Thames, there is no reason to exclude him wholly from the north. If he was a sort of battle-overlord, he might well at times have been called thither; there were roads available for his horsemen. Though, at this period, the events in the north are obscure, the Saxons must have been consolidating their hold in Yorkshire and penetrating further northwards. The earliest sure reference to Arthur, indeed, comes in the *Goddodin*, which deals with an heroic episode in the north, when the Goddodin or Menau Gudodin sallied from Edinburgh to fight the invaders of Bernicia and Deira at Catraeth, identified as Catterick. The date seems to be late 6th century. The battle ended in disaster for the Goddodin. One of their warriors is described as performing noble feats before the wall of the Caer, "though he was not Arthur".

Also there is a Welsh tale, traceable back to the 11th century, of a feud between Arthur and a chief of south Scotland called Caw. Caw was a robber giant living in Pictland, north of a

mountain Bannawg (Peaky) and was killed when making a raid
south of this mountain (clearly the range of hills from which
Bannockburn rises and which almost closes the narrow isthmus
between the Forth near Stirling and the Clyde near Dumbarton).
The tale goes that Caw was brought to life again by St. Cadog
and fathered his son Gildas in Strathclyde. (14)

It is also significant that in the late 6th and early 7th centuries
two Celtic princes appear with the previously rare name of
Arthur, one of them belonging to the dynasty of Dalriada, the
other located in south-west Wales. (15)

In Wales we find our Arthur set in the south-east as early as
the 9th century. Nennius in his *Marvels* says that in Buelt is a
heap of stones, on the stone on the top is the print of a dog's
foot. "When he hunted the boar Troynt, Cabal, who was the
dog of Arthur the Soldier, impressed his footprint on the stone
and Arthur afterwards collected a pile of stones under the stone
whereon was the footprint of his dog, and it is called Carn
Cabal. And men come and carry the stone in their hands for the
space of a day and a night, and on the morrow it is found upon
its pile." (16)

Another locality which is persistently cited by the Welsh
chwedleu and triads is that of his court at Kelli Wic in Cornwall
—probably the hillfort of Kelly at Egloshayle near Padstow. (17)
There seems little likelihood, however, that the historical Arthur
had any settled point in Cornwall, which was far to the rear of
the threatened areas. In the later 5th century, however, Cornwall must have been an area of much activity through the
migrations to Brittany and the new importance given to the
south-west sea-routes; and there is no reason why the supreme
war-chief should not visit the region.

From the 6th to the 11th century the importance of Arthur
as a national figure increased, concentrated in poem and tale.
In the Triads he is often interpolated, simply because such an
outstanding figure is felt to be needed everywhere even when it
is only a question of the Three Red Ravagers or the Three
Scurrilous Bards. (18–19)

We are not concerned here to follow in detail the legendary
developments of Arthur, but their general shape and direction
are important for us. The interest of Arthur lies both in the

historical figure which we can excavate from the shattered
fragments of his buried age, and in the great stimulus that that
figure gave to his people—in Wales, Cornwall, and Brittany—
so that out of their national aspirations, so often disappointed,
they created an heroic image which dominated large areas of
medieval culture.

Arthur became on the one hand the symbol of national
triumph and resurrection; and because many frustrations and
setbacks had to be explained, a drama of treachery and dissen-
tion had to be built round the great leader, giving him a tragic
end and making a prophecy of his return and restoration. On
the other hand, as a result of his merging with the myth-world,
Arthur became also a sort of divine figure, a culture-hero
bringing up plenty out of the underworld and wielding irresistible weapons.

For this latter development we may take the theme of the
Hunt which is already found in Nennius. In the triad of the
Three Mighty Swineherds we hear that the three swineherds of
Britain were Drystan (Tristan), Pryderi, and Koll. Drystan
minds the swine of March ap Meirchiawn while the herdsman
goes with a message to Essyllt, and Arthur tries to get a pig
from the herd, by guile or force, but fails. One of Koll's sows
is with pig, and the prophecy is made that Britain will suffer
from her litter. Arthur goes in a great chase of the sow Henwen
from Cornwall across Wales to Anglesey. Here "we get a note
of the culture-myth, for the pig dropped grains and a bee at
spots which were afterwards productive of corn and honey".(20)
In the tale *Kulwch and Olwen*, the hero has to accomplish
various tasks to win his bride. In the hunt for two magic boars
Arthur intrudes, and his dog Cabal kills one of the boars. A
highly elaborate account of the itinerary of the hunt is given,
from Ireland across south Wales till the boar is driven over the
Severn and drowned in Cornwall. The swine is an underworld
creature, an earth-rooter, and the hunt is a great fertility
sweep. (21)

Arthur becomes the Lord of the Otherworld Feast, the dis-
penser of plenty, especially associated with pigs and the cauldron for cooking them. (22) And it is this cauldron that ultimately becomes the Grail of medieval legend. (23) We can

pursue the imagery of the Feast back into Irish and Welsh myth or forwards into medieval romance; but for us here it is perhaps most relevant to point to the close relation of the myth-complex gathered about Arthur, and the cult of Nodens, Nudd, which was so strongly developed in the Severn area in the period round 400. The offerings show that the dog was extremely important at Nudd's healing shrine with its great hostel for pilgrims; and the god's name seems at root to refer to catching, bringing home from the hunt or field—with a secondary meaning of acquisition, having the usufruct of.

Whether the god was called the "snarer" or the "catcher" or the "hunter" in some sinister sense, or merely as being a lord of venery, mere etymology can hardly say. It is suggestive, however, in this connection that the most remarkable thing about Nuada was his hand, and that without his hand his power was lost. Even in the dimmed memories of Welsh legend in Llaw Ereint we hear still an echo of the ancient fame of the magic hand of Nodens the Catcher. (24)

Nuada of the Silver Hand was king of the Túatha dé Danaan of Irish legend, who seem to a large extent divine figures. In Wales his counterpart was Lludd of the Silver Hand (the ultimate origin of King Lear); and his daughter Creiddylad (Cordelia) was carried away after her betrothal to Gwythyr by Gwynn vab Nudd, who has connections with the underworld. Creiddylad seems to have had an ancient link with the eternally renewed fight of the Year, the May-battle between life and death, in which the young victor bears off the earthbride and ensures the return of flower and seed and sunlight. Both her father Lludd and Gwynn vab Nudd seem ultimately the same figure. "Certainly the normal Welsh form of Nuada-Nodens would be Nudd. The fixing of the father's name as Lludd may have owed something to alliteration with his surname" Llaw Ereint (of the Silver Hand). (25)

Nudd as a saviour-god, with his close affinities to Irish otherworld gods, and with his deep hunt associations, shows us the root in the 4th and 5th centuries of the sort of beliefs that gathered round Arthur as culture-hero carrying on the magical hunt that ensured prosperity. In the strange poem *The Spoils of Annwn* (other world), which goes back at least to about 900, Arthur and his men raid Annwn after the Cauldron:

My first utterance, it is from the cauldron that it was spoken.
By the breath of Nine Maidens it [cauldron] was kindled.
Even the chief of Annwn's cauldron, what is its nature? . . .
and before the gateway of hell lamps were burning,
And when we went with Arthur—glorious hardship—
Save seven none returned from the Fortress of Carousal . . .

Beyond the Fortress of Glass they had not seen the prowess
  of Arthur.
Three score hundred men stood on the wall.
It was difficult to converse with their sentinel.
Three shiploads of Prydwen went with Arthur;
Save seven none returned from the Fortress of Frustration. (26)

As the saviour of the people, Arthur, like Charlemagne, takes the place of Christ at the Round Table; and the dish used at the Last Supper appears as the Holy Grail—though it takes in fertility magics and fuses with pagan cauldrons in the process. Finally, Arthur takes over the sword of light, the lightning-sword. The lightning was "regarded as a flashing sword. The sword of Nuada was such that, when it was unsheathed, it was irresistible and none could escape from it. In addition to his huge spear Mac Cécht [sun-god] wielded an immense sword, from which broke forth fiery sparks which illumined the house". (27) One of its names was in Caladbolg. The Welsh counterpart is Caledvwlch, which in *Kulhwych and Olwen* is wielded by Arthur; Geoffrey of Monmouth Latinised it as Caliburnus. All the accounts of how Arthur obtained the sword imply an other-world origin. (28)

THE BACKGROUND

ARTHUR had averted the threat from the upper Thames. There are, however, signs of uninterrupted Saxon occupation there. Some groups may have accepted British overlordship—a thesis supported by certain cultural borrowings—or we may have failed with our present knowledge to note a gap in the burials. The one Saxon confession of a bad defeat is made by an omission. Under Aelle (*c.* 514) a sort of supremacy had developed. But after him there is a pause of nearly fifty years with no claimant to the position. Then comes Ceawlin of Wessex (*c.* 560–91), and thereafter is no repetition of the empty period. Significant, too, is the fact that round the time of Badon the Saxons were emigrating back in large numbers to the Continent. Frankish visitors in the East told Procopius about it. They said that Britain was held by three races, Angiloi, Frissones, and Britons, each with its own king. Each race was so fertile that it yearly sent many of its people to the land of the Franks, where they were planted in the less-populated areas. As a result, the Frank Theodebert (*c.* 534–48) had asserted a claim on Britain itself and had included Angiloi in an embassy to impress the emperor at Byzantium. (1)

The situation in Britain was now very different from that in Gaul. The Gallo-Roman magnates had made the best of a bad job and were amalgamating with the tribal nobles; the barbarians in Gaul were Christians even if many were at one time Arians; a steady fusion of cultures went on. The relatively high level of the invaders made all this possible; the Burgundians, for instance, crossed the Rhine to get jobs as carpenters. (2) And so the Church could play a rôle far beyond its powers in Britain. The town-bishops assumed the powers let fall by the secular officials and held together what was possible of the municipal system; in effect they became *defensores civitatum.*

In all the *civitates* that became episcopal seats, urban life went on and was preserved. The contrary case is none the less conclusive. Some Roman cities, partly ruined in the great invasions, had not gained a bishop. They thereby signed their death-warrants and their decadence was irresistible. (3)

In Britain there was nothing like the fortified manors or castles such as Sidonius describes at Burgus on the confluence of Garonne and Dordogne: the central point of the *regna* which Ausonius attributed to the rich Paulinus. It was a luxurious country-house and stronghold on a high rock, with granaries and stores, porticoes, baths, summer and winter apartments, spinning-room, frescoed walls depicting the history of the Jews. (4)

If we look at the genealogies in Britain we find several princes whose position put them in the 5th century and who have names like Honorius, Marcianus, Gerontius.

There is often a fork in the first half of the century; and we hear at times of more than one king in a kingdom. Hereditary possession seems accepted; most dynasties have an unbroken line from the 5th for several centuries; the lines are rarely carried further back unless descent is claimed from Maximus. (5) Under the loose supremacies there were many of these sub-kingdoms, which helped to bring about the strains and periods of anarchy at which Gildas rages.

In Ireland and in the wilder parts of Britain the form of living was mainly pastoral. Land was held by the kindred and had no connection with military tenures; in Ireland we find the king giving his men stock, not land. During the 5th century in general there must have been a steady shaking-down of social conditions to the level of the more tribal areas, under the revived kingship. In the laws of Hywel Dda of the 10th century the kindred is still vigorously functioning:

For purposes of *galanas* [value-of-a-life] payment or receipt it was limited to kin within seven degrees, for giving a woman in marriage the consulting members of the kin were confined to four degrees. In *galanas* payment and receipt the *cenedl* [kindred] may be counted upwards from the murderer and the victim through the father . . . to the great-great-great-great-grandfather. Collaterally it is counted through the first cousin . . . to the fifth cousin, who is in the same

degree of relationship to the great-great-great-great-grandfather as
the murderer or the victim. . . . In older legal practice it seems that
nine degrees of kinship entered into land claims.

We may allow for Irish influences in the 5th–6th century; but
however we analyse the process bringing out medieval Wales,
it is clear that the tribal kindreds have their tenacious roots in
the pre-Roman Celtic past.

In the 5th century we must see the tribal forms becoming
more and more dominant, though modified variously where the
magnates maintaining a Romanised tradition held power. In
the east of the island there were severe dislocations, but elsewhere there may have been comparatively peaceful conditions
for long periods. The roads were at least usable. The western
sea-routes, increasingly active, linked the coastlands from
Cornwall to Strathclyde, and Ireland, with Brittany, Bordeaux,
probably Spain.

Dark-Age sites reveal the trade-nexus. The headland of Tintagel was occupied from the 5th to the 8th century. Here no
Roman coins or pottery are found, though two of the five
Cornish milestones come from nearby. (6) We meet, however,
two kinds of fine red ware and various amphoras, all of Mediterranean origin, with exotic sherds also imported—though
whence we cannot say—and bowls or mortaria not unlike some
late Romano-British vessels in form but with a clay and a
washed surface of their own. Among the fine red ware of friable
soft clay with a dark slip, five bases of wide, flat dishes had
impressed symbols, mostly crosses. Here the outer edge was
usually concave with lines of rouletting or of slight incisions.
The other red ware was hard, without impressed designs; a
hemispherical flanged bowl alone could be restored.

Similar imported wares have turned up at four more Cornish
sites: Padstow, where St. Petroc first settled and a Celtic monastery was built; Porthmeor, where pottery of late 3rd and 4th
century has been also found, with imitations like the native
wares of Tintagel; Castle Dore, where one sherd is linked with
the early medieval palace supposed to be King Mark's (6th
century); Gwythian, with wares ranging from 400 to 1100.
Devon has examples at Bantham; Somerset at South Cadbury
in the ramparts of the hillfort (traditionally the site of Arthur's

Camelot). In Wales examples come from Dinas Powis (Glamorgan) and from Dinas Emrys (traditionally associated with Ambrosius Aurelianus). Further up the western coast, more examples come from Dunadd the capital of Dalriada (remains from 5th to 9th century); from sandhills at Elie (Fifeshire); and from the tall Mote of Mark with its wall-enclosed top in Kirkcudbrightshire (remains from 6th to 8th century). Also a piece recorded from Catterick in 1849 seems to belong to the series of stamped Christian ware. (7)

There are further four sites in Ireland that show the same kinds of imported pottery: Nendrum in Co. Down, and Garranes, Garryduff, and Ballycatteen in Co. Cork. The last-named site is a ring fortress; and so is Garranes, which is larger and perhaps earlier, with triple ramparts—the external diameter being about 350 feet. There were several gates and the place held a metal-working community—indeed, it yielded on excavation more crucibles than the whole of Ireland had previously produced. They were mainly pyramid-shaped; in some the traces of bronze were found. But a semi-spherical kind was also used, made of soft stone, for the preparing of enamel. Rods of millefiori glass as well as rods of single-coloured glass used for making millefiori were also found, and moulds for casting metal objects. Apparently the workers carried on their metal and glass work under the aegis of the king of the fort.

St. Finnebar was born here in the 6th century to one of the metal-workers. (8)

There are many foreign parallels for the stamped ware, which stretches from the early 5th to the second quarter of the 6th century and perhaps later. Nendrum and Tintagel were both Celtic monasteries, and we may date them from mid-5th century—a date which will also fit the finds from secular sites like Garranes and Dunadd. The wares from Tintagel and Garranes may come from Egypt—though similar wares are very common also at Carthage. Examples have been found near Marseilles and in Nantes near the mouth of the Loire, suggesting the route by which the wares came to Britain. (9)

Glass also gives us some indications of the trade of the period. The Cologne factories had ceased producing by the early 5th century, but some parts of the Rhineland and north Gaul continued producing in the early Dark Ages—perhaps even as far west as the Somme valley. The workers were very mobile, as the makers of "forest-glass" have always been, and some may have crossed into Kent. The bulk of Saxon glasses thus came across from the Continent along the old routes which, however, were now closed to the Britons. (10)

At Tintagel some pieces of glass seem from Egypt, though one fragment is of Western make. Others of the pottery sites already mentioned show glass of Western make; and the Mote of Mark was rich in Merovingian types (6th to early 8th century). Glass of the same origin has been found on the Irish Dark-Age sites. (11)

In the west of Britain and in Ireland, then, the 5th century saw no break in trade relations. (12) The relative volume o trade to the whole island of Britain must have shrunk con siderably, but for the remoter western regions it had probabl increased. Certainly the connections there with Brittany an south Gaul, mercantile and ecclesiastical, were extremely vigor ous, and the Visigothic churches of Aquitaine and Spain have left marks on Celtic Christianity. (13)

In the *Life* of St. Philibert, abbot of Noirmoutier, we hear of *Brittones nautici* who came to sell a young bull in his monastery; another time a ship with a crew of Irish, full of merchandise, arrived to sell shoes and clothes to the monks. (14) This is later 7th century, but there is no reason to think the connections ever ceased. Certainly in the 6th century they were busy.

The Atlantic and Channel ports kept up a certain activity. A list has been drawn up of the products that were made the object of exchanges and were transported in boats on the Atlantic routes: salt of Saintonge and of Noirmoutier; copper, unworked wool that Ireland exported in return for Gaulish wine; tin was also brought from Cornwall and copper from England. Coasting trade seems carried on between Bordeaux and Rouen in the Merovingian epoch. (15)

The *Life* of St. Ciaran of Cluain, who died about 550, tells of harvest festivals when merchants from Gaul came along to fill the great vessel of the monastery with wine. At Whithorn the Peter Stone witnesses that relics were carried from Rome by a member of that northern community; and St. Adamnan (who died about 704) took down the story of Palestinian holy places from a pilgrim Ataulf in Iona. (16)

Most interesting of all is the story in the *Life* of Humble John the Almsgiver of Alexandria, which was drawn up by contemporaries, Sophronios and Leontios. John had been appointed to the patriarchate in the first decade of the 7th century, when his Church had its own corn-ships. Once in a bad Adriatic storm the fleet had to jettison a cargo of silver, water-proof garments, etc. On arriving home, the captains took asylum in church, till John sent word not to be afraid. Another time he gave five pounds of gold to a foreign captain in trouble; the man bought a cargo but was wrecked outside the Pharos; John gave him ten pounds of gold and this time the ship was blown ashore. John said that the first time the Church money had been mixed with unjustly-got money; the second time the ship itself had been unjustly gained. He gave the captain one of his Church-ships, a swift sailer with some 20,000 bushels of corn. For twenty days and nights she sailed before a strong wind. The sailors had no idea where they were going; but the helms-man saw John at his side holding the tiller. On the twentieth day they sighted the Islands of Britain, where a famine was raging. The chief man of the town (*protos*) offered to buy corn at a *nomisma* a bushel or give a freight of tin. The captain took half and half. On his return the tin was tried in the brazier and found to be fine silver. (17)

There is no reason to doubt that the facts of Mediterranean trade lie behind this tale. Seven Byzantine coins were found, we may recall, at Caerwent.

With what articles, then, was trade still carried on? Wine and oil, and at times wheat, were needed in Britain, together with small precious articles for the services in church and for the luxury-demands of rulers. The return trade was in Cornish tin, probably Irish gold and copper, dogs and slaves, perhaps hides as well. (18)

A sidelight on the use of oil is given by Gregory of Tours and Paulinus of Périgueux, who mention that the faithful put vessels full of oil by the bodies of saints or on miracle-sites; the oil was thought to be infused by grace—on the lines of the virtue that Victricius claimed for relics. In the ruins of a villa at St. Martin-de-Fraigneau (Vendée) a fine black vase was found, inscribed on shoulder and side: ✠ *Divi Martini Antistitis Balsamum Oleum Pro Benedictione.* The date is 5th century.

Besides the wider trade movements there must have been much exchange within the area of Ireland and west Britain. A large number of metal objects found in Wales over these years seem Irish in origin. (19)

About 450 there would still have been current a fair amount of Theodosian copper coins, much worn. And there would have still been a fairly high proportion of silver, which it was profitable to clip.

Did the Romano-Britons perhaps dispense old hoards of radiates to the newly arrived Anglo-Saxon peoples, by whom these coins, nearly two centuries old, and not conveying to the Romano-Briton the sense of political realism inherent in the Theodosian issues—were accepted, imitated, cut down and overstruck? It might have been just at such a time that hoards could be deposited like those of which we have many examples—hoards containing a proportion of minim or near-minim pieces, with a varying mixture of larger pieces, sometimes halved or quartered. And it is not difficult to imagine the melting down of the larger coins of the early empire to supply metal for a poorer, regressive age. (20)

The post-450 period might, then, have seen a tendency to hoard the Theodosian issues, now badly worn, and the production of radiate copies on the model of obsolete pieces handed out to the newcomers. In Gaul, we may note, the problems of paying the Federates were often acute: Avitus (455–6) tried to lessen the number of mouths to be fed, but first had to melt down bronze statues which had escaped the ravaging vandals, to get coin.

The long-distance trade in the West at this period seems fallen almost wholly into the hands of the Syrians. (21) They were present in Gaul in considerable numbers and in some towns like Orléans they formed definite colonies. Other Easterners, Jews and Greeks, were mixed with them. Sidonius shows that Jews were prominent as letter-carriers, no doubt as a sideline for their commercial journeys. A Jew, client of Magnus Felixus of Narbonne, carried letters between his patron and Sidonius, who himself sends a letter to the bishop of Nantes by a converted Jew. (22) There is also a Jew taking a letter to bishop Eleutherius.

Slaves were an outstanding item in commerce. A Frank Samo, under Dagobert, travelled to Bohemia on a trading mission and ended by becoming King of the Wends. (23) He had been concerned with the international slave-market (our word *slave* derives from the Slavs who abundantly supplied that market, while the old term *servus* was changing into our *serf*). At the same time, no doubt, "he himself sold arms to the barbarians as did the interloping traders of the frontier, against whom the Cartularies so often legislated". (24) Britain was often raided for slaves and the Anglo-Saxons were known for their readiness to sell their own fellows. (25) Later, according to St. Boniface, English prostitutes and bawds littered every town of Italy, Gaul, and Germany (along the main roads). Frisians, though specialising in cloth, also dealt in slaves. Saint Eloi, minister of Sagobert, used to buy batches of 50 or even 100 Britons or Saxons on the landing quays. (26) The Church did not forbid the practice. (27)

The *Life* of John the Humble mentioned the corn-ship arriving in Britain at the time of a famine. We know of such a famine in Gaul in 473–4. (28) The towns in Britain must have been thrown more and more back on their local resources. The system of dykes that we have noted for Silchester and other places may mark the limits of the land upon which the food supply of the town depended. (29)

Though we cannot trust the Saints' Lives to any extent, they often embody ancient material, and it is worth noting that famines occur in many of them. Thus, St. Cadog came back to Wales from a visit to Ireland and found in Brycheiniog "a great famine". He wanted to be taught by a rhetorician Bachan newly arrived from Italy, but Bachan demurred through the difficulties of providing food. Cadog prayed. A mouse came from its hole with a grain of corn in its mouth, which it set on a writing tablet; then returned with six more grains. Cadog caught it, tied its foot, and showed the grains to Bachan. He then borrowed a long thread from a widow, attached it to the mouse's foot, let the mouse go, and located the creature's lair, "a very beautiful house underground, built of old and filled with clean wheat", inside a tumulus. Cadog then suggested that the corn be distributed to the poor and the hungry, lest the judgment of the wise man come upon them: "He who hides away his corn is cursed among the peoples, but a blessing rests on the head of those who distribute it." He gave the corn to the people, to each according to his need. (30)

Again, St. Ileud, born in Brittany, wanted to visit a church there and ordered his stewards to thresh and store the corn cramming his three barns. He found men stricken by a famine in Brittany and prayed for his corn, which was miraculously fetched. From the harbour where it landed "the whole of Llydaw (Brittany) fed itself and sowed its cultivated lands". (31)

In the *Lives* of Patrick we get a glimpse of the peasants' hate of taxes, and their difficulty in meeting them. The saint made milk and butter out of snow to meet the king's demands; as soon as the king had been paid, the goods turned back into snow. (32)

Since we found the question of armour and weapons of primary importance in the reconstruction of his forces and tactics, it would be as well to consider further what had been happening in the Roman Army. At the start of the 3rd century, equipment was still classical. By 450 every element of that equipment was gone—the *pilum* (the heavy javelin of the infantry), the *gladius* (a pointed cutting sword), the cylindrical buckler, the cuirass and the helm, not to mention the *cingulum* or belt that from the early empire had been the emblem of the military. At the start of the 5th century the Army had two typical arms: the Infantry in a long-sleeved tunic, long, clinging breeches, closed shoes, without helm or cuirass, but bearing a big flat buckler, oval or round, and armed with the long sword, *spatha*, and the lance— or else bow, sling, or crossbow; (33) and the Cuirassier, cov- ered in iron from head to foot or wearing chain-mail with a hood. The Eagles have given way to the Dragons. (34)

Missiles grew more prominent, ranging from sling-balls to arrows. The axe, though it does not seem to have entered the legions, was introduced by Germans and Franks, and became one of the main weapons of both foot and horse in the Byzan- tine army. (35)

The old oval shield went, but another type, without the convex shape that gave the original shield its value, was brought in by barbarians. (36) Other barbarian forms were round, or scutcheon-shaped, or based on the pelta, the amazonian shield. The decoration wholly changed. Winged thunderbolts, bay-wreaths, and sidereal emblems went. On a buckler shown on a disk from Geneva we see two animals reminding of classical dolphins but more like the dragons of the legionary ensigns; the commonest ornaments, however, are geometrical—i.e. juxta-posed triangles alternately light and dark, curved spokes, or scales.

The failing techniques of army equipment appear clearly in the helmets. From the 4th century the infantry did not generally wear them; the barbarians were not used to them and no doubt felt them oppressive. Gratian courted popularity among the German troops by letting them leave off helm and breastplate, and carry the spiculum instead of the heavy pilum. Cavalry-helms degenerated. We find the classical form turned out in barbarised construction, e.g. a specimen from Worms made out of four sections united by a nailed band which formed a longi-tudinal crest, while a band round the lower edge and guards for neck and ears were riveted on. In the later 4th century, or at least in the 5th, the armourers could not beat out the whole shape; we approach the epoch of odd pieces riveted together—a method still being carried on in the 12th century. (37)

The heavily armoured cavalry, found first among the Par-thians, Persians, and Sarmatians, appeared in the Roman Army from the time of Alexander Severus. Ammianus des-cribes the Persians: "Ironclad bands so thickly covered with small bits of metal that the solid jointures fit the joints of the limbs." We see the same sort of thing in the Sarmatian cata-phracts on the column of Trajan, rider and steed alike encased in mail. The only written account comes from the emperor Julian, addressed to Constantius:

You led a host of horsemen like statues mounted on horseback, on whom the various parts of armour, constructed on the model of the human frame, exactly fitted—from the end of the wrists to the elbows, thence to the shoulders, together with the segmented cuirass and the iron helm covering even the face.

The effect is of a shining polished statue; for neither the thighs nor the legs nor the ends of the feet remain unprovided with this equipment. As these various sections are adapted to the cuirasses by a kind of web made of little rings, one does not see anything of the body left bare, since even the hands are protected by the chain-mail made so as to follow the fingers in their movements.

Such is the picture that my words try to bring to life, but I feel that I am far from success. Whoever wants to know more, had better (to acquire knowledge of this armour) go and look at the reality rather than listen to my description. (38)

A bas-relief of Taky-Bostam in Persia shows a Sassanid cavalier whose horse has its head, neck, and chest protected by mail made of juxtaposed pieces of metal. The rider, helmed, is clad in a long mailcoat which covers the arms to the elbow, goes below the knees, and hides throat and face to the eyes. (39) A similar equipment is worn by several cavaliers painted in the Vatican *Virgil*. (40) Mail descends to mid-thigh and covers arms to the elbow, ending above in hood of mail for the head. Mail-coats reaching down to the instep are worn later by the Byzantine cavalry; and as the hawberk or broigne, this kind of armour, often completed with the hood or camail, was one of the commonest armours in the West from the 11th to the 16th century.

It is argued there were no nailed horseshoes, as no horse-collars. The throat-and-girth harness strangled an animal trying to pull a heavy weight. The Romans made efforts to protect the hooves of horses with metal hippo-sandals, strapped-on plates with hooks and heel-pieces. Also leather or straw shoes were used for mules, horses, and camels on hard or slippery ground. Both horseshoe and collar seem developed by nomads of the steppes and taken over by the Germanic and other tribes to the West, coming into general use by the early medieval period. (41)

Cavalry which were not cataphracts, according to the monuments, wore leather cuirasses. Vegetius says that their defensive equipment had been bettered in imitation of the Goths, Alans, and Huns, but gives no details.

The Roman party in Britain, closely in touch with their Gallo-Roman fellows, could easily pick up ideas about the most modernised armament—that of the cataphracts—and to see how to use it against the Anglo-Saxons with their weak defensive equipment. No doubt the ironwork was crude, but it would be none the less effective.

In Gaul Syagrius the patrician, centred on Soissons as *Rex Romanorum*, had been trying to carry on the Aetian work, in deteriorating conditions. For a while, with Reims the seat of his archbishop, he made headway, and the Seine valley and the central plain of Gaul were still Roman. But by the early 6th century the union of Gaul under the Franks had been achieved under Clovis (Chlodovech), king of the Salian section. Clovis took over what remained of Syagrius' system; notaries, doing the secretarial work, preserved what was possible of Roman usage and method in administration. This period is roughly that of Arthur. During it the Gallo-Roman party, which is strong under Aetius and which survives weakened under Syagrius, is swept away; but the connections maintained between Gaul and Britain in the 5th century would have been sufficient to keep alive and well informed the Romanising tradition of Ambrosius and Arthur.

One of Sidonius' letters, written in 474, gives us indeed the very picture we want of the sort of development that we have conjectured to be going on in Britain. He is writing to his brother-in-law Ecdicius of the latter's daring relief of Clermont.

Never can the image slip from the hearts of our citizens who crowded, men and women of every rank and age, on our half-tottered walls to watch you cross the level space between us and the enemy. In mid-day, through the midmost of the foe, you rode with your band of scarcely eighteen horsemen across some thousands of Goths—a deed that posterity will find it hard to believe.

At the sound of your name, at the sight of you in person, a stupor overwhelmed those battle-scarred battalions. Their chiefs (*duces*) could not tell in bewilderment how numerous were they, how few were you. Their whole line was withdrawn headlong to the top of a sharp hill; they, who had been besiegers, were unable with you in view to move into battle-order. You cut down some of their best men, whom rashness not laziness had put in the rear. With not one man lost in the important clash, you remained master of a quite exposed plain with less henchmen at your side than you usually have guests at table.

There we have exactly the sort of exploit which Arthur carried out on Badon. (Gregory of Tours, telling the story later, reduces the band to ten men.) Fortunately, Sidonius gives us a fairly thorough account of the equipment which enabled the handful of Gallo-Romans to scare and break through a host of lighter-armed Goths; he also mentions that Ecdicius had himself gathered and fitted out the band at his own cost.

My vows can better conjure up than my words depict the crowd streaming to meet you on your casual way citywards, the salutes, the applause, the tears of joy. We beheld the most auspicious ovation of your mobbed return, the courts of your spacious house thronged, some welcomers kissing off your battle-dust, others removing the foam-and-blood-slippery bridles, others turning up and ranging the sweat-drencht saddles, undoing the flexible cheek-pieces of the helm you longed to take off, or unlacing your greaves.

We saw folk counting up the nicks on swords blunted with many deaths or measuring with trembling, pale fingers the holes broken in cuirasses by cut or thrust.

Though many people joy-wild hung upon your comrades, on you the main torrent of popular delight was gathered. At last you had come into an unharmed host; but not with all your arms could you have driven them off, you bore with tactful grace the stupidities of the congratulators; and pulled to and fro amid the furious surge of embraces, you came to the point in your patriotic response to the public love that you showed the most overflowing politeness to those who took the most damaging liberties with you.

Finally, I remark nothing of your services in raising from your private resources—with very little aid from our magnates—what amounted to a public force, with which you have held up the inroads of the barbarians and chastised their devastations. I remark nothing of surprise attacks wiping out whole squadrons with the loss of only two or three men. (42)

Sidonius uses *cassis* for helmet, *ocrea* for greave or legging, *gladius* for sword, *lorica* for cuirass. He is carried away by the epic occasion rather than attempting accuracy of description; but we may accept the impression given of heavy cavalry without pressing the terms too far.

He adds (perhaps misunderstanding) that to hide their losses the Goths in the dark decapitated the dead whom they could not bury, but next day felt their trick futile. They collected the heaped corpses in dripping waggons without washing, shrouding, or interring them; and as Ecdicius went on harrying, they bore the bodies into houses, which were set on fire as hasty pyres.

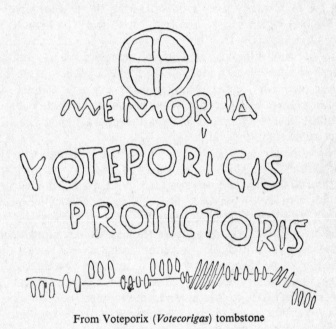

From Voteporix (*Votecorigas*) tombstone

THE PELAGIAN AFTERMATH

WE may now return to investigating the developments in Gaul which can be connected with those in Britain; for there were yet many fruitful connections between the two areas. First, the after-effects of the Pelagian struggle. We saw that the extirpation of Pelagian ideas in Gaul and Britain was no easy matter, and for long a strong resistance was made to pure Augustinianism. The groups of individuals who carried on the modified attack against Predestination and Original Sin have been called Semi-Pelagians. (1)

The second stage of Gallic monasticism came with the foundations of Lérins and St. Victor. Lérins lay on an island south of Marseilles and was founded by St. Honoratus early in the 5th century or maybe a little before, and is called in the *Life of Hilary of Arles* an Earthly Paradise. It became a centre of learning and produced some of the best thinkers and writers of the day. Its source of inspiration seems to be Greek rather than Egyptian. Honoratus was born on a great estate in north Belgic Gaul, where he struggled against his pagan father. The words which his disciple Hilary puts in his dying mouth conclude with a call for the exercise of freewill and the rejection of money, which is semi-Pelagian in tone:

You can see that you will be compelled to lose the world. It's best then to turn from it now of your own free will. Let no one give himself up to riches, let no one be money's slave, let no one be seduced by the empty show of wealth. It's a crime to turn what could be used to buy salvation [i.e. by giving it up] into the instrument of one's damnation; to be taken captive by what could have ransomed one.

John Cassian, founder of St. Victor, seems to have come from a Balkan province; he had an extensive knowledge of Egyptian monasticism and was ordained deacon, probably by St. John Chrysostom in Byzantium. (2) He was a blithe, calm spirit who assumed that Christians renounced the world and therefore naturally "must seek a dwelling-place in a *coenobium*" or community of monks, fellow-renouncers. Throughout, his attitude was communal in its values. "Whatever is claimed by one of a few or a few in a community of religious, and is not held in common by the whole body of the brothers, is either superfluous or vain, and therefore to be considered harmful."

The revulsion that many Christians felt against what was dour and rigid in Augustine's thought soon found wide expression in Gaul. Provençe and Aquitaine seem the main areas of this semi-Pelagianism. Vincent of Lérins wrote about 434 his *Commonitorium*, which gives a summary of heresies; he cautiously but scornfully tries to include Augustinianism in the catalogue of errors.

The heretics . . . dare to promise and teach that in their own church (that is, in the little society of their communion) there abides a certain great and special and indeed personal Grace of God—so much so that without any toil, without any struggle, without any effort, even though they do not see or search or knock, anyone at all counted among them receives such dispensation from God that, lifted up by angels' hands, guarded by angelic protection, they cannot dash their foot against a stone—that is, be caused to stumble. (3)

Then there are several poets who stoutly come near to setting out the Pelagian case. Marius Victor, orator of Marseilles, in his *Alethia* described the events of *Genesis* to the death of Abraham; his approach is philosophic, concerned with the implications and inner meanings of the events. In his introduction to the poem he cogently sets out the argument for Free Will. In the poem itself the Fall appears begetting a sense of loss which urges towards the reattainment of harmony:

> Ah, with what eyes, what feelings do they look,
> in whose hearts yet paradise lives. (4)

and again: "Better to conquer death than never experience dying."

Orientius, in his *Commonitorium*, seems to be drawing on both Lactantius and Pelagius in his attacks on lewdness, envy, greed; he has the Pelagian touch in his wish to show the accordance

between the natural law of human brotherhood and the law of
love in the Evangel.

> "Ah true, but these are difficult things you state."
> Hard are our precepts: climb from earth to heaven . . .
> Great is the toil but great the toil's reward . . .
> What will be lofty, what will be hard for you?
> Nothing is difficult when hope's our helper.

The anonymous author of the *Carmen de Providentia* derives
even more emphatically from Pelagius; he stakes everything on
the rights and responsibilities of the will, the theory of the
natural law written on our hearts, the justice and salvation open
to all without distinction of place or time:

> Let the enemy cram all things with endless terrors
> and clamp the closed doors with armed sentries,
> yet, beaten and harried, if the old flesh we strip
> and renew our bodies in Christ and ask the victor
> for all the powers of conquering ourselves,
> he, mating ours with his, mates his with ours,
> till, trusting naught human, Man returns in wholeness
> to him: without whom those who seem to stand
> totter, with whom the scattered are brought together,
> the broken rise again.

He sees the great powers latent in man:

> Water your servant is here and fire the consumer:
> stretch out your hand to whatever you wish. Equal lies
> the power for all . . .

Nothing can check the movement of human freedom:

> And vain would be the promise of God's own mouth
> if external force may control this will of ours. . . .
>
> Why am I not good? You don't want to be. Why wicked?
> You want it. Why do I want the wrong and not
> the right? You are free . . .
>
> Lo, Man, how great the power you are freely offered:
> You can be Son of God, if you wish. The omnipotent
> Spirit created you with the Word's virtue shadowed. (5)

Even the badgered and bewildered Paulinus of Pella meditated awhile "a task beyond his strength",

> of venturing to live too loftily
> after the perfect pattern of the monk
> though with a housefull of dear relatives . . . (6)

Prosper, whom we have already seen as the chief anti-Pelagian of his day in Gaul, wrote a long poem, *De Ingratis*, which is an attack on the "Enemies of Grace". It consists of versified *sententiae* from Augustine, a pedagogue's poem, which was much used in the medieval schools. (7)

A dissident thinker who was a friend of Sidonius may have been son or grandson of Vortigern: Faustus, bishop of Riez. Nennius says that Vortigern had three sons, but then adds "the fourth was Faustus, who was born to him of his own daughter, and saint Germanus baptised him and reared him and taught him. And he built a great *locus* [Welsh *llog*, monastery] on the bank of the river called Renis and it remains to this day." This seems on the face of it an interpolation, with the charge of incest as a theological deduction from heresy (which we have surmised to be Pelagianism). But the existence of a Faustus (Britu) is further upheld by the inscription on Eliseg's Pillar and the genealogies; the Pillar even supports the blessing by Germanus; so we may assume that there really was a Faustus, son or grandson of Vortigern.

Sidonius, writing to Faustus of Riez, refers to "your Britons". He no doubt means Bretons; but at this early phase of the migration, his words bring Faustus as much into a British as into a Breton context—the Bretons being still recent Britons-come-overseas. Further, Sidonius had been visited by a friend or relation of Faustus, whose name is the Celtic Riocatus, which accords with Riagath or Riagat in the genealogies. Riagath was a grandson of Vortigern. It is tempting, then, to see in Faustus and Riochatus two members of the Vortigern dynasty; but we cannot prove the connection. What, however, is clear is that Faustus has close Briton-Breton relations and that he belongs to the Gallo-British cultural nexus. Avitus, bishop of Vienne also calls him *Britannus*. He may indeed have been one of the foreigners whom pope Celestine noted as filling high church offices in Gaul and against whom he protested in his decree *Cuperemus quidam* of 428. (8)

Though he became a bishop after his abbacy at Lérins, Faustus maintained the monastic attitude. "An abbot still unchanged into priest: you have not relaxed the rigour of your old discipline by the gaining of a new dignity," Sidonius remarked. (9) And in a poem he depicted his works:

> Are you among your people? they, lower-class,
> dare, with you there, to scorn the great ones' pride.
> Or do you anxiously scan the sick man's food,
> the stranger's food, or his who lanks in prison
> till loose his legs go sliding in the fetters?
> or are your thoughts on burying the dead,
> as you unshrinking to the graveyard carry
> a poor man greening in his livid corpse?
> Or do you sit on the holy altarsteps
> gazed-at by all the zealous people crowding
> to drink the Medicine of the expounded Law?

Faustus, though opposed to ideas of Predestination, was careful to separate himself out from Pelagius, whom he calls *pestifer doctor*. But his own views were as controversial. He carried on the tradition of Christian materialism which had found important expression in Tertullian. He declared that to call the soul immaterial was to claim for it a quality belonging only to God. Also his work on Free Grace was condemned by pope Gelasius. (10)

Mamertus Claudianus, another of the Sidonius' circle, replied to Faustus's thesis of the materiality of the soul in a treatise "which in its subtlety and formal elaboration of proof has the tone and atmosphere of the scholastic theology of the Middle Ages". (11) Sidonius praised both men impartially, with no sign that he understood what the argument was about. (Faustus wrote also against the Arians.) (12)

The influence of the Semi-Pelagians long persisted. Monachism in south Provençe, we saw, began near the Rhône mouth and the islands to the south; towards the century's end, it spread north up the river; and about 512 Caesarius founded a monastery for men at Arles and a nunnery under his sister (the first such house known in the West) on a Rhône island. His *sermones seu admonitiones* give us information about the pagan cults of tree and spring, and he cites Faustus of Riez, so that his modern editor has to note: *Cave semipelagianum*. His Letters to his sister reproduce more or less exactly Pelagian passages; the first has reminiscenses from the treatise for Demetrias; the second draws on a source now lost, and seems to be linked with letters from Pelagius (preserved in fragments) to one Livania.

In his letter, written about 475–8, Sidonius tells how Riocatus, after visiting Faustus at Riez, called on him during the return journey to Britain (or Brittany), having been forced to stay at Clermont through the Goth-disturbed state of the roads. Sidonius mentions to Faustus that "I had read those works of yours which Riocatus, bishop and monk (thus twice a stranger and pilgrim in this world), was taking back from you to your Britons" or Bretons. Riochatus remained at Clermont two months, keeping secret that he had some special work by Faustus with him. Word, however, got about, and he hastily went off. Sidonius followed with horses capable of cancelling out the day's start of the fugitive, caught him up, clasped his knees, opened his baggage, found the precious text and "began reading and dismembering it by long excerpts from the main chapters". He dictated full speed to his secretaries "they could skip wholesale, using concentrated signs that need no letters". Finally, tearfully embracing, he and Riocatus parted. Sidonius in his letter proceeds with an inflated, lengthy account of the book's contents, which gives no idea of what it was about, except that it concerned philosophy.

There are further writings, strongly Pelagian, which belong to the Gallo-British milieu. Some of these, together with works by Pelagius himself, have been attributed to a British writer on the strength of an entry in Gennadius:

Fastidius, a bishop of the Britons, wrote to a certain man Fatalis a book on *The Christian Life* and another on *The Preservation of Widowhood*, sound in doctrine and worthy of God.

From the writer's place in the lists it seems that he flourished about 430; and in one of the oldest MSS. he is described as *Britto* instead of *Britannus episcopus*. We can, however, dismiss him as the author of the works in question; and if we must make a guess, that author is more likely to be the Pelagian son of Severianus. But it is best to admit that we do not know who he is. (13)

He has gone on a long journey against his father's wishes, taking one of his two young daughters with him. He had wanted to live in lands that he felt nearer to God, the holy East; and his father had argued that God was everywhere. "God is in Francia and in Saxonia and in all the heathen world, but there are no worshippers of God there," the son retorted. From these words we gather that he came either from north-east Gaul or from Britain. (*Francia* means not France, as it did later, displacing *Gallia*, but merely the northern area inhabited by the Franks: in this sense it is used by Ausonius and Claudian.)

At home, the son says, he complacently thought himself a worshipper, despising things lawful (such as marriage) and sometimes doing unlawful things (lying, cursing, swearing, defaming, flattering, considering of persons, eating with fornicators, covetous men, drunkards, hating enemies and hitting back). Now in his travels overland and sea he has found the truth.

He mentions two people. A widow in Sicily who convinced him that there was no need to go East and that he could live the good life anywhere; with her he left his young girl to be educated in virginity. And a "saint", Antiochus, who has been defamed and whom he defends. As a *sanctus*, Antiochus must be of the school of Martin, and the truth that the traveller has found is the Pelagian way. (14)

The author insists on the need to base one's ideas on one's own experience. "I have found no evil in him and I can retain in my consciousness (*intra conscientiam*) only what I have myself experienced." He accepts without question the idea of general crisis. "You will cite the popular saying: Then the whole world is dying." He bids his father be virtuous and above all to keep chaste. And, incidentally, we learn from him that boys were sent away from home to be educated. "Look upon her [the girl] for the time being as a boy who for education's sake must be taken away for the time being from those who love him." (15) In the midst of his rejection of the family he tenderly remembers his absent girl and begs his father to look after her well so that she will not feel his absence.

A second letter may be by the same man, though it has also been attributed to Pelagius. It takes the position that the rich are debarred from heaven; and is strongly rationalist. "I assert there is no real ignorance when a man knows where his ignorance lies." The person addressed is a young man of consular rank, and a friend of his, a *sanctus* named Martyrius, is cited. There is the same insistence as in the previous letter on the need to test things by personal experience. It is "hard for human nature to trust another as oneself".

It ends, "I pray you may live ever and rejoice in the perpetual honour of consulship." As we do not know where the man addressed is living, it is not easy to know what to make of the final phrase. It may mean only: May you always remain in your honoured rank. But, conceivably, if the young man is someone like Aurelius Ambrosianus in Britain, it may refer to a sort of dictatorship conferred on the leader of the *civitates*. (16)

But important as the after-effects of Pelangianism were, they represent only one section of the wide contacts existing between Gaul and Celtic Britain in the 5th century.

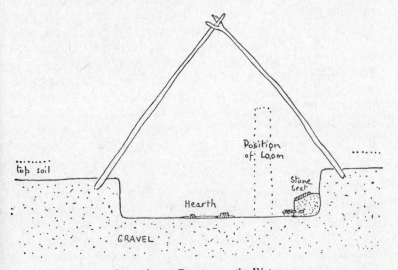

Saxon hut at Bourton on the Water

GAUL AND CELTIC CULTURE

IN a glossary of Latin words at Leiden, contained in an MS. of the 12th century, it was stated:

All the learned men on this side of the sea fled away, and in transmarine parts, i.e. Hiberia, and wherever they betook themselves, brought about a great advance of learning to the inhabitants of those regions. (1)

There seems to be strong evidence for much connection of Ireland with Gaul from the second half of the 3rd century, when Gaulish mercenaries were said to be coming over. Various tribal groups claimed descent from Gaulish ancestors. (2)

In the later 5th century there were close connections of Wales with the region of Vienne and Lyon in Gaul. Probably many Gauls moved out at the time of the Burgundian settlement and came to Britain or Ireland via Bordeaux or Brittany. At Penmachno is part of a rough pillar-stone with a Latin inscription: "(the stone of X) son of Avitorius: in the time of Justinus the Consul." Justinus was consul in 540; he and Basilius, consul in 541, were the last consuls to be named on monuments in the West; and their names went on being used retrospectively until the early 7th century in Burgundy (when consular dating had died out in the rest of Gaul). The use of Justinus' name was limited to monuments of Lyon and district, that of Basilius' to those of Vienne and district.

On seventeen Welsh monuments the formula *hic jacit* is found. This formula was adopted by Christians to replace the pagan *Dis Manibus*; it appears in Italy in the late 4th century and was carried into Gaul, where it had a restricted use in the first half of the 5th century—in two regions, round Lyon and Vienne in south Gaul, and in the Rhineland, especially at Trèves. The normal form in Wales, *hic jacit*, appears occasionally on the Continent, where *hic jacet,* however, predominates. Four Welsh monuments have the allied formula: *hic in tumulo iacit*—thus at Llanerfyl: "Here in the tomb lies Rosteece, daughter of Paterninus, 13 years. In peace." (Near St. David's a pillar-stone had *nomina,* apparently in the sense of relics: *nomina* with that meaning is found in north African epitaphs of the 4th century and later, usually commemorating martyrs.) An Anglesey stone, to be considered later, seems to mention a man from the region of Angers on the Loire. (3)

At Llandysilio West "(the stone) of Clutorix son of Paulinus Marinus of Latium" is built into the outer nave-wall: *Latium* probably means Brittany or a Snowdonian locality, since in Irish Latin it meant both Latium in Italy or any area

Trecastle
pillar-stone
(Nash-
Williams
No. 71)

called Letha (Irish) or Llydaw (Welsh). At Trecastle was found a pillar-stone inscribed in Latin and ogam: "(The stone) of Maccutrenus (Maquutrenus) Salicidinus"—which, shortly after its erection, was decorated with incised linear symbols or pictographs in three vertical panels with border-lines: (i) a traverse division into two sections, with a small human figure at the top by cruciform, dotted, and hatched devices, with opposed triangles below (filled with reticulated or scroll-like forms); (ii) small figure apparently running to front with arms out, between parallel zigzags, with small crosses and dotted and scroll devices; (iii) small frontal figure with bent staff or crook held across his body in his left hand and a bag (?) in his right, with various devices. The nearest analogies come from the prehistoric decoration of megalithic and later monuments, especially those in Brittany and along the Atlantic seaboard, with elements perhaps derived from the popular art that flourished in the Celtic West during the empire (e.g. bronze sceptre-mounting from the Romano-Celtic temple of Farley Heath, Surrey). The Trecastle stone may thus reveal a movement from Brittany and

Gaul—though the Irish may also have been responsible for it. In any event the movements to and fro between Brittany and Wales or Cornwall is not in doubt. (4)

The lettering used on the stones derives from the Roman monumental style in its less formal or rustic variations, with certain post-classical touches (i.e. letter-forms adapted from the cursive or written hand and epigraphic forms of Greek or Graeco-Roman origin). These intrusions represent the plebeian and Oriental aspects of early Christianity. "While thus basically akin in epigraphic style to the monumental lettering of the antecedent Romano-British period, the script used in Welsh Early Christian inscriptions was not in fact derived from it, but represents a reintroduction of Roman epigraphic practice, now Christianised, probably from Gaul in the sub-Roman period." Out of these elements, by the 7th century, emerged a new Celtic script, rounded in its forms and quite unlike the angular rune-like characters developing on Merovingian Gaul's monuments. (5)

The Gaulish reputation for eloquence was pre-Roman. Under the empire rhetorical schools flourished in Gaul. The severe scholar Jerome admitted that in his day studies were "most flourishing" there, and referred to the "richness and glitter of Gallic speech". (6) The Gauls, he said, were fertile in orators. The senator Symmachus at Rome had been trained in Gaul and wanted a Gaulish tutor for his son. During the 4th century the main centres of learning had moved from Marseilles and Autun to Trèves in the north and Bordeaux in the west. In particular the prose panegyrists of the emperor were linked with Gaul. It is not altogether unfitting that when Argobast set up a puppet emperor in 391–2 he chose a former teacher of rhetoric. (7)

In the ancient system of education, Philosophy was divided into three parts, Ethics, Physics, and Logics. But by now all sections had been weakened and flattened in mechanical, stereotyped ways. The essential aspect was Declamation. The speaker needed to have apt allusions ready from all spheres of thought, to master a set diction, to construct extempore passages from his stock of materials, to blend the tricks he had learned for exciting, stimulating by unexpected collocations, contrasts, inversions, repetitions, all working up to a calculated climax.

He attempted hyperboles based on stale elements, tried to fabricate the picturesque out of dull and trite ingredients. Set descriptions and catalogues were part of the stock-in-trade of accumulative devices.

We see the effect in the work of Ausonius and Sidonius, where a native talent keeps breaking through but is continually twisted and made vapid by the tricks of which they are so proud. Ethics is a set of copy-book maxims. Philosophers are ticked off by labels, by feeble vulgarisations of their thought: if you know that Democritus laughs and Heraclitus weeps, you have those thinkers fixed in their meagre frames. History consists of anecdotes quotable in letter or speech, so that things are liable to get mixed: Sidonius describes Caesar fighting the Irish in Britain and equips Vandals of his day with the weapons of Aeneas. (8) Geography, despite all the surveying work done by officials, has not developed in the schools. The East is a place where you find Aurora with a red torch, the Phoenix in its nest, ivory, and elephants. The Franks once lived by the marshy Elbe, so, when they move about, they still have the Elbe attached to them. (9)

The rhetors, who taught in the secondary schools, divided their work into three stages: the Virgilian, where the students paraphrased some Aeneid speech; the Soliloquies, where the students spoke as historical or legendary persons; the *Controversiae*, where at last an approach to normal social life could be attempted—though generally in stilted and remote terms: against a man refusing to support an aged father, against a man putting a statue of Minerva in a brothel, and so on. (10) We see from the textbook of Aphthonius of Antioch how the elements of eloquence were divided and subdivided: he has the headings of Pointed Saying, Aphorism, Refutation, Confirmation, Commonplace, Praise, Censure, Comparison, Characterisation, Description, Thesis. (11) Thus, Refutation means proving your opponent's argument Obscure, Incredible, Impossible, Illogical, Improper, Inexpedient. Take the myth of Daphne. She was born from a River and the Earth. "If a human being is born from a river, why not a river from a human being?" and so on: it's obscure and incredible. Where did the girl live? In the river or inside the earth? Impossible. How could a god love her, since it is absurd to attribute such a terrible thing as love to a god? Improper. How could a girl beat Phoebus in a race, since women are inferior to men, therefore even more inferior to gods? Did her mother help her for fear of a mis-alliance? Illogical. Why does Earth, after taking away her daughter, offer a laurel with which the god crowns his tripos? Inexpedient. All poets are fools: avoid them; we had better stop talking of them or, like them, we'll talk nonsense. The student then, to show his skill in Confirmation, would take the same myth and prove it Manifest, Probable, Possible, Logical, Proper, Expedient. (12)

Was there no organic element at all in this rhetorical culture? There was little evident in the system; but to some extent there were dominant ideas growing up in society which vitally affected the use to which rhetoric was put. Apart from Chris-tianity, which could provide a living centre, a point of funda-mental criticism and transformation, there were certain trends in later imperial society, in its religions and its philosophies, which attempted a unified approach to experience and which saw man in relation to the universe of which he was a part. And these trends in turn strongly affected Christian ideas and attitudes.

The solar henotheism, linked with imperial centralisation, was one such effort to draw the various aspects of life into a single focus; but even when partially merged with ideas of death-and-renewal from the mystery-religions, it could not escape the compromising and deadening effect of its relation to the State—by which one means not only the direct organisa-tional ways in which it became connected with emperor-wor-ship, but also the indirect ways in which it reflected and butt-ressed a blind acceptance of the State and its oppressive needs. More creatively useful was the sense of a living link between man and nature, expressed at times in allegory, which had developed out of the breakdown of the earlier forms of ancient religion, and of which Neoplatonism was in one aspect an expression.

In the 3rd and 4th centuries the mosaics of Gaul and Britain show this feeling, pantheist and allegoric, in artistic imagery: Orpheus as the power of harmony tuning men and nature in a single song, and yet meeting a tragic fate when the civilising music somehow grows jangled. Bellerophon or Perseus as the Redeeming Hero against the Monster. The Seasons as the eternal round of nature which is turned by the redeeming act into an image of unending life. And because these images stir in men their deepest sense of what is happening in history, in human life, they become to a large extent as much Christian as pagan. Orpheus plays in the catacombs and Hermes Ram-bearer becomes Christ the Good Shepherd. (13) Bellerophon gives way to St. Michael or St. George with their similar iconography.

Ideas and practices of magic thread these new ideas, whether Christian or pagan; and men turn both to Christ and to Astrology to gain power over the predestinating Stars. We saw astrologic and mystery imagery in the Brading villa of the Isle of Wight. Origen had been the great Eastern thinker who brought the allegoric method into Christianity; and Hilary of Poitiers introduced his method into Gaul after being exiled in the East. (14) The only philosopher who wakes Sidonius to anything like fervour is Pythagoras, whose theory of numbers suggests the interrelations of astrology; and he tells the story of the rhetor Lampridius who "consulted those African astrologers whose nature is fiery as their clime," but who could not evade his own death—his slaves strangled him and threw him face down on the floor so as to seem dead in a sudden haemorrhage.

There can be no doubt that the Irish, and the Welsh, took over the methods of Gaulish rhetoric—the set descriptions, inventories, catalogues. When Sidonius tells us that the prince Sigismer went amid his bodyguard "in flame-hued mantle, with much glint of ruddy gold and gleam of silk snow-tunic; his blond hair, his red cheeks, his white skin in accord with his three-hued equipment", he is stressing the three-colour contrast which becomes one of the set devices of Irish and Welsh narrative. (15) Ausonius, too, uses the trick.

The style known as *retorics*, constructed on a metrical basis, developed mainly in south Ireland: used for genealogies, but also for panegyrics and satires. It probably had a 5th-century origin and was finally driven out by the rimed verses that also came in from the Continent, deriving metrically from the Latin hymns. (16) In the *retorics* we can trace the characteristics of

Gaulish prose, the *rhetoricus sermo* of Sedulius. (17) There is antithesis, parallelism, artificial word-order, archaism, neologism, rhythmical cadence, elements of rime and alliteration.

The Irish saga-form seems certainly derived from the *retorics* in which occur earliest allusions to the persons of the Irish heroic age (in particular to the heroes of the Red Branch Cycle and of the Deidre tale). The Norse saga material is ultimately based on the skalds with their panegyrics and elegies; Ireland alone in Europe has a corresponding traditional prose of an elaborate kind, which seems certainly also to derive from the panegyric poets and their metrical form, the *retorics*. (Wales, too, once had such a body of prose, we can claim with assurance.) The Irish panegyrists were the *filid*, who seem to correspond to the *vates* or seers who were linked with the Druids in Gaul; they were organised in strict groups and had to· reach a high level of learning in saga, genealogy, law, rules of metre and composition. (18) The bards in Wales are clearly of the same type; and it was against them that Gildas fulminated as the panegyrists of king Maelgwn Gwynedd:

> With your prickt ears caught, not the praises of God in the tuneful voice of the followers of Christ, with its flowing rhythm and the song (*neuma*) of church-melody, are heard, but your praises, which are nothing, the voice of the villainous gang belching forth like Bacchic revellers full of lies and the foam of phlegm so as to smear everyone around. (19)

There was some close relation between the *filid* and the Druidic system of the Celts which had been put down by the Romans in Gaul and Britain in the 1st century A.D. Even within the provincial boundaries Druidic remnants may have continued in the remoter highlands; and in Ireland and the further North the full system went on, modified in various ways by the development of strong kingships. (20)

It is possible that in Britain during the later 4th century, with considerable Irish immigration in the west, there was something of a Druidic revival, for instance in connection with the cult of Nudd. It is to Britain that Cuchulainn and other Ulster heroes come in Irish saga to be educated by two British queens in the arts that include the use of arms, wisdom, gnomic maxims, and magic. In Rhygyfarch's *Life of St. David* the main opposition to the saint comes from Boia of Clegyr, whose wife is called a Druid. She invites her step-daughter to go gathering nuts, gets her to lie in her lap to have her hair combed, and then cuts her throat—from the blood arising the spring called the Martyrium of David. (21)

Adamnan mentions a Druid, Broichan, at the Pictish court of King Bruide. The name seems Irish. (22)

At least in a sort of antiquarian way Druidic traditions seem to have survived among the Gaulish learnèd; for among Ausonius' friends we meet a family who prided themselves on a descent from the Armorican Druids. (23) Phoebicius was keeper of the temple of Belenus and obtained a chair at Bordeaux University with his son's aid. The son Patera is described as a man of remarkable powers of eloquence and of teaching, scion of the line of the Druids of Bayeux. Patera's son Delphidius was named from Apollo's shrine (Patera himself has the name of the sacrificial dish). A poet almost from the cradle, Delphidius began in youth with a Hymn to Jupiter and composed epics quicker than anyone else could tell the same tale in prose. Jerome, testy and exacting, mentions him thrice with high praise. In 359 he conducted a case in which the governor of Gallia Narbonesis was accused of embezzlement before the emperor Julian. (24) His wife and daughter, we saw, became Priscillianists, and the wife, Euchrotia, was executed.

Druidism seems to have been mingled with medicine at Bordeaux. Early in the 5th century Marcellus Empiricus there composed a book of prescriptions, and amid many provincialisms he gives plant-names in Celtic and magical procedures. Certain herbs are to be picked with the right hand, or while muttering a formula like *rica rica soro*. And there may be something of a ritualistic self-dedication in the career of Ausonius' aunt Aemilia Hilaria, sister of his mother, who loathed her "female part" and was "malely busied in the medical art". (25)

Among the commonfolk, Druidism certainly survived as a form of magic and soothsaying. The elder Pliny mentions that Druids still carried on in his days; Flavius Vopiscus in the 3rd century speaks of wise women who called themselves *dryades* (*mulier dryas*, *drysada*). Aurelian consulted the wise women about the future of his imperial office, and Diocletian was told that he would gain the throne "after killing the boar". Alexander Severus, preparing for his last expedition, met a female Druid who prophesied his death in Gaulish speech, *Gallico sermone*—presumably Celtic, though it might mean provincial Latin.

We can recognise the traditional importance of women as prophets in a heresy reported in north-west Gaul early in the 6th century:

From a report by the venerable priest Speratus we learn that you do not cease from taking among various fellow-citizens, from cottage to cottage, certain tables on which you celebrate the holy mass with the assistance of women whom you style *conhospitae*—while you distribute the eucharist, they take the chalice and dare to administer to the people the Blood of Christ.

That is an innovation, an unheard-of superstition; we have been deeply saddened to see reappear in our times an abominable sect which has never been introduced into Gaul. . . .

The "innovators" are suspected of Montanism, which in Asia Minor likewise did not banish women from the services and gave a high importance to the female prophet; but we are much more likely to be meeting a Celtic usage—perhaps a Breton or British one. (26)

The strange and contorted forms that classical learning was liable to take under the furious pressures of a world breaking up and coming together again in new ways, is exemplified supremely in the work of Virgilius Maro, his *Epitomes*. It is difficult to be sure if Virgil is a parodist or a slightly demented enthusiast—though some commentators have thought him a highly educated man. As Virgil had strong effects on Celtic culture, he is worth considering at some length. We see in him the kind of tension that was developing in the late 5th or 6th century between the old systems and the new needs. At first glance his ideas may seem futile and distracted; but the fact that he could so richly fertilise his world should make us think twice and look deeper for the needs he answers. (27)

He may have come from Toulouse as Abbo of Fleury (*d.* 1000) declared—though that statement may derive from one of his comments which can be read cryptically: "I will speak in the vulgar tongue of Bigorre" (maybe meaning, "I will speak double-Dutch"). In his 15th epitome he explains:

The first then was an old man of the name of Donatus who lived at Troy, it's said, for a thousand years. When he came to pay a visit on Romulus, who founded Rome, he was welcomed with cordiality and stayed four years, setting up school and leaving numberless works. . . .

There was also at Troy one Virgil, a pupil of that same Donatus, who was a very busy prosodist and wrote seventy volumes on Metre and a letter Explaining the Word which he sent to Virgil of Asia.

I am the third Virgil.

Now Virgil of Asia was the pupil of the first Virgil. . . . I have seen him with my own eyes. He set me my copies when I was a child. He wrote a well-known book about the Twelve Kinds of Latin. . . .

Troy, you see, means Rome. Rome means—Toulouse? Virgil cites many books all quite unknown to fame outside his pages; but then with such a mystifier we have no proof that he isn't referring to something quite different from what he seems to be. A Gregory the Egyptian wrote 3,000 volumes on Greek History; Galbungus wrote *Praise of the Roman Emperors and Soldiers* and a *Letter to Gurgilius Assianus*; Glengus, *Exposition about the Gods*; Terrentius, *On the Computation of Syllables*; Donatus, 70 volumes on metres; Gergesus, 27 on *The Sun, Moon and Stars and Especially the Rainbow*; Galbarius, *On Commentaries of the Universe* (*Creatum Seculum*). There were three Lucans: of Araby, India, and Africa. The last-named taught Aeneas, who taught Virgil himself. Aeneas mentioned in one of his books a Maro who lived before the Flood, and, seeing promise in Virgil, remarked, "This my son shall be called Maro, for in him the spirit of the ancient Maro lives again."

They are a closely-knit and violent community of scholars. Galbungus and Terrentius for fourteen days and nights argued about the vocative of *ego*. Regulus of Cappadocia and Sedulius of Rome kept it up a day and night longer on frequentative verbs, taking no food or drink and sensibly providing themselves with three soldiers to carry on if the discussion led to blows.

The aim of these grammarians was to acquire all divine and

human knowledge, thus becoming worthy of the name of philosopher. The main arts of philosophy were poetry, rhetoric, grammar, *leporia* (graces), dialectic, geometry, and "others which seek less to be useful than to satisfy curiosity". Virgil admits: "A small amount of lying is perpetrated by rhetoricians and leporicians" (beautifiers). Dialectic has a bite; it submits to rigorous criticism all words capable of being read, pronounced, and written; it penetrates somehow right in "to the bowels of sentences, the marrow of senses, the veins of sounds". "Poetry, satisfied with its proper variety, is constricted and difficult; rhetoric, delighting in its charm, spreads its amplitude and beauty, not without a showy use of metres, feet, accents, tones, and syllables."

In grammar Virgil takes over the terms of the schools, but uses them in his own way, which may be the exact opposite of the accepted. He is particularly interested in breaking words up and putting them together in odd ways. He recommends the scholar to try new words for those in common use, to set a letter in place of a sound, a word in place of a phrase, and vice versa; also to employ the same word in different senses. Using the roots of epithets related to fire, he builds eleven synonyms for fire, and so on. (28)

The practice of stenography had to some extent helped his attitude. (29) But the aim is to create a secret group, "to protect the mysteries". The Art of Cutting-up Words, he claims, was used in the schools of Italy and Africa. It exercised the wit of the pupils, ornamented and constructed discourse, and kept certain mysterious themes from the crowd. Its method was to upset the normal order of words, cut the words up into syllables and scatter them. In its simple form it turns *regnum* into *germen* or *is* into *şi*, *dono* into *nodo*, *lego* into *gelo*. In its more complex forms (the text is from Galbungus) it turns, for instance, *primae partis procerae partes pleni pupis erant* into PPPP PPP RRR RRR LM SSS NN TTT C IIII AAAAA O EEE EEE. The Learned Cutters, *Scindentes Periti*, were concerned not to be understood.

The epitome about metres is extremely interesting as showing the crisis in the old systems with their basis in quantity. Virgil still uses the old terms, and he never explains the rôle of accent, but clearly he deals with verses that are developing quite new laws. The verses he cites are rhythmical and reveal a strong element of riming. (30)

The poems have a doggerel touch and are so simple that one can scarcely translate them:

> Phoebus surgit, caelum scandit,
> polo claret, cunctis paret. (Aeneas)

"The sun doth arise and climb the skies, on high he is bright, in everyone's sight."

Lupus, a Christian, writes: "True Truth, equal Equity, large Largesse, faithful Faith, tranquil Times hold the daily Days": (*Veritas vera . . .*)

There are many poets, all on this level. But these grammarians are sure that they inherit the wisdom and creative powers of the ages. "We trust in Mitterius as in an oracle." "Aeneas cannot err." "Then he spoke as though inspired by some prophetic breath." (31)

With Virgil, we may say, medieval scholasticism in its schematic aspects is meticulously founded. The debates which we have noted, and others such as that on the distinction of *hic* pronoun and *hic* adverb, "would have made the reputation of the grammarian-dialecticians of the 13th century." (32)

The epitomes were widely read in Ireland. Virgil may even have travelled to Ireland; he has some knowledge of the country; he notes that the Irish verb is placed first in a sentence. Among his friends is Bregandus Lugenicus or Lucenicus—the latter part of his name being the name of a tribe of the Luceni, settled then on the south coast of Ireland. Bregand itself is an ancient Irish name; and there are indeed a large number of names in the epitomes that seem to be of Celtic origin. (33) The epitomes themselves have been preserved through Irish intermediaries; and they may even have been first written in Irish script. (34)

There grew up out of the tendencies present in Virgil and his friends what is called Hisperic Latin, based in south-west Britain and Ireland: a tangled bristling speech, which can reveal many new vigours but which can also be heavy and harsh. (35) In virtues and vices alike it has little relation to classical Latin. (36) We see it at its strongest in Columba's hymn *Altus prosator*; at its most obscure in the *Hisperica Famina*. As an example, we may take the *Lorica* ascribed to Gildas—*lorica* or breastplate being a name for certain hymns against dangers of all sorts. (37)

> Help me, Unity of Trinity.
> Trinity of Unity, pity me.
> Help me, beset, I make my plea
> as in the perils of a great sea.
> Let not the world's vanity snare me,
> nor this year's Plague tear me.
> And this petition, I cry
> to the powers of heaven's army on high:
> Let not harrying foes rend me,
> with your strong armour defend me.
> Let heaven's soldiers, row on row,
> before me into battle go,
> Cherubim, Seraphim in thousands follow,
> Gabriel and Michael with their fellows.

The poet calls further on powers, thrones, archangels, principalities, dominions, angels, patriarchs, prophets, apostles (watchmen in Christ's ship), athlete martyrs, virgins, widows, confessors:

> Christ strike a firm pact with me,
> whose Terror makes the foul hosts flee.

Then he calls on God to protect his body and names every portion of his anatomy for some fifty lines, missing nothing out, "paps, stomach, navel, belly, reins and genitals" . . .

> From soles to crown let me quicken,
> in no part, inside-outside, sicken,
> let my life be cast out never
> by pest, frailty, anguish, fever,
> till, with the gift of age from God,
> my sins through my good works I shed . . .

Note that last line. It is at root Pelagian in the modified form that the creed of free will and good works had taken in order to escape persecution as a heresy. (38)

Most interesting, however, for its diversity and for its information is *Hisperica Famina*, Western Words. The material is as follows:

1–48 glorification of rhetors and their school, and of the speaker himself as able to beat all his contemporaries.

49–86 a grazier who has tried to be a scholar is told to go home to his family.

87–115 illustrations of the speaker's superiority in Latin.

133–357 description of a day and its occupations, followed by passages on various subjects: sky, sea, fire, wind, and so on. (39)

The lines are of varying length with a cesura occurring very irregularly; the ghost of the classical hexameter seems to haunt the metrical ruins. The lines have been taken as riming internally, but this is not quite correct, though an illusion of rimes is gained by marking breaks after an adjective or noun which agrees in case with an adjective or noun at the close of the line —the like endings then give a faint jingle.

Thus the west wind is described:

> Now well reared oaks in this weather go down to
> the sounding Zephyr,
> old knotty holmoaks it harrows flat to furrows,
> stoutly-snorting it harms thatch crested farms,
> cracks topmost tiles on chimneystacks,
> raves threshing water with blue waves,
> swings high marine foam-drops on starry sky.

The poet asks:

> Do not Ausonian fetters hold fast my wits?
> Therefore no creaking Irish blarney I speak—

scottigenum eulogium. Another Irish reference is in the lines:

> Our gnashing teeth in the mealy cakes we sheathed,
> and Irish fat in spreading sauce we ate;
> our jaws we plied and the fleshy joints chewed.

A characteristic word of this lingo is *tethys* for sea; it is found in Gildas as well as the *Famina*:

> has the foamflood pouring of tethys riproaring
> crashed down on fagged-out rowers who drown?

But there are odder words than that—*idumae* for hands and *gibrosus* for human, *sennosus* for toothed and *gigra* for head, for which a Hebrew or Semitic origin has been vainly sought. Greek words appear in Latin spelling, *somata, troni, pe pompo* (*pepompa*), *pantes, migrus* (*mikros*). There is also a trick of using a phrase for a noun, with the adjective holding the substantive meaning:

> Ample joy through the breastly cavern blows:

runs the first line of the poem. (40)

Much argument has gone on as to whether the work was composed in south-west Britain or in Ireland, and whether the poet was a Briton, an Irishman, or a Gaul from the south-west of his land come in exile to Ireland. The essential point is that the poem comes from a cultural complex embracing all the suggested areas. (41)

The tumultuous Hisperic Latin directly reflects the disintegrations of its world and seeks to bring together in a new way a large number of conflicting factors. The Celtic poets—the exiles from Gaul, the Irish and British—were attracted by the way in which prose-rhythms were being reorganised as verse and given the previously-prose decoration of rime. Taking over the experiments of Gaul, they developed them and then fed the forms back into the general stream of Latin culture:

It is clear that the Irish poets did much to further the development of rimed and rhythmical verse. They took it in its rudimentary form from the Continental poets and gave it a whole-hearted welcome. They were familiar with rime, not only in hymns but in the rhetorical prose of ecclesiastical writers, and in the contestationes or prefaces of their mass-books. The writings of Isidore and of other Spanish churchmen must have been well known in Ireland in the seventh century, and Columbanus knew all the devices of rimed prose. This love of rime passed from the Irish to the Anglo-Saxons, and thence back again to the Continent. (42)

But we cannot thus limit the development to the Irish. The Britons of south-west Britain and of Wales also played their part in this early period when the cultures of all the Celtic regions in the islands were closely connected. Saints like David and Gildas visited Ireland, and the Irish wandered in all directions.

OGAMS AND SAINTS

W E have earlier come across evidences of Irish infiltrations
and irruptions in south Wales: for instance, Tewdrig who
founded the kingdom of Brycheiniog. An Irish glossary mentions joint kingdoms in Ireland and Britain held by Irish kings,
with the more important section in Britain, and cites Dind map
Lethain, seemingly on the north coast of the Dumnonian peninsula of the Severn Sea: "and they held that power long after
Patrick's coming". In Breton tradition Rheval, founder of
Breton Dumnonia, ruled "on both sides of the sea; and Cono-
marus, who held Dumnonia at the time of the Frankish Hilde-
berht, has his name on a cross-shaft near Fowey in Cornwall:
Drustanus hic jacit Cunomori filius". (1)

Fedelmid, son of Loiguire, was high-king of Ireland at the
time of Patrick's mission; he was married to a British princess.
When Patrick's nephew Lomman visited his residence at Trim,
the prince Foirtchernn took him to his mother, who was
pleased to see a man from her own country. Fedelmid, who
spoke Welsh, gave up the residence to Lomman and entrusted
Foirtchernn to his care. As Foirtchernn is the Irish cognate of
Vortigern, it is possible that the queen was a daughter of the
British high-king and had given her father's name to her son. (2)

The Scottic attacks on the western shores in Wales and further
north had no lasting consequences; but a little after the mid-
5th century a Scottic settlement was established in Argyll and
the islands to its west. It was an offshoot of the kingdom of
Dalriada in north Ireland, and was said to be the work of three
princes:

It has been suggested that the Dalriada of Scotland came into being
through a colonising movement carried out with the co-operation of
the northern Welsh people who lived near the western end of the
Antonine Wall and whose capital was at Dumbarton on the Clyde.
According to this conjecture, the purpose of the move was to inter-

rupt the western sea-communications of the Picts, and by confining them to their mountain territories, to reduce the menace which they offered to the security of the northern Welsh. (3)

The main strongholds of the new Dalriada were at Dunolly Castle, Oban, and at Dunadd in the Moss of Crinan.

An early saint in south-west Wales was Tathan, perhaps an Irishman from Caernarvonshire, who moved south around the coast after the coming of Cunedda; he may, however, belong to the next generation and have come across the sea. His *Life*, though of the 12th century, has a pastoral simplicity. A king's son, he sails after a dream to the Severn and lands "at the haven called after the name of people arriving". A stag holds the rope and stops the ship from floating away, then extends its neck to be killed for the saint's dinner. All the miracles are everyday matters. His horse stamps a spring out; he resurrects his cow which robbers have stolen; he deals with sheep-stealers and a shepherdess, a swineherd worried by a wolf-bitch and needing a spring, a miserly peasant who won't make a gift of a bit of fire. Horses of the court damage his cow's meadow, they die and the king comes barefooted from Caerwent, so the saint revives them. On the land that the king grants he founds a collegiate church. (4)

The ogams in Wales further testify to the Irish connection. As far east as Silchester one has been found, the tombstone of Ebicatos, with inscription in an Irish form of Celtic. The man had died there and friends had set up an epitaph in his own tongue; there must have been an Irish colony in the town. (5) We may note that the road from south Wales to the Continent was from Abone at the Avonmouth, running via Bath, Marl-borough, and Silchester to London, then on to Richborough. (6)

Ogam letters are made up of notches cut on the edges of memorial stones so as to form a stroke-alphabet. In Ireland the stones have ogams alone; in Britain, and especially in south Wales, there are many bilingual stones, in ogam and Latin. (7) The distribution of ogams in south Wales follows closely the pattern in Pembrokeshire and west Carmarthenshire made by the early-Christian inscribed stones and the dedications to the family of Maximus. (8) There are few ogams in north Wales.

A definite link appears with the trade-routes using the south of Wales and the Bristol Channel, with the Roman road system.

Ogam is a sophisticated alphabet, the work of a grammarian who was something of a phonetician and who was able to make his abstract construction on the basis of a developed analytic tradition. Its inventor was a man learned in grammar as taught in the schools of the late empire; possibly it was created in south-west Britain by an Irishman who took it back to his homeland. Its origin would then be linked with the Irish settlements on the west coast of Britain, where Irish was a living language through the 5th and 6th centuries and perhaps into the 7th.

In Ireland there are somewhat over three hundred monuments with ogams, five-sixths of them in the south counties of Kerry, Cork, and Waterford, with an extension through Kilkenny, Carlow, Wicklow, and Kildare of some thirty. About half the south ones are in Kerry; so the concentration is in south-west Ireland. They may have begun in the 4th, but they mostly belong to the 5th and 6th centuries, straggling on into the 7th— a few are later still, agreeing in language with the Old Irish of the 8th century or later. The British examples range from mid-5th to early 7th century.

In Wales the ogams more or less coincide with the area of stones with Roman inscriptions; but that does not prove the latter to be Irish. There are often British and Latin names on them. The epitaphs of the 5th–7th centuries, with or without ogams, are in Roman letters cut for the most part on rough slabs; they are almost all funerary. They give the name of the dead man (rarely woman) in the genitive with *filius* or *filia* and the father's name—though occasionally the *filius-filia* section is left out. The formula is *Hic Jacet* or simply *Jacet*—though we also find *Memoria, In Pace, In hoc tumulo,* chi-rho or cross; elaboration is rare. Only one has a date, that of Justinus Consul. (9)

The genitive occurs on pagan Roman stones, where *dis manibus* (to the Shades) is given or understood; but it is not found in Christian inscriptions in Gaul. The mention of father or other relations is also not from Gallic or Roman custom. In Gaul the concern with the parents went out in obedience to

Matthew (xxiii. 9): "Call no man your father." The Welsh formula is Celtic. (10)

The Roman epitaphs had to accommodate themselves to the narrow stone that would suit ogam, which needed a long edge and generally began on the left, went up and over, ending down on the right.

Why was ogam invented? Perhaps we can find the answer if we think of the passion of the circle of Virgilius Maro for secret communication. Grouping the alphabet in fives, it is clearly connected with a finger language; all the signs could be made by laying the fingers along a straight line—even the nose or the shin. Irish literature reveals a very strong magical nexus around ogams, and so we may take it as a sort of marriage of late Roman grammar and Druidic Irish spell. All our examples are on stone (or bone in the Pictish examples); but obviously the notching technique would better suit wood. The wooden examples, probably used casually, are all gone. (11)

In the tales, ogams exert a strong power against spirits. They are used in funerary ritual, and in their original wand-form they are connected with various trees—each group and each sign had its relation to tree or plant. At the beginning of the *Tain*, Cuchulainn, before meeting Fedelm Noichride, sets a bough of oak in a circle round a pillar of stone after inscribing an ogam. Fergus reads the ogam and interprets it with the aid of a Druid. In one version the procedure of Cuchulainn is minutely described: he cuts the wand with one cut, using one foot, one hand, one eye. Then, when the horsemen of Ailill meet the pillar, Ailill takes the "barbarous circle" and hands it to Fergus, who says that it will be dangerous for the army to pass the pillar and calls on the Druids to interpret the ogam. A Druid recognises the hand of Cuchulainn. A little later Cuchulainn enters a wood, cuts a four-pointed wand with one blow, sharpens it, and passes it through fire, then cuts an ogam on it. On the four points he sets the heads cut from four of his foes and buries the bough in the middle of the ford. As before, the ogam is given to Fergus who calls on the Druids.

It would seem, then, that the ogam was a secret mode of communication, a finger language which could be transferred to wands. On wands it had considerable magical power over living and dead, especially of an apotropaic kind. When its secret aspect was dissolved, it still held enough magical feeling to seem of use in inscriptions protecting a dead man or property.

The Latin inscriptions, at which we glanced earlier, have much interest. They establish the close links with Gaul and show us something of the system of society. A stone at Llanael-hiarn states: "Aliortus the Elmetian lies here". Elmet was a British kingdom corresponding roughly to West Riding; Aliortus must have migrated from there to north Wales, where he died. At Penbryn was "(the stone) of Corbalengus: (here) he lies, an Ordovicium". In Roman times the Ordovices were a tribe in north-central Wales; Corbalengus must have moved down to Cardiganshire. His stone shows that the tribal divisions of Roman and pre-Roman days still survived.

More important revelations are made by a stone from Pen-machno: "Cantiorix lies here: he was a citizen of Venedos, cousin of Maglos the magistrate." *Cives, consobrinos*, and *magistrat*—are the words used. Venedos is the Celtic form of the Welsh Gwynedd, the old name for north-west Wales. This region (roughly Caernarvonshire and Anglesey) was thus already defined in the sub-Roman period. *Consobrinos* is a plebeian form of *consobrinus*, cousin; *magistratus* is a noun of the fourth declension drawn into the commoner second through sharing the *-us* ending. It seems that an administrative area has been constituted, centred on Caernarvon, Segontium, the town linked with Maximus.

In Llangian churchyard is a stone: "Of Melus the Doctor (*medicus*), son of Martinus: he lies (here)." The inclusion of a secular profession is unusual in an early-Christian epitaph, as incongruous with a rejection of worldly matters; the name Martin suggests either an immigrant from Gaul or someone whose family revered the saint of that name. (12)

At Cynwyl Gaeo a fragmentary slab records:

> He served the Faith and his Homeland ever loved,
> here lies Paulinus, devoted to Justice he lived.

The two hexameters are barbarous in form, with stock phrases. Paulinus was a common name; but we may reasonably take the praised man to be the saint who was said to have taught St.

David and who died about 550. The stone comes from the area associated with him. There is no special reason to identify him with the Paulinus who was father of the Cantusus recorded on a stone near Port Talbot—the stone having originally marked the repairs or reopening of the main south-Wales roadway under Maximinus (309–13). But we possibly meet him again at Llantrisant:

. . . iva [or ina] a most holy woman lies here, who was the very loving wife of Bivatig [irnus] servant of God, sacerdos, and disciple of Paulinus, by race a . . . docian, and an example to all his fellow citizens and relatives both in character [and] rule of life [as also] of wisdom [better] than gold and gems [or gold from stones].

Famulus dei was a favourite term among early Christians, found in Italy (not often), in Gaul, and especially in Spain; in epitaphs it seems used only of the dead. *Sacerdos* generally means a bishop, but can be used for priest. *Vasso Paulini*: *vasso* is a Gaulish word for servant, here meaning disciple. Bivati-girnus is described as *andoco* or *avdoco*: which may be equivalent to Andescavo. He would then be an Andecavus, one of the Gaulish tribe centred on Angers; *vasso* also suggests a Gaulish origin—though the language is rather that of African inscriptions of the time, the later 6th century. (13)

At Aberdaron on a boulder used as a pillar-stone was found: "Senacus the presbyter (priest) lies here with the multitude of the Brothers." The Latin is barbarous (*cum multitudinem*), but we see that Senacus was one of a monastic community in whose cemetery he was buried. At Penmachno we meet a cairn system of burial: "Carausius lies here in this heap of stones" (*in hoc congeries*). On the highway near Bodafon: "Sanctinus Sacerdos in Peace."

At Llansadwrn in the churchyard was found "Here lies buried blessed (*beatus*) . . . Saturninus and his holy (*sancta*) wife: Peace be with you (both)." Beatus or Beatissimus is common in early Christian epitaphs, particularly for martyrs, confessors, bishops; *sancta coniux* occurs often in pagan epitaphs and so has no specifically Christian meaning, but in this context a saintly element is doubtless intended. Saturninus has been taken as Sadwrn Farchog, brother of Illtud and founder of the church where the stone was found.

At Llanddewi-Brefi was found an inscription: "Here lies Idnert, son of Ia . . ., who was killed near the farm (*praedium*?) of holy (*sanctus*) . . ." (14)

At times we detect relations. At Llandeilo lay Curcagnus ("son of . . . urivus); at Maenclochnog, Curcagnus son of Andagellus; at Llandeilo again, Andagellus son of Cavetus, and Coimagnus son of Cavetus. At Llanuwchllyn lay Salvianus Bursocavis son of Cupetianus; at Llanymawddwy, the daughter of Salvianus, "Ve . . maie, wife of Tigirnicus," and her sister Rigohene, wife of Oneratus. At Defunnog lay Rugniatis, son of Vendonius; at Clydai, Solinus, son of Vendonius.

At Llandanwg was buried Equester in the 6th century; we know no other example from Roman or post-Roman inscriptions for the use of this adjective (equestrian, belonging to the order of *equites*, knights) as a name.

Roman names were common: Turpillius, Martius, Eternus son of Victor, Vitalianus, Salvian, Honoratus, Paulinus, Saturninus, Avitus, Severinus and Severus, Vitalis, Secundus, Pompeius. Also Irish names. And at times a British name has a long history. From Margam comes a four-sided stone: "Of Bodvoc: here he lies, son of Catotigurnus, great-grandson of Eternalis Vedomavus." The date is 6th century; but *Bodvoc* is met on British coins of the 1st century B.C. in the region of Oxfordshire-Gloucestershire. There was also a potter at Lezoux in Gaul in mid-2nd century named Bodvocus. (15)

We move into history with the stone at Castell Dwyran: "Memorial (*memoria*) of Votepori the Protector (*protictor*)." With "of Votecorix" in ogam. The formula *memoria* with an encircled chi-rho or its derivative ring-cross (as here) occurs in Italy, at times in Spain or Gaul, but especially in north Africa in the 4th–5th century. The title *protector* was at first used for members of the imperial bodyguard, but later became honorific; Voteporix's family probably inherited it from Roman times. Voteporix seems certainly the king of Demetia (south-west Wales) whom Gildas abused as a tyrant full of guile, guilty of various parricides and adulteries, the wicked son of a good father, who did not slacken in his bad deeds with greying hair.

Finally, at Llangadwaladr on Anglesey we meet "King Catamanus, Wisest, Most Renowned of All Kings". Catamanus was the Welsh Cadfan, king of Gwynedd (north-west Wales) in the early 7th century, son of Iago. "The magniloquent phraseology of the inscription plainly echoes the formal language of the imperial Byzantine court, which was copied by the courts of the barbarian kings." Cadfan was the last prince of the highland region to get a Latin epitaph; in this sense he was the last of the Romano-Britons. (16)

There are inscribed stones also in the north: four in Lothian and the Merse, three at Kirkmadrine in the Rinns of Galloway, two at Whithorn. One or two are perhaps late 5th, the rest are early 6th century: apart from one Whithorn stone, which may be 7th. The Kirkmadrine and Whithorn stones are Christian; two of the eastern series seem linked with Christian graveyards and another has a cross. The Yarrowkirk stone has been read: "This is the Everlasting Memorial, in this place lie the most famous princes Nudus and Dumnogenus, in this tomb lie the two sons of Liberalis." (17)

We cannot here pursue the history of the Celtic Church, but we must have some idea of the lines on which it grew. Substantially we may call Celtic Christianity the Church of St. Martin developing in still largely tribal society. Not that the Celts set themselves to a special imitation of Martin, though it is likely, we saw, that his example was potent in Britain round 390–410. For various historical reasons the Celtic Church shared and extended his independent attitude with its simple evangelism and its rejection of the existing world. It was a law to itself, making no submissions or compromises, and by its very nature opposed to the regimentations by which, under the rules of Basil and Benedict, the monastic revolt was controlled inside the centralised Church. One plain reason why the Martin kind of church could carry on among the Celts was the lack of a state system at all comparable to that which survived, however imperfectly, in Gaul and elsewhere. (18) Because of this lack the Roman Church was unable to impose any control of the situation and use the secular power to insist on uniformity, while the tribal level favoured the cenobitic form. The barrier of pagan Anglo-Saxons left the Celts free in the spaces beyond to work out their own strange world.

The bishop still existed for purposes of ordination, but was otherwise unimportant. The key-figure was the abbot, who was a kind of tribal chief; indeed, he was often a son or brother of the tribal head. There was no diocesan bishop at all; the abbot directed all the community's affairs, though in important matters he called a council of his monks. (19) The loose organisation accorded equally with the desire to seek the desert or to move among men with the evangel, to live as hermit or as member of a brotherhood.

The social background was that of free tribesmen, semi-nomadic pastoralists who also carried on temporary tillage. These freemen lacked settled houses and set up shacks that could be easily taken down and moved. In areas of particularly good agricultural land the freemen's place was taken by non-free tribesmen in a more settled and nucleated system of dwellings, with a strong arable basis to the economy. Between the 9th and 13th centuries the free tribesmen gradually took to living in clusters of a permanent kind (later dispersed into the kind of picture given by the modern *tyddynod*). (20)

In the monks' outlook there were wild elements, a desperate conviction of loss, a bewilderment but, deeper still, a great sweetness and love, a hope of human relations thriving without the limits and distortions felt to rule in the world.

The early monastic elements in Wales continued to be linked with the Roman roads, with the areas where classical culture was undergoing its deep-sea changes. Refugees, contributing, had come in from Gaul as well as the Silchester–Cirencester region. St. Dubricius (Dyfrig), one of the earliest figures, who appears in the *Life of St. Samson* written by a Breton monk of Dol in the early 7th century, seems to represent the primary concentrations in south-east Wales; he is in fact more like a diocesan bishop than a Celtic one. (21)

More important still was St. Illtud, said to be born in Brittany, who founded a monastery at Llantwit in Glamorganshire. The monk of Dol thus describes the master:

Now this Illtud was a disciple of St. Germanus and St. Germanus himself had ordained him priest in his youth. And in truth Illtud was of all Britons the most accomplished in all the Scriptures, namely of the Old and New Testaments, and in those of philosophy of every kind, of geometry namely, and of rhetoric, grammar and arithmetic, and of all the theories of philosophy. And by birth he was a wise magician, having knowledge of the future. I have been in his splendid monastery. . . . (22)

The monk thus states that he had visited Llantwit and talked of Illtud with the monks there. The claim about Germanus is the usual invention, for Germanus died about 445 and Illtud was born about 436; but we may assume there was truth in the tradition of Illtud's learning. The *Life* of St. Pol-de-Léon (called both Paul and Paulinus), written by a Breton about 884, also refers to Illtud as a great master to whom disciples flocked, including both St. Paul and St. David.

The remark about his birth is odd and perhaps means that he was of Druidic descent. Indeed, there seem several connections between the Celtic Church and Druidism. We cannot ignore the link traced "between the monastic establishments and the preceding Druidic colleges". Fruitfulness of crops depended on obedience to the monks, and they claim the Druidic prerogative of exemption from taxes. The Celtic tonsure seems to be Druidic. According to a MS. of Hibernensis, they shaved the forepart of the head from ear to ear, leaving a lock in the front—"thus one may distinguish Christians from Simon Magus": Simon standing for the mage or Druid, the father of heresy.

The form of the tonsure is not quite clear, but it seems that in the front a crown of hair was left connecting the ears—while the Roman style was to shave the whole head. Patrick seems to have had the latter shave: hence the way in which the Druids called him Adzehead. That the Druids had a tonsure is certain, but it seems that other Celtic classes also shaved their heads in ritualistic ways. The Breton warriors of Weroch were tonsured; and the Saxons of Bayeux who fought on their side were tonsured "in the British way" (*ritu*) so as not to be recognised. (We learn from Sidonius that the Saxons were used to shear the whole forepart of the head, so that at a distance they seemed to have very long faces and scanty heads.)

The earlier name of Illtud's monastery, Llan-yltwyt, is Irish in form and attests the strong Irish element in this area at the time. The site, like that of St. Cadog at Llancarfan, brings out also the relation to Roman times; Llantwit is close to a large Roman villa. Both Llantwit and Llancarfan, here in south

Glamorganshire, were in effect Channel ports, though in the lower reaches of small river-valleys, hidden from the look-out of roving pirates. They were high enough up the Bristol Channel to make an easy crossing, and near enough to the Roman roads across the sea-plain to be in touch with other settled areas of south Wales. Further up the estuary the northern shores grew marshy. (23) Cadog, like Illtud, is described as an inheritor of the Roman tradition, descended from a long line of emperors reaching back to Augustus, and regretful that he will not be able to meet his admired poet Virgil in the hereafter. Throughout their history the schools of Illtud and Cadog flourished and maintained their scholarly tradition.

If the Celtic Church was in a sense the church of Martin developing under tribal conditions, it was also in another sense the church of Pelagius under those same conditions. The Celts were not in any conscious way heretics, despite their obstinate practices in regard to tonsures or Easter; but they remained theologically rather at a pre-Augustinian level, though accepting in a general way the ideas of Original Sin and sanctifying Grace. We are indeed told of David of Wales and Kentigern of Glasgow putting down Pelagians. (24)

Yet practically they live as Pelagians. They have the sense of the triumphant apostolate, an effective hate of sin, the ambition of the sinless state. They have enough confidence in free will to expose themselves voluntarily to perilous temptations; the most extreme renunciations—the white martyrdom of sacrifice and the green martyrdom of penitence—seem to them natural; they compel those whom they "regenerate" to a total conversion, one without circumspection or stages; they follow the rules of a perfect life and want to make a whole people into a people of "saints". These men, who besides might have read *De Vita Christiana*, have realised the most lofty ideal of Pelagius. (25)

We can therefore recognise a general truth, though theological precision might be lacking, in the letter of pope John IV to the abbots of the north of Ireland in 640, in which he complains of having heard that "the Pelagian heresy, extinguished for two centuries, is in way of reappearing". The Roman Church was now at last in the position of being able to interfere. (26) Also certain Irish chronicles of 455 seem to assimilate the Pelagians to the upholders of the Celtic Easter. (27)

To estimate how far the Celtic Church had moved from the Roman controls we must note that in 451 the Council of Chalcedon in its fourth canon laid down that "the monks of the country and the town come under the jurisdiction of the bishop". For Gaul the position was defined at the third Council of Arles in 455. A result was that while among the Celts the bishop was subordinated to the abbot, in Gaul of the 6th and 7th centuries the bishops rode roughshod over the abbots with a series of vetoes that left all effective power in their hands.

Before we leave the Saints, we may touch on their relations to Arthur in the *Lives*. Cadog, Illtud, Carannog, Padarn, and Gildas are all represented as meeting him. Though we cannot expect historicity here, the tales have interest in showing the various sorts of traditions that had grown up about Arthur. In the *Life of Padarn* the *tyrannus* Arthur chances on the saint's cell and covets his tunic; the saint makes the earth open and swallow him up till he begs pardon. Here Arthur simply stands for the world that the saint rejects. Cadog has a more complicated relation. His father, a Glamorgan king, is fleeing with king Brychan's daughter Gwladys when he meets Arthur and his knights (*equites*) Kei and Bedwyr gambling on a hilltop. Arthur is enamoured of Gwladys, but his knights remind him that it is their custom "to aid the needy and distressed". So the three of them defend the runaways. Later, when Cadog is abbot of Llancarfan, Arthur seeks a man who has killed three of his knights. Cadog hides the man for seven years, then persuades Arthur to accept arbitration. On the banks of the Usk he, with other monks (David, Teilo, and others), award Arthur a hundred cows for the dead knights. Arthur insists that each cow must be red before, white behind. Cadog enchants an ordinary herd to look red and white; but when Kei and Bedwyr lead them over the ford, they turn into bundles of fern. Arthur, humbled, dedicates the spot as a sanctuary.

Carannog is described as coming from Cardigan to south Wales, led by a floating stone altar. He goes across the Severn Sea to Dindraithov where Arthur rules, and meets Arthur, who is looking for a ravaging serpent. Arthur promises to find out where the altar has come ashore, in return for aid against the serpent. The saint prays; the serpent hurries up to be tethered with his stole and to follow him like a lamb. Then Arthur produces the altar; he has wanted to use it as a table, but everything put on it is flung off. He gives the site of Carrum to the saint and later builds a church there. The saint goes off again after his floating altar.

The *Life of Illtud* states that he sailed from his home in Brittany to the court of his cousin Arthur, where he saw a great host of knights. He is called a "magnificent soldier" and the author says vaguely that "he was honourably revived and rewarded as to his military desire. His desire to receive presents also being satisfied, he withdrew highly gratified". He then became Master of the Soldiers of the King of the folk of Glamorgan, Poulentus, till converted by a miracle. Courtiers on a hunt, eating a meal extorted from St. Cadog, were swallowed up in the earth.

The most involved of the saints was Gildas. Caradoc of Lancarvan composed the *Life* about 1130–6 and wrote in the vein of the romances, though before Geoffrey of Monmouth. Arthur is king of all Greater Britain, much loved by Gildas. But Gildas' twenty-three brothers will obey no lord and resist the *rex rebellis*, especially the eldest, Hueil, who keeps raiding from Scotland till Arthur kills him in the Isle of Man. Gildas, then in Ireland, is deeply grieved; but on his way to Rome is reconciled to Arthur, who undergoes penance. Later, Gildas is at Glastonbury, writing his history. Melvas, king of Summer Land, who has carried off the wife of the *tyrannus*, brings her to the marsh-enclosed sanctuary. After a year Arthur finds where she is, and brings all the forces of Devon and Cornwall against Melvas, but Gildas and the abbot of Glastonbury make peace between the kings. (28)

RESISTANCE AND SURVIVAL

W E have neither space nor need to carry the inquiry further into the 6th century, for the latter part of the first half of which we have the passages of Gildas denouncing five princes.(1) The Saxons, despite their heavy check in the Thames valley, were strengthening their hold along the east sections of the island. In Kent the Frankish elements of the culture were becoming dominant after 525, and after 494 there was a new threat in Wessex:

In the year when 494 winters had passed from the birth of Christ, Cerdic and Cynric his son landed at Cerdices-ora with five ships.

The Haestingas, the South Saxons, and the Jutes of Hampshire were established along the Channel, though in the chalk uplands of Hampshire and Wiltshire the British villagers still carried on. The Wealden forest was still mostly ignored by everyone, Celt or Saxon. In East Anglia the invaders had gathered under the rule of the Wuffingas. North of the Fens there may still have been the gap of Lincoln between the incomers round Sleaford and Ancaster, and the Humbrenses of the north. In Derbyshire valleys occupation was becoming settled, and across the wooded Midlands riverside-invaders were tackling Britons and clearance problems. The south of the Thames valley was filling in; and by mid-century maybe there were intruders into the backlands such as the Hycga who left the mark of his Chiltern estate in Hitcham, Hedgerley, and Hughenden of Buckinghamshire.

In Kent was the highest level of political organisation, with the king's hall raised in Canterbury, and rents paid and law administered in the *villa regalis* of each lathe (often set in a broken-down Roman town). Here the native populace had probably been to a large extent assimilated, and the self-contained farms at times made use of the bounds already set up between the Roman villas.

It was only a question of time before the Britons were dislodged from all their lands except the difficult highlands:

In this year [577] Cuthwine and Ceawlin fought against the Britons and slew three kings, Coinmail, Condidan, and Farinmail, at the place which is called Dyrham; and they captured three cities, Gloucester, Cirencester, and Bath.

The work of Arthur was undone.

Why had the Britons failed, despite the fact that they owned so many superior elements of organisation and technique? They failed in the final resort for the reasons that Gildas upbraided them. Their inability to unite and to remain united. For behind this failure there lay their inferiority to the Saxons in clan-spirit, in the ability to fuse a resolute independence and a sense of community. The free village-group of the Saxons represented a level of social and economic integration with richer possibilities of development than the Celtic social system. The States built up on the Saxon basis had a strength and a tenacity, a power of growth, which the Celtic kingdoms lacked.

But this does not mean that the Celts made no important contribution or that the Saxon world could have developed as it did without the Celts. In Gaul, medieval society arose from the merging of the Gallo-Roman estates with the tribal system of the invaders: the towns surviving in the interstices under the bishops to play after a while an increasing economic rôle. In Britain there was no such steady merging of the two systems. The Roman world collapsed, though various aspects of it were taken up by the *civitates* and the tribal kingdoms; the barbarians were pagans and there was no easy meeting-ground of the two cultures. What seemed, and often was, a war to the knife went on. Thus was created the whole body of specific characteristics which England carried on into medieval history and which still vitally affect our tradition.

But at the very heart of the ruthless conflict a series of meetings and mergings were in fact going on; and directly and indirectly the Celts made an invaluable contribution to the Saxon world.

In some places they were doubtless killed off. In others they were seized as slaves, were sold abroad, or kept to work the land. Place-names can give us some indication as to the survival of British groups even in areas overrun by the Saxons, but clearly their evidence is not final. Generally, however, they do conform to historical fact in the way that Celtic forms grow as we move westward. River-names survive in all parts, sometimes in forms suggesting that the new settlers had a fairly good acquaintance with British. Names with the element *weala* are of interest, as from *foreigner* it came to mean *British* and later *slave*.

A surprising detail is the number of Celtic personal names among the Wessex royal family. That this suggests intermarriage between Saxons and Britons at a high level is often pointed out; and that if the kings took British wives, the commoners probably also did so. Probably Britons in some parts joined the Saxons to fight against their fellow-Britons. We have seen how in Gaul the farmers of the 5th century went off in large numbers to join the barbarians. Why should things have been different in Britain? The paganism of the Saxons no doubt made fraternising more difficult; but the British peasants of the invasion-era were not likely to be ardent Christians. (2)

The towns in Britain did not survive as in Gaul, for reasons already noted. The Kentish king lived at Canterbury, and there must have been a sort of continuity in economic and social life there between sub-Roman days and Saxon. The Roman street-plan was lost except at surviving gates, though the early Church seems linked with the Roman plan. At Lincoln a *praefectus civitatis* was converted later by Paulinus, and at Carlisle a *civitatis praepositus* showed St Cuthbert "the wall of the city and the fountain once wonderfully built there by the Romans". Clearly elements of Roman organisation lingered long, but certainly in slight ways, unaffecting the later town systems. This is probably true even at London. Gildas, looking from the west, saw only desolation; but towns like Canterbury, London, Lincoln were out of his view.

The case for a valuable inheritance, carried over into later Saxon-Britain, does not, however, rest on the question as to whether or not anything of Roman municipal organisation survived. Nor does it rest even on the similar question as to whether the Roman villas affected Saxon agriculture. (3) Certainly the lay-out of fields, the clearances, the relation to roads, the boundaries, must have had influences in various places in various ways; and even small aspects of Roman technique may have filtered through, in tools and the craft-skill of British slaves. The *laetas* of Kent have often been thought to represent a British element.

The language spoken in medieval days in Britain was not a well-preserved Germanic tongue, but a lingo "characteristic of the imposition of a foreign language on an alien population. The rulers may have spoken relatively pure Anglo-Saxon for 500 years; the common people apparently did not". The kingdoms of the Heptarchy, which grew up, were certainly not settled at the outset by homogeneous groups of Saxon or Angle origin; they were composed of mixed elements coming together from diverse areas on the Continent; and the folk-culture that each built up must have been created in the years after the invasion. "There is reason, too, for thinking that these folk-cultures were at least in part a mixture of late provincial Roman with Teutonic fashions. It is even possible to question whether they, and the little kingdoms with which they are more or less associated, represent tribal districts formed by the Anglo-Saxons." The boundaries remain much what they were at the time of Roman conquest, those of the Iceni in East Anglia, the Trinovants in Essex, the Cantii in Kent, and so on. "Anglo-Saxons no doubt provided the rulers, the moving spirits, and the large farmers, replacing their bankrupt or murdered predecessors; but the tribal boundaries remained more or less as they had been for five hundred years." (4)

Even in the earlier years there is much evidence for exchange and influence in the art-field among Celts and Saxons. Both sides were in varying ways developing motives from the repertory of late Roman artists and craftsmen. The Germans were working out their animal ornament. This, combining with late Roman forms and the revived curvilinear style of the Celts, created the Hiberno-Saxon art of manuscript and stone-crosses. Probably an important area of reborn or expanding Celtic crafts lay in the borderlands, in the Severn valley and the

Cornovian area. Thus, penannular brooches are found mostly in Anglian cemeteries and in the Saxon ones nearest to the Severn, and are rarest in south-east England. Their concentration in Warwickshire and the Avon valley suggest contacts with the Britons there—with effects spreading east along the Fosse Way, towards East Riding in Yorkshire and into the Cambridge region; though direct contacts with British groups in the Pennine area is also possible. Whether gained by loot, by trade, or by employing British craftsmen:

it does seem probable that the penannular brooch became the normal dress-fastener in sub-Roman communities established on the western flank of the zone of early Anglo-Saxon settlement, and particularly in the Severn and Bristol Channel area: (5)

the area where we have found the lively centre of early Celtic Christianity in Britain. The liking for the brooch goes back, it seems, to the late Roman period here, and reflects the revival both of native arts and crafts (including metallurgy) and of British modes of dress—with stimulation probably from areas looking out on the Irish Channel where Roman influences had always been slight. What the penannular brooch is in the west, the Germanic crossbow types of brooch are in the east of Britain.

There are also kinds of Irish pin in the 6th century, coming to the Welsh coast and spreading via the Severn valley into Saxon areas—pins with double spiral heads and zoomorphic derivative penannulars with splayed terminals. There were possibly also borrowings the other way: e.g. the Romano-Germanic brooch found at Lydney. (6)

Then there is the yet-unsettled problem of the fine hanging-bowls with enamelled escutcheons found in Germanic graves. Whether manufactured in the west Midlands or in Ireland, they belong generally to the phase of Celtic revival we are considering, and point to cultural and trading contacts between the peoples. And it has been surmised that the combs and tweezers, brooches and bags with imported ivory handles, girdle-hangers and the like, of this period, reached the invaders from a craft-centre somewhere in the south-east, probably London.

The coinage question is still obscure for the later 5th and the 6th century; but on grounds of probability we may argue that the debased issues were still being issued, and indeed never ceased till the arrival of Anglo-Saxon mintings in the 7th century. (7) Such designs as the cross and pellets, found on the minims, on Anglo-Saxon brooches, and on sceattas, are strongly suggestive.

The Roman roads and the tradition of a single rule over Britain played their part in the political conceptions of the newcomers, in making them feel that the island (or at least the lowland part of it) composed a single unit. But the crucial contribution of the Celts came when the Irish missionary zeal spilled over in the north, driving down from Iona to Lindisfarne, making it possible for Anglo-Saxon scholars like Bede and Aldhelm to achieve their comprehensive and rapid advances, and bringing about the fusions of Hiberno-Saxon art. (8)

This book, however, is not the place to labour or extend those points. What we have been concerned is to show how late-Roman Britain became sub-Roman or Celtic Britain, how under Arthur the Britons drove back the invaders and gained a precious breathing-space, and how the Celtic Church with its special forms and attitudes developed, at least on one side, out of the struggles embodied in Martin, Victricius, Pelagius, and the Gallo-British Semi-Pelagians. It was a strange, violent, furiously-changing world over which a Gildas might well weep, and yet a world with all the fascination of stark conflicts, rapid breakdowns, and drastic reorganisations. Despite the uncertainties and difficulties, a clear pattern emerges out of the stormy rack, and we seem to look down into the very matrices of history, the very moment of deep and powerful formative activities, in which a vast arc of human development collapses and another begins to take its place.

ENDPIECE

IN 1113 certain canons of Laon were on a visit to England. They carried a shrine with the relics of Our Lady of Laon, hoping to raise money for rebuilding their cathedral. From Exeter they went westwards, were told that they were on the very land of King Arthur, and were shown Arthur's Chair and Arthur's Oven. Then at Bodmin an argument arose between one of them and a man with a withered arm, who had come to be healed. "Just as the Britons are wont to wrangle with the French on behalf of King Arthur" (says Hermann de Tournai, who tells the tale, referring to Breton wars), the cripple maintained that Arthur still lived. The argument became a brawl. An armed crowd rushed to defend the honour of Arthur and bloodshed was with difficulty averted. Our Lady of Laon did not heal the cripple.

This event, which antedates the great expansion of Arthurian Romances, shows how deeply the memory of Arthur had sunk into the minds and hearts of the Celtic peoples of Wales, Cornwall, and Brittany, kept alive by their long struggles for independence. Arthur still lived—as a raven or a chough, as leader of the Wild Hunt, as Maimed King, as a Warrior Chief guarding treasure in a Hollow Mountain. He was waiting in the otherworld lair of Avalon, in Sicily, beyond the Red Sea. He was Lord of the Antipodes (another form of the Otherworld). Many are the sites in which he has been located as the Sleeper awaiting the Trump that calls to the last battle, the final achievement of freedom. (1)

It is not long since a party of antiquaries, visiting an ancient hillfort, were accosted by a frightened old man asking if they had come "to take away the king". (2)

In one sense at least his fears were unnecessary; for the archaeologists of recent years have done much to re-establish Arthur as historical fact, to put him back into hill and valley.

He sleeps in the cave of Craig-y-Dinas in Glamorgan; on

Snowdon his men are hidden, but not he. He lies under a cairn in Bwylch y Saethau where he fell driving his enemies from Cwmllan (doubtless taken for Gamlan). He lies in the hollow hill of Cadbury Camp in Somersetshire; under Richmond Castle in Yorkshire; under the Castle Sewingshields near the Wall in Northumberland. In medieval days he lay under Etna in Sicily.

But in time he became more than the leader fated to bring victory and freedom to Breton or Welsh. Through Geoffrey and the Romance writers he became a European property, the medieval king under whom life rose to its noblest height of glory and fulfilment. And the prophecies of Merlin, old and new, entered into the daily life of men who knew little of the Romances. (3) The old ones dealt with events in Wales or Brittany from about 700 to 1200: whenever hopes throve of some leader who might prove another Arthur—Cadwaladr Owain, Arthur of Brittany. Then even among the English there were whispered prophecies attributed to Merlin whenever there were deep stirrings of change, right into the 16th century. (4)

The extraordinary history of the legend of Arthur, with the attached one of Merlin, is a tribute to the Celts' longing for independence and freedom. In making Arthur a universal figure, they lifted him from the war against the Anglo-Saxons and put him in what seemed the only satisfactory setting—that of the Roman Empire. He then had a worthy foe. In overthrowing the Emperor of the Romans and in driving on like Alexander into Asia itself (as he does in *Kulwych*), he became a universal champion, a hero slumbering in the hearts of the peoples till awoken by the trumpet of freedom.

Such was the remarkable heritage from the struggles of the Dark Age which we have traced, a period of deep change when all the old forms were breaking down and the faces of men are glimpsed in a strange stormlight of fear and hope.

NOTES

Introduction

1. Hence perhaps the tradition in Nennius (cap. 23) of Severus as the Wall-builder, though the source seems Jerome, year 2221 from Abraham; A. S. Chronicle (E), a. 189; Spartianus, *Sev.* xviii.

2. Appointed "to pacify the sea in the neighbourhood of Belgica Armorica (i.e. from Rhine mouth to Brittany), which the Franks and Saxons were raiding," Eutropius, ix, 21; D. Atkinson, "Classis Britannica," in *Hist. Essays in Hon. of J. Tait*, 1933. 1 ff.
Large numbers of Carausius coins in Malton fort, esp. in N.E. gate, suggest his use of Humber as naval base; lacking a Hadrianic frontier, he secured his entry there by reconstructing the fort: P. Corder (2). He affected the Celtic tradition. Nennius knows, before Maximus, only Julius Caesar, Claudius, Severus, and Carausius.

3. In Wales garrisons were reduced after Hadrian, though there was a continued or renewed occupation of some auxiliary forts; only one town developed at all; known villas are few; the natives largely went on in settlements of prehistoric type. H. J. Randall in Nash-Williams (1), 80 ff. For later defences: Nash-Williams (2), 71–3; Nash-Williams (3), 142 f.
The movement in Ireland to a central monarchy appeared in later 3rd c. under Cormac, who formed a sort of praetorian guard, the Fianna, and based his rule on Tara, with a good road system radiating and a triennial assembly or Feis for homage, lawsuits, athletic and bardic contests. Though R. contacts were indirect, developments in Britain must have contributed to the system: E. Curtis, *A Hist. of Ireland* (5th ed., 1945), 4 .In the Rath of the Tara Synods have been found R. glass and pottery of 2nd–3rd cs., and other R. objects (e.g. a seal and a lock); some things came from Britain, some from Gaul: Sean O'Riordan, *Times* (Dec. 10, 1953), 11.

4. R. Laur-Belart, *Congress of R. Frontier Studies* (1952).

5. See, for example, Rostovtzeff (2), 15.

6. Picts, north of the Forth, were Celts or partly Celtic, probably not Brithonic though closer to the Britons than the Goidels of Ireland. Ammianus (xxviii, 8), writing of 367, says they were divided into two, Dicalydonae and Verturiones. The first name is associated with Caledonia (Tacitus' term for the north of Britain) and with Kaledonioi (in Ptolemy). The second survives in Fortrenn, that part of the Pictish area immediately north of the Antonine Wall. It seems that by the end of 4th c. the Picts were dominant over all Scotland north of the Forth–Clyde isthmus: H. Blair (1), 4, K. Jackson (1), 77.

7. For poss. signs of 367 see Copley, 30: accidents, arson by peasants or Saxons? Nectaridus is called Count of the Maritime Tract, not of the Saxon Shore. Atecotti are found in Spain and Gaul; two regiments were called the Honorians: Orosius, vii, 40 (*c.* A.D. 400), calls them "bar-

barians who when received into treaty and taken into the army are entitled Honoriaci". Collingwood calls them Irish; Blair suggests British (2), 20; Richmond (1), 64, locates them on "the western littoral of Scotland"; Lethbridge thinks their name Irish meaning Wizards (*Aith* as *Sith*), just as other units had names like Thunderers (4), 140 f., (1), 128 f; Jerome thought them cannibals. (Note names of 4th-c. regiments: Constantiaci-Feroces, Petulantes, Leones, Mauri Tonantes, Exculcatores.)

8. For aspects going back to Caracalla, Richmond (1), 58–60.

9. "Are they responsible for some of the very early Germanic brooches which are identified from time to time? Did they inspire the late Roman pot-forms with Germanic ornamentation? . . . If it could be shown that such cemeteries as Sibertswold, Kingston, Uncleby, Camerton, Burwell, and the rest originated in these Alemannic settlements, the whole conception of A.S. archaeology would have to be revised. We may yet have to turn our sequence of art styles and typologies upside down, accepting some of Kendrick's views," Lethbridge (3), 129.

10. The historian Socrates (*H.E.* vii, 12) states that Chrysanthus, after several offices about the Palace, was raised to consular rank in Italy and appointed by emp. Theodosius as Vicar of Britain; later drawn against his will into the episcopate at Constantinople. (He was a Novatian in creed.) As his ecclesiastical work began in 407, he held office in Britain before that; Socrates says that he governed efficiently.

11. Irish records show the royal house of Dyfed in S.W. Wales were thought to come from people driven out of Meath in the 3rd c., Blair (1), 5. Anyhow, the Irish Deisi had occupied the Gower peninsula and nearby by this time.

12. *De B.G.*, 414 ff.; for the "legion," Haverfield, *C.M.H.*, i, 379; Foord, *Last Age of R.B.*, 122–6.

13. Rostovtzeff (1), 212; Collingwood (2), 303 f.

Chapter 1

1. For Gaul: Brogan, 222. The Theodosian Code mentions re-use of stones; a law of Honorius permits use of sculpture, etc., from dismantled temples in town walls, and some attempt is made to stop vandalism. The Urso charter in Spain (*CIL*, ii, 5439) forbade demolition unless house-owner gave sureties to rebuild or the permission was made at town council with quorum of 50. Defaulters pay the building's value; anyone may sue and prosecute "for that amount". See also Dill, 243.

2. *T.C.* xii, 19, 1 (Mommsen, 733). But for Caistor, see *Med. Arch.* 1959, 330.

3. Summarising Corder (1), citing his p. 42; Richmond (4) 79 f. Corder thinks the first walls the work of Clodius Albinus, 194–7, while awaiting civil war; Sept. Sev. would have his hands full with York and the Wall. In any event, we can roughly call the walls Severan. (The ballistae-platforms needed lateral windows for enfilading fire.)

4. Rivet, 32. For Bath Gorgon: *Med. Arch.* 1959, 331.

5. G. S. Keeney, *A.A.* (4th), 1934, xi, 158–75.

6. Richmond (1), 63.

7. York, *J.R.S.*, xviii, 98; Malton, *Antiq.*, March 1928 (base of Yorks. signal system), and Corder (2), Speech: Jackson (2) 98 f.

8. Keeting, *Hist. of Ireland* (*c.* 1633), transl. Dineen (1908), ii, 137; *Antiq.*, xviii (1944), 138; no refs. in Ireland to mill before 7th c., Fahey, *J. Cork H. & Arch. Soc.*, lxi (no. 193), Jan.–June 1956, 13–57, esp. 47.

9. Rivet, 32, and notes 18–21; 54.

10. Richmond (1), 133 f. Old Durham, founded, it seems, in the Antonine period (pottery), represents the north movement of R. agriculture through the north move of the frontier, Tyne to Forth: *A.A.* (4s), xxii (1944), 1–21; xxix (1951), 203–12; xxxi (1953), 116–26. Rudston, *Arch. J.*, xxxi (1934), 366–76; xxxii (1936), 214–20; xxxiii (1938), 81–6, 321–8; Richmond (5). Corder (3) for Langton. Ribchester Fort (Lancs.), and Calder basin: Richmond (1), 134. Almost everywhere were small native farmers or crofters, sometimes living in caves, as in the Pennines or Wales (e.g. on Caldy Island): *Arch. Camb.* (1916), 172 ff.; (1917), 71 ff.

11. Rivet, p. 33; Espérandieu, v, 4044; Mariën, *Anns. de l'Inst. Arch. du Luxembourg*, 76 (1945), 75, fig. 27.

12. Clipsham; *J.R.S.*, xxx (1940), 169; Rivet, n. 33, 55.

13. The inscription by a Gallic notable (who was court-assessor at York) records among his salary, not only payment in gold, but also "a wrap of Canusine wool, an embroidered Laodicean dalmatic, a gold brooch with gems, two thick rugs, a British *tossia*, and a sealskin" (*CIL*, xiii, 3162: first half 3rd c.); *tossia* was some sort of wrap or rug. Diocl. *Edict*, xix, 36; *Notitia Occ.*, xi, 60. Eumenius in his panegyric of Constantine praises the sheep-flocks of Britain and their heavy fleeces: *Paneg. vet.* (1828), iii, p. 1336. Glossaries say that the cloth for such mantles as the *birrus* was of goats' wool: Richmond (1), 163. For the carpet: *Arch. N.L.* (1955), v, 12, suggesting a relation to the A.S. needlework tradition.

14. *V.C.H. Hants*, i, 353, but the date is uncertain. Linen was much used in the finely-woven shrouds in the York district.

15. Rivet, 34, noting also Longstock.

16. Hawkes (1), 33–5, 48, 58, 71; for Ditchley villa with a similar change, Richmond (3), 44, and Radford, *Oxon.*, ix, 472.

17. *Not. Dignit.*, *Occid.*, x (Boecking, 49, 5); 10, 72; and *CIL*, xv, 4097–4141. State intrusions are post-200 on the whole in Spain: Van Nostrand, 198 f., on *CIL*, ii, 1180.

18. Fens: *Arch. J.*, xxxv, 1955, 202. Holland: Hettema, *De Ned. Wateren* (1938), 105; Volgraff, *Ned. kon. Akad. Wet A'dam* (1938), 12, 555–76, and (1939), ii, 6, 141–3.

19. G. Webster, *Antiq. J.*, xxxv (1955), 200 f.; *Arch. N.-L.*, v, 100; *J.R.S.*, xliii, 121 (Caister); *A.A.* (4s), xi (1934), 92 ff. (S. Shields). In Wales, only at Brecon fort; at four Antonine Wall-forts. Salt by brine evaporation at Welney (Webster, 203); in gen., Collingwood (1), 105 f. At least where convict labour was used, the State controlled; Birley (1), ch. ix.

20. Rivet, 32; *CIL*, vii, 62.

In the north pre-Roman agriculture was sparsely developed; the seething cauldrons then, as in Roman days, were one of the main manufactures, showing the basis in cattle (Richmond (1), 132 f.). At Irchester, in an area of good horse-pasture, was a *strator* or remount-officer.

21. Hawkes (1), 62–81. He points to earthworks or stone walls in Gaul and Rhineland of a similar character; parks or ranches (maybe at times for hunting) protected against raids by "brigands" or enemies. Often the date is hard to prove; but the huge enclosure of 220 sq. km. in limestone Eifel country round the Kyll valley north of Trèves, secured by the so-called Long Walls of Bitburg, seems 4th c. The area would have had guard-troops and have included perhaps studs for army and draught horses, also cattle and sheep producing for the imp. leather and textile works (*gynaecia* at Trèves). See Hawkes for refs. An eventual use as imp. hunting-park is suggested by G. Lafaye, Daremberg-Saglio, *s.v.* vivarium.

22. Hawkes, 71 f., citing Sutherland for coins.

Chapter 2

1. *Arch.*, lix (1905), 210–14; *V.C.H. Oxfordshire*, i, 316–18, and *J.R.S.*, xxxiv (1944), 81; S. Lysons, *Reliq. Brit.-Rom.*, ii (1813), pt. 1.

The new nobility (ultimate basis of Constantinian State) came up out of 3rd-c. turmoils with much land. Gaudentius of Brescia: "They usurp nobility of lineage by the heaping-up of wealth" (Migne, xx, 945). Salvian: "Rich and noble, it's all one; if they're rich without nobility, their fortune makes up for it." Note Sulpicius on Priscillian: *Familia nobilis, opibus praedives.*

2. *Arch.*, lxxi (1921), 140–98. Some ninety babies have been found buried inside the residential area, examples of the infanticide of slave-children.

3. *Arch. J.*, civ, 27 ff.

4. Maybe at least one villa in north Somerset was owned by emp. F. Haverfield, *Romanisation of R.B.* (1923), 64; *V.C.H. Somerset*, i (1906), 311 f.

5. For legal bases, see E. G. Turner, *J.R.S.* (1956), 115–18, on the tablet from Chew Stoke, Somerset, which seems based on *jus Italicum*—the territory then maybe being that of a community with the *jus* (i.e. Glevum, the nearest *colonia*). Or the formula may be wrongly used. Or the Constitutio Antoniniana (by creating large numbers of new citizens able to act according to the *jus civile*) encouraged these citizens to act on forms of *jus civile* for their transactions, even though there was no explicit change in the distinction of Italian and non-Italian soil.

The tablet may not refer to the local estate, but it shows in S.W. Britain a concern for careful property definitions.

6. Scramuzza, 363–7; Heitland, *Agricola*, 405; Holm, *Gesch. Sicilians* (1870–98), iii, 272 f., 496.

7. Stevens (3), 41.

8. Brogan, 125. The villa was destroyed 275–6, later rebuilt; it was of

corridor type. Cf. the huge domain of St.-Ulrich-Lolring: M. Lutz, *Les cahiers lorrains*, 1952, iv, 46–8.

9. *Arch. Camb.*, cii (1953), 89–163.

10. *V.C.H. Hants*, i, 313–16.

11. Rivet, 34 and ns. 43–5, 55. Note Little Milton with its enclosures or paddocks, plus a suggestion of earlier elements: *J.R.S.*, xl (1950), pl. vi, 2; Richmond (3), 44.

12. R. Latouche, 35. Cf. P. Classen, *Archiv. f. Diplomatik*, i (1955), 45–8; E. Holmberg, *Zur Gesch. d. C.P.* (1933), ch. ii; Rostovtzeff (1), 332–40.

13. Collingwood (2), 224; Rostovtzeff (1), 209, 212, who adds (213) that Britain was not a land of "peasants and small proprietors".

For the colonate's origin on imperial *saltus*: E. Beaudoin. *N. Rev. hist. de Droit* (1897), 554; for a *lex saltus* (Trajanic), Henchir-Mettich, *the same* (1947), 373–415.

14. *De Gub. Dei* (ed. Pauly), 115.

15. Crawford (2), 303. Ditchley was an ex. of tree-felling; it stood in a clearing of Wychwood Forest, in this complex; the first timber house was Flavian or even earlier. It has a drive and ditches, and a seemingly earlier Celtic field system (Richmond (3) and *Oxoniensia*, i (1936), 24–69; *Antiq.*, ix, 472). We must beware of generalising about enclosures.

16. Fineberg, drawing on Rostovtzeff (1), 629; Collingwood (2), 209 f., 220, 224. See also my note 12, Introduction.

17. Applebaum (1) on the distribution of the R.B. population in the Basingstoke area; see also Rivet, n. 46, 55, for criticism.

18. Called Walwell: from the remains of a wall (Lyson) or from Wealh (Welsh, Britons)?

19. Fineberg, 23 f., in a very useful essay; *Arch.*, xviii (1817) 112; *J.R.S.*, xxii (1932), 214; *Gentleman's Mag.* (n.s. 1864), xvi, pt. 1, 86–8; xvii, pt. II, 85–7.

20. Applebaum (2). The Ravenna order is Lindinis, Canza, Dolocindo, Clavinio, Morionio, Bolvelaunio, Alauna, Coloneas, Aranus, Anicetis, Melezo, Ibernio. Lindinis is Ilchester (*Somerset N.H. & A.S. Trans.*, xcvi, 188); Alauna is almost certainly Shaftesbury. For the plural form of Anicetis, cf. Sullonnacis and Vagbiacis in the Antonine Itinerary (471, 4; 472, 2). Other British exs. of *acum* names are Eburacum (see Jackson (2), 39, n. 2); Brovonacis, Bremmentennacum, Epeiacum, Cantiaci, Colonea(cu)s, and maybe Baldock, Herts (Applebaum, 2). For Coloneas, Richmond (2), 23, no. 35. Ibernio may be the farmhouse dug by Pitt Rivers (Hawkes (1), 55), not the temporary fort, Hod Hill. For Tarrant Hinton, Hutchins, *Hist. Dorset*. i, 319.

21. Nero: *E.E.*, ix, 1267. Silchester no doubt had its own city-land, and in A.D. 61 the British nobles owed much to the late Claudius and to Seneca; Nero probably inherited from Claudius. Bath: *E.E.*, vii, 828. Abascantus: *V.C.H. Derby.*, i, 228 f., 232, no. 11.

22. *Epistle* xxvi. He refers to Cicero's 3rd speech against Verres, dealing with Sicilian corn, and cites Plautus' *Pseudolus*.

23. For barter in 5th c., Rostovtzeff (3), 239; for a different view, G. Mickwitz, *Geld u. Wirtschaft in rom. Reich des vierten Jahrhunderts* (Helsingfors), 1932.

24. Summarising Stevens (4), whom see for refs. and details.

25. Summarising W. H. Frend (1). (For another case of Phrygian elders, *J.H.S.*, lvii (1937), 1 ff.; Philadelphia, *Or. Graec. Insc.*, ii, 488.) In N. Africa they were made responsible for the anti-Donatist decree of 26 June, 411 (*P.L.*, xi, 1418).

For *saltus* in west: *C.T.L.*, xii, 2250-1, 2272, 2604; Pelham, *Imp. Domains and the Colonate* (1892), 27.

Rescripts of Commodus at Souk el Khmis and Gasr-Mezuar show the extension of customary rights on large tracts of Africa for the colons, and the vindication of usages against imp. stewards: *CIL*, viii, 10, 570; viii, suppl. 14, 428.

Rescripts of Philippus for Araguene in Phrygia and of Gordian for Scaptaparene in Thrace reveal the readiness of the peasants to take a collective stand against abuses; the latter threaten a mass exodus.

26. P. Fiebig, *Zeits. f.d. Neutest. Wiss.* (1917–18), xviii, 65. See Frend, 54, with various refs. for the oppressive weight of *angareia*. For the *mansiones* as places of *annona*-delivery, H. G. Pflaum, *Mém . . . à l'acad. des Inscs. et B.L.* (1940), xiv.

British *mansiones* or admin. centres of pagi: Alchester, Dorchester (Oxon), Irchester, Horncastle and Caistor-on-the-Wolds, Kenchester, Chesterford, Caistor-by-Yarmouth, Catterick, and Norton (a *pagus* centre of Parisi). Others, maybe post-road stations: Rochester (Kent), Towchester, Baldock, Great Casterton, Chesteron, Wall, Mildenhall (Wilts.), Droitwich. Walled post-stations not important enough for *pagus*-centres: Penkridge, Mancetter, Ancaster and Littleborough, Leintwardine, East Stoke. See Richmond (1), 96 f. (*Portorium*, S. J. de Laet, 1949, 283 for customs?)

27. Summarising Stevens (2) on *C.T.*, xi, 7, 2, of 20 Nov. 319, to Pacatianus Vicar of Britain; Seeck (1), vi, 172–6, in *P.-W.*, vi, 30–3, and in (2) 1–18. Lot uses the item as proof of the fiscal solidarity of colon and proprietor: (5), 35, n. 6.

28. J. G. Milne, *J.R.S.* (1931), xxi, 101–9.

29. *Field Archaeology, Ordnance Survey* (1951), 42. For Gaul: Espérandien, nos. 3224, 4861, 616; F. Oswald, *Index of Fig. Types of T.S.*, pl. xlvii, 965; Jullian, v, 152; Duval, 195. Brean Down: JRS 1959, 129.

30. Certain small settlements in Gaul, with houses well back from a main road, seem places for rural markets and fairs: Oelmann, *Bonn. Jahrb.* (1923), cxxviii, 77 ff. For hawkers: Sumner, *New Forest Pottery Sites* (1927), 82. For industrial life in towns note Silchester's two hoards (second half 4th c.) with many tools of smith and carpenter, etc. (Boon, 185–7).

31. Milne, *l.c.*, Collingwood (2), 240.

A.H.T.—10

Chapter 3

1. A. E. van Giffen, *Congress of R. Frontier Studies*, 1949 (1952), ch. iv.

2. Brooks and Glasspoole, *British Floods and Droughts* (1928), 148; Bede, *H.E.*, iv, 13.

3. *Arch. Camb.* (1939), xciv, pt. 2, 163–99; (1948), c, pt. 1, 104–6.

4. *E.H.R.* (1938), liii, 385–411, esp. 391. Siculus Flaccus describes the intermixture of holdings as seen in many parts of R. world (Seebohm, *The Eng. Village Community*, 4th ed., 1890, 278). The use of fallow was well known: Varro, Virgil, Columella, elder Pliny. For heavy ploughs: coulter of Great Witcombe villa; share with slanting ears and long shanks, Box villa; two hoards of scrap at Silchester with six more coulters; five from the Great Chesterford hoard—(Box) *W.A.M.*, xxxiii, 236; xlv, 12; (Chesterford) *Arch. J.*, xiii, 6, fig. 18; F. G. Payne, *Arch. J.* (1948), civ, 96 f.; Hawkes, *Antiq.* (1935), ix, 339–41.

For R. strip systems in Fenlands and Housesteads: C. W. Phillips, *Aspects of Arch.* (1951), 267. Twyford Downs strip lynchets are thought Belgic.

5. Leeds (3), 139 ff.; Collingwood (2), 257 f.

6. Lethbridge (2), 142. An Ashtead tile has the imprint of a 1st-c. cloth; at Huntcliff was a scrap of herringbone weave. In general see *P.P.S.* (n.s.), xvi (1950), 136, 139.

7. *Dialogues*, ii, 1.

8. Jackson (3), 61 f.; (4) and (2). From Q Celtic came Goidelic, parent of Irish, Scottish, and Manx Gaelic; from P, Gallo-Brittonic.

9. Levison, *Antiquity*, 1941, 350; N. Chadwick (1), 199.

10. Chadwick (1), 201. Hilary of Poitiers seems in contact with Brit. bishops, prefiguring the rôle of Victricius and Germanus.

11. Nash-Williams (4), 235. This church may be of Dark Ages; N.-W. suggests a Byzantine origin. Gallic churches, too, were small, *Gallia*, 1954, xii, 567. For Sulpicius: *Chron.* xl–xlv.

12. Nash-Williams (5), 255.

13. *Arch.* (1920), lxix, 198; *B.G.A.S.* (1935), lvii, 157; Carcopino (2); H. Last, *J.R.S.*, 1954, 112–14.

14. Nash-Williams (6), 1; Jackson (2), 162 f.; coffin, *C.I.I.C.*, no. 332. See also n. 5, ch. 23 here. A half-way house to the full monastic rejection is seen in refusal of curials to marry and beget lawful children; a Novel of Justinian denounces as the most impious thing of all: *a nuptiis legitimis abstinentes* (*Nov. Just.*, xxxviii, pr. 1).

Chapter 4

1. *J.R.S.*, 1921, xi, 101. For versions of the poems with others from *Parentalia*, Lindsay (1), 70 ff.; for epigrams on Silvius Bonus (showing literary contacts with Britons if not with Britain): Lindsay (2), 247, 336 f. Note the 2nd-c. mag. of Narbo holding honorary magistracies in Sicilian ports where he doubtless had trading branches: Espérandieu, *Inscr. Lat. de G. Narb.*, no. 573. Also, inscr. at Rome of C. Sextius Regulianus,

diffusor olerarius ex Baetica, negotiator vinarius Lugduni, nauta Araricus: *CIL*, vi, 29722.

2. *Famous Cities*, xx; Paul. of Pella, *Thanksgiving*; Brogan, 108, 193.

3. *Parentalia*, vii, viii; he calls Britain Rutupian from Richborough Rutupiae, entry port in Kent.

4. N. Chadwick (1), 232; *ep*. xiv. Holiday is Vacuna, goddess of Leisure; the last line cites the Pirate of Laverna (goddess of gain, so of theft). Spindlefish: sort of tunny. Some contorted bit of scholarship makes the Muses 8 (for 3 see *Gryphus*, 21). Sturgeon (*corroco*): may be turbot. The hooks seem sewn on long line for sea-fishing, worm-baited. Feather-bunches tied to cord scared prey from breaking through gaps (Grattius, 75 ff.). Narycian: conventional epithet from Naryx, town of Ozolian Lokrians.

5. N. Chadwick (2), 64; *Carm*., xxi, 416; ep. 35. Constantine and sons were baptised on their death-beds; Valentinian II was strangled while still catachumen. Compare Augustine, *Confessions*. Ambrose was not bapt. till forced to become bishop; Theodosius, at age of 40, and so on.

6. C. Jullian (3), 59; *Rév. hist.*, xlvii, 263, xlviii (1892), 29.

7. For figures on wall-paintings, J. Liversidge (2), 48.

8. Sid. *carm*., vii, 495–8; *ep*. iv, 22, 3, and viii, 6, 13; Hydatius, *Chron. Min.*, ii, 156; Allard (1), 32, and (2), 23; L. Schmidt, i, 290. Also Greg. Tours, *H.F.*, iv, 46; Sid., *ep*. v, 5. For close knowledge of Virgil in Sulpicius, Paulinus: Glover, 287. Alcimus Ecdicius Avitus, bishop of Vienne like his father, wrote a readable hexameter poem (Raby (1), 109 and (2), 69; Manitius (2), 242); he was upset when Viventiolus, rhetor of Lyon, spread report that he had made a false quantity at ded. of the new basilica, and cited Virgil in his defence (Peiper, *M.G.H.*, *A.A.*, vi), *ep*. lvii (85 ff.).

9. Note the baths at Well (R. Gilyard-Beer, 1951) which may rep. a source-cult or a hunting-lodge of some rich man. For Lullingstone, note at Cologne the church of St. Pantaleone came with its fundus from a villa. The same sort of thing happened at Tours and Auxerre, where the atria of great men's houses became basilicas: R. Louis, *Bull. soc. nat. antiq. fr.*, 1950, 26; *Les Eglises d'Auxerre*, 1954. In the 5th c., when the Arles church was brought inside the walls on a high spot, with baptistery and atrium, the bishop's apartments were on first floor, the clerics' on ground floor: J. Hubert, in Le Bras, 15–23. Britain in gen., *J.B. Arch. Assoc.* 1953, 1–24.

10. *Ep.* iv, 9; iv, 13.

11. *Ep.* v; *Mosella*, 68 ff., W. T. McIntire, *C. & W. A.A.S. Trans.* (1941), n.s. xli, 41–9. There may have been a market for the pearls at the R. fort-port of Clanoventa, Ravenglas.

12. *Dial.* i, 4.

13. The *Corpus* has many examples: Blümner, *Röm. Privatalterthümer*, 321; Bucheler, *Carm. Epig.* 219, on a boy "now skilled to gather the herds of letters and of words, with running pen to note the sounds from some-one's throat"; Sid., *ep.* v, 17, 10. For original protocols of *Acta*, Hardy, *Studies in R. History*, 151; Watson, *Hilary of Poitiers*, intro. xl. (Origen

also; and see Jerome, *ep.* cxviii); Prudentius, *Peristeph*, ix, 21–4 (Migne, lx, 434). Possidius (*Life of Augustine*, xvii) mentions a debate with Arians when "what was said on either side was taken down".

14. J. Hawkes, ch. ii, in *Vineyards in England* (1953), ed. by E. Hyams; also Forbes, iii, 119 ff. The cask is northern. J. H. notes that in A.S. graves the dead have glass vessels, esp. in Kent; some were made in Rhineland and N. France, 5th–6th cs., where the barbarians imitated R. forms; among the types are small beakers and cups originally made for wine, possibly still being used for it, esp. if the drinkers were Franks from N. France.

For wine and vine in Gaul, *Gallia*, xii, 1954, 555 f. By 2nd c. Burgundy was growing its own wine; wine-amphorae go, though Spain still supplies oil (from Baetica, e.g. family of Aelii Optati, *c.* 160, in region of Aṣtigi, Ecija): E. Thevenot, *Rev. arch. Est.*, iii, 1952, 224; *Bull. soc. nat. antiq. fr.*, 1949, 187 f.; *Archivo espan. de arqueol.*, 1952, 225 ff. The big landlords of Burgundy went in for vineyards to make up for lack of good riverways; in the early empire such as could develop vine-growing domains were given admin. or honorific functions obliging them to stay in the capitals of the *civitates*—thus came the close link of metropole and high-class vineyards, which still drew the attention of Gregory of Tours. With Bordeaux it was the facilities for waterborne trade that led to the vineyards. At Montans (near Gaillac-sur-Tarn), the point from which in the Aquitanian basin river-traffic can descend to the Garonne, to the sea, we find the growth of commercial viticulture, uniting vine-grower and potter: R. Dion, *La Rev. des Deux-Mondes* (15 Oct. 1952), 672 ff. The vineyard-survivals in Alsace may be taken to show a survival of Gallo-R. population: R. Lantier, *Ampurias*, 1952, xiv, 218 ff.

Chapter 5

1. Note how long Flavian silver was in circulation—indeed throughout the 2nd century. "The presence of Flavian silver, for ex., on a R. site in Scotland, even if it is in good condition, does not of itself prove that the site was occupied in the Flavian rather than in the Antonine period," A. S. Robertson in *Essays in R. Coinage* (1956), 270; *P.S.A.S.* (1950), lxxxiv, 138 f. See also Bushe-Fox, *Sec. Rep. Richborough* (1928), 8: coins there (383–95) may well "indicate an intensive occupation well into the 5th c.". (H. Mattingly for 3rd c. econ. crisis and Bacaudae).

2. For selective bases of hoards: coins with certain reverse types, the issues of one emperor, etc. A. S. Robertson, *l.c.* 274 f. For this chapter in general, J. P. C. Kent, ch. xi, in the same *Essays*.

3. M. Bloch, "Le problème de l'or au moyen âge," in *Ann. hist. éc. et soc.* (1933), v, 1–34.

4. A. Grenier, 641; Ammianus, xxxi, 6, 5–7; Zos. v, 22, 6.

5. Latouche, 151.

6. Kent, 193 f.

7. Kent, 194–7, and *The Office of the Comes Sac. Largit.* (1951), 69 ff. In the East, John Chrysostom calls officials brigands and beasts, and keeps his worst language for the tax-collectors. See St. Basil, xlvii, for Athanasius

agaınst the tyrannic governor of Libya; note also the stand of Synesius of Ptolemais against the *Dux*.

8. Grenier, 635 f.; Brogan, 159. *Nautae* must have been organised on the main waterways in Britain, e.g. to carry the masses of flints that built Caistor-by-Yarmouth.

9. *Ep*. viii, 7; ix, 4; vi, 8; vii, 2; vii, 10.

10. E.g. Birley (1), 81–3; J. Lindsay (2), 247–9.

Chapter 6

1. For Picts: O'Rahilly, 353 ff., 529 ff., 535; their matrilinear system, 538, 364, 367. Against this thesis, J. Fraser in *Med. Stud. in mem. G. S. Loomis* (1927), 407–12. Jackson (1), Lethbridge (1). In general: Wainwright. Also, R. Radford, Arch. *N. L.* vi (1) 18.

2. Tribal and place-names show them P-Celts. In the area was Tadoriton, Ford of the Father; Maporiton, Ford of the Son; and Blatobulgium (Birrens), meaning the Sack of Flour: Jackson (1), 79; Richmond (2), 15, for *loca*. Locus Maponi seems the ancient enclosure at Lochmaben (C. A. Ralegh Radford elaborating R. C. Reid's identification): Richmond (1) thinks Lochmabenstone. No trace of 3rd-c. occupation in even so promising a site as Inveresk (*J.R.S.* (1948), xxxviii, 82). For Euidensca of Rav. List and Urbs Guidi of Bede: Richmond (2), 14.

3. Collingwood (2), 245; *C.A.H.*, xi, 518; Drexel, *Germania Romana* (2nd ed.), 1924, ii, 12, with Richmond (6), G. Macdonald, *P.S.A.S.*, lii, 250–2; D. Young, *Romanisation in Scotland* (n.d.), 83–5, 88 f.

4. A. H. A. Hogg, *Aspects of Arch.* (1951); Richmond (1), 84 f.

5. Dion, *Hist.*, lxxvi, 12–13, and 16, 5; R. W. Chambers, *Eng. before the Norman Conquest*, 47 f.

6. Jackson, in Wainwright, 138: Veda's ded. to the Victory of Our Lord Alexander the Pious and Fortunate suggests a philo-Roman feeling: *Arch. J.* (1946), ciii, 64, n. 55. He may just have been a canny trader, or a cavalry-man concerned with remounts—he was on the direct route to the middle Rhine where *Brittones gentiles* were then quartered, recruits from the tribes.

7. We saw above (Intro., n. 7) the Atecotti. Whence the Scotti? from N. Ireland, Argyle, or N. Wales? Note Dumbarton lies on north side of Clyde, supporting the thesis that Scott settlements in Argyll were made as act of policy to cut Picts from Britons. See Bede's opening chs.

8. Amm., xxviii, 3, 5, and 8; J. C. Rolfe, Loeb ed., iii (1939), 134, n. 2; C. E. Stevens, *Latomus*, xiv, 394 f. on Areani. Theodosius was ferocious in discipline: E. A. Thompson (5), 91; on four occasions in Africa deserters were burnt alive or had hands cut off (Amm., xxix, 5, 22, 24, 31, 49); Africans and R. officials suspected of co-operation with foe were tortured and then burnt alive (xxix, 5, 40, 50, cf. 39). Theodosius, himself a big landowner (Soc. *H.E.*, v. 2, 2) spared the landlords so much that the army food was not good (Amm., xxix, 5, 11, cf. 10).

9. *C.T.*, vii, 1, 1; Amm., *l.c.*; xxx, 5, 3; Ausonius, *Ep.* xiv, 22–7.

10. Jackson (1), 80; Blair (2), 27.

11. *L.P.* 31; *C.I.L.*, vii, 481. Père Grosjean, *Anal. Bol.*, liii, thinks Concessa invented by 7th-c. hagiographer who knew the Hexham stone; but the prefect may have been a real ancestor of Patrick's mother: note connections between troops of Wales and the building of the Wall. (Pringle suggests P.'s father and mother were cousins in some degree.) We cannot accept the tradition that Pat. was born in the Brigantian area, i.e. north Cumberland or rather the land either side of the Solway.

12. Kent, *Trans. C. & W.A.S.* (n.s. 1952), li, 4 ff.: asking if Valentinian coinage did not supply the main currency till *c.* 400. See A. H. M. Jones (in Carson, 24) on the Gallic silver coins near the Mendip silver-mines.

13. Stevens (5); *Chron. Min.*, i, 646, 7; Greg. *H.F.* 1, 4, 3; Gildas, 14 f. (adding the detail that it was then the soldiers were sent and the Wall built). The usurper put down would be Valentinus in 369. For envy: Zos., iv, 35, 2, and John of Antioch, frag. 186, 2. For his office, Zos., iv, 23, 4. Stevens suggests that Max. was governor of now-formed Valentia (taking it to be Wales).

Note Aegidius, Master of Soldiers in Gaul, who seems for a time the king of federate Franks: *Y Cymm.*, xxxiii, 91. The Wledig suggestion is from Stevens. For Protictor Vorteporix: *E.E.*, ix, 1030; Macalister, *C.I.I.C.*, i, 358 (no parallels, but cf. *I.L.S.*, 2813); *Y Cymm.*, ix, 1; Chambers, 176. Stevens cites Dinorben as a repaired hillfort (with coins from Constantine to Gratian).

14. Pacatus, *Paneg.*, xxxi, xxxiv, lxii; Aus., *Famous Cities*, ix.

15. *Carm.*, iv, 16, 9; Sid. *Carm.*, v, 203–6; Loyen (1), 16, n. 1. For pillar: Nash-Williams (6), 123–5.

16. N. Chadwick (1), 20, 94; Parry, 273; W. Stokes, *Life of St. Meriasec* (1872). R. S. Loomis (1), 4, on pedigree that states he "killed Gratian King of the Romans". For the Irish basis in the Dream of Oengus, Loomis (1), 8. The vision in a dream was a popular Celtic motive.

17. *Y Cymm.*, xxxiii, map opp. 176; J. E. Lloyd, *Hist. of Wales* (3rd ed., 1939), i, 67, 74, 78; W. J. Gruffydd, *Math* (1928), 346; Fisher and Baring-Gould, *Lives of Brit. Sts.* (1911), iii, 258; *Breuddwyd Maxen* (ed. 1. William, 1908), 27. *The White Book Mabinogion* (J. G. Evans, 1907, i.e. 1909), 94, and Ellis and Lloyd, *Mabinogion* (1929), i, 147, for explanation that "the men of the island would never have assembled those great hosts for anyone but her". It is best taken as a cult title of which the meaning was lost. For Ahés, N. Chadwick, "Cantr'r Gwaelod and Ker Is" in *The early cultures of N.E. Europe* (1950). Note the legendary Brunehaut of the R. roads in Gaul.

18. J. J. Parry, 271 ff. Geoffrey uses the title *Dux* for Vortigern, whom he seems to regard as ruling the same territory as Octavius. See Loomis, 5 f., for further confusions in Geoffrey and the *Dingestow Brut*, with relation to the Dream; also N. Chadwick (1), 135, 109, 126; Nennius, caps. 26–9.

19. Math, 346. Cf. Chadwicks, *Growth of Lit.* (1932), i, 297–9.

20. Wheeler, *Y Cymm.* (1923), xxxiii, 70 f., 89, 91.

21. *Ibid.*, 106. For Caer Seint in the mabinogi of Branwen, Loomis, 4 f.

22. Parry, 273 f.; Baring-Gould and Fisher (1913), iv, 373.

23. Parry, 274 for refs. The text of the stone might be all in genitives, in the Welsh manner, e.g. *Constantini fili Maximi*, which could lead to some of the confusions. Also, Lot (7), 59.

Constantine son of Maximus has no firm authority for existence, but is worth recording to show the play of thought round Maximus and Elen.

Chapter 7

1. Amm., xxxi, 10; Zos., iv, 35; Themistius, *or.* xviii is fulsome on his beauty. He was mad on archery; as Ausonius' pupil, he cared for letters. Sulp. *Chron.*, ii, 49, says that at his court, "through the will and power of a few men all things were for sale". Zos. says Max. fomented the revolt.

2. Theodoret, *H.E.*, v, 12, calls him "a certain Maximus". Ruf., *H.E.*, ii, 13, says he won by treachery rather than might. Orosius calls him vigorous (*strenuus*), upright, and worthy of a throne except "that he was not born to it".

3. Zos. says Master; Soc. and Soz. say Duke. A variant of G.'s death makes him rush, he thinks, to his wife: i.e. monkish moral against uxuriousness.

4. *Ep.* xx.

5. Oros., *Hist.*, vii, 34; Zos., iv, 53; Hodgkin, *Italy and her Invaders* (1st ed.), i, 401; Soc., *H.E.*, v, 11; Prosper, *Chron.*; Soc., v, 14; Ambrose, *ep.* xxiv; Migne, xiii, col. 592.

6. *Paneg.*, ii (xii); *Pacati Theod. Aug. dicatus*, xxv, 1, Grenier, 619.

7. LXIX, xxvi.

8. Zos., iv, 37.

9. *CIL*, ii, 4911.

10. *Dial.*, iii, 4 and 8. He must be the man of Amm., xxvii, 7, 1, who in 363 was Vicar of Africa. Note the terror of the dark. Apart from the heretics, Max. seems to have executed only the barbarians Merobaudes and Vallio; for Gratian he could disclaim responsibility.

11. *Vita*, xx; *Dial.*, ii, 6 f. For dinner as a sort of communion, Ep. to Corinth. i, 7; for stibadium or sigma, Sid., *ep.* i, 11. The consulate was now an honorary dignity given by emperor. Evodius was consul 386, but that was not necessarily the dinner's year.

12. For problems raised by excavs. at Ligugé: F. Eygun, *Gallia*, xii (1954), 380–9: a villa ruined *c.* 275 and a large later building (a sort of semi-circle, some 30 m. diam.) of good Roman work, which, however, can hardly have been there when Martin settled in.

13. *Dial.* ii, 16.

14. *Dial.*, ii, 14; *Vita*, xxii, xxiv; *Chron.*, ii, 3, 6 f. Jerome accused Sulp. of Millennarianism: *Comm. in Ezech.*, xi, 36; Migne, xxv, col. 339; Le Blant, *I.C. de la Gaule*, ii, 83 n. Note formula *iudicii adventum tremendum* on 5th–6th-c. tombstones in Italy (Diehl, *I.L.C.V.*, iii, nos. 3863, 3866–7, etc.) with variants in Gaul, *I.C.G.*, ii, nos. 478, 551a. In Wales (7th–9th c.) at Llanlleonfel (Nash-Williams (6), no. 62): "Silent in the shroud Iorwert,

and Ruallaun in the tomb await in peace the dreadful coming of Judgment." *In sindone* is found in Book of Kells (Sullivan, 19). The epitaph is metrical, with two incised Greek crosses with barred terminals.

15. Sulp. recalls the episode in Luke; *Dial.*, ii, 6 f.

16. Lavertujon, 561 and cxxxiv. This book is a strange medley of expositions, but with some useful points. Coustelier, *Ep. Summ. Pont.*, i, 641.

Ruf., *H.E.*, ii, 6, says his zeal was to cover his crimes; also Sozomen. Ambrose admits to Val. II (*ep.* xvii) that Max. had defended orthodoxy (cap. 16), though he had wildly accused him of paganism, Judaism, impiety (*ep.* xxix).

17. Soc., v, 14; Symm., *ep.* xv; Zos., iv; Amb., *ep.* lxxix, xxiv.

18. Soc., v, 11; Themistius, xviii; Zos. mentions proclamations at Alexandria.

19. Ambrose would not have gone, "had he not realised that the situation threatened danger to the integrity of ecclesiastical liberty and prerogative," N. Chadwick, 44; 112, n. 6. Justina hoped to net him in a charge of treason or conspiracy. On his second embassy he reminded Max. of his project to enter Italy "companioned by barbarian ranks", *ep.* xxiv.

20. Accusations of magic were common. Among those accused: Emps. Maxentius, Julian; philosophers Edesius, Maximus, Chrysanthius, Libanius; bishops Athanasius, Ambrose; Jerome, Origen, even Augustine was not untouched; the minister Sopiter. Note that Sulp. in *Chron.* stresses the heresy came to Spain direct from Egypt. For Gnosticism forcing orthodoxy to an exegesis: Labriolle (3), 57.

21. N. Chadwick (2), 35 ff.; A. d'Alès; G. Schepps, *Prisc. quae supersunt op.* (1889): Dom Leclercq, *L'Espagne chrét.* (1906). Jerome mentions a Julian among the beheaded (*de vir. ill.*, cxxii). See also E. C. Bahut, *Priscillien et le Priscillianisme* (1909), and *Concile de Turin* (1904); Sulp. *Chron.*, ii, 46.

22. *Ep.* xi.

23. *Chron.*, 1, 4.

24. It is clear that P. had studied astrology. Note a canon of the Council of Laodicea: "clergy charged with the holy offices must not be magicians or sorcerers, and must not make phylacteries" (xxxvi: Labbe, i, col. 1546).

25. *Dial.*, iii, 11–13.

26. Pacatus calls the bishops "accomplices, indeed butchers", xxix. For the temporary reaction, see n. 2 next chapter.

27. Oros., vii, 35 (Migne, 1150); *Vita Amb.*, xix.

28. Ambrose, *ep.* xl. Also in general his *ennaratio in Psalm* lxi; *de obitu Val.*; Greg. Tours, *H.F.*, i, 43; Prosper and Marcellin, *Chron.*

29. Stevens (5), 86.

30. Lavertujon, ii, 158 f.; he notes how Sulp. rationalises his summary of Biblical history. For Sulp.'s attitude to Martin's miracles (credulous or obliquely smiling): Delehaye, *Anal. Boll.* (1920), xxxviii, 73 ff., and P. de Labriolle (2), 383 f.; N. Chadwick (2), 100. For Sulp. himself: Kappel-

macher, *P.-W.*; C. Helm, *S.S. libri qui supersunt* (1866); M. R. Ricaud, *S.S. et ja ville* (1913). For the *Chronica*: J. Bernays, *Gesammelte Abhandlungen*, ii, 81 (cap. xxix). For sacristy and chasuble in the story of the poor man: Hoare, 101 f.

31. Nash-Williams (6), 7, n. 1.

32. Bowen, 22; Wade-Evans (1), 57. Later Dyfrig was said to be descended from King Erb and so linked with Maximus family: Bowen, 37. For deds. in west of N. Wales, Bowen, 68. Note that when Constantine crossed in 407, he was welcomed by several bishops, including disciples of Martin, such as Heros of Arles. In the Moselle area, where M.'s cult is strong, it spread along the rivers, not by the roads: Morhain, *Mém. Acad. Nat. Metz* (n.s.), 1951, 16 f.

Chapter 8

1. N. Chadwick (2); A. d'Alès; G. Schepss, *Priscilliani quae supersunt opera* (1889); Dom Leclercq, *L'Espagne chrétienne* (1906). Jerome (*De Vir., Ill*, 122) mentions a Julian among the beheaded. Drepanius: G. Baehrens, *XII Paneg, tat.*, 87 ff. (esp. 114); N. Chadwick (2), 29, 43. E. C. Bahut, as in note 21 above.

2. Jerome, *l.c.*, 122 f. (*tumenti compositoque sermone* in his *Apologia*); Aus. *Comm.*, xxi. Pacatus was made proconsul of Africa after his speech. There was a certain rehabilitation of the P.'s after the death of Maximus; Ithacus lost his see, Hydacius was exiled; the matter was widely discussed (Ambrose, *ep.* xxvi). The movement did not end till the synod of Braga, 563. (Pacatus' grandson, a poet, meant to write a poem on the life of Paulinus of Nola; we do not know if he did: Migne, liii, 681.)

3. M. Chadwick (1), 221 (cf. 219 f.).

4. *Antiq. J.* (1955), 187–98, P. Ashbee. For a Celtic hermitage on St. Helens: *Times*, Aug. 6, 1956. Signs of early-Christian graves (i.e. west-east orientation) with an early rectangular building that may be a Celtic chapel, on St. Teons.

5. N. Chadwick (3); W. Levison, *Antiq.* (1940), 280–91; K. Strecker, *Neues Archiv.* (1922), xliii, 1–26; Duke, 22 ff., 36–8, 144 f. For authenticity, W. Simpson, *St. Ninian* (1940), reviewed A. O. Anderson, *Scot. Hist. Rev.* (1948), xxvii, 25–47. Besides the Latin poem considered by Levison, there is a ref. Alcuin, *ep.* no. 273 (Migne, iv, 431). See also Jackson, *antiq.*, ix, 492; Duke, 144 f.

6. Ailred, cap. iv; Adamnan, *Vita*, i, 15 (Reeves (1857), 43), giving Tothail (Irish is Tuathal). *Math*, 183, 343 f., for place-names in Wales.

7. Collingwood, *C. & W. Trans.* (1925), xxv, 9, and (2), 310, makes a case for N. working in Irthing valley, blazing the trail along which the Irish missionaries went in the 7th c. (from Iona to the Tyne). For evangelisation in Scottish Lowlands at this time: Crawford, *Antiq.* (1948), xxii, 51 f.; Bowen, 72, for link with Maximus family.

8. Owen Chadwick in N. Chadwick (1), 181. There was some myth worked up in connection with the white stones which gave the place its name of Candida Casa (Bede, *H.E.*, iii, 4).

For Paulinus: *C.S.E.L.*, xxix, 257 ff.: *ep.* xxxii, 2. This epistle gives many details of church decoration at the time.

9. Gildas, cap. 4; Sulpicius, *Vita*, 13–15; *Dial.*, iii, 8; iii, 7. In Pat.'s *Confessio* there are two refs. to sun-worship (caps. 20, 60) which may show the persistence of Roman Invictus Sol, but may deal with the Celtic sun-cult (O'Rahilly, 470).

10. Dessau, 1153; E. A. Thompson (1), 21, n. 12 (with ref. to remnants of Clodius Albinus' army). In general, *P.-W.* (1896), ii, 2, col. 2766 (Seeck); Jullian (1), viii, 174–6; F. L. Ganshof, *Hist. Essays.*, *J. Tout* (1933), 111. The Circumcelliones of N. Africa were the same sort of revolting peasants with a strong religious idiom directed against the State: C. Saumagne, *Ann. d'Hist. éc et soc.* (1934), vi, 351–64; W. H. C. Frend (2); A. Pincherle, *J.R.S.* (1954), 138 f.

11. Eutropius, ix, 20; Aur. Victor, *Caes.* xxxix, 17; Jerome, *Chron.*, a. 2303; Orosius, vii, 25, 2; *Chron. Min.*, s.v. Bacauda. For mid-3rd c., Rostovtzeff (1), i, 620; N. Chadwick (1), 228.

Events of *c.* 284: troubles at Reichenstein (near Arlesheim) and Champagnes and Geneva: E. A. Thompson (3), 73; *Genava* (1924), ii, 127; Staehelin, 266.

12. Amm., xxvii, 2, 11; cf. xxviii, 2, 11. Throughout this section I owe much to Thompson (1).

13. *De R.B.*, ii, 3; Amm., xxviii, 2, 10; Merob., *Paneg.*, ii, 9 f. They did raid towns, but did not burn Autun: P. le Gentilhomme, *Rev. des ét. anc.* (1943), xlv, 233–40.

14. Collingwood (2), 303 f.; Amm. says that Theodosius prohibited close inquiry so as not to stir up further trouble.

15. *Vita*, v. We hear of Bacaudae active in Alps early 5th c. (Zos., vi, 2, 5). At Noyon, Germ. Inf., a municipal officer, *praefectus arcendis latrociniis*, was set up, *CIL*, xiii, 5010 (where another is also cited from Dhaun: cf. *CIL*, xii, 21 f., Dessau 2646). Compare the Greek *lēstodioktēs*. No doubt there were "brigands" all over Gaul: Amm., xxvii, 2, 11; xxviii, 2, 11; *De R.B.* ii, 3; Aus., *ep.* xiv.

16. The Irish Revolt of the Vassals may have been influenced by the Bacaudae (N. Chadwick, 249); but what was the date and did it really occur?

Chapter 9

1. Vacandard; Migne, xx, 443; E. Griffe, *La Gaule Chrétienne* (1947), 226 ff.; L. Duchesne, *Fastes Episc. de l'anc. Gaule* (1899), ii, 205; N. Chadwick (1), 221 f. A. Anscombe (*Eriu*, vii, 13 ff.) oddly tries to make V. the Victor (Victorinus) of Pat.'s *Confessio*.

Paulinus (Migne, xx, col. 443, n. C), *ep.* xviii, 4. Note in the same *ep.* Paulinus writes "in remotissimo Nervici littoris tractu quem antehac spiritu fides veritatis afflaverat".

2. Lactantius (Migne, vi, col. 707 f.) says that if God forbids to kill, there can be no exceptions. St. Maximilian had stated to the proconsul

who tried to enrol him, "I cannot enter the army, I am a Christian" (*Acta Martyrum*, ed. Ruinart, 1713, 300).

3. *Ep.* xviii.

4. *Dial.*, iii, 2; Paulinus, *ep.* xviii, 242; Greg. of Tours, *De Gloria Confess.*, c, 10; Cabrol (xv, 1) *s.v.* Rouen; Foedula: *CIL*, xii, 2115; Buecheler, *C.L.*, no. 1445; Marche, 328; Cabrol, 2661 f.

5. Ambrose, *De Virginibus* (ad Marcellam) (377); *de Virginitate* (378); *de instit. virginum* (391–2). V. himself joyously laboured with his hands at the new church.

6. Augustine, *Sermons*, 286, 4; see Gibbon, ch. 27; Ambrose, *ep.* xxii, and *Conf.*, l, 9, 7. Ambrose was told in a dream to dig.

7. *De Laude Sanctorum*, 1, 2–3.

8. There were relics of saints from Pamphylia at Bologna: Vacandard, 69, 65 f. for relation to relics gathered by Gaudentius who became bishop of Brescia. V. calls the relics *domicilia passionum* (ii, 4).

9. Vacandard, 122 ff.; Paulinus, xviii, 5. For Limouzin: R. Limouzin-Lamotte, *Le diocèse de Limoges des origines* (1951).

10. Duchesne, i, 89 f. For Martin: *Vita*, ix; *Dila.*, ii, 3; Origen against Celsus, vi, 75.

11. Duchesne, *Origines du Culte chrétien* (2nd ed.), 32–7.

12. N. Chadwick (2), 95 f. Note for ex. the picture of Brictio (prob. the Brice who eventually succeeded Martin at Tours): *Dial.*, ii (iii), 15; i, 21—with bishops as devils? (N. Chadwick (2), 115).

13. Jaffé, *Regesta*, 286; Migne, xx, 468, and xiii, 1155 (*Regesta* 258 for decretal used). Note that canon viii deals with Novatians and Donatists.

14. Vacandard, 145–8.

15. Vacandard, 135 ff. Paulinus in *ep.* xxxviii; cap. 6 speaks of Apollinarism in the West.

16. Vacandard, 95–103, 175–9: though V. tilts at the dialecticians (*De L.S.*, ix, 17 f.), and "the vain sophisms of the philosophers fitted only to deceive" (xi, 23).

17. *De L.S.*, xii, 27; ix, 8.

18. x, 20 f.; vii, 13; ix, 17.

19. Thus, viii, 15 f., after arguing that God is spread in all parts, and that the martyr is the primary absolute virtue, he adds: "But by favour and not by property, by adoption and not by nature."

20. ix, 19; x, 20 f.

21. E. J. Holmyard, *Alchemy* (1957), 30; Archelaos is *c.* 715.

22. Raby (2), i, 4; Eusebius, *H.E.*, v, 1; F. Wieland, *Altar und Altargrab der christl. Kirchen im 4. Jahrh.* (1912), 46. For Deuil (next century a Priory of St. Denis): M. Roblin, *Mém. fédér. hist. et arch.*, Paris et Île-de-Fr. (1952), ii, 7–19; cf. *Syria* (1934), xv, 210.

23. *Conf.*, viii, 6 (Pusey).

24. Two further points. Rouen was the residence of a prefect with troops, under the Dux tractus Armoricani et Nervicani (*Notitia*).

25. Aus. *Order of Noble Cities*, xix, Narbo; Grenier, 468 f.; Brogan,

88 f.; Sidonius, *Carm.*, xxiii, 37 ff. Cf. a 418 constitution of Honorius about Arles and its trade (*Corp. leg. ante Justinianum latarum*, Haenel,⸴238). Aus. (x) says of Arles: "You make a bridge of boats your central street, gathering the trade-goods of the Roman world, then scattering them for other towns and peoples."

Vita Caes. i, 19 (*S.S. Rev. Merov.*, iii, 462); Greg. Tours, *H.F.*, viii, 1; viii, 15; x, 26 (cf. vii, 31). In general, Pirenne, ch. ii, 2; P. Charlesworth, *Trade-routes and commerce of R.E.* (2nd ed., 1926), 178, 202, 220, 238; Bréhier, *L'art en France des invasions barb.*, 36, 38; E. Leblant, *Inscr. chrét. de la Gaule*, i, 207, 328 (cf. nos. 225 and 613a): at Eure near Seine-mouth (? trading with Britain), i, 205 (no. 125).

26. L. Armand-Calliat, *Gallia* (1953), xi, 85–9 with refs. A sistrum that seems decorated with a cat, found at Saint-Rémy-de-Province: M. H. Rolland, *Bull. de la Soc. Nat. des Antiq. de France* (1948), 35. E. Male, *La fin du Paganisme en Gaule* (1950), 9–14. Christianity entered Spain via Guadalquivir. Weasels: G. Jennison, *Animals in Anc. Rome*, 19, 129.

The cat seems the favourite of small girls in Gaul. *Cattus* appears in Palladius (*de re rustica*, iv, 9). For bronzes and ceramic decorations: Armand-Calliat, 87 f. For cats in Silchester, *Arch.* liii, 287; G. C. Boon, 173.

Chapter 10

1. *Fourth Cons. Hon.*, 26 ff.; *Stil. Cons.*, ii, 247 ff. (see also *Ruf.*, i, 131 ff.; ii, 147 ff.); *Goth War*, 414 f., 568 ff., 201 ff.; *Stil. Cons.*, iii, 148 ff.

See also poems translated in Intro. and ch. 5. (Drepanius (A.D. 391) has the line on 369: "Shall I cite the Scot hurled back upon his marshes?")

There is also (*Against Eutropius*, i, 393): "The Saxon is conquered, Tethys calm, and Britain secure with Picts broken." (*Epith. on Hon. and Maria, c.* 398); the use of Moor and Saxon as south and north; cf. *Gildo*, 17 ff. In *Stil.*, iii, 300, British dogs "sinewed to break the backs of brawny bulls". (Cf. Strabo, iv, 5, 2; Grattius, 175 ff.; Nemesianus, 225.; See J. Lindsay (1), 61, 71, 368 f. for the idea of Britain as "another world".

2. O'Rahilly, 209 ff.; Chadwick also takes a later date.

3. Zos., vi, 3, 1; 2, 1; Olymp. frag. 12; Sozomen ix, 11, 2; Oros., vii, 40, 4 (omitting Marcus); *Chron. Min.*, i, 465, a. 407, and ii, 70, a. 411 (omitting Marcus and Grat.). For 407: *Chron. Min.*, i, 465; E. A. Thompson (2) to whom I owe the main argument, 163, n. 3. For Olymp. *Class. Q.* (1944), xxxviii, 43–52.

For Rhine-crossing: N. H. Baynes, *J.R.S.* (1922), xii, 217–20 and *Byz. Studies* (1955), 338–42. Against: S. Mazzarino, *Stilicone* (1942), 278, and C. Courtois, *Les Vandales et l'Afrique* (1955), 38.

4. Jerome, *ep.* cxxiii, 16; Courtois, 42 ff. Bury's thesis (3), 138, that the revolt was based on hate of Stilicho (as that of Maximus on hate of Merobaudes) is not necessarily inconsistent with the view I give.

5. Olymp. frag. 12 and 16; Procop., *B.V.*, iii, 2, 32; Zos., vi, 1 f., and 5, 2. (The daughters of Gerontius, disinherited, appealed to Pelagius, who sought to strengthen them: Plinval (1), 175, 191.)

6. *Chron. Min.*, i, 654, a. 408; Thompson, (2) 164.

7. Zos., vi, 5, 3; Rutil., i, 213 ff.; *Querolus*, ed. Peiper, 86 f.; Thompson (1), 11–23.

8. *Chron. Min.*, i, 660, a. 435; Rutil. *l.c.*; Merob., *Pan.*, ii, 8 ff.

9. *Chron. Min.*, i, 652–4, with Mommsen's emendation.

10. Zos., vi, 10, 2. "Mr. C. Hawkes . . . gives it as his opinion that this at least (the coin evidence) seems to leave the way clear for 'a Pictish-Bacaudae' (if we may transfer this Gaulish nickname to revolted British peasants) combination in the region in the early 5th c.". T. D. Reed (2), 21.

11. Holder, 1, col. 204; Loyen (3), 501 for Armorica. Constantius: Sundwall, 65; Seeck (2), 326, 344; Oros., vii, 43, 1. Probably after the fall of Constantine he went to Africa, and "generals of Honorius" defeated Jovinus and followers 413: Loyen (1), 37, n. 5. In 415–16 he fought Visigoths in Spain, and Vandals. In 416, to help the settlement of the situation in the West, which was coming under control, a general amnesty was offered for all who had joined marauding bands: *C.T.*, xv, 14, 14.

12. Carcopino (1).

13. Bury (2).

14. See refs. in Collingwood (2), 476 f., including Stein and Schultz; N. Chadwick (1), 32, 10 ff.; Polaschek, *P.-W.* (1936), xvii, 1077–1116; Nesselhauf (1939), *Die Spatröm. Verwaltung* (1938); Stevens (5); Birley (2), 190 ff. Stevens holds no returns after 367.

15. Collingwood (2), 296 f.

16. Collingwood (2), 313, for the few who would go in an evacuation. "At the end of the 4th c. the *Not. Dig.* lists an impressive number of Dukes and Counts; but this account should not create an illusion. It has been calculated that for all Gaul, all these chiefs with deceptive titles muster not more than 30,000 soldiers under their orders," E. Thevenot, *Les Gallo-Romains* (1948), 122.

17. The same route took on a fresh significance later in 5th c.: Copley, 23.

18. Richmond (1), 185, but also (6), 67.

19. Eugipp., *Vita Severini*, 4, 2; 20, 1; 3, 3; H. S. Schultz, *J.R.S.* (1933), xxiii, citing Stein and Egger. One gold of Arcadius at Heddon on the Wall, *Arch. J.* (1914), lxxi, 35; one gold of Valentinian III (*J.R.S.* (1922), xii, 98) paralleled by *solidus* of same at Alzey fort (*Germania* (1929), xiii, 185). A check is the find at Barrington, Cambs.

Chapter 11

1. Levison, *Vita G.*, 280, n. to ch. xl; Salv., v, 22, 26 f.; Oros. vii, 41, 7; Zos., vi, 5, 3.

2. Salv., *ep.* i; Gennadius (2), 67; Ebert., *Lit. des Mittelalters*, i, 447, n. 4.

3. Dill, 137, 318, 231.

4. *De Gub.*, v, 25; iv, 21; vii, 91; v, 18; v, 30 and 35. Also for the curials, *C.T.*, xii, 1, 117; Symm., *ep.* ix, 10; *C.T.*, xiii, 10, 1, for collusion with *tabularii*.

5. *De Gub.*, v, 51–6; *Ad Eccl.*, iv, 22. He is esp. sharp against the rich towns of Aquitaine: vii, 16.

6. *De Gub.*, vi, 72. *Vidi ego ipse*, etc.

7. *Antiquity*, viii (1934), 315. Even the laws denounce the landlord *Nov. Th.*, xxi: "Gratified with so great domestic gains, they forsake the common good."

8. *De mort. persecut.*, xxiii, 1 ff. Aurel. Victor (*de Caes.*), xxxix, "the immense evil of tributes" under Diocletian. See A. Piganiol, *Constantin*, 179 f. Things bettered under Julian, worsened under Valentinian. "The fisc intervened to complete the work of the brigands," Jullian (1), vii, 15; viii, 33 f. See Lot (1) 201 f.

9. *De Gub.*, v, 37; v, 46; Thompson (1); J. Lindsay (2), 181 ff., 190 ff.

10. *De Gub.*, v, 28, 38, 44 f., 24 f., and 21.

11. Note Aus. epigs. on branded runaway, xxxvi–xxxvii. *Eucharisticus*, 329 ff.; *Comm.*, ii, 174; Jerome, *ep.* cxviii, 2, and cxxiii, 4.

12. Sid. *ep.*, iii, 2; ii, 1; v, 13; vii, 7; Schmidt (1), i, 261. The people of Auvergne brought Seronatus to justice, and he was condemned to death.

13. *Ad Eccl.*, iii, 49; iv, 23. This is an earlier work than *De Gub.* (dated 435–9).

14. Migne, lii, col. 691 ff.: Hom. iv, 6, 7 (col. 705), and xvi, 5 (743). Céméle was a fair-sized town near Nice; N. Chadwick (2), 140.

See J. Lindsay (2) for Orientius with his picture of Gaul burning like a single pyre, etc. (p. 200); also Paulinus of Béziers on the vain effort to build up ruins to a world that's lost. Raby (2), 68 with further refs.; *J.R.S.* (1956), 65; Dill, 316.

15. *On His Return*, lines 497 ff., 205 ff., 29 ff. For monks, 515 ff.; Labriolle, *Rev études lat.*, vi (1928), 30.

Note that Avienus (late 4th c.: Jerome in 420 speaks of him as having made a translation *nuper*) writes of the *harsh* Britons (*Desc. O.T.*, 416–18); cf. lines 745–60 on the rich soil and spacious pastures inhabited by the *horrible* Britons. (If the A. in Macrobius' *Sat.* was the poet, he was a pagan with the same sort of outlook as Rutilius.) For date, Carcopino (3); Duff. *Minor Lat. Poets* (Loeb), 755.

16. L. Havet (1880), 2 and 4; P. Thomas, *Mélanges L. Havet* (1909), 531–5; Jullian (1), viii, 176, n. 3; Lot (7), 472 f.; Ganshof tries to refer it to Alans settled by Aetius, others see a Germanic people, but they would not be *rustici*. L. Hermann in his ed. (p. xix) sees it is Bacaudae, but thinks they copy barbarian law; Thompson (1), 23, n. 46; 19.

17. Editions of Havet, Peiper, Hermann, G. Ranstrand (1951), with refs., p. ix. Also W. Johnston, *The Q.* (1900); S. Cavellin, *Eranos* (1951), xlix; Raby (2), ii, 59; Wernsdorf in Peiper; Pichon, ch. iv; N. Chadwick (2), ch. v, for Rutilius and Querolus.

18. *De R.S.*, lines 201 f., 267, 603 ff. for his interests; Cavallin, 139 f., for correspondence of *De R.S.* and *Q.*—e.g. the Harpies and Circe. Salvian, iii, 50.

19. *Chron. Min.*, i, 660; Const. *Life of Germanus*, xl.

20. *Chron. Min.*, i, 469, a. 419; ii, 19, a. 418; G. Kaufmann, *Forsch. zur deut. Gesch.* (1866), vi, 441–4; Thompson (3), 65. In 507, defeated by the Franks, the V.s went back to Spain.

21. Amm., xxvii, 5, 4–7; Zos. iv, 10 f.; Thompson, 66, n. 15.

22. Thompson, 74 f. In Italy the peasants were also up in arms. Symmachus remarks casually that he cannot go to his country seat through the abundance of brigands (*ep.* ii, 22). In mid-4th c. the use of horses was forbidden, not only to colons and shepherds, but even to landlords (with some specified exceptions) and their agents (*C.T.*, ix, 30, 1 and 2, a. 364); in 399 Honorius denied to shepherds of Valeria and Picenum the right to use horses (ix, 30, 5). In 391 the right to bear arms, jealously denied to civilians, was conceded for use against brigands (ix, 14, 2). A law of 383 threatens bailiffs of the big estates in collusion with brigands (ix, 29, 2). Laws against deserters gone in for loot, 403 (vii, 18, 14), again 406 (vii, 18, 15).

In Brittany excavation has shown throughout the Romanised area "signs of fire, everywhere thick beds of ashes covering the soil, charcoal in masses, calcined stones . . ." (Cabrol, ii, pt. i, 1247; cf. A. de la Broderie, *Hist. de Bretagne* (1896), i, 222–4), dated as 406–16. The historiàns have taken these to represent barbarian incursions, but they must be largely Bacaudan.

Chapter 12

1. St. Paula, F. Lagrange (transl. 1934); Hedibia, *St. Jerome* (1875), A. Thierry, 412; N. Chadwick (1), 206; (2), 17 ff.; Glover, 134.

McClure and Felton, *The Pilgrimage of Etheria* (1919); W. Heraeus, *Silviae vel potius Aetheriae Peregrinatio* (1929); E. Lofstedt, *Kommentar* (1936). Silvia came from Elusa in Aquitaine; Etheria (mentioned by Valerus, life of St. Fructuosa, as "sprung from the furthest shore of the Western Sea, the Ocean").

For a Bordeaux pilgrim (*c.* 333): *Palestine Pilgrims Soc.*, i (1887), transl. A. Stewart. (Note the advent of the title of Augusta and the growing importance of women of the imperial house, 5–6th cs.)

2. It may not be mere confusion that makes the *A.S. Chron.* (Parker, a. 381; Laud, a. 380) say of the exploits of Maximus, "at that time arose the heresy of Pelagius throughout the world".

For Chrysanthus, see n. 10 to Intro. above. He took Ablantius out of the school of Troilus the sophist and made him a minister: Soc., vii, 12. For Novatians, Augustine, *Contra Ep. Parmeniani*, iii, 19, 24; *Exp. II Cor.*, ii, 11.

3. Plinval, 61, 58. I follow him generally as to the works to be attributed to Pelagius, and in the historical narrative; Ferguson and Souter also are useful.

4. Aug. *ep.* clxxxvi, 1; Mercator, *Liber subnot. Juliani* (Migne, xlviii, 111); Orosius has *Britannicus noster*, *Apol.* xii; Kenny, 1, no. 26; Jerome, *Comm. in Ierem.*, i, prol. 4 (Reiter, p. 4); iii, 1 (p. 151). Further refs. in Ferguson.

For Ireland: Zimmer (3), 20; *P.-W.*, x (*Kelt. Kirche*), 211; Kenney,

157–60; Bury, *Pat.* 296; Gougoud, *Le Chrét. Celt.*, 32; Haddan and Stubbs, i, 15 f.

5. Plinval, 64. For time at Rome: *diu* (Aug. *ep.* clxxvii, 2); *diutissime, de grat. chr.*, ii, 24). Plinval conjectures a clash with Jerome in early years, 51 ff. and 64, n. 5; Ferguson, 44, 77.

6. Plinval, 65 f. *Homo latinissimus* (Jerome, *ep.* l—ironically?).

7. Plinval, 67–9 for refs.

8. Plinval takes the date about 383, but it could be nearer 400.

9. Plinval, 199 f. for refs. A monk Jovinian, prob. with Arian affiliations, attacked the Ambrosian cult of Virginity: W. Haller, *Iouinianus* (1897); Harnack, *Dogmengesch.*, iii, 53 f.; Jerome, *adv. Iouinianum*, ii (Migne, xxiii); Aug. *de remissione*, iii, 13; *P.-W.*, ix, 398 ff. Pope Siricius condemned him, also a Council of north Italian bishops. Iovinian replied that he succumbed not to the arguments but the conspiracy of the bishops (*non est ratio, sed conspiratio*: apud Jerome, *ep.* 1, 4).

10. Salvian, *De gub.*, viii, 2; Mercator, *l.c.*, ii; Gennadius *de vir.*, xlv; Migne, xxx, 278 ff., could be by him.

11. Augustine contrasts the Catholic Mean: *Contra ii ep. Pelag.*, 1, 3, 14. They omitted *Dimitte nobis* and *ne nos inducas* in the Pater.

12. P. C. Martini in *Antonianum* (1938), xiii, 319–34; Plinval, 125 ff. He stressed the abasement of Christ in the sufferings of the Passion.

13. For studies of Paul in east and west, Plinval, 130; Souter (1), 3 f.; Ferguson, 120.

14. E.g. for *Ep. to Romans*, Plinval, 154 f.

15. Refs. Plinval, 221 ff. He divides mankind into the rich, the poor, and those with a sufficiency. Ferguson, 147–53, stresses that the comments on Wealth apply to all forms of power.

16. *Ep.* cxxx, 2 and 8.

17. Note how the argument for and against the Perfectibility of Man raged during the period of the French Revolution. P. makes much use of terms *proficio* and *profectus* for progress in moral life: Ferguson, 131; Souter (1), 70, 108 f. Note a like use in Rufinus' version of Origen on *Romans*, and the verb in Ambrosiaster (*J.T.S.*, xx (1918–19), 148; Souter (2), 129 ff.).

18. Cyprian had composed a similar collection; Pel. seems also to have known the *Ethica* of St. Basil.

19. *Ep.* cxxx, 6.

20. His earlier work is harsh, wholly concerned with logic of argument. For his style see Plinval (2). Here, to Demetrias, he has reminiscences of Ovid and Juvenal.

21. Caps. viii and xiii: a remarkable psychological insight.

22. Cap. iv, *in animis nostris naturalis quaedam* (*ut ita dixerim*) *sanctitas*.

23. Cap. iii.

24. *Ep.* cxxxiii, 5. The first serious clash, it will be seen, arose through C. challenging one of the sacraments; the issue ceased to be one of general theological controversy and had to be sharply dealt with.

25. The defence of *apatheia* had been made by Evagrius Ponticus; Rufinus, translating maxims of Pythagorean Xystus, had helped the infiltration of Stoicism. The pretext for Jerome's attack was Pelagius' effort to come to friendly terms with him through Ctesiphon (a rich partisan of P.): Jerome, *ep.* cxxxiii, 1; *Dial.*, ii, 11.

26. Migne, lxxviii, 363; Oros., *Apol.* xii.

27. Also *Comm. on Job*, and on *Constancy*: Plinval, 330 f.

28. The deacon Sixtus at Rome succumbed, Plinval, 334. (In the troubles at Rome that led to the imperial measures, one anti-Pelagian, Constantius, an ex-vicar "bore many things", says Prosper, *Chron.*, a. 418, without defining his persecution.)

29. Julian said the terms were tampered with: apud Aug., *Op. imp.*, i, 18. For Julian's letter denouncing Manicheism: Plinval, 339.

30. Plinval, 344.

31. Migne, li, 594; *Contra Collatorem*, xxi (Migne, li, 271). Collingwood thinks no local roots (2), 311 f.; Williams thinks there were, 196, 209.

32. For some confusions, Plinval, 354.

33. For Arnobius the younger: Migne, liii; Morin, *Études, Textes et Docs.*, i, 308 ff.; Plinval, 378 f.

34. *Lib. de vir. Ill.*, xix.

35. Pelagius, like Martin, seems to have been a millennarian, expecting at any moment world-end: Plinval, 184.

For his appearance: a Goliath (Orosius, ii) broad-shouldered as wrestler (same, xxxi; Jerome, *Dial. adv. Pelag.*, i) and bull-necked (Orosius, xxxi); a great alpine hound (*Comm. in Jerem.*, iii, 1); large and bulky (Orosius, xxx) by 415, with tortoise steps (xxxi). Jerome adds the jeer about porridge; Orosius (xxxi) about luxurious living, and calls him full of face, also says he liked to go bare-headed; Jerome calls his brow stern (*Adv. Pelag.*, ii, 10), and speaks of him butting with horns (i, 29 and *ep.* l, 4). For Augustine's praises and refs. to friendship with Paulinus of Nola: Ferguson, 45 f.

Chapter 13

1. J.R.S., xxi, 232.

2. Hull (1), 37.

3. B. H. St. J. O'Neill, *Antiq.* (1944), xviii, 113 ff.

4. Myres, *Antiq.* (1935), ix, 456; A. Fox, *Camb. Arch. Assn. Cent. Vol.* (1939), 109; *Arch. Camb.* (1939), 40.

5. Collingwood, cited Hodgkin, i, 157.

6. *Antiq. J.*, xvii, 159–61. See further n. 15 of my ch. 2.

7. *Arch. J.*, cii, 30; *Antiq. J.*, xvii, 349; *Sussex A. Colls.*, lxxviii, 27 f.; *J.R.S.* (1956), 133 f.; ditto, 144; ditto, 135 f.

8. Sulp. Sev. First letter on Martin.

9. Lethbridge (2), 62; Collingwood (2), 312.

10. *Antiq.* (1937), 39–45. The date is hardly before 420.

11. O'Rahilly, 218 f.; for Eochu as sun-god, 218.

12. *Z.f.C.P.*, iii, 463; xiii, 378; O'Rahilly (1), 219, n. 3. For the im-

portant part played by Niall and his sons in destroying Emain, building up vassal states. The conquest of Ulster increased the power of the Tara dynasty; probably the claim of Tara's king to be King of Ireland arose at this time: O'Rahilly, 234.

13. Lethbridge (2), 61. All seem much later than 367. Grosjean (*Anal. Boll.*, liv (1936), 196–9) thinks the account in cap. xix is of Gaul in 407–9; so P. (then in his 22nd year) was born about 385. But however we date his return, my main point holds.

14. The same, 62.

15. *Arch.*, xl (1866), 411; Barker, *Brislington* (1901), 15.

16. The Dyke is post-R.: *Camb. A. S. Com.* xxxi-ii, xxxv; *Antiq.* iii, 148.

17. Hornsby and Laverick, *Arch. J.* (1932), lxxxix, 202–19. One of the skeletons in the H. ditch was a woman.

For the relation of the pottery to Crambeck (with clean break in wares of the stations *c.* 370): Hull (2) and *J.R.S.*, ii, 215.

For coin-evidence, Craster, *Arch. J.* (1932), 251–3.

18. Sutherland (1), 6; J. J. Hatt, *Cahiers d'Arch. et d'Hist. d'Alsace*, (1948), cxxix, esp. 191; Sutherland (2), 116, 120.

19. Collingwood (2), 308 for York. For R.-Saxon wares: Myres (4), citing, 39; for Salonae: Diehl, *Ins. lat. christ. vet.*, i, no. 185.

20. *E.H.R.*, lvi, 353 f.

21. *Arch. J.* (1933), xc, 282–305; xcii (1935), 74; *B.G.A.S.* (1934), lvi, 133–9.

22. *B.G.A.S.* (1933), lv, 329, 366; lvi (1934), 108.

23. Fineberg, 29 f.; Hawkes (2), 294.

24. *Ep.* iv (the carriages are *petorritum* and *cisium*); *ep.* vi (recalling Horace, *ep.* ii, 2, Lucretius, i, 354, Juv. iii, 236, Mart. xii, 57).

25. *Ep.* viii, 8 (also v, 5); i, 6; ii, 14. His grandfather had been consul in 381, friend of Ausonius and Symmachus: Seeck (3), p. čix; Dill, 376. Sidonius cites exs. of Roman Republican heroes who were also good farmers; the woman was the wife of Camillus.

26. N. Chadwick (2), 320.

27. *Ep.* xxvii, 90–8. The threefold rivers: Garonne, Durance, and Charente.

28. Matthew Paris (*Chron. Maj.* Rolls, series i, 186, 2), citing Bede, glosses the site as Verulamium.

29. Wheeler (4), 31 f. Note the trouble Paulinus took at Nola to get rid of hovels before his church; then one was burned down and the owner pulled down the other: N. Chadwick (2), 86

30. Wheeler, 34, 199 f.—5th-c. ware? Compare *Richborough, Third Rep.*, 182 (no. 334).

31. Wheeler, 35 ff.; M. Paris, *Vitae Abb.* (1684), 994.

32. Bury (p. 23) works out his name as Patricius Magonus Sucatus (Sochet, Muirchu).

33. Probus read in his copy of Muirchu, *Nentriae provinciae*; an ancient note on the hymn *Genair Patraicc* identifies Nemthur with Dumbarton; the preface (B) to the hymn of St. Sechnall gives the same birthplace. See

also Dukes, app. iv. Boulogne has found supporters (Lanagan). See Bieler (3), 56, for the readings. In defence of Daventry: O'Neil (*Arch. J.*, xc, 295, n. 1) and Hawkes (1), 78, n. 227. Note Bewcastle? Banna.

34. Bury, preface, x, and 322–5. N. J. D. White takes Banavem (Bonavem) as River's Mouth (Todd, *St P.*, 357) and Taberniae as from Taberna "a tavern. It is not a fatal objection to this theory that it is inconceivable that a Celtic town should have only one taberna in it," 111. But *taberna* means a shop; *taberna vinaria* is a tavern.

35. E. MacNeill, *P.R.I.A.* (1926); R. D. Pringle, *Trans. Cymmrod.* (1956 for 1955 session), 23–35, esp. 28; L. Bieler (1) gives Bannaventa Taburniae). Collingwood (2), 305, sees that the site cannot be in the north. For St. David's, Bowen, 60. (Bury, MacNeill, Rhys, Pringle support a site near the Severn; also Bowen, cited Pringle.)

36. Pringle, 32; *Archaeologia* (1944), xciii, 48.

37. Note two Pembrokeshire sites with his name (Pringle).

38. Crawford, cited Bowen, 25, on 12th-c. MS based on older trads.

39. Bowen, 26 f. and fig. 4; J. Lloyd, *Hist. of Carmarthenshire* (1935), i, 118.

Chapter 14

1. A Council of the Province is mentioned early in the occupation, but never again. For Gaul, see n. 34, ch. 17 below.

2. The old *ri(g)* seems to have grown early obsolete.

3. N. Chadwick (1), 27, 47 f. The dynasties of Powys and the Upper Wye (S. Powys) claimed descent from him. For Cair Guorthigirn: Jackson (5), 47.Vortigern was doubtless a magnate, not a war-king, but anti-Roman.

4. N. Chadwick (1), 53; Bromwich in same book, 125 f.; Ifor Williams (3) str. 85 of *Gododdin*.

The high prestige of Vortigern is shown by his name entering the calculus in Harl. 3859 beside Roman emperors; also he is the most important figure in Nennius. For forms of his name, Chadwick, 26; ancestor of the kings of Built, 18 f., 28. For Procopius: *Vand.* i, 2; *de bello Goth.*, iv, 19.

5. W. Levison (1); Bollandist, *Acta Sanct.*, May 1st, s.v. Amator. There are two versions of C.'s biography: Levison holds the shorter to be more genuine. See also H. Williams, 216 ff.; Le Bras and Gilson; N. Chadwick (2), ch. ix.

C., probably a presbyter (poss. of Lyon), wrote his work at the request of Patiens (bishop of Lyon, 449) who was at synod of Arles with Faustus of Riez *c.* 475; he died *c.* 494. The *Vita* was written *c.* 480 or a little later: Levison (1), 97 ff.; N. Chadwick (2), 250.

6. The *ducatus culmen* was mainly military, concerned with control of the Armorican and Nervian areas, including the coastal parts from Somme to Gironde and the interior of Aquitaine and Lugdunensis 1. It would have taken in the province of Senonia with Auxerre (Seeck (4), *occid.*, 45, no. xxxvii, 205). For anomalies in G.'s career: Gaudenet in Le Bras and Gilson, 111 ff., and N. Chadwick (2), 263 f. The latter suggests that G. followed Exuperantius in the Armorican Dukeship. For the possible

combination of civil and military functions, *C.M.H.*, i, 30; Hoare, 287.

7. Autun was never the seat of the *praefectus praetorio Galliarum*; and the name here, Julian, is not known of any prefect of the time, Levison (1), 159.

8. Constantius says the election was by unanimous vote (acclamation?) of clergy, nobles, commons; in *Life of St. Amator* election by consent of bishops appears. We see the transition from the old democratic form to the authoritarian one in Sidonius, *ep.* iv, 25; N. Chadwick (2), 247, 252, 291; Stevens (1), 122 ff.; R. Laprat in Le Bras, 156, n. 12; Beck, 15 ff. (The details about the Tree and Amator do not occur in the shorter text of Levison, *M.G.H.*, *S.R.M.*, vii.)

9. But the foundation seems of later date: Levison, *Vita G.*, i, 254.

10. A possessed is cured, a man converted, plague ended, thief (possessed) found.

11. Lupus plays a minor part: N. Chadwick (2), 276 ff. (for his rels. with Attila). He was still alive while C. wrote, and in touch with Sidonius, friend of C. "These men were in fact members of the same circle, and C. himself was a man of considerable literary gifts," Chadwick, 251. Prosper does not cite L. going with Germanus (note Sid. links L. and G. as models in letter to Prosper of Orléans). C. was perhaps trying to weld two rival traditions (Auxerre, Troyes).

12. Chadwick, 257. Efforts to locate the battle (e.g. at Mold) are mere guesses. The union of Saxons and Picts may be a touch to enhance things; but there is arch. evidence for Saxons in E. Midlands before 429, and they have joined Picts (whom Gildas makes come by sea) in a Chilterns skirmish: Hodgkin, 61, 66, 116 (window urns and equal-armed brooches). The Alleluia maybe suggests magic. Round the churches on festivals "the people shouted with all the might of their lungs those Hebrew words they did not understand and perhaps for that reason attributed a magical virtue to: *Hosanna! Alleluia! Amen!* Long after leaving Rome, Jerome recalled with emotion those noises of the Christian throng," Plinval (2), 116. The Alban shrine was prob. near Thames: Stevens (6), 273.

13. The *Vita's* first miracle concerns theft of the bag of the prov.'s chief tax-collector (called a man of good morals); in the bag was his silver. In Anon. Gaulish Chron. (entry 114, a. 433): "Germanus bishop of Auxerre is famed for his virtues and austerity of life." For the Breton rels. of this chronicle: N. Chadwick (2), 274.

14. Levison (1), 127; Stevens (6), 365, n. 10; Chadwick (2), 255. The *Vita* reads as if with no gaps between first return, Arles visit, second journey. *Interea* . . . N. Chadwick is sceptical of second visit; but the verbal parallels with the first no doubt merely show C. gravelled for matter. Note the way in which the voyage links in with the Armorican deputation. C. does not grasp what was at stake in Britain apart from the P. question (or in his age's way sees political issues subsumed in theological). His reliability is proved by many details: the prefect Auxiliaris (xxiv) is known otherwise by a single milestone (Levison, *Vita*, 232), Peter is bishop at

Ravenna when G. dies (xxxv, xlii), Segisvult is Master of Soldiers (xxxviii) though C. antedates his patrician rank. C. knows about Val. and Placidia, Goar, Tibatto. For Severus: Levison (2), 268, 270, n. 3; Bede, *H.E.*, i, 21; N. Chadwick (2), 255, 277 f. For Prosper at Rome: Plinval (1), 369 ff.; L. Valentin, 403; Letter, Migne, lv, 413.

15. Among late deeds are the bearing of a crippled old man over mountain torrent (men are going home after work, bowed with burdens), the order to his deacon to give all the gold to the poor, the freeing of prisoners condemned to torture and death (chains fall off, bolts draw back).

16. Levison (1), 127; Stevens (6), n. 10.

17–18. N. Chadwick (1), 27.

19. Chadwick (1), 229 f., 34–6.

20. Collingwood thinks he had effects (2), 312; G. H. Doble, *St. Paul of Leon* (1941), 3. For west: Crawford in *Custom is King* (1936), 190.

21. Ifor Williams (4); Bowen, 32. We can set no trust for this early period on a statement of the 9th c. (Heiric, *Miracula Germani*, i, 54, 80) that Britain worships G. with special devotion.

22. N. Chadwick (2), 266.

23. Migne, l, col. 430 (Mansi, iii, 264).

24. N. Chadwick (1), 46–9, 38, 259 f.

25. Blair (2), 28–50. For Votadini still in north in 6th c.: Ifor Williams (3), 1 ff.

26. Blair (2), 36; H. M. Chadwick, *Early Scotland*, 146; Jackson (1), 79 f. Blair, 27 f., for Cunedda's kingdom, urbs Giudi and Gildas "Transmarinae." Hogg (*Antiq.* (1948), xxii, 201–5) for the argument dating *c.* 400. Nennius, xiv, lxii; F. Lot (8), 158, n. 2; genealogies, N. Chadwick (i), 18. In Glossary of Cormac mac Cuilenáin (late 9th c.) the Irish are said to have occupied Dind map Lethain in land of Cornish Britons.

27. Bowen, 31; W. F. Grimes, *Guide to Coll. Illust. Preh. Wales* (1939), 110.

28. Hemp and Gresham, *Antiq.* (1944), xviii, 183–96; Bersu and Griffiths, *Arch. Camb.* (1949), 173–204; Hogg, "The Votadini" in *Aspects* (1951), 200–20. For concentric hut circles: Ralegh Radford, *Antiq.* (1944), xviii, 205 f. For 6th c. links with north: *Arch. Camb.* (1934), lxxxix, 18–20.

29. Among the Cunedda-line saints were Einion Frenhin, Seiriol, Meirion, Eugain, and Edern: Bowen, 72 f. and fig. 18. For speech effects, Bowen, 100; Jackson (2), 171–6.

30. Charlesworth, 27–39.

Chapter 15

1. *Chron. Min.*, 660, a. 435; Thompson (1), 21, n. 1. Bacauda is used both of a rebel peasant and of the movement.

They are called *rusticani* (Eutrop., ix, 20), *agrestes* and *latrones* (Aur. Victor, *Caes.*, xxxix, 17), *rustici* (Jerome, a. 2303, Oros., vii, 25, 2).

2. *Chron. Min.*, a. 437; John of Antioch frag. 201, 3. For Gallia Ulterior: Levison (1), 133, 136.

3. *Paneg. Avitus*, 246–8; Loyen (1), 45–7; A. Coville, *Réch. sur l'hist.*

de Lyon (1928), 107; Sundwall, 36, 96; Jullian, iii, 430; iv, 566; v, 93; Prosper, a. 436.

Huns were at this time a part of Roman army of the West, Waitz, i, p. 1.

4. Forms are Gochar, Gohar, Goar: Olympiodorus, *Thebaeus*, s. v, 412; Levison, *Vita*, 271, n. 5; C. Zeuss, *Die Deutschen u.d. Nachbarstämme* (1904), 468, 704 f.; Levison (1), 133 ff. It seems that Goar was the chief with whom P. of Pella made his pact during the siege of Bordeaux.

5. E. A. Thompson fixes date of G.'s death at 445 (communication).

6. *Paneg.*, ii, 8–12; Loyen (1), 66 (not the first day of 447).

7. Loyen (1), 66; Levison (1), 133–6; *Chron. Gall.*, 133, a. 448; Bury (3), i, 250, n. 2 (taking this revolt as the same as 441–2), but see Levison, Lot, Stein, Loyen.

8. Loyen (1), 68; Sid., *Paneg. Avitus*, 210 f.; Stein, 493; Dubois, *Hist. crit. de l'estab. de la Monarchie fr.* (1742), i, 430.

9. Thompson (1), 16 f.; Hydatius, *Chron. Min.*, a. 441, 443, 449, 454, 456; Salvian, *De Gub.*, v, 23.

10. Thompson (3), 66, n. 13; Levison (1), 136 f.; Jordanes, *Get.*, xxxviii, 194; *Chron. Min.*, i, a. 442, 440.

11. *Chron. Min.*, a. 443; Thompson (3), 65 f.; Schmidt (1), ii, 293 f.; Loyen (1), 51 f.

12. Lot (4); Loyen (1), 42. For Visigoths taxing Romans: Thompson (3), 68, n. 22; Lot (9).

13. Thompson (3), 73; Zos., vi, 2, 3–5; *Chron. Min.*, ii, 22, a. 430; Sid. *carm.*, vii, 233 f. Merobaudes fought in Alps before 435: *ILS*, 2950.

14. Sid., *carm.* xii; T. Hodgkin, ii, 362; Stevens (1), 66, n. 1. Orosius (vii, 32) says the B.'s were mild and treated their Gaulish subjects as brothers (Bury-Gibbon, iii, 350 n.).

15. Lot (3), 17, 23 f.; Sid. *carm.*, vii, 361 ff.; Loyen (1), 53 f.; Blair (1), 4. Saxons were settling near Boulogne and Bayeux: near the latter lay Otlinga Saxonia (Greg. Tours: H. Prentout, *Essai sur les Origines et la Fondation du Duché de Normandie* (1911), 51–76, 280 f.).

16. For the question whether the Armoricans fought under Aetius in 451, Thompson (1), 20, and (2), 167; Jord. *Get.*, xxxvi, 191, and Sid., *ep.*, i, 7, 5. No, says Lot (2), 108—but were they the same Armoricans? See later.

17. *Ep.* vi, 4; Dalton (1), ii, 240; *Lex Salica*, xiv, add. 5, and lv, 2; Dill, 379.

Chapter 16

1. *Liber contra Collatorem* (Migne, li, col. 271); Duke, 31 f.

2. Not an uncommon name. He can hardly have been the Palladius of Rutilius' poem, as N. Chadwick (1), 223, suggests.

3. *Conf.*, xlvii, l–liv; Bury (1), 160 ff. The four Munster bishops are claimed as before Patrick, e.g. *Vita S. Ciarani*, vv; Plummer (2), i, 220; Todd, *St. Pat.*, 198–211, rejects the claim. For Ciarán as senior saint, *Fél. Oeng.*, 88 f.

4. Latinising Irish Fethgna: Haddan and Stubbs, ii, 289; *Martyrology of Donegal*, 12th Feb. (p. 416).

5. K. Meyer, using Zimmer's materials (1), 23 f.; N. Chadwick (1), 219. Jackson (2), 4th ch. for secular words (for gold and wine) from pre-Christian period into Irish; the later loan-words are from British Latin and not from British. For P. and the Latin loan-words: T. A. Watkins, *Arch. Camb.* (1955), 175 f.

6. Fol. 9, r.a. Tirechán's *Memoir* was written *c.* 675 (Ultan his teacher); Muirchu's *Life* about the same time or shortly after.

Bury, 367, tries to fit in the "visit" to Rome (Tirechán) with Leo's pontificate. (For *insula Aralanensis* and rel. to Germanus' monastery on isle of Yonne: R. Louis, *Mél. L. Halphen*, 445–51—for rel. of this site to British or English missionaries, and possible site of *insula A.* at Arles in monastery founded by St Hilary: F. Benoît in Le Bras and Gilson, 181–9.

7. Victoricus: for the Victor names, N. Chadwick (1), 218. Amathorex: Zimmer, *Nennius Vindicatus*, 123; Bury, 347.

8. N. Chadwick (1), 215.

9. Muirchu. i, 8 f.; *H.B.* l. N. Chadwick (3), 9 ff. Ebmoria is unknown; Bury suggests Ebroica, Evreux, 347. Muirchu says Auxilius and Iserninus were with Pat.; *The Annals of Ulster* (a. 439) says that they reached Ireland seven years after Patrick.

10. N. J. D. White, 16 f.

11. This thesis fits the facts better than that of "two Patricks".

12. *Confessio*, xxvii–xxiii. Note that Sulp. (dealing with the persecutions of Martin) is as vague (First letter and *Dial.*, i, xxvi) with remarks about envy, etc.

13. xxx, ix–xii. For the rhetoricians not in Ireland: E. MacNeill, *Studies* (1931), xx, 458, "The Beginnings of Latin Culture in Ireland". The dream-motive: N. Chadwick (1), 217.

14. I, 27.

15. Migne, xxxix (app. Aug. *Serm.* x); cf. Aug. *in Psalm* 36.

16. I, 4; ii, 18; ii, 38 (Sid. *ep.* iv, 16; v, 15; *carm.* xi). Cf. Jerome on Hilary (Migne, xxii, 585, *ep.* lviii; cf. 395, 459, 534); Vincent of Lérins, *De vita contemp.*, xxiii. Jerome, however, attacks the *rusticus et tantum simplex frater* who can only help himself, *ep.* liii, 9 and 3; on the need to live like the apostles if one wants to write like them, *ep.* lvii, 12.

17. Symm., *ep.* vii, 9: *ingeniorum varietas in familiaribus scriptis neglegentiam quondam debet imitari*.

18. *Ep.* vii, 2, 1; viii, 16, 3. Pacatus (*Paneg.*, xii, 1, 2), speaking before the Roman Senate, deprecates the rustic style of his transalpine eloquence.

For the struggle against eloquence: Haarhoff, 157 ff.; N. Chadwick (1), 216 f. and (2), 110; R. E. Prothero, *The Psalms in Human Life* (1904), ch. ii; Loyen (2) and Raby (2), chs. 1–2 for the extent of its dominance.

19. He seems to know the *Commentary on the Apocalypse* of Victorinus of Pettau (White; 12, 112 f.), and there may be links with Irenaeus (F. R. M. Hitchcock, *Irenaeus of Lugdunum*, 348 ff.) in a Latin version. His scrip-

tural texts: Old Latin, Vulgate, and a transitional version: Bieler (4).

A collection of P.'s letters existed at least by 7th c.; two survive: Bieler (3), 6, 28—with some fragments; Bury, 207, thinks *Conf.* composed at Saul in Ulster.

20. Marianus Scotus makes P.'s mother a sister of St. Martin, "a kinswoman of Martin's" (*Vit. Trip.*, i, 9). "Lupait and Tigris were his two sisters" (*Preface B* to *Hymn of St Sechnall*).

Muirchu (i, 10) has the adze-head taunt that is taken to refer to a Roman tonsure: White, 124 f.

21. Letter, 2, 3, 14 f., 19.

22. *Chron. Min.* (*M.G.H. Auct. Ant.*, ix, ed. Mommsen, 660 f.)—*latae* amended to *late vexatae*.

23. Gildas: Stevens (6); H. M. Chadwick (2), 140 ff.; J. F. Kenney, i, 150–2; Lot (10), 229–64.

There may be a memory of Stilicho's reconstruction and of the sub-Roman earthworks in his account.

24. Lethbridge (1), 48 ff., considers the picture of the Picts wriggling out of their brochs or wheelhouses to come from someone who had looked down from above and seen the likeness to a wormcast.

Chapter 17

1. *Ep.* vii, 6: by *fides* if not by *foedus.*

2. Cap. xx. The appeal is doubted by Lot (11).

3. Not clear what is referred to (certainly not Anglesey): Paul. Diac., *H.R.*, xii, 17 (Droysen, *MGH*) says "not ever after could they be driven out thence."

For Bede's use of Gildas: Blair (2), 11 ff.

4. See Stevens (6)—and in effect Myres (2)—for taking the Three Groans of Britain as made to Count Theodosius (or after Maximus' death: Hawkes (3), 92), Stilicho, Honorius (misplaced as Agitius). It may well be that the third appeal fuses memories of Groans to both Honorius and Aetius, but the appeal to Aetius (whose name is given correctly in Nennius and Bede) in his Third Consulship is convincing—Collingwood (2), 293 f.; Blair (2), 3–6.

5. Stevens (6), 363. See Gildas (cap. iv) in which he remarks that he will do his best with lack of British records which, if they ever existed, have been burnt or "carried off in the ships that exiled my countrymen" (? to Brittany). He has thus to use non-Brit. sources (transmarine) which are full of gaps and obscure. (Collingwood (2), 294; Blair (2), 8–12; Stevens (6); Stenton, 2; N. Chadwick (1), 22.

6. This entry seems independent of Gildas and Bede.

7. Bede gives the same reason about the Huns as the *Chronicle*. The name of the Proud Tyrant is not given in 2nd ed. of Gildas (Joscelyn, 1568) based on the earliest (lost) MS.; the name Vortigern inserted in later codices from Nennius or Bede? or originally in Gildas?

8. Cap. xxxi. Vortigern seems to rep. transition from anti-R. magn? to tribal king proper.

9. For the Advent date: (441–2) R. Thurneysen, *Eng. Studien* (1895), xxii, 174; Lot (1), 236, and (12). For criticism, R. V. Lennard, *History*, xviii (1933), 204 ff.; for an odd view, A. Anscombe, *Brit. Num. J.* (2nd s., 1927–8), ix, 20 f.

Also, Collingwood (2), 352, 446, 451; Hodgkin, 66–8, 81; Plummer, *Bede*, ii, 27; Chambers, 237 f.; F. W. B. Nicholson, *Z.f.C.P.* (1907), vi, 439 ff.; Myres (2); Hawkes (3).

For the *A.S. Chronicle* and the relation of its dating to Easter Tables: R. L. Poole, *Chronicles and Annals*, ch. i; T. D. Reed (2), 4 ff.

10. Bede, *H.E.*, i, 15 (cf. ii, 5 and *de temp rat.*); Myres (2). Note Bede seems to draw on Kentish sources as well as Gildas: Stenton, 8 f.

Gildas, xxiii; Nennius, xxxi and xxxvi ff. N. calls the Britons unarmed, as all weapons were taken by Maximus. Bede omits the marriage tale; unlikely that N. invented this, it must have grown up in Welsh tradition. For N. (Nemnivus, etc.): see Hodgkin, i, 79 (citing Libermann). He put together bits of what he called the Tradition of Our Elders with bits from Jerome, Isidore, the *Life* of Germanus, plus Saxon and British pedigrees and the Wonders of Wales. (Thurneysen, *Z.f.C.P.* (1933), xx, 97–138; Kenney, 152–5; Hodgkin, i, 371.) Gildas thinks in his strange but expressive Latin; Nennius has to translate out of Welsh: Jackson (2), 121; Ifor Williams (4), 55 f.

11. Myres (2), 232–4; Bede, *H.E.*, i, 15. It would be rash to say that Hengist already led in 443: E. G. M. Fletcher, *Antiq.* (1943), 91–3; Myres, 232; Blair (2), 18 f.

12. Myres (3) and (2), 238 f.

13. Myres (2), 238, n. 33.

14. Blair (2), 38–43, with refs. 39; Hodgkin, 159, pl. 29. York was a *colonia* as well as H.Q. of the Duke of the Britains at least till 395: Stevens (7), 141.

15. Stevens (7).

16. For a Soemil who may have led a Saxon revolt in the North that led to Deira being taken over in whole or part: Blair (2), 44. Coroticus to whom Patrick wrote was king in Strathclyde about this time. Coel Hen, too, perhaps somewhat earlier, founded a dynasty in territory forming part of Strathclyde kingdom: Blair (2), 45 f. He is Coel the Old, also Gautepauc taken as equivalent of Voteporix (name of a king known to Gildas). But it is unlikely that *Coel* comes from *Caelius*: Jackson (1), 80.

17. Lethbridge (3), 116, and *A Cemetery at Lackford* (1951), fig. 7; Myres (3); for remains at Dorchester: Myres (1), 356, 394.

18. G. Ward, *Hengist* (1949); Myres (2), 233; Stevens (6), 368; M. G. Clarke, *Sidelights on Teut. Hist. during the Migration Period*, 186 f.; Chadwick, *Origin*, 53; R. W. Chambers, *Beowulf* (1932), 443 ff. The Finnesburg frag. links with the Finn Lay (*Beo.* 1071 ff.).

19. In W. Kent and Surrey, Saxon leadership may have wholly or partly taken the place of Anglo-Jutish. For Frisians: Procopius, *Bell. Get.*, iv, 20. For the Cornovian area as a Celtic stronghold: Savory in Harden, 56 f.

20. T. D. Reed (2), 22, and (1), 20 f.; Hawkes (1), 78. The Benli legend

may hold a trad. of slaves becoming kings: G. as anti-V. becoming the patron despite his Roman position. (The Benli tale is a variant of the Balor tale, found also in Muirchu (xii) about Patrick.)

21. Bede gives 450–5 for the settlement. The Channel fleet was still active later in century (Sid. to Admiral, *ep.* viii, 6; Lindsay (2), 375), but was not likely effective just now.

22. *Carm.* vii, 359 ff.; Sid. claims that Avitus as Master of Horse controlled things. "The Saxon's raid abated, the marshy Albis confined the Chattian." But in fact tension went on.

23. Cap. xxv. For chanteys, Jerome, *ep.* xiv, 10; Paulinus, *carm.* xvii (sailors sing hymns instead); also Sid. *ep.* ii, 10, 4. Note Gildas uses the hoary rhetorical paradox of "living tomb", also he seems to connect *coloni* with *coloniae*! Bede follows Gildas in general. (He, even more than Nennius or Muirchu, was writing propaganda to ensure the Roman triumph, in a difficult Northumbrian moment.)

24. Nennius, xliii; Wade-Evans, 67.

25. D. C. Whimster, *Arch. of Surrey* (1931), 177; Hollingworth and O'Reilly, *Girton*, 15–17.

26. Nennius tells how G. bade his men bury him in the harbour whence the foe made exit. Then, "though they may hold a harbour elsewhere in Britain and shall have dwelt there, yet they shall never remain in this land". But his men "despised his command".

27. It is argued that Hengist and Horsa are legendary names (Stallion and Mare, though Horsa means Horse) and the mon. to Horsa an etymol. myth. But Hengist was a well-known name (Horsetead in Kent near Aylesford, Horstead in Angle N.E. of Husum). (The 473 entry in the Chron. has the note of a poem). See Hodgkin, i, 371; Ekwall, *Oxf. Dict. E.P.N.* 240, also Collingwood (2), 358, n. 1; Blair (1), 16; and Hawkes (3), 94; T. D. Reed (1).

28. Collingwood (2), 312 f. For the traditions: N. Chadwick (1), 250.

29. Hodgkin, i, 181.

30. Thompson (2), 167. Whether the appeal was in 446 or slightly later does not affect the argument.

31. *Ep.* iii, 9. For Riothamus: Greg., *H.F.*, ii, 18; Journandes, *Get.*, xlv; Dill, 302, 316. Journandes speaks of a fleet.

32. Loth (2), 93. The founders of the Breton bishoprics were all monks of British origin: T. Taylor, p. xxix; Anderson, p. xii.

33. N. Chadwick, 251.

34. The same, citing *Vitae*, SS. Gurthiern and Ninioc in the cartulary of Quimperlé. The earliest ref. to Cornwall in Britain (as Cornubia) is in poem to Aldhelm by an anon. cleric (*Aldhelmi op.*, *carm. rhythm*, i. 11, 9 ff., ed. Ehwald (1919), 524).

35. *Carm.* vii, 543 ff. The meeting at Viernum was of Gaulish magnates; it was not the representative assembly of Gaul meeting at Arles: Bury (3), i, 207; Anderson, p. xii. The rousing of Armorica, etc., refers to gathering forces against Attila.

Chapter 18

1. *H.E.*, i, 15; Myres (1), 337–51.

2. Hodgkin, 2–19, 158–61; Stenton, 4 ff.; Blair (1), 6 ff. K. Malone (*Rev. Eng. Studies*, v, 174) shows that Bede follows Pope Gregory in using *Angli* as English, not as Angles. For the growth of the name English and England, Blair (1), 11 f.

3. *Ep*. viii, 6; he speaks of them going home *de continenti*—to Britain or to islands off the Schleswig coast? In *ep*. viii, 9, Sid. refers to "blue-eyed Saxons, lords of the seas".

4. The terpen or mounds built on the Frisian coast were the main defence against the sea till dykes were made about A.D. 1000 Excavation shows in the period 400–50 a strong Saxon element intruding on Frisian, both in pottery and houses: Blair, 10.

5. Hawkes (3), 99; Myres (1), 359–61. The two main cultures: Kendrick (2). Two groups of archaeological goods between the advent and the emergence of the Franks: Hawkes (3), 104.

Other Jutish areas: Myres (1), 364 f.; Hodgkin, 99 f. Also Stenton, 23; Hodgkin, 82 f., 88–93.

6. Joliffe; Hawkes (3), 105 ff. The unit of land (*sulong*, ploughland) and its quarter-share (*jugum*, yoke) are also all its own.

7. Myres (1), 364; Joliffe, 88, n. 5; Hodgkin, i, 101.

8. Myres (6), 156 ff. and Hawkes (3), 108 f.

9. Hawkes the same; n. 108 for Myres' error about Canterbury, which means Town of the Kentfolk.

10. Style 1, out of late Roman animal forms (at least to a large extent); these forms were still being used in Kent. Also we find bracteates in the Danish manner till mid-6th c., with square-headed brooches of Kentish form. Hawkes (3), 109.

Jutes in Gaul are also there connected with Franks: Stenton, 59.

11. Stenton in *E.P.N. Soc.*, vi, 14.

12. Myres (1), 364; Hodgkin 105 f.; Blair (1), 17. For Stuf and Wihtgar who seem Jutes: Myres, 365 f.; Blair, 33.

13. Hodgkin, 107 f.; Stenton, 17–19, 55, 58; Myres (1), 368–71. For lower Thames: Myres, 405–8.

14. Copley, 27 f.; Hodgkin, 106.

15. The arch. evidence is poor: cemeteries at Feering and Kelvedon, remains round Colchester; Kentish-type goods at Shoeburyness, Southend, Broomfield. For *-inga* names: Hodgkin, 95 and 216 f.; Stenton, 314.

London: Hawkes (3), 121 f.; Stenton, 55 f.; Myres (1), 372–7; Hodgkin, 137–47; Wheeler (5), 65.

16. Myres (5), 250–62.

17. Myres (1), 386 f.; *Antiq.*, viii (1934), 185 ff. for geog.; Lethbridge (3); Stenton, 49–53; Hodgkin, 114–18.

18. C. Fox (2), 224, 274 f., 296 and maps.

19. Myres (1), 413, 416: see last chapter also here.

20. Hodgkin, 148–53, 194–200; Myres (1), 411–12, for rel. to Frisians;

413, for line between civilian and military areas in R. days. Lindsey: Myres (1), 413 ff., 456.

21. Cemeteries at Ipswich and Snape; Rendlesham, between them, the only *vicus regius* of the E.A. kings in 7th c. on a known site.

22. Myres (1), 394. Also Copley, 57 f., 79 ff., 104 ff., 112 ff.; Savory, 57 f.; Stenton, 26–8.

23. Kirk, 126 f. The British custom of inhumation may have affected the newcomers; there is a rel. of river-sites and cremation; in most of area the Saxons spread in small groups; by or near the river are the more solid settlements. For problems of dating: 126 (Osney). For Bucks: Myres (1), 407.

24. In the Damendorf peat, a man in large woollen cloak almost 2 yds. sq. with trousers, shoes, puttees, belt. The women could weave diamond pattern, etc. Jessup, 34 f.; *Ant. J.* (July–Oct. 1953), 188 f. On the Franks casket are warriors with tunics (like kilts), garments like sleeved jackets, cloak brooched to shoulder; putteed or bare-legged (or with hose); cross-gartered breeches to ankle. For fashions: Leeds (2), 79 ff.; Lethbridge (6) and (8), 27–9. The splendours of Taplow and Sutton Hoo do not concern us here.

For arts, e.g. brooches in chip-carving technique: Hodgkin, 33; Jessup, Baldwin Brown, etc.

25. In the bog (probably then a lake) were boats with holes cut, swords bent, spear-shafts broken: offerings to a god or "killed" to accompany the dead? or merely a war-dump after a campaign? We know from Tacitus the Earthmother's procession with the slaves thrown into the sacred lake.

26. For disintegration in migration of the primitive aristocracy: Stenton, 301. The king's councillors were more or less his nominees; his court was composed of seniors and juniors, tried soldiers already rewarded with land or officials (eorls, etc.), and young warriors in constant attendance: H. M. Chadwick (1), 157. Hodgkin, i, 155 f., overstresses the confusions of the migration period, but we must not undervalue them.

27. There is no need here to enter into details of wergild.

28. Stenton, 294.

29. Stenton, 310.

30. We must not interpret early Saxon religion in terms of the late Norse poems, etc. For pagan place-names, see, for ex., Copley, 104 ff.

31. xvi, 2.

32. In the three-room house, room 3 seems built as kitchen for 2, and then 1 added as extra living-room; the floor of 3 had risen six inches with pottery and rubbish. In room 1, a bone stiletto, a comb, broochpin, skeleton of middle-aged man buried in floor under thin layer of clay; with him a knife and double-toothed ivory comb. In room 2, a circ. hearth (2½ ft. in diam.), frags. of grey R. pottery and R. glass, and equal-armed brooch of 5th-c. pattern (close to those in lands between Elbe and Weser). Leeds (4), (5), and (1), 21–8. For other sites: Hawkes (2), 323 f.; Lethbridge (7) and *V.C.H. Cambs.*, i (1938), 299 f. Car Dyke: *Ant. J.*, vii,

(1927), 141; Bourton, Hodgkin, 224 and pl. 34 (weaver's hut). A dog was buried inside at Car Dyke.

33. Also knives, chisels, pins, awls of iron; pins, prickers, bodkins, and combs of bone. Too poor for metal buckles, they used bone toggles for girdles.

34. Gröber, *Grundriss der rom. Phil.*, i, 387; Masmann, *Z. f.d. Alt.* i, 379 ff.

35. *Carm.* v, 251-3; the wedding is 218 ff. To Philagrius he writes, "You shun barbarians as bad folk; I, when they're good," *ep.* vii, 14. He jeers at the uncultured Visigothic court, *ep.* iv, 8. He has ready-made epithets: speedy Herulians, javelin-throwing Huns, skilled-swimmer Franks, scimitared Gelonians, skin-clad Goths, ferocious Alemanni, bulky Vandals, etc. But often his pictures are direct and striking.

36. *Ep.* viii, 3.

37. R. K. Gordon, 67-70; R. W. Chambers, *Widsith*. Ealhhild seems to have been the wife of Eormanric; the story went that he murdered her.

Chapter 19

1. Sidonius, *ep.* iii, 7, and vii, 10.

2. *Ant. J.* (1931), xi, 149 ff. No exact date, but suggesting the war-chiefs rather than *civitates* of the R. period. Collingwood (2), 316.

3. *J.R.S.* (1956), 141; for Arthurian assocs.: Chambers, 184.

4. Collingwood (2), 320. Hillforts (defended homesteads less than two acres in extent or HQ of estate) in Wales still held or even built in Wales during R. period; the small concentric enclosures and rectangular defended homesteads on low plateaux and slopes seem native settlements of late R. or Dark Ages. Savory (*Bull. Board Celtic Studies*, xiv, pt. i (1950), 70, argues for Iron Age origin: differing from larger hillforts only in that they were occupied through R. period and on into Dark Age. Bowen, fig. 31, 113 f. For Dark Age refortifications on the fringe of the Black Mtns. of Brecknockshire: Savory, 69.

5. Collingwood (2), 320. See Crawford (1), 282, on six earthworks defending highland zone (two double) all facing south, south-east, east or north-east—from Manchester via Derbyshire to Sheffield and on by Leeds and Aberford to Richmond. Four straddle Roman roads. See further, Crawford (1), 282.

6. *Antiq.* (1944), xviii, 113-22; *Arch. J.*, c. 177-87; Peake, *Antiq.* (1943), xvii, 199-93; R. Gilyard-Beer on Little Heath section *Berks. Arch. J.* (1954-5), liv. At Padworth signs perhaps of timber revetment (Peake).

7. Wheeler (2), 83, argues that earthworks in Chilterns, Middlesex, Kent are "tangible evidence for the effective survival of London through the Dark Ages". See him also (3), 262. For the Deserts of Chiltern: Collingwood (2), 438, n. 2. See further, *J.R.S.* (1936), xxvi, 87-92; *Antiq.* (1934), viii, 437-42. We must await the verdict of forthcoming excavations.

8. Hawkes (1), 78.

9. Hawkes (1), 77, with refs. to Pitt-Rivers; *Wilts. A.M.* (1891), xxvi, 335-42; T. D. Reed (1), 11, 149-58, 197; Copley, 65-8. Oman's idea of a

mere boundary is impossible: see Hodgkin, i, 376, n. 39 for refs. The Woden name suggests that the Saxons returning to the upper Thames had forgotten the origin.

10. Caps. xlvii f.

11. Note that Vortigern also has a pedigree linking him with the Roman *colonia* of Gloucester, gateway to the villa-area of the Cotswolds: *Antiq.* (1946), xx, 16 ff.; N. Chadwick (1), 30. See also Lot (8), 188.

12. N. Chadwick, 31; also for the site of Vortigerniana as a commote between Wye and Ieithon.

13. Caps. xxv f. Geoffrey makes him son of the usurper Constantine, brother of Uther and uncle of Arthur; in Nennius he is Embreis Guletic (Emrys Wledig in Welsh lit.); Bede simply follows Gildas. (The praet. prefect wore a purple robe, *mandye*, though shorter than the emperor's, as well as having a big silver inkstand, a 100-lb. gold pen-case, and high chariot as symbols of office. Eusebius compares the relation of God the Son to God the Father with that of p.p. to emperor; Johannes Lydus sees p.p.'s office as encircling ocean.)

14. For the purple dragon of the Roman standards, Amm. xvi, 39; see also Sid., *carm.* v, 402 ff., Anderson, 96: the serpents were made of cloth or flexible skin, hollow, with a silver mouth through which the wind entered.

In the tale (*H.B.*, xlii) the Welsh can be seen through the struggling Latin: Ifor Williams (4), 44 f.; N. Chadwick (1), 111, 101.

15. Ifor Williams, 46; Chadwick, 125 f.; H. M. Chadwick (5), i, 123 ff.; Jackson (6). Note that in the *H.B.* Germanus never contacts Saxons or Ambrosius.

16. Cap. lxvi; P. P. Graves, *Antiq.* (1938), 474–6; also Crawford, *Antiq.*, v, 236–8; vi, 83, 480; vii, 479 f.

Note the fount Galabes in regione Gewisseorum where Geoffrey says the messengers of A.A. find Merlin. Ekwall takes Wallop as from A.S. Wiell-hop or Waell-hop, valley of the stream. *Y Cymm.* (1892), xi, 24 f., for attempt to take Wallop as Voluba of Ptolemy and as Golden near Grampound, Cornwall. Ambrosius may have given the name to Amesbury as likely as an unrecorded A.S. name *Ambr* postulated on strength of Ambrosden, Amesbury, Ombersley, and O.H.G. Ambricus, Ambrico, personal name (*Concise Oxford Dict. E.P.N.* 9). (For Aurelii as a R.-B. name from the 2nd c., see N. Joliffe, *Arch. J.*, xcviii (1941), on Dea Brigantia.)

Chapter 20

1. Cap. lvi. Bede had no Celtic sources; the A.S. Chronicle was not interested to record reverses. For Octha: Crawford (1), 284.

2. Collingwood (2), 321–3: I follow his brilliant conjectures, which alone make sense of things, though they cannot be proved.

3. Thompson (6). Chronology: see discussion, P. K. Johnstone *Ant.* June 1962.

4. Lot (13), i. 92. Couissin, 516 f., for the cataphract as the precursor of the medieval knight.

5. Crawford (i); Phillimore, *Y Cymm.* ix; N. Chadwick (1), 124;

Jackson (7) (8). See Crawford for refs. It has not seemed to me worth while to pursue the guesses further.

"The Old Welsh Linnuis (which would be Llynnwys in medieval Welsh) can then come from Lindensis (provincia) or Lindensia, presumably referring to the Roman town of Lidum Colonia, Lindensia would explain the O.E. Lindissi, the modern region called Lindsey", Jackson, cited Crawford, 286.

For *celli* names: note Calleva Atrebatum, Silchester: E. C. Curwen suggests that Bigbury was Calleva Cantiacorum: *Antiq.* (1937), xi, 1041. It has been suggested Cheltenham has the root.

6. Wade-Evans (3), 24 f.; Crawford, 289. There is no proof all the battles were against the Saxons: cf. the Battle of Wallop, also that of Camlann.

7. *History*, xxx, 133 f.; Chambers, 199; Copley, 67; Hodgkin, 123, n. 19.

For Bath: Leeds, *Ant. J.* (1933), xiii, 233; *H.B.* (Mommsen ed.), 130 and the gloss in one Gildas MS. "qui prope Sabrinum ostium habetur"; Chambers, 197.

8. T. Stephens, *Lit. of the Cymry* (1849), 17.

9. I have not laboured this vexed point: Collingwood (2), 460 f.

10. *CIL*, iii, 303, 2131; Chambers, 170; Lindsay (2), 296 for full version.

11. Chambers 210 f.; Crawford (1), 278. Note Beowulf as a bear-character (his hugs, etc.) whose tale is that of the Son of the Bear: Aarne-Thompson Tale-type, no. 301. For Gildas having A. in mind in a cryptic passage: A. O. Anderson, *Z.f.C.P.*, xvii, 404–6.

12. Harl. MS. 3859, integral part of *H.B.*

13. Crawford (1), 289 f.

14. Jackson (1), 81; N. Chadwick (4). Geoffrey makes A. die by his nephew.

15. Chambers, 169 f.; O'Rahilly (1), 362, 504. Chambers cites two more Arthurs in Irish sources.

16. Cap. lxxii; Wade-Evans, 120.

17. N. Chadwick (1), 125.

18. The same, esp. n. 2.

19. Chambers, 79 f.

20. Chambers, 80. Note also the dark side: as ravager, he kills all things where he treads for 7 years, the others for 3.

21. Cf. the animal-lifting epics of Ireland. Nennius already shows (*porcus Troit*) the link of A. with Twrch Trwyth.

22. O'Rahilly (1), 526 (121, 282 for other aspects).

23. R. S. Loomis (1), ch. ii and p. 156.

24. Tolkien in Wheeler (1), 137.

25. Same, 133; O'Rahilly, 527. There seems a relation of the Nodens cult to the Irish influx into S.E. Wales: note that in the mosaic inscription there is ref. to an Interpreter.

26. Loomis, ch. ix. For Grail and Table: A. A. Barb, "Mensa Sacra" (*J. Warburg and C. Inst.* (1956), xix, 40–67).

27. O'Rahilly, 67–9; cf. the weapons of Cuchulainn and Finn.

28. From a lady under a lake; cf. tale of Kei in *Kulwych*. For Arthur and the Gatekeeper: N. Chadwick (1), 18; same, 58 for rels. to Gereint, also 118. For early Arthur: T. Jones, *Bull, Board Celt. Stud*. 1958, May.

Chapter 21

1. Stenton, 5 f.; H. M. Chadwick (1), 61–4, on Frisians; Proc. *de bell. Goth*., iv, 19; Chadwick, 97–9; Britons are going to Brittany, *E.H.R.*, xiv, 44 f. There is also the trad. stated by monk of Fulda shortly before 865 that ancestors of Continental Saxons came from Angli of Britain; Stenton, 7, for extent to which fact in this: *Translatio S. Alexandri* (Pertz, *MGH Scriptores*, ii, 673 ff.); Chadwick, 96, 112.

2. Soc. *H.E.*, vii, 30; Latouche, 34, 83; Hoare, 274.

3. J. Lejeune, *La principauté de Liège* (1948), 17 ff., giving exs. For *defensor*, Bury (3) 27, 34; the turning-point appears in the 409 rescript of Honorius giving bishop and clergy power to participate in nominating the *defensores*; *Gallia*, xi, 563.

4. *Carm*., xxii. For still leisurely life of villas: *ep*. ii, 9 (cf. iii, 5; vi, 5); ii, 12; ii, 2; viii, 4.

5. N. Chadwick (1), 20. For Hywel: Richards, 8 f., for 10th c. nucleus, 127 for kindreds.

6. *V.C.H. Cornwall*, ii, 27. For stone at Gwennap: *Antiq. J.* (1944), xxiv, 65.

7. Ralegh Radford (1), 60 f. for full account. There are also pitchers like vessels of S. France. A. Fox on Bantham, *Antiq. J.* xxxv, 55–67.

8. *Antiq*. (1938), xii, 94–9; *P.R.I.A.*, xlvii (C. no. 2) (1942); and xlix (C. no. 1) (1943), 1 ff. for Ballycatten.

9. Radford. The harder ware began in 4th (even late 3rd) c. as copy of *terra sigillata*; certainly survived into 5th c.

10. D. B. Harden, 147 f.

11. Same, 70, 149.

12. Irish trade with empire is highest in early period, then in 4–5th cs. Of late period, R. coins: 2 in Galway, 1 in central Ireland; also 1 on Uist, one on Islay. *P.R.I.A.*, li (C. no. 3), (1947), 35; Lethbridge (2), 55. Scotland: *P.S.A.S.* (1931), lxvi, 177—here Eastern trade route important. Colour-coated sherds at Ballybunnion in Co. Kerry and Keil Cave in Kintyre, Argyllshire.

13. Radford, 68.

14. After late 5th c. no effort control waters till Charlemagne. *Vita S. Filiberti* (*SS. Rer. Merov*., iii, 603); A. Lewis on Atlantic trade 5–8th cs. in *Le Moyen Age* (1953), 249–398.

With rise of Frisians, Quentovic and Duurstede became important.

15. Latouche, 155 f.

16. *Vita S. Ciarini*, xxxi (Plummer (2), i, 214); Adamnan, *De Locis Sanctis*, praef.

17. *Acta Boll*., ii, 495 (Jan. 23); Migne, xciii, 1625; Leontios, *vita*, ix.

(In a later version Byz. is substituted for Alex. and zinc and lead are the metals gained.)

18. *P.S.A.S.* (1931), lxvi, 396, for earlier hides; Bowen, 16, Caerwent. Martin: Marche, 489–91; E. Garnier, *Hist. de la Céramique* (1882), 134, fig. 70; H. Leclerq, *Man. d'Arch. chrét.* (ii), 1907, 529, fig. 351.

19. A. Fox in Nash-Williams (1), 108, n. 112, 121; cf. *A Survey and Policy of Field Research in Arch. of G.B.* (1948), i, 69.

20. Sutherland (1), 7.

21. L. Bréhier, *Byz. Zeit.*, xii, 1 ff.

22. III, 4 and iv, 5; viii, 13; vi, 11. For clerics also as letter-carriers: N. Chadwick (32), 314 f., and for name Victor: (1), 218. The merchants of Verdun were in an association by 6th c. (Greg., *H.F.* iii, 34). For Jews: Pirenne, 82–6 (their centre, Marseilles). A hermit near Nice ate only root, imported from Egypt, Greg. vi, 6. For papyrus widely needed: *Pirennes Comptes-Rendus des Séances de l'Acad. des Inscr. et B.L.* (1928), 178–91; F. Vercauteren, *Études sur les civitates*, 211 ff.

23. M. Verlinden, *Rev. belge de philol. et d'hist.* (1933), 1095.

24. Pirenne (1), 79.

25. Lot (2), 1935.

26. *Vita Eligii* (SS. Rer. Merov. iv, 677). The trade increased after the advent of the Saracens.

27. Many chains of slave-gangs have been found in Britain of the R. period, see *Arch. J.* (1932), lxxxix, 108 ff.

28. Sid. to the bishop Patiens of Lyon, *ep.* vi, 12: another of the very rich bishops making best of both worlds, impressing the Burgundian king with his feasts, the queen with his fasts.

For dangers of river-travel in Gaul: *Vita S. Apollinaris*, bishop of Valence (SS. Rer. Merov., iii, 200); Greg. Tours, *H.F.*, iv, 48. By Saint Martin's aid a trader taking salt from Metz to Tréves could sleep, Latouche, 161. Also, F. Vercauteren, *Les civitates de la Belgique Seconde* (1934), 448 f.

29. Richmond (1), 105.

30. Wade-Evans (2), 50 f.; G. H. Doble, *Iltut* (1944), 13. The tale is linked with a land-gift for a monastery.

The *Vita Domitiani* gives some details of baking, about 4th c. The *clibanus* (vessel for slow cooking) was heated above and below amid embers. It seems in 5th c. the Gaulish peasants used brown bread: the names for bread are borrowed from the German (*simila, meca, bolling,* etc.). P. Lebel, *Mém. comm. ant. Côte d'Or,* 1952, xxii, 571.

31. Wade-Evans, 228 f.; Doble, 25, 32, 42. Cf. *Vitae,* 264, for St. Padarn on a famine.

32. For rel. to Celtic magic, Gruffydd (2), 334.

33. "Pedites constat esse nudatos," Vegetius, i, 20. For this section, Couissin, 517 f., 494–6, 501, 509, 512–17.

34. Barbarians took over Roman Weapons, e.g. pilum-agon in Germany; the gladius in Britain (Déchelette, *Manuel,* ii, 1126).

35. Leon, *Tact.*, vi. On the Arch of Constantine the axe-men are Asiatic.

36. The oval shape, lost in the West, persisted in Byzantium: A. Goetze in *Nachrichten über deut. Altherstumstunde* (1900), 43.

37. Couissin, fig. 190, with further exs. p. 150 f. The cassidarii made the helms; barbaricarii decorated armour, esp. helms with gold and silver.

38. Amm. xxv, 1, 2, and Julian, *In Constantii laudem*, i, 37d; Talbot, *Oeuvres de J.*, ch. xxxii, 32. On the hands seem mittens with no separate spaces for fingers.

The one rep. of a R. cataphract, at Lyon, is much mutilated (S. Reinach, *R.R.*, ii, 227). For the old R. parade-mask, Couissin, 506 on Amm. xxv, 1, 12 (the Persian cataphract-mask).

39. R. Menard, *Vie privée des anciens*, iv, fig. 228. For Dura graffito: *C.A.M.* vol. of plates iv, 26 f.

40. *Cod. Vat.* Fos., lxxi Ro, painting 47, and lxxiii, 49. Leon, *Tact.*, vi; Veget. *l.c.*

41. Lefébre des Noëttes, *L'attelage et le cheval de selle* (1931); G. Carnet, *Lé fer à cheval* (1951); Forbes, ii, 85. The nomads had both breast-strap or postillion harness and collar. The horse in the anc. world could not draw more than 62 kgr. With the collar it began displacing the ox, though it needed costlier food like oats. Yoking in line tandem also came in in early medieval days. R. horseshoes: there is more yet to be worked out. See e.g. Johnson, 423-9.

42. *Ep.* iii, 3; Greg., *H.F.*, ii, 24. In the earlier part of the letter Sid. says if the nobles have left the *squama* (scaliness, roughness) of Celtic speech, it was owing to Ecdicius. He reminds him that it was at Clermont he first swam a river, hunted in the woods, played ball and cast dice, sported with hawk and hound, horse and bow, and went to school. (Ecdicius tried to use the Burgundians against the Visigoths.) For the use of *celticus*: Hoare, 100, n. 3 on *Celtice aut . . . Gallice* of Sulpicius.

Chapter 22

1. Theologians have disliked the term Semi-Pelagian, as it seems to infer that Vincent, Cassian, etc., were semi-heretics; but here, where we are concerned with cultural developments, the term excellently describes the strong Pelagian element in their thinking. See N. Chadwick (2), 180, esp. ns. 2 and 3; O. Chadwick (2), 109 ff.

2. *Institutes*, i, 2; he is probably not directly affected by Pelagius, but builds on somewhat similar bases. The influence of John Chrysostom also helps to give him the active positive outlook. "It is not possible to be victorious without a struggle," *Coll.* xviii, 13, 4. Note that Hilary of Arles in his Discourse on Honoratus (Migne, 1. 1249–72), cap. 19, calls Salvian "one of those dearest to him, an eminent man most pleased in Christ".

3. *Common.*, xxvi: ed. by R. S. Moxon (1915), trans. T. H. Bindley (1914). See A. C. Cooper-Marsdin in *History of the Islands of Lérins* (1913), 50 ff.

4. Raby (2), 68; Plinval (1), 239; *Corp. Scr. Eccl. Lat.*, xvi, 381. *Alethia*, ii, 15 ff. and v, 95 f.

For Orientius: *C.S.E.L.*, xvi, 205; Manitius (1), 199. He borrows from Virgil, Ovid, Horace, Lucan, Juvenal, *Dist. Catonis*.

5. Migne, li, 617 ff.—lines 960 ff., 652–7, 554 f., 500–2. For natural law, see 412–22; universal salvation, 452–9; righteous pre-Christians, 265–367.

Hilary of Arles in his poem on the Creation (*C.S.E.L.* xxiii, 231) seems more interested in Lucretius than Genesis: Raby (2), 69.

6. Lines 453 ff.

7. Migne, li, 499 ff.; Manitius (2), 202; cf. Ausonius on the Caesars, Paulinus of Nola using *De Regibus* by Suetonius.

8. *H.B.*, xlviii; N. Chadwick (1), 226, 256–63; H. Williams (1), 242 f. The place-name Renis (taken by Irish Nennius as on the Rhine, sceptically) has been linked with Riez (Regiensis, Reiensis) where F. was bishop in 452, or with Lerinensis (abbot 433).

The ref. to Mother in Sid.'s poem is certainly to the Church.

9. *Ep.* ix, 3; *carm.* xvi, 116.

10. Dalton (1), lxxxi, clxviii; Engelbrecht, *C.S.E.L.*; Dill, 220; Gennadius, *De Scr. Eccl.*, lxxxv. In the poem Sid. refers to F. in his retreat, "an unfriendly wilderness . . . a marsh thick with green slime . . . deep gloomy caves", with steep alps trembling before the anchorite. He is said to have been influenced by the desert fathers, but no doubt Cassian played a part.

Jerome (*comm. in libr. Job*, xxv) and Cassian (*Collat.*, vii, 13) are not unfriendly to the materialist thesis; Augustine attacked.

Avitus, bishop of Vienne (*ep.* iv, migne, lix, 219) has him *ortu Britannum, habitaculo Regiensem*; Possessor in Africa calls him *Gallus* (*Concil. Gall.*, iv, 1520)—no doubt merely knowing that he was a Gaulish bishop.

11. Dill, 220. It seems during the abbacy of Faustus that Vincent wrote his work.

12. There he grew friendly with Ruricius who in 484 was bishop of Limoges (Sid., *ep.* iv, 16; v, 15; viii, 10). Ruricius, admiring but somewhat puzzled by Sid.'s style, wrote two books of Letters himself. For F. preaching at Patien's new church: Sid., *ep.* ix, 3. Caesarius: ed. Dom Martin (i) (1937), p. 797, n. 26. See index for cults. For Letters, Plinval (1), 30 f.

13. N. Chadwick (1), 211 f.; Haslehurst; Plinval (1), ch. i; C.-P. Caspari; Dom Morin, *Basler Z. f. Gesch. u. Alt.* (1927), xxvi, 208, 234–41, and *Rev. Bénéd.* xxxiv (1922), 265–75 (cf. *l.c.*, li (1939), 138–36). Morin, *R.B.* (1898), xv, 483; on Fatalis as woman: cf. B. Czapla, *Gennadius als Literarhist.* (Kirchengesch. Stud. iv, i, 114–16) for mistakes of G. Gennadius, *de Vir. Ill.*, lvi (Haslehurst, vi).

14. *Sanctus* used thus of a living person implies something of the Pelagian belief in perfectibility: cf. the *sancti* at Marseilles, who were friends of Paulinus of Pella (line 521).

15. Girls were flogged like boys: Aus. pictures to his grandson the bustle of the benches, the cane, birch, strap, and offers the consolation that both father and mother went through it all before (*Protrep*, 33). Sid. corroborates the beatings: *ep.* ii, 10—and mentions that even the

prof. of philosophy at Lyon used to mould his pupils *castigatoria severitate* (*ep.* iv, 1). Augustine puts his punishments at school in the same category as *temptationes martyrum* (*Conf.* i, 8 ff.; xii; i, 16, 17). Students were often rowdy: Libanius, *Or.* i, 199; i, 63; *ep.* cccxlviii; Amm., xiv, 6; xxviii, 4; Aug., *Conf.*, v, 8 (14).

16. Caspari, 343, cites Gildas for clergy going abroad by sea and land. Plinval includes Letter II among works by Pelagius (1), 44, but I think it is more likely to be by the writer of Letter I.

Chapter 23

1. Kenny, i, 142; K. Meyer (2), 117 ff. and (1), 5 f. Hiberia = Hibernia (cf. Pat.'s Hiberio).

For Greek in Ireland: M. R. James, *Camb. Med. Hist.* (1936), iii, 502 ff.; G. S. M. Walker, *Arch. Lat. Med. Aevii* (1951), xxi; Meyer (1), 26, n. 35; L. J. D. Richardson, *Hermathena* (1943), lxiii for the thesis of ogam from agma. For use of adonic by Irish: B. Bischoff in *Stud. zur lat. Dichtung . . . f. K. Strecker* (1931), 9.

2. Moinne (= Gaulish Moenius) appears in older version of Wanderings of the Dessi as a Gaulish soldier, *mil*, in 2nd half 3rd c. (Meyer (3), 208). He has a fellow-servant Grainne (= Gaulish Grannius). Irish groups (Moinrige) from Moinne, (Grainraige) from Grainne. Also lists of Dessi descendants include three with Gaulish ancestors; two other Irish tribes seem to have Gaulish ancestors; and the great Eoganacht dynasty of Munster may have originated in a peaceful settlement from Gaul, 5th c.: N. Chadwick (1), 249 f. on Meyer.

3. Nash-Williams (6), nos. 104, 9, 294, 370.

4. Same, nos. 315, 71: for memoria, p. 10. Dates lack in the British examples as in Gaul till the 2nd half of 5th c.

For barbarisations, p. 13; for Celtic elements, 7 f.

5. Same, pp. 10–13. Also, for the break, see no. 27 (Llangeinwen) for a lead coffin, the only one of the 5th c. in Wales. Fairly common in Britain and Gaul in 4th c. (though rarer elsewhere) in long box-form with separate overhanging lids, as distinct from the more tapering form of pagan period (inhumation coming into vogue from the 3rd c.), with decoration of bead-and-reel, scalloped and cabled motives, or combined Alpha-Omega and chi-rho (as here).

6. *Ep.* xcv (Migne, xxvi, col. 355); Dill, 406; Caes. *B.G.*, vii, 22, and iv, 5; Diodor., v, 31; Juvenal, i, 44 and xv, 1; Tac., *Hist.*, iv, 73; Suet., *Calig.*, xx; Lucian, *Hercules*. Claudian can use *docti* for Gauls (*4th Con. Hon.*, 582); cf. exaggerations of Clement of Alex. (*Stromat.*, i: Migne, viii, 776 f.).

Agricola flattered the Britons as being even more naturally gifted: Tac., *Agric.*, xxi (cf. Juvenal, xv, 111): Haarhoff, 34 f.

There was a counter tradition of Gallic boorishness: Haarhoff, 49. The Pictavi are represented as backward, 51.

7. Symm. (Seeck, 1883), ix, 83; *ep.* vi, 34; Aus. *Comm.*, i.

8. *Carm.*, vii, 90; v, 402 ff.

9. xxii, 22, and ii, 407; Loyen (2), 24 f. Greek little known, Loyen, 26 ff. Geography: there were maps on walls of porticos of Autun university: Eumenius (Baehrens, Galletier, caps. xx–xxi), who refers to "Britain lifting her squalid head above woodlands and waves". Ausonius refers to maps in *Grat. Actio* (cap. ii): Haarhoff, 66 f. The agrimensores now were in guilds, and there may have been schools for them in Gaul (e.g. the Theodosian Code with its laws about surveyors). The Code makes them judges in controversies about a locus: *C.T.*, ii, 26, 1; ii, 26, 4 (330 and 385). Yet they play no part in general education. Mommsen, *Die Schriften der röm. Feldmesser*, ii, 174; i, 29, 50, 136, 307, 353, 368, etc.

10. Denk, *Gesch. des gallo-fränk. Unterrechts-u. Bildungswesen*, 133. Note already the attack on the remoteness-from-life in Petronius, *Sat.* 1–3.

11. *Rhetores Graeci* (Spengel), ii, *Progumnasmata* and *Fables*.

12. Claudian and Statius are main influences. Scripture for him is mainly marvellous tales which he embroiders with conceits, e.g. flames wet with dew mocking the Children in the Fire.

Loyen (2), for preciosity of Sidonius and Ruricius; Mamertus Claudianus as a would-be opponent. For literary meetings: Chadwick (2), 208 f.; Roger, 80. See also H. Hagendahl, *La Corr. de Ruricius*, 1956.

13. In the 4th c. Rome's sarcophagus workshops often keep to neutral imagery like the Seasons.

14. Origen was translated by Rufinus (*R.E.A.* (1909), xi, 337, for effects of allegory on Sid. and friends: La Ville de Mirmont). For the arch-allegory of Martianus Capella: Raby (2), i, 100 ff.; Roger, 246.

Ep. viii, 11; *carm.* xv, 51 ff. and Bouché-Leclerq, *L'astrologie Grecque*, 311; Loyen (2), 16; Dill, 317, 51–3.

15. N. Chadwick (1), 236 f. Ausonius: see p. 53 of this book.

16. Chadwick suggests carry-over of genres seen in Celtic themes of marriage procession, the *Dinnśenchas* (from *Mosella*, etc.) and itineraries (Twrch Trwyth in *Kulhwch*: Rutilius and Avienus), the Death Tale (development out of *Passio*: Britain had at least one, of St. Alban).

17. Sedulius, *Ep. ad Macedonium*, pref. to his prose version of Carmen Paschale (Huemer, 171); Meyer (1), 20. The rimed prose of Isidore affected Ireland: Polheim, 292 ff., 312 f.

18. Macalister, 11 ff.; N. Chadwick (1), 95 ff., 242 f.

19. G. Murphy, *Eigse (J. of Irish Stud)*, ii, 200 f. For schools of *filid*: stimulated by rhetors from Gaul—no, E. MacNeill, *Studies* (1931), xx, 458 f. For rels. to Druids: Chadwick (1), 96; Macalister, 11 f.

20. In general, N. Chadwick (5). See med. romance *Peredur* for suggestion of Welsh hero-schools.

21. F. Jones, 41, 25.

22. O'Rahilly, 533 f. In Ireland Druids were still kept by king Diarmait (*c.* 558), though he was patron of monasteries: Macalister, 72.

23. N. Chadwick (2), 31 ff., for full account. Belenus, however, may be antiquarian for Apollo.

24. Amm. xviii, 1.

25. A.'s father, Julius, was court physician to Valentinian I. Galen twice mentions Claudius Abascantus of Lyon (Kühn, xiv, 177; xiii, 71), and Eutropius of Bordeaux wrote in 4th c. (Helmreich, Marcellus, *de Medicamentis*). For M.E.: Galen, xiv, 459, and Geyer, "Traces of Gallic Latin in Marcellus," *Archiv. f. lat. Lex.*, viii, 4, 419; Haarhoff, 88, for rels. with State. Doctors were mainly Easterners; Ammianus (xxii, 16, 18) describes the growing fame of the Alexandrian medical school in the 4th c. Ausonius, *Par.* vi (see also *Prof.* xxvi). One Crinas (1st c.), who seems of Massilia, introduced astrology into medicine (Pliny, *N.H.*, xxix, 1, 5) and did well.

26. Pliny, *N.H.*, xxx, 1, 4; xvi, 249; xxiv, 103; xxx, 13; *Script. Hist. Aug.*, xxvi, 44, and xxx, 14; also *Alex. Sev.*, lx.

P. de Labriolle, *Sources de l'hist. du Montanisme* (1913), no. 187. Addressed to Louocatus and Catihernus: perhaps in the Breton area.

Avienus (*D.O.T.* 751–7) says that in the two islands of the Britons women danced in bacchic orgies, madder than Thracians or Indians. Cf. Priscian on the women of the Nesides islands (? Hebrides): *Periegesis*, 584–6.

27. Roger, 110 ff.; Raby (2), 153 ff.; D. Tardi, *Les Epitomae de V. de T.* (1928); edition, Huemer; Huemer, *Wiener Sitzungsber* (1882), xcix, 509 ff.; Macalister, ch. iii; P. Lehay (rhythms), *Rev. de Philol.* (1895), xix, 45 ff.; M. Manitius (2), i, 119 ff.; Kenny, i, 143; G. Calder, *Auraicept na N-Eces* (1917).

An MS. of Milan makes him *presbyter Hispanus*. Ennodius, bishop of Pavia, calls him *fatuus homunculus*. (For Bigorre speech, cf. *Gurdonius homo* of Sulp. Dialogues, 1, 27, meaning Bonehead and app. referring to a Spanish locality for fools: cf. Gotham or Coggeshall.)

28. Raby, 154. Compare the preface to the "African Anthology" of Codex Paris. 10318, made up of strange words dug from the glossaries; and the fashion for epanaleptic verses and centos.

He admits forms like *magnissimus*; with the school of Galbungus adds an *i* to *docti*, cites a new declension of *vis*, yet protests against some Gaulish usages. He quotes from the poet Virgil only one parodied line; seems to have no Greek.

29. "Assena hoc est notaria," *ep.* xv (Huemer, 89).

30. Raby, 155; W. Meyer, *Rhythmik*, i, 199 ff. No sign of strophic structure; rime links pairs of verses; close rel. to Irish poets. The new rhythmic basis is being grasped by the theorists: Fl. Mallius Theodorus (*c.* 400), *De Metris* (Keil, *Gramm. Lat.* v, 586). Examples: Manitius (1), i, 200 f.; Raby, 157.

Virgil complains that verse and rhetoric are oft confused as both rhythmic (iv).

A poem by Auspicus, bishop of Toul and friend of Sidonius, in rhythmical iambic dimeters, makes us realise that much more was going on under the surface than we might think: Raby (2), 86; W. Meyer, *Gött. Nachr.*, 1906, 194.

31. He had read the Fathers, cites Bible (in version not Itala or Vulgate), says that study of pagan sciences right only if oriented towards understanding divine law.

For his circle of "oracles": cf. Sidonius, who "mentions 20 incomparable geniuses" (Roger, 81).

32. Roger, 122; he sees in V. the start of scholasticism, break with past. For the "two libraries" (pagan, Christian) in monasteries, 124.

33. Meyer (1), 8, 24, n. 20 and n. 22; Calder, Orosius, i, 2, 81, for Luceni.

34. N. Chadwick (1), 244; Macalister, 86; Roger, 125 f.

35. Note the Celticisms in Sidonius: Haarhoff, 17; Dalton's intro. and Baret in his edition, 106 ff.; Roger, 73 f.

36. N. Chadwick, 246, for British exs. and the Irish *Little Primer*; for jargon: Macalister, 74, 76; L. Wiener, *Contribs. toward a Hist. of Arabico-Gothic Culture* (1917), i.

37. Gildas, 289 ff.; *Irish Liber Hymnorum*, ii, p. xxi. The *Lorica* attributed to Patrick is far superior and seems to incorporate Druidic elements: "I arise today: in the might of Heaven; Splendour of the Sun; whiteness of Snow, irresistibleness of Fire; the swiftness of Lightning; the speed of Wind; Absoluteness of the Deep; Earth's stability; Rocks' durability . . ." (But cf. the catalogue in "the most elegant poem" by Plastus in *epitome* iii, 151, *limo solubili, lympha meabili, igne ardibili, aura mutabili* . . .") For style: Raby, 167.

38. Williams in his *Gildas*, 313, notes the divergence from the Augustinianism of Grace and Original Sin.

39. F. J. H. Jenkinson, edition 1908; Kenney, i, 255 ff.; Roger, ch. vii; Manitius (2), 157; Raby, 153; MacNeill, 457 ff.; E. S. Duckett, *The Gateway to the Middle Ages* (1938), 444 ff.; Hélin, 22; Zimmer (1), 336; (2), 1119 (first: sites in S.W. Britain; second: in Ireland by exiles from S.W. Gaul). For *famen*, Gildas, 301.

40. Macalister, 82 f.; Roger, 242–8; Gildas, 301–3; Raby, 167 f.

41. Jenkinson thinks Irish; E. K. Rand, "The Irish Flavour," *Stud. z. lat. Dichtung . . . f. K. Strecker* (1), 31, 137 ff.; Roger, 249 f. (Spain). For Irish alliteration in Aldhelm, Raby, 171.

42. Raby, 163 f.; Polheim, 292, 312 ff.; Macalister, 73 f.; Diod., v. 31; K. Meyer, *Arch. Rev.* (1888), i; *Z.f.C.P.* iii, 229.

Chapter 24

1. Ascribed to Cormac of Cashel *c.* 900; Dind = Fortress. *Vita of St. Leonorus*: B.-G. and Fisher, iii, 342, n. 2. Macalister, Corpus, 465 f.; Hencken, *Arch. of Cornwall and Scilly* (1932), 227; N. Chadwick (1), 251 f.; Jackson (2), 155 f.

Also Dind Tradui (prob. Din Draithov, Cornwall, in *Life of Carannog*: cf. Cair Drait(h)ou in Nennius' List): under Crimthann (prob. legendary king of Ireland in 4th c.). The Sons of Liathan app. are the Ui Laithain (Div. of Érainn in east Cork) neighbours of Deisi (Nennius, lxii).

2. Memoir in *Book of Armagh*: Chadwick, 27. Cf. the mill story.

3. Blair (1), 6. It grew and led in 9th c. to the kingdom of Scotland.

4. Bowen, 15, 31; Wade-Evans (1), 57; A. Fox in Nash-Williams (1), 108.

5. *V.C.H. Hants.*, i, 279.

6. *Arch.* liv, 223, 241; Crawford (3), 188.

7. Nash-Williams thinks the persons commemorated were not Christians on arrival in Wales, then were converted (6); Bowen, 29.

8. Bowen, 24, 23, 31, 67; Fox and Hyde, *Antiq. J.* (1939), 382 f.

9. Jackson (2), 138 f., 152 ff.: Nash-Williams (6). Ogam seems based on alphabet associated with Donatus. Macalister argues for Greek basis, 20 ff. There are 2 in Scotland; 6, I.O.M.; 40, Wales; 6, Cornwall; 2, Devon; 1, Silchester; 44 have also Latin. Jackson, 171–3.

10. Le Blant, *Inscr. chrét. de la Gaule* (1856), p. viii; *An Invent. of Anc. Mons. of Wales and Mon.* (1937), viii, p. cvi.

11. J. Vendryes; Thurneyesen, *R. Celt.*, vii, 169, and *Beitrage*, 192–6.

For Picts, Macalister, *Essays . . . to E. MacNeill* (ed. J. Murphy) (1940), 184–226. For property: *R. celt.*, xl, 387. For Ogmios, Vendryes, and Macalister (*Sec. Lang.*); Calder, *Auraicept*, 272. For the dead, Vendryes on rites and the tale of Lug mac Ethlenn's wife.

Later forms of ogam were devised on birds, colours, etc., etc.

For relation to runes, Vendryes and Wheeler, *Rome Beyond the Imp. Frontiers*, 44.

12. Nash-Williams (6), nos. 87, 126, 103, 92. For *hic jacet* in no. 87, cf. nos. 94, 153. For Elmet: Crawford, *Antiq.*, ix (1935), 282; for literary evidence of rels. of Wales and north England in this period: *Cymmrod. Trans.*, 1909–10, 95 ff.

For chi-rho by western sea-route: Hencken, *Cornwall and Scilly*, 212 ff.; Collingwood, *Northumbrian Crosses*, 1 f.; R. Allen, *Early Christ. Mons. of Scotland* (i), xvi; Henry, *Irish Art*, 33; Jackson (2), 163 ff.; *Antiq.*, viii (1934), 49. For Cantiorix: *J.R.S.*, xxviii (1948), 55. For Segontium: Wheeler (6), 64.

For doctors on the Continent in this period: Nash-Williams, 90, n. 2.

13. Nash-Williams (6), nos. 139, 258, 33. No. 139 has *servatur* for *servator* and *fidaei* for *fidei*; the lengthening of vowel into diphthong was African: Nash-Williams, 107–9.

Cultor aequi is the phrase for his justice-devotion; it is in the key of inscriptions from Gaul and Italy; Le Blant shows the rel. to Lucan and Ovid.

14. Nos. 78, 101, 83, 32. Less certain saints are Vendesetl (Gwynhoedl), no. 96; Cunegnus (Cynin), nos. 142, 172 (no. 142 is of his daughter Avitoria, and is also in ogam). Irish: e.g. nos. 115, 124.

15. Nos. 153, 345, 313–14, 283–4, 44, 307, 279, 229.

Note no. 271 "of Aeternus and Aeterna?"; no. 272, "of Caelextis (Caelestis) Monedorix"; no. 354 "of Vitalianus Emerito(s)"; no. 89 "of Anatemor son of Lovernius"; no. 106, "Jaconus son of Minus (? Minius)"; no. 68 "of Nemnius (? Numnius), son of Victorinus".

Double names are rare. (No. 285 has Barrectus Carantus with the Roman formula *DM*.) The names Carantus and Cupitianus (no. 283) occur on Scottish stones (P.S.A.S., lxx, 1935–6, 35). At Towyn is "of Pascentius", no. 286. Ireland has Vitalin and Sanctus (Sangti); for Latin names in British: Jackson (2), 160 f., 78–80.

16. Nos. 138 and 13. For *protectores:* Grosse, *Röm. Militärgesch.*, 13 ff., 138 ff.; for the use of the title on early Christian mons. in Gaul: *I.C.G.* (Le Blant) ii, no. 606 (Toulouse); *Nouveau Rec.* (Le Blant), p. 122 (Rhineland); Lloyd, *Hist. of Wales*, i. 133. For a 10th-c. record of V.'s genealogy: *Y Cymmr.*, ix (1888), 171. See N.-W., p. 57, and index "Byzantine", for Byz. relations.

17. Simpson, figs. 3–6; Duke, 139–42; J. Anderson, *Early Christ. Mons. of Scotland*, i. p. xvii; Jackson (1), 80 f. For Britomaglos: Blair (2), 20–4; Collingwood (2), 319 f.; Macalister, *Corpus*, i, 493–501.

18. For Martin as *peregrinus:* N. Chadwick (2), 105; Bowen, 19, for the spread of Martin's monasticism to Britain.

19. Duke, 119 ff. An abbot could be, and often was, a bishop, save at Iona. There was a strong hereditary principle: Todd, 149, 155 f.

The Celtic Easter was that of the Council of Arles as modified by pope Leo I in 455; after that the Celts were unaffected by the R. system.

20. Bowen, 144; T. Jones-Pierce, *Trans. Anglesey A.S.* (1), 51, 1–33; G. R. J. Jones, *Inst. of Brit. Geog. Trans.*, no. 19 (1953).

21. Dyfig deds. Bowen 37–9; Samson, p. xxi, 19, 37, 44, 67. For the struggle against paganism: F. Jones, 44, 67; Samson, 49, 75; etc.

22. Samson, cap. vii; Doble, *Iltud*, 6. *Samson* also brings in David. The Latin of the odd sentence is *genereque magicus sagacissimus* (seven MSS. read *magnificus*).

Druidism: Macalister (cited), 64, 68. Also Cabrol, xv (2), "tonsure"; Bury, 240–2; Rhys, *Lectures on the Origin . . . Religion* (1888), 263; on Tirechan, 367; L. Gougaud, *Christ. in Celtic Lands*, 201 ff. Weroch: Greg. Tours, *H.F.*, Migne, lxxi, 537; Haddan and Stubbs, ii, 328. (One cannot accept that Pat. fought the Celtic style.) The tonsure survived in Brittany till 818 (Haddan, ii, 79; Dom Morice, *Hist. de Bretagne*, i, col. 228; de Jubainville, *Mél. hist.* (1886), 539.)

The Sigambrians wore their hair long at the back; the old warrior seen by Sid. at Bordeaux will not feel a man till his hair grows: *ep.* viii, 9, line 28 of poem; Dalton (1), p. cix.

23. Crawford (3), 191 ff.

24. *Acta Sanct.*, i, 819 (13 Jan. Kentigern); vi, 45 (1 March) David; Haddan & Stubbs, i, 116 f.; Mansi, viii, 581 f.

25. Plinval (1), 406: Columban, *Ep.* v, (*M.G.H. Epist.* iii, 170), for apostolic faith. For perils: D. Cabrol, *L'Angleterre Chrét. avant les Normands*; J. Chevalier, *Essai*, 275; Gougaud, *Les Chrét. celt.* and "La conception du martyre chez les Irlandais," *Rév. Bénéd.*, xxiv (1907). People of saints: Bede, *H.E.*, iii, 5; Chevalier, 402. Note the importance of works in the predication of St Aidan and Gildas' *Lorica*.

For Chalcedon: H. B. Bittermann, *Speculum*, xiii (1938), 198–203; Hefele, ii, 779. The Arles position was based on agreement between abbot of Lérins and bishop of Fréjus, 419–26. (Yet the Celts had R. contacts up to 455.) For Welsh *filius*-stones and Pelagianism: *Arch. Camb.* cv, 141.

26. Kenney, i, no. 58; Bede, ii, 19. Bede, *H.E.*, ii, 2, gave rise to legend that the 2100 monks were Pelagians (Bangor near Chester).

27. *Annals of Clan-macnoise*: Zimmer, *Pelagius in Ireland*, 22

28. Chambers, 80 ff.; Faral, 236 ff. For Caradoc, Loomis, R. S. (1) 812 f.; Tatlock, *Speculum* (1938), xiii, 139; (1939), xiv, 350.

Chapter 25

I am sparing of references in this chapter which deals with things in a summary way.

1. Aurelius Conatus may be a descendent of Ambrosius: N. Chadwick (1), 55; for later kings: 84.

2. Jackson (2), 244: Celtic are Caedmon, Cadwalla. There are Celtic names also among the Humbrenses.

3. I began a list of sites with a link of some sort between Roman and Saxon sites, but it would bulk too large and only underline what appears from other evidences.

There was nothing like the territory of the *civitas* of the Parisii in Gaul, where the left bank of the Seine, the Marne valley (between Saint-Denis and Sevran) and the middle course of the Marne was well cultivated by Gallo-R. farms and where little change shows in occupation of soil and its productive level—even if there were changes in ownership. The new element is the orientation of traffic towards the Rhine valley and Germany, which encourages the settlement on the right bank. M. Roblin, *R.E.A.*, liii (1951), 301 ff. and *Le terroir de Paris aux epoches g.-r. et franque* (1951).

4. Lethbridge (3), 118 f., citing Wade-Evans, *Coll Prydain*; doubting impassable forests of clay uplands.

5. H. N. Savory, 541.

6. Note also "applied" variety of saucer brooch and silver bulla pendants: Lethbridge (3), 120 f.

7. Sutherland (4). They suggest more than small local issues.

8. Glastonbury and other south-west sites played their part.

Endpiece

1. Loomis, ch. v; Chambers, 157, 185, 227; 188–93, 221–5; 187, 229. Arthur as cave-sleeper links with a wide series of heroes awaited for by various peoples, including Bruce in Scotland: Chambers, 225 f.

2. Collingwood (2), 324. Also, C. Hole, *Eng. F. L.* 1948, ch. iv.

3. Tillyard and others have shown the complex political rôle of the Arthurian legend in the 16–17th cs. Note Milton's attraction to the theme, which he gave up as compromised by attachment to the cou~t; Blackmore used it to symbolise William the Liberator; Tennyson anctify Victorian society; Morris to vindicate life   ed   ld) against Tennyson's values.

4. M. E. Griffiths, *Early Vat*   h *Parallels*
  ~7); *Ballad~*

REFERENCES

Books cited once only are mostly named in the notes. I have used the usual abbreviations: *J.R.S.* is Journal of Roman Studies; *Z.f.C.P.* is Zeitschrift für Celtische Philologie; *Arch.* is Archaeologia; *Antiq.* is Antiquity; *E.H.R.* is English Historical Review; *A.N.L.* is Arch. News-Letter; *P.S.A.S.* is Proceedings Society of Antiquaries of Scotland, etc. Brit. = British or Britain; R. = Roman; A. = Arthurian.

Alès, A. d', *Priscillien et l'Espagne Chrét.*, 1936.
Alliez, *Hist. du Mon. de Lérins*, i (1862).
Anderson, W. B., *Sidonius* (Loeb, i), 1936.
Applebaum, S. (1) *P. of Hants. F.C. & A.S.* (1953), xviii, pt. ii. (2) *J. of Brit. Arch. Assn.* (1954), xvii, 77–9.
Arnold, C. F., *Caesarius von Arelate*, 1894.
Aymard, J., *Gallia* (1953), xi, 249–71.

Baldwin Brown, *The Arts in Early England*, 1903 on.
Barger, E.; *E H.R.* (1938), liii, 385–411 (field systems).
Baring-Gould and Fisher, *Lives of Brit. Saints.*
Beck, H. G. F., *Pastoral Care of Souls in S.E. France during the 6th c.*, 1950.
Bede, *Hist. Eccl.* (Plummer, 1896).
Bieler, L. (1) *Life and Legend of St. Patrick*, 1949. (2) "The Mission of Palladius," *Traditio* (1948), vi, 1–32. (3) *Libri Epist. SS. Episc.* pt. i (1952). (4) *Biblica* (1947), xxviii, 31 ff., 236 ff.
Birley. (1) *Brit. & the R. Army*, 1953. (2) *Trans. Cumb. & Westmor. A. & A.S.* (n.s. 1939), xxxix.
Blair, P. H. (1) *Intro. to A.S. England*, 1956. (2) *Arch. Aeliana* (4s) (1948), xxvi. (3) In N. Chadwick, 1, ch. vi.
Boissier, G., *La fin du Paganisme*, ii (1894).
Bowen, C., *A.N.L.*, vi (no. 2), 35–40.
Bowen, E. G., *The Settlements of the Celtic Sts. in Wales*, 1954.
Bruce, J. D., *Evolution of Arthurian Romance*, 1923.
Bury, J. B. (1) *Life of St Patrick.* (2) *J.R.S.* (1920), x. (3) *Hist. Later R. Emp.* (2nd ed. 1923), 1.

Cabrol and Leclerq, *Dict. d'arch. chrét. et de liturgie.*
Carcopino. (1) *R.E.L.* (1928), vi, 180 ff. (2) *Études d'Hist. Chrét., Le Christiantisme secret*, 1953. (3) *Rev. ét. lat.*, vi, 180–200.
Carson, R. A. G. (and Sutherland), ed. *Essays in R. Coinage*, 1956.
Caspari, C. P., *Briefe, Abhandlungen und Predigten*, 1890.

Chadwick, H. M. (1) *Origin of Eng. Nation*, 1907. (2) *Early Scotland*. (3) *Studies on A.S. Institutions*, 1905. (4) *Heroic Age*, 1912. (5) *Growth of Lit.*, i (1932) (with N.K.C).

Chadwick, N. K. (1) *Studies in Early Brit. Hist.*, 1954. (2) *Poetry and Letters in Early Christ. Gaul.* 1955. (3) *Trans. Dumfries. & Galloway N.H.A.S.* (1950), xxvii. (4) *Scot. Gaelic Studies*, 1953. (5) *Yorks. Celtic Studies* (1946), iii, 22 ff.

Chadwick, O. (1) In N. Chadwick, 1, ch. vii. (2) *John Cassian*.

Chambers, E. K., *Arthur of Britain*, 1927.

Collingwood, R. B. (1) *R.B.* (Econ. Survey Anc. Rome, T. Frank), iii, 1937. (2) *R.B. and the English Settlements* (with Myres), 1937.

Copley, G. J., *The Conquest of Wessex*, 1954.

Corder, P. (1) *Arch. J.* (1956, for 1955), cxii, 20–42. (2) *The Defences of the R. Fort at Malton.* (3) *R. Villa at Langton*, 1932 (with Kirk). (4) *The R. Pottery at Crambeck*, 1928.

Couissin, P., *Les Armes Romaines*, 1926.

Crawford, O. G. S. (1) *Antiq.* (1935), ix, 277–91. (2) *Antiq.* (1930), iv. (3) Western Seaways in *Custom is King*, 1936.

Curle, J., *P.S.A.S.* (1931–2), lxvi, 326–9.

Dalton, O. M. (1) *Letters of Sidonius*, 1915. (2) *R. Lit. Theory and Crit.*, 1931.

Delachaux, A., *La Latinité d'Ausone*, 1909.

Dickinson, W. H., *King A. in Cornwall* (uncritical), 1900.

Dill, S., *R. Soc. in Last C. of West Emp.*, 1925.

Doble, G. H., *St. Iltut*, 1944.

Duff, J., *The Letters of St. Jerome*, 1942.

Duke, J. A., *The Columban Church*, 1932.

Duval, P.-M., *La Vie Quotidienne en Gaule*, 1952.

Faral, E., *Légende Arth.* (1926), i.

Ferguson, J., *Pelagius*, 1956.

Field Arch. (Ord. Survey), 1951.

Fineberg, H. P. R., *R. and Saxon Withington*, 1955.

Frend, W. H. C. (1) *J.R.S.* 1956, 45–56. (2) *The Donatist Church*, 1952.

Forbes, R. J., *Studies in Anc. Technology* (ii, 1955).

Fox, A., in *Camb. Arch. Assn. Cent. Vol.* (1946), 109.

Fox, C. (1) *Personality of Brit.* (2) *Arch. of Camb. Region*, 1948.

Ganshof, F. L., *Hist. Essays . . . Hon. J. Tait* (1933), 111–20.

Glover, T. R., *Life and Letters in 4th c.*, 1901.

Gordon, R. K., *A.S. Poetry*, 1954.

Gregory of Tours. (1) *Opéra*, Arndt and Krusch, *MGH*, i, 1884–5. (2) *Hist. Franc.*, Omont, Collin, Poupardin, 1913.

Grenier, A. (1) *La Gaule Romaine* (T. Frank). (2) *Manuel d'archéol.*

Gruffydd, W. J. (1) *Welsh Rev.* (1947), vi, no. 4 (2) *Math*, 1928. (3) *Rhiannon*, 1953.

Haarhoff, T. *Schools of Gaul*, 1920.

Haddan and Stubbs, *Councils and Eccl. Docs. rel. to G.B. & Ireland.*

Harden, D. B., ed. of *Dark Age Britain*, 1956.

Hawkes, C. F. C. (1) *Arch. J.* (1948). (2) *Arch. in Eng. & Wales*, 1932 (with Kendrick). (3) In Harden.

Hefele, J., *Hist. des Conciles* (ii, 1), (1908), 168–90 (Pelagian).

Hélin, M., *Hist. of Med. Latin Lit.* (trans. J. C. Snow), 1949.

Hoare, F. R., *The Western Fathers*, 1954.

Hodgkin, R. H., *Hist. of A.S.*, 1952.

Hodgkin, T., *Italy and her Invaders*, 1931.

Holder, *Altcelt. Sprachschatz.*

Holmes, Scott, *The Church in Gaul.*

Hull, M. R. (1) *Short Guide to R. Colchester.* (2) *Arch. J.* (1932), lxxxix, 220–50.

Jackson, K. (1) *Antiq.* (1955), xxix, 77–88. (2) *Language and Hist. in Early Brit.*, 1953. (3) In N. Chadwick, 1, ch. iv. (4) In *Med. Studies Hon. J. D. M. Ford*, 1948. (5) *Antiq.* (1938), xii. (6) *Féil-Sgríbhinn Eoin Mhic Néill*, 1941, on threefold death. (7) *Listener*, Feb. 17, 1956. (8) *Mod. Philol.* (1945), xliii, "Once again A.'s Battles". (9) In Wainwright. (10) *Antiq.* (1935), ix, 492.

Jessup, R., *A. S. Jewellery*, 1950.

Johnson, W., *Byways in Brit. Arch.*, 1912.

Joliffe, J. F. A., *Pre-feudal Eng., the Jutes*, 1933.

Jones, F., *The Holy Wells of Wales*, 1954.

Jullian, C. (1) *Hist. de la Gaule.* (2) *Ausone et Bordeaux*, 1893. (3) *Hist. de Bordeaux*, 1895.

Kendrick. (1) *Arch. in Eng. and Wales 1932*, (with Hawkes). (2) *Antiq.* (1933), vii, 429–52.

Kenney, J. F., *Sources for Early Hist. of Ireland* (1920), 1.

Kent, J. P. C., in Carson, ch. xi.

Kirk, J. R., in Harden.

Labriolle, P. de. (1) *La Corr. d'Aus. et de Paul. de Nola*, 1950. (2) *Latin Christianity.* (3) *La Réaction Païenne*, 1950.

Latouche, R., *Les Origines de l'Écon. Occid.*, 1956.

Lavertujon, A., *La Chronique de Sulp. Sev.* (1) 1896. (11) 1899.

Le Bras and Gilson, *St. Germain et des Temps*, 1950.

Leeds, T. E. (1) *Early A.S. Art and Arch.*, 1936. (2) *Arch. of A.S. Settlement.* (3) *Celtic Ornament*, 1933. (4) *Arch.* (1923), lxxiii, 147. (5) *Arch.* (1926), lxxvi, 59–80.

Lethbridge, T. C. (1) *The Painted Men*, 1954. (2) *Herdsmen and Hermits*, 1950. (3) In Harden. (4) *Merlin's Island.* (5) *V.C.H. Camb.*, 318–20. (6) *P. Camb. A.S.* (with Tebbutt) (1933) xxxiii, 133–51. (7) *A Cemetery at Shudy Camps*, 1936.

Levison, W. (1) *Neues Archiv.* (1904), xxix, 95 ff. (2) *Vita Germani, MGH, SRM*, vii (1920).

Lindsay, J. (1) *The Romans were Here*, 1956. (2) *Song of a Falling World*, 1948.

Liversidge, J. (1) *Furniture in R.B.*, 1955. (2) *A.N.L.*, vi (no. 2), 46–9.

Loomis, C. G. *Speculum* (Oct., 1933), no. 4, viii.

Loomis, R. S. (1) *Wales and the A. Legend*, 1956. (2) *A. Trad. & Chrétien de Troyes.*

Lot, F. (1) *La Fin du monde ant.*, 1927. (2) *Les Invasions Germaniques*, 1935. (3) *Rev. hist.*, cxix, 1–40. (4) *Rev. belge de Philol. et d'Hist.* (1928), vii, 975 ff. (5) *La Destinée de l'emp. en Occ.* (with Ganshof and Pfister), 1928. (6) *La Gaule*, 1947. (7) *L'Impôt foncier et la capitation personelle.* (8) *Nennius et l'H.B.* (*Bull. de l'Ec. des Hautes Ét.*, cclxxiii). (9) *Mélanges P. Fournier* (1929), 467 ff. (10) In *Med. Studies in Mem. G.S. Loomis* (1927), 229 ff. (11) *Mélanges G. Schoepperle*, 1926. (12) *P.B.A.* (1930), xvi, 327–45. (13) *L'art militaire et les armes au moyen âge*, 1946.

Loth, J. (1) *Rev. Celt.*, xxx, 270 ff., and xxxiii, 258 ff. (2) *L'émig. bretonne.*

Loyen, A. (1) *Récherches Hist. sur les Paneg. de Sidione*, 1942. (2) *Sidoine et l'esprit précieux*, 1943. (3) *Bull. de la Soc. arch. et hist. de l'Orlandais* (1935), xxii.

Macalister, R. A. S., *The Secret Languages of Ireland*, 1937.

MacNeill, E., *Studies* (1931), xx, 457 ff.

Manitius, M. (1) *Gesch. der christ.-lat. Poesie* (1911), i. (2) *Gesch. der lat. Lit. d. Mitt.*

Marche, L. de la, *St. Martin*, 1881.

Mattingly, H., *in Stud. in R.Econ. and Soc.Hist.*, ed. Coleman-Norton, 1951.

Merobaudes, ed. F. Volmer, *MGH* (1905), xiv.

Meyer, K. (1) *Learning in Ireland in the 5th c.*, 1913. (2) *Z.f.C.P.* (1913), x. (3) *Eriu*, iv.

Myres, J. N. L. (1) With Collingwood 2. (2) In *Aspects of Arch.*, 1951. (3) *L'ant. class.* (1948), xvii, 453 ff. (4) In Harden. (5) *History* (1935), xx, 250–62. (6) *Arch. J.* (1933), xc.

Nash-Williams, V. E. (1) Ed. *Hundred Years Arch. in Wales*, 1949. (2) In *Congress R. Frontier Studies*, 1952. (3) *R. Frontier in Wales*, 1954. (4) *Arch.* (1930), lxxx. (5) *Arch. Camb.*, (1938). (6) *Early Christian Mons. in Wales*, 1950.

Norden, E., *Die ant. Kuntsprosa*, 1898.

Nostrand, J. J. van, *R. Spain* (T. Frank), 1937.

O'Neil, B. H. St. J., *Antiq.* (1944), xviii, 113 ff.

O'Rahilly, T. F. (1) *Early Irish Hist. and Mythology*, 1946. (2) *The Two Patricks*, 1942.

Palanque, J.-R., *St. Ambroise et l'Emp. rom.*, 1933.

Parry, J. J., *Speculum* (1938), no. 3, xiii.

Payne, F. C., *Arch. J.*, civ, 82 ff.

Phillips, W. A., ed. *Hist. of Church of Ireland* (1933), i.

Pichon, R., *Les derniers Écrivains Profanes*, 1906.

Pirenne, H., *Mohammed and Charlemagne*, 1939.

Plinval, G. de. (1) *Pélage*, 1943. (2) *Essai sur le style et la langue de P.*, 1947. (3) "Les Luttes pélagiennes . . ." (1937) in *Hist. de l'Église* (ed. A. Flèche, V. Martin), iv (with Bardy, Bréhier, de Labriolle).

Plummer, A. (1) Bede. (2) *Vitae SS. Hibern.*

Polheim, *Die lat. Reimprosa*, 1925.

Raby, F. J. E. (1) *Hist. of Christ. Lat. Poetry* (2nd ed.), 1953. (2) *Hist. Sec. Lat. Poetry*, i (1934).

Radford, C. A., Ralegh (1) in Harden. (2) *Antiq.* xviii.

Reed, T. D. (1) *The Battle for Brit. in the 5th c.* (2) *The Rise of Wessex*, 1947.

Richards, M., *The Laws of Hywel Dda*, 1954.

Richardson, L., *Wells and Springs of Gloucestershire*, 1930.

Richmond, I. A. (1) *R.B.*, 1955. (2) *Arch.*, xciii (with Crawford). (3) A.N.L., vi, no. 2, 43–5. (4) *City Walls of Imp. Rome*, 1930. (5) *R. Pavements at Rudston*, 1935. (6) In Robson, *Kirkcudbrightshire*, 14–35. (7) *Policy of Brit. Arch.*, 1948.

Rivet, A. L. F., in *A.N.L.*, vi, no. 2, 29–34.

Robertson, A. S., in Carson.

Roger, H., *L'Enseignement des lettres classiques*, 1905.

Rostovtzeff, M. (1) *Soc. & Econ. Hist. of R.E.*, 1926. (2) *Mélanges H. Pirenne*, 1926. (3) *Musée belge* (1923), xxvii.

Savory, H. N., in Harden.

Schmidt, L. (1) *Gesch. d. deut. Stämme* (2nd ed.), 1934. (2) *G.d. Vandalen*, 1901.

Scramuzza, V. M., *R. Sicily* (T. Frank).

Seeck, O. (1) *Gesch. d. Untergangs d. ant. Welt*, vi, 1920. (2) *Regesten d. Kaiser u. Päpst*, 1919. (3) *Symmachus*. (4) *Notitia Dig.*, 1876.

Simpson, W. D., *Celtic Church in Scotland*, 1935.

Soutar, A. (1) *Texts and Studies*, ix. (2) *Study of Ambrosiater*.

Staehelin, *Die Schweiz in röm. Zeit.* (3rd ed.), 1948.

Stevens, C. E. (1) *Sidonius*, 1933. (2) *J.R.S.* (1947), xxxvii, 132–4. (3) *A.N.L.*, vi, no. 2, 41. (4) *Arch. Ael.* (4s) (1934), xi, 138–45. (5) *Études celt.*, June 1938. (6) *E.H.R.*, 1941, "Gildas sapiens". (7) *Arch. J.*, xcvii.

Sundwall, J., *Weström. Studien*, 1915.

Sutherland, C. H. V. (1) In Harden. (2) *Coinage and Currency in R.B.*, 1937. (3) In Carson, ch. x (4) *Antiq. J.* xciv, 117–23.

Taylor, T., *Life of St. Samson of Dol*, 1925.

Thompson, E. A. (1) *Past and Present* (Nov. 1952), 11–23. (2) *Antiq.*, no. 119 (1956), 163–7. (3) *J.R.S.*, 1956. (4) *A.R. Reformer and Inventor*, 1952. (5) *Hist. Works of Ammianus*, 1947. (6) *Attila*.

Vacandard, E., *St. Victrice*, 1903.

Valentin, L., *St. Prosper d'Aquitaine*.
Vendryes, J., *Études celt.* (1948), iv.
Vinogradoff, *Growth of Manor*, 1911.

Wade-Evans, A. W. (1) *Welsh Christ. Origins*, 1934. (2) *Vitae SS. Brit. et Genealogiae*, 1944. (3) *Nennius' History of the Britons*, 1938.
Wainwright, F. T., ed. *The Problem of the Picts*.
Waitz, *Der Kampf d. Burgunder u.d. Hunnen*, in *Forsch. z. deut. Gesch.*, i (1861), 1 ff.
Watson, *Celtic Place-names of Scotland*, 1926.
Wheeler, R. E. M. (1) *Report . . . Lydney*, 1932. (2) *London and Saxons*. (3) *Antiq. J.* (1934), xiv, 254–63. (4) *Verulamium*. (5) *R. London*. (6) *Y Cymm.*, xxxiii.
Whitaker, T., *Macrobius*, 1923.
White, H. G. E., *Ausonius* (Loeb).
White, N. J. D., *St. Patrick*, 1920.
Wilamowitz-Moellendorf, *Hermes* (1900), xxxv (Asianismus u. Attick.).
Williams, Hugh. (1) *Christianity in Early Britain*, 1912. (2) *Gildas*, 1899.
Williams, Ifor. (1) *Welsh Rev.*, vi, no. 4 (1947). (2) *The poems of Llywarch Hen*, 1932. (3) *Canu Aneirin*, 1938. (4) *Trans. Cymmrod.* (Chwedlau), 1946–7.
Wright, R. P., *Cat. R. Insc. & Sculpt. Stones . . . Chester*, 1955.

Young, D., *Romanisation in Scotland* (? 1956).

Zachrissen, *Romans, Kelts and Saxons*.
Zimmer, H. (1) *Nennius Vindicatus*. (2) *Sittz. d. Preuss. Akad. d. Wiss.*, 1910. (3) *Pelagius in Ireland*.

INDEX

Further Notes: p. 154, Caradawc, Chadwick (1) 48 ff., Wade-Evans (2) 318 f.; p. 284, n. 7, 2nd c. Wales *Y. Comm.* xxxiii, *J. R. S.* xiii, 68 f. (Sept. Sev.), mosaics at Carmarthen; p. 285, n. 9, but we know Alemannic ornament and the sites are 7th c.; p. 289, n. 24, Petuaria, capital of Parisi (vicus, mid-2nd c.) means Fourth, see Strabo on allied Gallic tribe Allobroges for change from village-community to town; p. 294, n. 18, confusion too of Maxentius Max. and our Max. in pedigrees; p. 300, n. 2, cat at Lullingstone; p. 301, n. 9, alternative reading, "devastated Gaul"; n. 15, Bury simply conjectures about the Count, but the imports of Argonne ware, mainly in S.E., with few exs. out N. and W. (York, Wroxeter, Cirencester) support coin-evidence, Chenet, *La Céramique g.-r. d'Argonne*, 147, and *Antiq.* no. 125, 22, for ex. at Moel Fennli (Benli).

R. Radford (*Antiq.* no. 125), examines Vortigern, suggests value in *Annales Cambriae*'s dates 425–8 (rule and Saxon coming) and the link of Germanus with Garmon; sees V. as landlord, not warrior, perhaps with M. Max. as patron —this may be so; also the association of Powys (Pagus) with Cornovii (not Ordovives) and Wroxeter, Chester. We may still see V. as representing the more Celtic sections and the transition to tribal kingdoms. R.R. notes sub-Roman occ. of I. A. hillforts (Breidden, Old Oswestry, Eddisbury: all Cornovian). Jackson (2) 116 f., notes "certain features of Celtic civilisation connected with the institution of chieftainship and tribal govt. managed to survive 400 years of Romanisation."